T0325473

SCIENCE-BASED INDUSTRIAL INNOVATION

www.royalcollins.com

SCIENCE-BASED INDUSTRIAL INNOVATION

Wang Ling
Zhang Qingzhi
Lei Jiasu

RC
Books Beyond Boundaries
ROYAL COLLINS

Science-Based Industrial Innovation

By Wang Ling, Zhang Qingzhi, and Lei Jiasu

First published in 2024 by Royal Collins Publishing Group Inc.
Groupe Publication Royal Collins Inc.
550-555 boul. René-Lévesque O Montréal (Québec) H2Z1B1 Canada

10 9 8 7 6 5 4 3 2 1

Copyright © Wang Ling, Zhang Qingzhi, and Lei Jiasu

All rights reserved. Without limiting the rights under copyright reserved above, no part of this publication may be reproduced, stored in or introduced into a retrieval system, or transmitted in any form or by any means (electronic, mechanical, photocopying, recording, or otherwise), without the prior written permission of both the copyright owner and the above publisher of this book.

ISBN: 978-1-4878-1168-6

To find out more about our publications,
please visit www.royalcollins.com.

Contents

List of Figures

List of Tables

INTRODUCTION

Science-Based Classification of Industries and Innovation

The Imperative of Focusing on Science-Based Innovation and Industry

Innovation research typically categorizes its driving forces into three distinct types: market demand-based innovation, technological progress-based innovation, and scientific discovery-based innovation. However, historically, academia has primarily recognized only the first two categories: market demand (demand-pull innovation) and technological progress (technology-push innovation). The neglect of the third category, innovation driven by scientific discovery (scientific discovery-push innovation), has led to significant misunderstandings about technological innovation within academic circles. This oversight is a key reason innovation research has seen limited advancement over the past decade. A comprehensive analysis of innovation types is essential for a deeper understanding of the associated challenges.

Science-based innovation (SBI), driven by scientific discovery, is critical for the emergence and development of innovation. This type of innovation, where new products and processes arise directly from scientific breakthroughs, is evident in sectors like biotechnology, chemistry, pharmaceuticals, and early microelectronics. Industries established and developed through SBI, such as biotechnology, the biological and chemical-pharmaceutical industries, basic chemical materials, the early semiconductor industry, current nanotechnology, certain new energy sectors, and novel materials, are typically the most dynamic segments of the economy. Their growth can spur industrial revolutions and even socioeconomic paradigm shifts. For instance, the transistor innovation and semiconductor industry post-1960s significantly influenced the global economic paradigm shift. Similarly, the contemporary biotechnology industry is catalyzing technological and economic paradigm shifts in several countries.

Conversely, technological progress-based innovation depends on the continual emergence of new technologies within existing knowledge systems. This form, also known as technology-based innovation (TBI), is seen in product and process innovations in machine tools, shipping, and petrochemicals, mainly from advancements in related fields. Industries founded and evolving based on technological progress, such as the machine tool, automotive, shipbuilding, petrochemical, and aircraft industries, have historically been central to many countries, particularly those in the early or middle stages of industrialization. Their growth plays a pivotal role in national economic development. For instance, these industries have seen substantial development in China, becoming pillars of the national economy and major contributors to the country's Gross Domestic Product (GDP).

The focus on SBIs and science-based industries is thus critical. Understanding their unique characteristics and impacts can provide valuable insights into future economic and technological developments.

First, the challenge for late-developing countries in advancing within science-based industries is considerable, often presenting seemingly insurmountable barriers compared to developed nations. This difficulty largely stems from the unique dynamics and principles governing the innovation and growth of science-based industries. These industries heavily rely on new scientific discoveries, which, in turn, depend on the accumulation of prior basic research, careful selection of research topics, increased investment in research and development (R&D), and the effectiveness of scientific endeavors. For instance, post-World War II, Japan shifted from a militaristic strategy to focusing on economic development. It managed to rapidly catch up with global leaders like the United States in industries such as electronics and automobiles, adopting strategies centered around technology, science and technology, and the creation of science and technology. Despite this success and producing nearly twenty Nobel laureates, Japan continues to trail behind the United States and Europe in science-based industries, including bioengineering and chemical pharmaceuticals. This example illustrates late-developing countries' difficulty bridging the gap in science-based sectors.

Second, the challenge of catching up with developed countries in science-based industries has been a long-standing issue for China. Over the past four decades of reform and opening-up, China has made significant strides in technology-based industries such as home appliances, daily chemicals, metallurgy, shipbuilding, and conventional machinery manufacturing, narrowing the gap with developed nations. However, in science-based industries like basic electronic components, biotechnology, chemical pharmaceuticals, and new functional materials, developed countries maintain a stable and robust competitive edge in these areas. Despite substantial efforts in policymaking, investment, R&D, and the industrialization of new technologies, including implementing scientific and technological advancement plans like the 863 and 973 programs, China still faces challenges in significantly reducing the gap in science-based industries. This persistent difficulty impacts the transformation of China's industrial structure and growth pattern, making it hard to achieve set objectives. Therefore, a focused approach to both theoretical research and practical application in science-based industries and their innovation is crucial to enhancing international competitiveness, achieving leapfrog development, and improving the quality of economic growth.

It is urgently necessary to develop strategic emerging industries, focusing on science-based industries and their innovation. Currently, a primary objective of China's economic development strategy is to transition its development model. A critical element of this transition is fostering strategic emerging industries to reshape the industrial structure. The 12th Five-Year Plan has identified key strategic emerging industries, including new energy, energy conservation and environmental protection, electric vehicles, new materials, new medicine, biological breeding, and information technology. A fundamental assumption underlying our commitment to these seven industries is their concurrent development alongside that of developed countries. This approach aims to position China at the forefront of the next wave of international competition and secure competitive advantages in these areas.

However, this strategy overlooks two significant challenges. First, many developed countries have conducted relevant basic scientific research and industrial technology development in these industries for ten to twenty years, leading to substantial knowledge accumulation and technological reserves. This historical head start presents a hurdle for China in gaining a leading position in certain areas. Second, some heavily rely on SBI within the subset of these seven industries. These include innovations in new material manufacturing technologies (such as nanotechnology and superconductivity), biopharmaceuticals, biomedical engineering, biological breeding, marine biotechnology, new information network technology, and advanced intelligent manufacturing equipment. Understanding the internal mechanics of science-based emerging industries helps to capture the "high ground" in the international arena.

So, what are the pressing concerns surrounding SBI and industry?

One illustrative example in China is the United Gene Group, from Fudan University, a typical example of a company driven by SBI. Since its inception in 1997, the Group has focused on "decoding life to benefit humankind." Through a series of SBIs, it has founded over thirty enterprises, including Extrawell Pharmaceutical Holdings Limited and United Gene Health Group Limited, based on the development of United Gene Technology Group Limited. This has positioned them as a leader group in China's high-tech industry, with a core focus on gene technology. Despite these achievements, the number of companies and institutions capable of implementing such innovations in China remains limited. This reality prompts several critical questions about SBI, both theoretically and practically, that need to be addressed to advance this sector.

First and foremost, the theoretical exploration of the intrinsic mechanisms behind SBI and its industrial development is imperative. Notably, current economic theories on a global scale have yet to address science-based industries and innovations specifically. For example, mainstream economists like Chandler and Krugman have focused on the concept of first-mover advantage, suggesting that early entrants into a market create entry barriers for subsequent competitors. Vernon and Porter have examined the product life cycle, proposing that industries migrate from one country or region to another as they mature. However, these mainstream economic theories often overlook the role and occurrence of innovation.

In evolutionary economics, scholars such as Henderson and Christensen have explored the phenomenon of technological development discontinuity in certain industries, suggesting that new, potent market entrants frequently challenge the innovative capabilities of leading firms. Korean economist Kim Linsu has delved into technological learning, advocating for the potential of latecomers to progress from imitation to innovation. Yet, studies in this field typically need to pay more attention to the variability in innovation across different industries. In China, since the early 1990s, there has been a gradual shift in the focus of academic, industrial, and governmental research toward innovation. However, most of these studies still need to differentiate between SBI and TBI adequately.

This leads to several urgent questions regarding SBI and its industry. First, what are this type of innovation's fundamental phenomena and characteristics? Second, what mechanisms drive the emergence and realization of such innovations? At a micro level, how do basic scientific research, commercial development, and manufacturing processes interact in the innovation cycle? At a macro level, which models—perhaps the Smith model or the Bacon model—are more effective in organizing this type of innovation? Third, among the existing and anticipated industries, which can be classified as science-based? What are their defining characteristics? Fourth, what mechanisms underpin the growth and international competitiveness of science-based industries? Fifth, what should the structure of the industrial innovation system look like for these industries, especially concerning the roles of government and universities?

A new industrial revolution centered around SBI has unfolded, garnering significant attention from these nations. As an emerging country, China should actively engage in this arena, with SBI as a cornerstone of its "innovation-driven development" strategy. This focus is crucial not only for the strategy's success but also for its effective implementation. To this end, the Chinese government needs to consider several key policy aspects.

First, what are the gaps between China and leading developed countries regarding SBI and industrial development? Second, what policies and mechanisms need to be established to facilitate the emergence and success of SBI in areas such as basic scientific research, industrial technology advancement, corporate knowledge acquisition, technology integration, and industrial innovation? Third, how should existing science, technology, and industrial policies be adjusted to support better the growth of SBI and its related industries? Fourth, policy focus should be on supporting those science-based industries where China already has a strong foundation and on regions that are hubs of research institutions to foster SBI.

Over the past two decades, Chinese academic research in technological innovation has yet to adequately focus on specialized, systematic, and in-depth studies of SBI. This lack of differentiated understanding between SBI and TBI has hindered the ability of academics to deepen their comprehension of technological innovation. Practically, China has faced challenges in keeping pace with developed countries in science-based industries. The development of strategic emerging industries now urgently demands a concentrated focus on science-based industries and their innovation. A preliminary analysis of the main characteristics of SBI and its industries reveals the need for a two-pronged approach: First, a theoretical exploration into the intrinsic mechanisms of SBI and its industrial development, and second, the adoption of more effective policies to promote the realization and development of SBI in practice. This book posits that addressing these areas is vital to overcoming the practical challenges of SBI.

The Exploratory Nature of SBI

Microsoft Research's report *Toward 2020 Science* posits that we are on the cusp of a scientific revolution, with SBI poised to usher in a new era that could redefine the last fifty years of technology-driven innovation. This shift promises to ignite a global wave of technological change and economic development. "Science has profoundly impacted society, the economy, and the world in unprecedented ways. SBI is expected to contribute to economic prosperity and development as significantly as TBI did in the 20th century."

This evolving dynamic between science and innovation is crucial. Traditionally, technological innovation was predominantly enterprise-driven, with scientists focusing primarily on the exploration of scientific theories and methods. Innovations were often propelled by advances in engineering technology following breakthroughs in basic science. However, by the late 19th century, with the emergence of foundational sciences like chemistry and physics—especially with the rapid development of the bio-industry—the distinction between scientific research and applied research began to blur, reshaping our understanding of technological innovation. This shift led to the recognition of SBI as a distinct paradigm, characterized by its reliance on new scientific discoveries and the direct impetus from basic scientific research.

Cardinal et al. (2001) delineated innovation based on the developmental stages of scientific knowledge. In some fields, scientific knowledge is well-established and encoded, having evolved over centuries. Researchers in these disciplines can access the necessary scientific knowledge through journals and patents, employing it alongside computer simulation programs and relevant human capital to develop new products. This approach, common in industries like electronics and steel, is referred to as "Developed Science." Conversely, "Developing Science" applies to fields without fully encoded knowledge, where innovations depend on interdisciplinary teams and experiential learning, typical in biotechnology and new materials technologies, with innovation being largely exploratory.

The current discourse on technological innovation, influenced by Jensen and others' categorization of two modes of technological innovation (STL mode: Science-Technology-Innovation; DUI-mode: Learning by Doing, Using, and Interacting), often conflates science-driven and technology-driven innovation. SBI, despite its significant contribution to the development of industries like biotechnology, biochemical pharmaceuticals, and the early semiconductor industry, has been under-researched and underappreciated. Yet, these industries, often the most dynamic sectors of the economy, have the potential to initiate new industrial revolutions and drive shifts in the socioeconomic paradigm. A dedicated and systematic study of SBI is thus of immense theoretical and practical importance.

This study aims to provide a theoretical definition of innovation based on science and to enrich the theory of industrial innovation. Traditionally, the concept of "SBI" lacked a clear definition in academic circles, influenced by the "Bush paradigm," which relegated scientific research to the realm of basic research with no commercial application. This perspective led to a linear model of innovation, from scientific research to application, development, and commercialization. However, as science evolves, it's increasingly recognized that basic scientific research not only seeks new knowledge but also addresses practical problems. Many Nobel Prize-winning scientific discoveries with practical applications have been rapidly transformed into commercial products, and numerous modern biopharmaceutical innovations stem from basic scientific research. This study systematically explores SBI, defines it, and analyzes its characteristics and patterns, thereby enriching industrial innovation theory.

Practically, the insights from this study could guide the adjustment of national science and technology policies and support the development of strategic emerging industries. The Bayh-Dole Act of 1980 in the United States, for example, greatly promoted the development of SBI in the US with stimulating the formation of related industries. A focused examination of SBI can elucidate its characteristics and principles, offering a theoretical basis for refining national science and technology policies.

As China aims to transform its economic development model, particularly through the development of strategic emerging industries identified, a thorough understanding of SBI is crucial for advancing new industries and boosting their international competitiveness.

Four Decades of Technological Innovation in China: Laying the Foundations for Exploratory Innovation

Over the past four decades, China has undergone a transformative journey in its scientific, technological, and economic domains. This period of reform and opening-up has propelled the nation into a position of significant global influence, establishing it as a major force in these fields. This advancement is reflected in various indicators of technological innovation, where China now ranks among the global leaders.

A critical aspect of this development is the evolution of the national innovation system. This system has seen considerable improvements, with a marked enhancement in the central role and effectiveness of enterprise-driven innovation. Concurrently, there has been a surge in major breakthroughs in basic research, complemented by significant advancements in strategic high-tech sectors. These technological innovations have been pivotal in elevating industries to the middle and high-end sectors, fostering the rapid growth of new, dynamic industries.

The quantitative evidence of this transformation is striking. Social R&D expenditure in China escalated from RMB 9 billion in 1988 to an impressive RMB 1.76 trillion in 2017, placing the country second worldwide in this metric. During this period, China's global ranking in national innovation capacity improved markedly, rising from 20th in 2012 to 17th in 2017. Another indicator of this growth is the substantial increase in SCI-indexed papers, a direct measure of innovation output. From a modest count of 5,600 in 1988, the number escalated to 735,600 in 2022, securing China the second spot globally in this regard.

Furthermore, the country's patent system, established in the mid-1980s, has seen a meteoric rise in domestic invention patent applications. From 4,780 applications in 1988, the number soared to 1.6 million patent applications in 2022, the highest globally. This growth trajectory is not just quantitative but also qualitative, as evidenced by the contribution rate of technological progress to economic growth. This rate, an indicator of the impact of innovation, grew from approximately 27% in 1985 to 52.2% in 2012 and further to 57.5% in 2017. According to the Global Innovation Index in 2022, China ranks 11th among the 132 economies.

The underlying reasons for these remarkable achievements can be traced back to the strategic roadmap of China's technological innovation over these forty years.

The Four-Stage Evolution of China's Technological Innovation over Forty Years

The period from December 18 to 22, 1978, marked a pivotal moment in China's history with the Third Plenary Session of the Eleventh Central Committee of the Communist Party of China in Beijing. This session, under the guiding principles of shifting the Party's focus to socialist modernization and embracing reform and opening-up, heralded the onset of a transformative era in China. It catalyzed significant reforms in rural and industrial sectors, laying the foundation for a comprehensive journey in technological innovation.

Spanning four decades from 1978 to 2018, China's trajectory in technological innovation can be delineated into four distinct stages, each representing a decade of evolution and a stepwise progression in technological advancement:

a. 1978–1988: Learning and introduction stage. This initial decade was characterized by the assimilation of foreign business concepts and the importation of overseas technologies, which were then adapted for domestic manufacturing purposes.
b. 1988–1998: Introduction, imitation, and improvement stage. This phase involved the continuous introduction, imitation, and refinement of foreign technologies. It was marked by the iterative upgrading of these technologies and their adaptation into new products tailored for the Chinese market.
c. 1998–2008: Integration of foreign technology and self-innovation stage. This period saw the amalgamation of domestic and international technologies and interests. The focus was on achieving "independent integrated innovation" through this synthesis and enhancing typical foreign innovations to suit the large-scale application scenarios in China.
d. 2008–2018: Self-innovation and iterative upgrading stage. The most recent decade has been defined by extensive independent R&D, complemented

by assimilating high-level foreign innovations. This stage emphasized rapid iteration and the strengthening of endogenous innovation outcomes developed in the preceding phases.

The empirical evidence supporting this categorization is detailed in Table 1.

Table 1 Climbing mode, corresponding stages, and patterns

Climbing modes	Learning and introduction stage	Introduction, imitation, and improvement stage	Integration of foreign technology and self-innovation stage	Self-innovation and iterative upgrading stage
Corresponding period	1978–1988	1988–1998	1998–2008	2008–2018
Basic methods and approaches	Learn foreign business concept ideas → introduce foreign technology → manufacture in China	Continuously introduce → improve imitation → iteratively enhance the imitated products	Integrate internal and external technologies and interests → seek integrated innovation and improve the application of foreign innovations in Chinese scenarios	Conduct extensive independent R&D and learn from foreign high-level innovation → enhance self-innovation by express iteration

An analysis of the trends in domestic R&D expenditure and technology introduction contracts (converted into RMB) from 1978 to 2018 offers a nuanced understanding of China's technological innovation stages.

1978–1988: Learning and introduction stage. During this decade, the alignment of domestic R&D expenditure with technology introduction expenditure highlights the intensive efforts in technology acquisition. A significant portion of the R&D budget was dedicated to "digesting and absorbing" these imported technologies. This period of active learning and assimilation of foreign technologies firmly establishes 1978–1988 as the initial "learning and introduction stage" of China's technological innovation journey.

1988–1998: Introduction, imitation, and improvement stage. Between 1988 and 1991, the expenditures on domestic R&D and technology introduction remained relatively stable. However, from 1992 to 1998, there was a notable shift with technology introduction contracts exceeding domestic R&D expenditure.

This shift, in conjunction with the implementation of the "technology for the market" policy and evident trends of "imitation improvement" post-1992, underscores the period of 1988–1998 as the "introduction, imitation, and improvement stage."

1998–2008: Integration of foreign technology and self-innovation stage. A significant change occurred post-1998, with domestic R&D expenditure surpassing technology introduction contracts, growing at a relatively rapid pace. By 2007, domestic R&D investment was 1.92 times that of technology introduction contracts. This era was also marked by a critical reassessment of the "market for technology" strategy and the adoption of the "endogenous innovation strategy" post-2005. The numerous instances of "endogenous innovation based on technology integration" corroborate the identification of 1998–2008 as the "integration of foreign technology and self-innovation stage."

2008–2018: Self-innovation and iterative upgrading stage. Post-2008, a remarkable increase in domestic R&D expenditure was observed, reaching 2.45 times (2008) to 7.68 times (2016) that of technology introduction contracts. Additionally, the ratio of R&D expenditure to GDP consistently exceeded 1.5% from 2008 onwards. This period, characterized by numerous examples of "iterative upgrading based on endogenous innovation," is aptly defined as the "self-innovation and iterative upgrading stage."

Unpacking China's "Four-Step Up Track" in Technological Innovation

Between 1978 and 2018, the evolution of China's technological innovation has unfolded across four distinct phases, culminating in its current stature. Presently, China competes on par with developed nations in approximately 20% of technological fields, matches their pace in 30%, and is rapidly closing the gap in the remaining 50%, as illustrated in figures 1 and 2. Collectively, these phases constitute a progressive "four-step ascent," delineating a strategic trajectory that might be termed the "four-step ascent trajectory." This terminology not only encapsulates the sequential advancement but also conveys the nuanced challenges overcome along this journey. From an international perspective, particularly for other emerging economies seeking to emulate China's success, this evolutionary path offers a viable "four-step ascent model." This model underscores the notion that the ascent has been anything but straightforward; it has been a climb marked by considerable challenges. The subsequent sections provide a detailed exposition of these four stages.

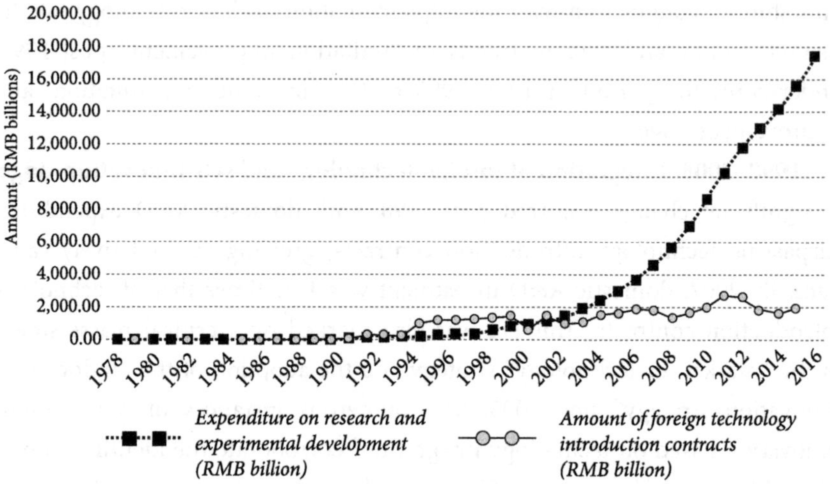

Figure 1 China's R&D expenditure and technology introduction contracts (expenditures) trend, 1978–2017

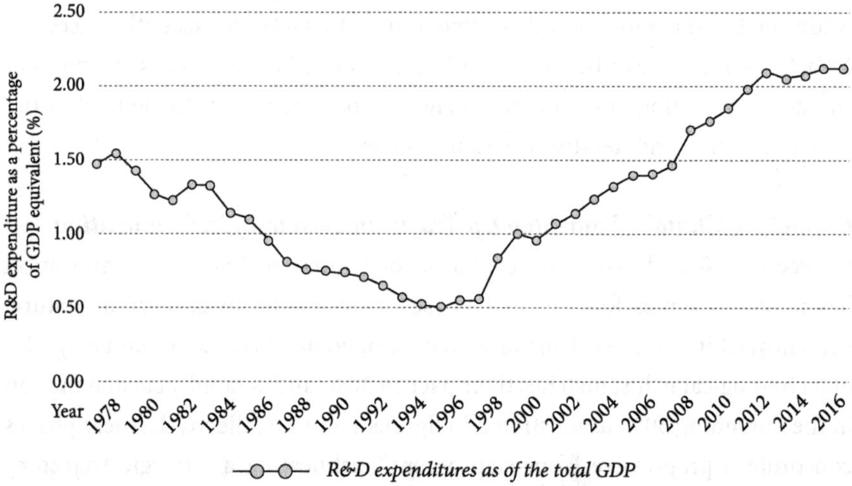

Figure 2 Trend of R&D expenditure as a percentage of GDP equivalent, 1978–2017

The decade spanning 1978 to 1988 marked the foundational "learning and introduction stage" of China's technological innovation practices, as outlined in Table 2. This period was characterized by a dual focus: addressing the economy's supply shortages and enhancing the nation's lagging innovation capabilities. The guiding principle of this era was encapsulated by a cycle of "learning, introducing, and re-learning."

Table 2 Stage 1 of learning: Learn, introduce, and strengthen

Stage	Period	Innovation model
Learn, introduce, and strengthen	1978–1988	Learn foreign business ideas → introduce foreign technologies → manufacture in China

The Third Plenary Session of the Eleventh Central Committee of the Communist Party of China, convened from December 18 to 22, 1978, in Beijing, served as a pivotal juncture in this narrative. The session's core agenda was to pivot the Party's efforts toward socialist modernization, heralding China's "reform and opening-up" policy, and initiate rural reforms. This strategic redirection facilitated an unprecedented level of personnel, academic, and commercial exchanges with the developed world. During this epoch, the influx of foreign scientific, technological knowledge, and consumer goods, particularly home appliances, through various channels—ranging from limited imports to items brought back by individuals from abroad—exposed the Chinese populace to the technological gap between China and developed nations.

The translation and publication of János Kornai's *Economics of Shortage* in 1986 was a watershed moment, prompting a collective awakening to the "shortage economy" plaguing China. The resolve to pivot toward socialist modernization, as decreed by the Third Plenary Session, became a catalyst for technological innovation in the ensuing era of reform and opening-up.

The approach to domestic technological innovation during this phase can be segmented into four main strategies:

a. International engagement and knowledge transfer. This involved both outbound and inbound exchanges where government leaders, business executives, and technical experts sought education abroad while foreign entities explored collaborative opportunities in China.
b. Technology importation. Heightened exposure to foreign market economies and their developmental ideologies, coupled with the urgent need to rectify the "shortage economy," spurred domestic demand for learning and assimilating advanced foreign technologies.
c. Joint ventures and local production. Recognizing China's burgeoning market, foreign companies eagerly established joint ventures, significantly alleviating the supply scarcity of certain industrial products. A notable example includes the collaboration between Volkswagen and the Shanghai

car factory to produce Santana cars, highlighting the minimal use of existing local components and the subsequent push for localization.

d. Development of domestic manufacturing capabilities. The era saw a surge in introducing foreign production lines, especially in the home appliances sector, marking a significant military-to-civilian transition in production capabilities.

The subsequent decade, 1988–1998, transitioned into the "introduction, imitation, and improvement stage" as detailed in Table 3. This phase transcended mere imitation; it was characterized by the substantive enhancement of foreign technologies through adaptation, leading to the development of superior products. The "market for technology" policy, pivotal during this period, not only expedited the technology transfer but also deepened the processes of imitation and innovation.

Table 3 Stage 2 of learning: Introduce, imitate, and improve

Stage	Period	Innovation model
Introduce, imitate, and improve	1988–1998	Continuous introduction → imitation improvement → iterative improvement of imitated products

In May 1988, the State Council sanctioned the establishment of China's inaugural national high-tech industrial development zone, the Beijing Haidian High-Tech Industrial Development Pilot Zone, which later evolved into the Zhongguancun Science and Technology Park. This initiative aimed to facilitate the translation of domestic research findings into commercial applications and to industrialize foreign high-tech technologies within China. In 1992, Deng Xiaoping, the principal architect of China's modernization, embarked on his seminal "Southern Tour," reaffirming the commitment to reform, opening-up, and laying the groundwork for the explicit adoption of the "market for technology" policy.

Subsequent policy frameworks, including the 1993 Communist Party of China (CPC) Central Committee's Decision to Establish the Socialist Market Economy System, delineated the blueprint for a market economy imbued with Chinese characteristics. The inaugural National Conference on Technological Innovation in 1999, underscored the strategic imperative of leveraging scientific and technological progress to enhance the quality and efficiency of economic growth. This era cultivated a conducive policy milieu for technological assimilation, emulation, enhancement, and indigenous innovation by enterprises.

Key practices during this stage are encompassed: First is creation of new market demands. Innovations by foreign companies and the localization of products by Sino-foreign joint ventures catalyzed the expansion of domestic markets for automobiles and home appliances, exemplified by the Santana vehicle. The second is technological acquisition and enhancement. Under the "market for technology" framework, a growing number of domestic firms engaged in technology acquisition, and this period witnessed an emphasis on refining previously introduced technologies, aspiring to develop proprietary technologies, and enhancing product offerings. The case of nine refrigerator production lines illustrates a spectrum of outcomes from such endeavors: three manufacturers, after adopting and refining foreign designs, captured a dominant market share; another three maintained their market presence through incremental technological and process improvements; while the remainder, failing to innovate, experienced a significant market share decline. This landscape encouraged a broader industry focus on improvement-led imitation to build innovation capacity.

The phase spanning 1998 to 2008 represented the "integration of foreign technology and self-innovation stage" of China's technological innovation journey, as detailed in Table 4. This period was characterized by the symbiosis of domestic and international technologies and interests, aiming for "independent integrated innovation" and the contextual adaptation of foreign innovations for large-scale application within China. The trajectory of technology introduction during this era, documented in Table 5, reflects a strategic pivot toward enhancing internal innovation capabilities.

Table 4 Stage 3 of learning: Integration of foreign technology and self-innovation

Stage	Period	Innovation model
Integration of foreign technology and self-innovation	1998–2008	Integrate internal and external technologies and interests → seek integrated innovation and improve the application of foreign innovations in Chinese scenarios

Table 5 Technology introduction in China, 1989–1998

Year	Technology introduction contract amount ($millions)	Number of technology introduction contracts (pieces)
1989	292,320	190
1990	127,399	103
1991	345,923	359
1992	658,988	504
1993	610,943	493
1994	410,576	444
1995	1,303,264	3,629
1996	1,525,700	6,074
1997	1,592,312	5,984
1998	1,637,510	6,254

Source: China Statistical Yearbook on Science and Technology, paper ed. (1997–2017)

Since its inception in 1992, China's "market for technology" strategy has facilitated the acquisition of a multitude of foreign technologies through various means—purchasing licenses for technology usage, establishing Sino-foreign partnerships and joint ventures, and leveraging the spillover effects of foreign direct investment in technology. While this approach has significantly enhanced China's technological landscape, it has also precipitated a dependency on foreign technology among numerous domestic enterprises. A notable repercussion of this dependency is the dissolution of internal R&D departments within some firms following the establishment of joint ventures. This trend is further exacerbated by a prevailing overreliance on foreign technology among some sectors, where domestic procurement competitions often disproportionately favor foreign technologies. Such practices diminish the opportunities for local enterprises and institutions to engage in and benefit from technological supply competitions, thereby impeding their capacity to innovate and compete.

Moreover, the implementation of the "market for technology" strategy has inadvertently contributed to an increasing technological divide among China's regions. Predominantly, the eastern regions, advantaged by superior geographical positioning, higher economic development levels, and a more open cultural outlook, have witnessed a greater influx and adoption of foreign technologies compared to their central and western counterparts. This disparity has not only magnified the technological gap between these regions but has also posed significant challenges to the harmonized technological advancement and economic development across China. The distribution and

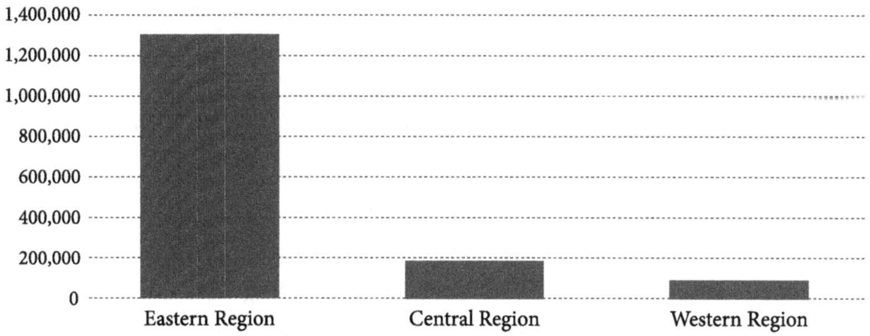

Figure 3 Regional differences in the amount of technology introduction (contract) in China in 2005

Source: China Statistical Yearbook on Science and Technology (2006)

impact of technology introduction across these regions, as depicted in Figure 3, illustrate the widening technological disparity, underscoring the need for a more balanced and inclusive approach to technology adoption and innovation across the country.

By the turn of the millennium, the debate over the efficacy and drawbacks of the "market for technology" strategy reached its zenith in China. The prevailing consensus, articulated through various discourses, acknowledged that while the strategy had facilitated the acquisition of crucial technologies and expedited the establishment of a modern technological infrastructure within two to three decades, it also entrenched a "double dependency" on the technology of developed Western nations. This dependency was twofold: an intrinsic lag in domestic technological capabilities necessitating reliance on foreign advancements, and a strategic control exerted by foreign entities through patents and standards that delineated the trajectory of China's industrial development. The imperative to recalibrate the "market for technology" policy became apparent, advocating for a dual approach that continued to leverage necessary foreign technologies while fostering a robust indigenous intellectual property (IP) landscape through endogenous innovation.

The concept of "endogenous innovation" was initially introduced during the "9th Five-Year Plan" in 1995, with a call for enhancing "endogenous innovation capability" echoed at the "15th National Congress" in 1998. The urgency for this shift was further accentuated by geopolitical events and global economic integrations, notably China's accession to the World Trade Organization (WTO) in 2000, which exposed domestic enterprises to direct competition with their developed-world counterparts. Consequently, in 2003, the National Program for Medium-to-Long-Term Scientific and Technological Development embedded "endogenous innovation" as a foundational guideline.

The implementation of endogenous innovation strategized on promoting three key modalities: original innovation, integrated innovation, and digestion, absorption, and innovation. Given the relatively nascent stage of China's basic research, a significant thrust was on "technology integration" to spearhead endogenous innovation across various sectors, including telecommunications, automotive, high-power generation, and high-speed rail, among others.

A hallmark of this strategy was the development of China's high-speed rail. Following the introduction of foreign high-speed rail technology in 2004, China rapidly progressed to inaugurate its high-speed rail service in 2007, a period marked by "independent integrated innovation based on technology integration." This endeavor was further bolstered by the national 973 Program in 2007, which funded pivotal research projects in high-speed rail technology. Similarly, the automotive industry witnessed a paradigm shift toward "independent integrated innovation," culminating in 2005 when China's automobile exports surpassed imports for the first time, signaling a significant leap in domestic innovation and global market penetration.

The epoch from 2008 to 2018 signified the "self-innovation and iterative upgrading stage" in China's technological innovation narrative. This phase accentuated extensive independent R&D, supplemented by strategic assimilation of high-level foreign innovations to enhance and elevate indigenous innovation capabilities, as documented in Table 6.

Table 6 Stage 4 of learning: Self-innovation and iterative upgrading

Stage	Period	Innovation mode
Self-innovation and iterative upgrading	2008–2018	Conduct extensive independent R&D and learn from foreign high-level innovation → enhance self-innovation by express iteration

The transition to the "self-innovation and iterative upgrading stage" of China's technological innovation landscape is set against a backdrop of significant milestones and global shifts. First, in 2008, China's domestic investment in R&D as a percentage of its GDP surpassed 1.5% for the first time, marking a critical threshold in the nation's commitment to fostering innovation. Second, the acceleration of a new round of the industrial revolution on the global stage, with projections indicating its maturation in developed Western nations between 2025 and 2030, has concurrently signaled the onset of a similar transformative wave within China.

In response to these developments, strategic directives from the central government have increasingly emphasized the imperative of innovation. The 12th Five-Year Plan, announced in March 2011, prioritized cultivating strategic emerging industries. This emphasis was further reinforced at the National Science and Technology Innovation Conference in July 2012 and the 18th National Congress later that year, where then-General Secretary Hu Jintao advocated for creating an innovation-driven economy and establishing a national innovation system with distinctive Chinese characteristics. Premier Li Keqiang's advocacy for "mass entrepreneurship and innovation" in 2014 and General Secretary Xi Jinping's explicit call for an "innovation-driven development strategy" underscore the government's commitment to this agenda. The Proposal for the 13th Five-Year Plan for National Economic and Social Development, issued by the CPC Central Committee in November 2015, encapsulates the policy framework guiding China's shift toward a more innovation-centric development model.

The practices characterizing this stage are multifaceted. Primarily, there is a concerted effort toward sustaining extensive independent R&D initiatives while assimilating high-level foreign innovations to facilitate the rapid iterative enhancement of existing indigenous innovations, particularly in the realm of integrated innovation. Additionally, the period has witnessed a surge in innovations driven by the Internet, artificial intelligence (AI), green technologies, new materials, and new energy sectors, signaling a broadening of the innovation spectrum. Financial technology, in particular, has emerged as a domain of notable advancement. This era is also marked by a significant uptick in the volume of domestic invention patent applications and grants, indicating a robust expansion in the nation's IP portfolio, as illustrated in Figure 4.

The evolution of China's high-speed rail system exemplifies the profound impact of "independent integrated innovation based on technology integration." From 2004 to 2007, the foundational phase was characterized by leveraging integrated innovations, significantly propelled forward by the national 973 Program's research funding in 2007. The subsequent increase in targeted research funding by the National Natural Science Foundation of China (NSFC) in 2008 marked a strategic effort to address industrial development challenges within the high-speed rail sector. By 2010, the NSFC's sponsorship of 26 high-

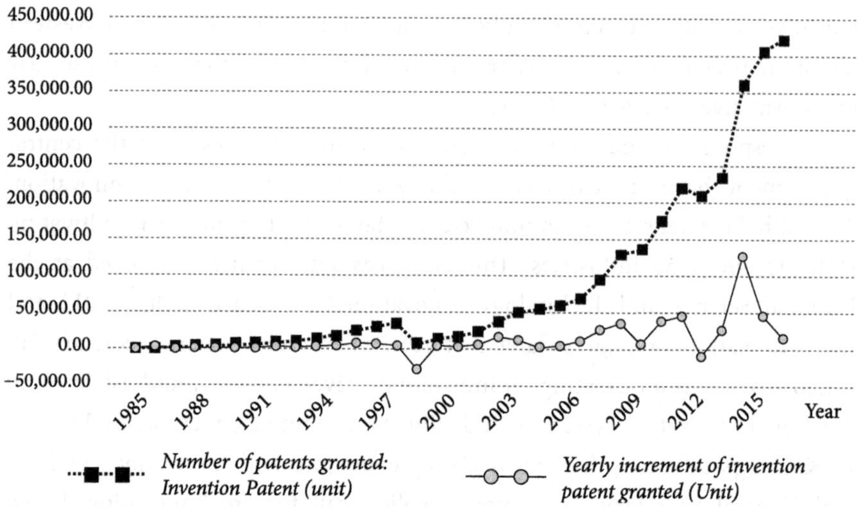

Figure 4 Increase in domestic invention patent applications and authorizations after 2008

speed rail projects underscored a concerted push toward surmounting technical hurdles, thereby accelerating the sector's innovative evolution.

Parallel to the advancements in high-speed rail, the realms of Internet+, AI, green technology, new materials, and new energy have witnessed pervasive innovation. Emblematic of this widespread innovation are the endeavors within the "mass entrepreneurship and innovation" ecosystem, prominently led by technological giants such as Baidu, Alibaba, Tencent, and JD.com. Financial technology innovation has permeated various sectors, including e-commerce, banking, securities, and insurance, extending even to public service infrastructures like transportation ticketing systems and institutional administrative platforms, with several initiatives embedding nascent AI applications.

Reflecting on the four distinct stages of technological innovation outlined previously, a coherent picture of China's innovation landscape emerges. Enterprises have ascended to the forefront of the innovation ecosystem; "mass entrepreneurship and innovation" has burgeoned across society, evolving into a pervasive mindset and practice, and the synergy among technological, institutional, business model, and organizational innovation has deepened. Technological entrepreneurship has emerged as a pivotal conduit for innovation, with numerous industries witnessing sustained growth in their innovation capabilities. Collectively, these developments underscore China's maturation into a nation that not only values but actively cultivates a culture of innovation.

Key Characteristics, Experiences, and Lessons from China's Forty Years of Technological Innovation

Reflecting upon the four-decade trajectory of technological innovation in China reveals three salient characteristics that distinguish the nation's approach to fostering a dynamic innovation ecosystem.

A distinctive innovation methodology and system. China's innovation strategy has been characterized by a multifaceted approach that includes learning from, imitating, improving upon, and integrating foreign innovations into the Chinese context on a large scale. This process of iteration and application has proven effective across different tiers of the innovation hierarchy. The innovation drivers in China range from industry elites with deep technical expertise, such as Ren Zhengfei, Liu Chuanzhi, Robin Li, and Ma Huateng (Pony Ma), to grassroots innovators like Jack Ma, an English teacher turned entrepreneur who founded the globally recognized Alibaba. Innovation agents encompass a wide spectrum from state-owned enterprises, particularly central enterprises, to private enterprises, which have evolved from imitation to leading innovation. This transformative journey is evident across the coastal regions, showcasing the vibrant innovation landscape. Moreover, research institutions and universities have emerged as critical sources of knowledge and as incubators for innovation and entrepreneurship, with the government playing a catalytic role in facilitating this ecosystem through strategic planning, financial support, and regulatory reforms.

The ascendance of high-tech enterprises. Over forty years, both private high-tech firms and central enterprises have become formidable forces in innovation. Private enterprises now contribute significantly to China's economic indicators, delivering over 50% of tax revenues, accounting for 60% of the GDP, and driving 70% of technological innovations. They also provide 80% of urban employment and 90% of new job creation. Concurrently, central enterprises have demonstrated remarkable innovation capabilities. The State Grid Corporation of China, for example, has consistently led in patent acquisitions among central enterprises for seven years since 2011, amassing 73,350 patents and securing numerous national science and technology awards. This highlights the pivotal role of central enterprises in China's innovation landscape, categorized into three main types: civilian enterprises activated by reform policies, military enterprises pivoting between civilian and military innovations, and newly established enterprises post-reform that have inherently focused on innovation.

The innovation ecosystem in China is marked by the dynamic evolution of its agents. Central enterprises, exemplified by the State Grid Corporation of China, China Aerospace Science and Technology Corporation, and China Mobile, among others, illustrate the broad spectrum of innovation sources. These entities span from historic establishments like the China Merchants Bureau, revitalized through reform, to military and newly formed central enterprises that have consistently prioritized innovation as a core aspect of their development strategy.

In the landscape of global innovation, certain Chinese central enterprises have emerged as frontrunners, particularly in the domain of complex system products. Notably, the Aerospace Science and Technology Group's development of the "Fengyun series of meteorological satellites" has significantly contributed to areas such as ecological observation, disaster prevention, and climate research. Similarly, the group's pioneering efforts in the "Beidou-1" navigation and positioning system positioned China as one of the few nations with an indigenous satellite navigation capability, alongside the United States and Russia. In the realm of energy transmission, the State Grid's ultra-high voltage transmission system represents the zenith of global high-voltage technology, while its "scenery storage and transmission demonstration project" sets a precedent as the world's inaugural large-scale initiative integrating renewable energy sources with advanced energy storage and transmission technologies. Furthermore, the China Mobile Group's advancement in the fourth-generation mobile communication system not only facilitated the global unification of the 4G standard but also established a new international benchmark, superseding the WiMAX standard championed by the United States.

Post-2005, the adoption of the endogenous innovation policy catalyzed a remarkable enhancement in the innovation capabilities of many central enterprises, propelling them to the forefront of their respective fields on the international stage. This period witnessed civilian central enterprises transitioning from reliance on foreign technologies to achieving parity with, or surpassing, international counterparts, exemplified by the State Grid's advancements in ultra-high voltage technology. Similarly, the innovations within military central enterprises have significantly bolstered national defense capabilities, ensuring readiness against modern military challenges posed by developed nations.

The role of academic institutions. As crucibles of innovation, academic institutions have achieved a pronounced effect. The establishment of "211," "985," and "double first-class universities," alongside the transformation of industrial institutes into high-tech enterprises, has underscored the pivotal role of universities and research institutes as repositories of knowledge and incubators of innovation. The exponential increase in SCI-indexed publications from 5,600 in 1988 to 324,200 in 2016, positioning China as a global leader in scientific research, alongside the surge in patent applications and authorizations, underscores the foundational role of academic research in fueling enterprise innovation. The widespread establishment of technology transfer offices, science and technology industrial parks, and innovation counseling services within over 3,000 public universities further exemplifies the systematic approach to nurturing innovation and entrepreneurship, culminating in the birth of numerous high-tech ventures.

China's forty-year practice of technological innovation has also accumulated some basic experience.

Mechanisms of innovation realization. The practice of technological innovation over four decades reveals distinct approaches based on the scale of innovation. Small-scale innovations typically rely on an iterative process, starting with a simplified "minimal viable product" that evolves through numerous iterations into a refined offering. This approach is exemplified by the evolution of Tencent's "Weixin" and Xiaomi's mobile phones. Large-scale innovations, on the other hand, necessitate an initial integration of relevant technologies to create a foundational product, which is then enhanced through integrated iteration. Systemic innovations require a national strategic directive, exemplified by projects like Peking University's laser phototypesetting system and the Chinese Academy of Sciences (CAS) Dawning computer. These innovations underscore the pivotal role of national support alongside the imperative for international engagement and learning.

The innovation subject and ecology. The experience of both state-owned and private enterprises demonstrates that innovation capacity is not confined to enterprise size. Large enterprises exhibit strengths in multidisciplinary systematic innovation and resource mobilization. The concept of "internal market testing" within conglomerates underscores the symbiotic relationship between different operational tiers, facilitating product refinement and market readiness. Conversely, small enterprises are advised to emulate the "invisible champions" by focusing on niche capabilities and core technologies, as noted by Professor Simon of Harvard Business School. This dichotomy addresses the long-standing debate in innovation economics regarding the optimal size for innovation, suggesting that both large and small enterprises possess unique advantages. Furthermore, the success of high-tech zones and science parks in fostering innovation is attributed more to their cultural atmosphere than to governmental incentives, challenging traditional notions of policy-driven innovation.

Innovation performance and impact. Empirical evidence suggests that both iterative and integrated innovation yield incremental returns on investment within a defined investment scale. Iterative innovation, embodying "lean innovation," has been widely recognized for its incremental investment returns. The concept of "incremental return on investment for integrated innovation" aligns with findings from the 1990s by Harvard Business School scholars, highlighting efficient technology integration as a crucial factor. This integration has been identified as a determinant of competitive performance and was instrumental in the resurgence of the US computer, electronic components, and software industries in the 1990s.

Since the 1990s, competitive advantage in the marketplace has increasingly been conferred upon companies proficient in selecting and integrating technologies, rather than those primarily focused on developing new technologies. This shift is particularly pronounced in an era where the array of technological options available to enterprises has expanded dramatically, leading to a significant increase in the breadth of technology incorporated into product design and manufacturing. Concurrently, product lifecycles have become markedly shorter, compelling enterprises to prioritize technology integration as a critical strategy for accelerating the commercialization of new technologies. Throughout China's four decades of technological innovation, the country has achieved remarkable successes, exemplified by advancements such as Tsinghua University's isotope container detector, the high-speed rail innovations within the railroad sector, and the development of the early warning aircraft by China Electronics Technology Group Corporation. These achievements can be attributed to two main factors. First, the integration of innovation—predominantly through the synthesis of existing technologies—has emerged as a vital source of revenue; second, the concept of innovation implantation growth has been identified as a key driver of high-quality economic expansion. This is achieved through various mechanisms: the catalytic role of innovation in stimulating economic growth, the expansion facilitated by imitative innovation, the enhancement brought about by iterative innovation, and the stabilization of growth fluctuations through successive innovation. Consequently, an innovation-driven development model has been realized, characterized by converting scientific and technological advancements into economic growth, transforming innovation into growth, and promoting entrepreneurship for development.

Over the past forty years, China's experience with technological innovation has been distilled into five crucial lessons.

The first of these lessons emphasizes that the institutional environment is a fundamental determinant of innovation's emergence and success. This period has revealed that for an economy (such as a city) to foster a setting where innovators feel content and see no need to seek change, at least three conditions must be met within its economic institutional framework. First, it must be challenging for both those who set and those who adhere to the system to gain extra benefits through "rent-seeking"; second, the return on investment for wealth creators, particularly innovators, should exceed the societal average; third, individuals should not have to engage in excessive "tug-of-war" to accomplish tasks, nor should they have to shoulder an undue amount of transaction costs. When such an institutional environment exists, dubbed a "satisfactory equilibrium," transaction costs for innovators in their innovative activities are lower, and the net benefits of innovation are higher. Consequently, the society at large tends to be more innovation-active. For instance, post-reform Shenzhen's economic institutional setting was in such a state, resulting in more vibrant local technological innovation than in other regions.

Conversely, if the institutional environment of an economy is "unsatisfactory and unimprovable," this can be termed a "non-satisfactory equilibrium" state. In such conditions, innovators may feel disinclined to innovate, incapable of doing so, or might even opt to "exit" the system. This leads to a dwindling group of innovators and a marked decrease in innovation activity. Following the reforms, certain innovators relocated to Shenzhen, escaping the "non-satisfactory equilibrium" of their hometowns.

An "unsatisfactory but improvable" state, or "unsatisfactory disequilibrium," presents a scenario where some innovators might wait for conditions to improve while others could engage in "rent-seeking" or "pseudo-innovation" to secure abnormal profits. Over the last four decades, some innovators on the mainland have pursued such extraordinary gains, influenced by local economic environments that needed to be more satisfactory and stable.

Drawing from these insights, to further propel innovation-driven development, local governments must prioritize creating a "satisfactory and balanced" institutional ecology. This involves implementing deeper reforms aimed at nurturing environments conducive to genuine innovation.

The second lesson from China's forty-year journey of technological innovation highlights a critical gap in the innovation and development of "science-based industries." When categorizing industries by their "knowledge sources," we can distinguish between "science-based" and "technology-based" sectors. The former relies heavily on new scientific discoveries for innovation, while the latter is more dependent on technological advancements. In recent times, "science-based industries" have surged ahead in many developed nations, carving out new international niches and securing unique global competitiveness.

Meanwhile, China has made commendable strides in closing the gap with developed countries in "technology-based industries," achieving both domestic and international recognition. The divide in these sectors is steadily narrowing and, in some cases, has even vanished. However, China's progress in "science-based industries" such as bioengineering, basic chemical materials, pharmaceuticals, and microelectronic devices has been less pronounced. This lag can be attributed to the nation's limited investment in basic scientific research, which stands at about 5% of R&D expenditure, compared to 18% to 20% in developed European and American countries. The shortfall in investment in basic sciences leads to slower scientific progress, which in turn impacts the innovation capacity within "science-based industries" due to a lack of domestic knowledge supply. This scenario not only hinders China's efforts to catch up with developed nations but also impedes the fundamental transformation of its industrial structure.

Given these circumstances, it is imperative for China to bolster its investment in basic sciences, overhaul the basic science research system, prioritize significant "remediation," and vigorously foster the innovation and development of science-based industries. Such measures are crucial for promoting a fundamental shift in China's industrial landscape and enabling it to match pace with developed countries.

The third key lesson from China's four decades of technological innovation underscores the critical need to focus on the emergence of "leading innovation" and the mechanisms driving its pioneering development. Innovation can be categorized into "leading innovation" and "non-leading innovation" based on its potential impact on economic and social development. “Leading innovations” inherently possess the capacity to spark new innovations and imitations, steering the direction and progression of economic and social evolution. In contrast, “non-leading innovations” lack this transformative potential.

A prime example from the 1990s involves Peking University’s development of laser phototypesetting technology by Wang Xuan, which emerged around the same time as Stone Company’s electronic typewriter. The former revolutionized traditional typesetting and printing, computer input and output, the press and publishing industry, and word processing habits, embodying the essence of a “leading innovation.” On the other hand, the electronic typewriter, despite creating a temporary boom in “typing stores,” was swiftly rendered obsolete by the advent of personal computers, representing a “non-leading innovation.”

To truly advance innovation-driven development, the government’s role should pivot toward primarily encouraging and supporting “leading innovations” that have the power to drive economic and societal progress. This approach allows “non-leading innovations” to be naturally sifted out or even phased out by market forces. Currently, the government’s general stance on encouraging innovation indiscriminately supports many initiatives that do not lead to significant development, resulting in the inefficient use of limited government resources. In advocating for “innovation leading development,” it’s crucial to depend on “leading innovations” rather than a blanket support for all forms of innovation.

The fourth critical insight from China’s forty-year innovation journey underscores the importance of nurturing domestic market demand for innovative products. While innovation is crucial to industrial advancement, the absence of domestic demand for new products can lead to their premature demise. A stark reminder of this came from China’s photovoltaic equipment manufacturing industry a few years ago. Encouraged by government incentives, companies in this sector pushed the boundaries of innovation, leading to rapid industry growth and a surge in exports. However, around 2014, when international restrictions on Chinese photovoltaic exports were imposed, industry giants like Wuxi Suntech and LDK experienced a sharp decline. This downturn was largely due to their failure to cultivate domestic market demand early on.

In light of this, future government strategies for guiding enterprise innovation and fostering new industry sectors must include initiatives aimed at cultivating market demand for these innovations. Reflecting on the economic landscape, China's GDP in the first half of 2018 stood at approximately $6.576 trillion. This was in comparison to the EU's GDP of about $9.428 trillion and the US GDP of $10.1 trillion during the same period, with China's GDP representing 69.75% and 65.11% of the EU and US GDPs, respectively. To mitigate challenges like anti-dumping, countervailing, or technical trade measure restrictions from entities such as the EU and the US, there's a strategic need to foster a domestic market that robustly supports China's innovative products.

The fifth lesson from China's four-decade-long innovation journey cautions that continuous, unchecked support for certain industries can lead to "industrial disasters." The "encouragement policy" serves as a vital tool for promoting and supporting the growth of nascent, underdeveloped industries. However, if such encouragement becomes excessive during the early stages of an industry's development, it invariably results in low-level overcapacity and intensified competition, potentially causing the industry's premature demise. When an industry faces nationwide overcapacity and the central government delays in adjusting these encouragement policies, while local governments persist in promoting the sector, it inevitably leads to industrial disasters characterized by further overcapacity, fierce competition, and unprofitable enterprises.

In 2000, the National Development and Reform Commission repeatedly issued warnings about emerging industries, such as photovoltaic equipment manufacturing and the aluminum industry, being plagued by overcapacity. Despite these cautions, some local governments continued to vigorously support these sectors. The current phase of "capacity reduction" is a drastic but necessary remedy for these industries. Therefore, going forward, it is imperative for central government departments to not only encourage the development of new industries but also to make timely policy adjustments and issue prompt warnings to industries at risk. Likewise, local governments must heed the industrial warning signals from the central government and promptly adjust local industrial development policies and plans accordingly.

In summarizing the trajectory of China's technological innovation over the forty years since the reform and opening-up, we delineate a progressive journey through "four ascending steps": the "learning and introduction phase," the "adoption, imitation, and enhancement phase," the "integration of foreign technology with indigenous innovation phase," and the "autonomous innovation and continuous improvement phase." Each phase is characterized by its own backdrop and distinct approach to innovation. Furthermore, we have meticulously outlined the main characteristics, foundational experiences, and critical lessons gleaned from China's technological innovation endeavors over the past four decades. Building on this analysis, the discussion advances the argument that, with the innovation-driven development strategy becoming increasingly ingrained, particularly with the growing focus by the state and industry sectors on "leading development through science and technology innovation," both government and academic circles must urgently address pertinent issues at this juncture.

First, intensifying trade disputes among numerous countries have changed the global science, technology, and economic governance structure and caused shifts in the global innovation competition and collaboration mechanisms. This vigilance is crucial in anticipation of adjustments or even a complete overhaul of the global governance architecture, enabling the emerging countries to navigate the evolving international landscape to further foster endogenous innovation and proactively devise response strategies. In this context, only "leading science and technology innovation" can inherently drive economic and social advancement and spawn new innovations, signifying our entrance into the era of big science and technology. Urgent priorities include understanding the emergence and mechanisms of leading science and technology innovation in this new era, discerning the optimal structure and institutional framework for a national innovation ecosystem suited to these advancements, and, upon clarifying these elements, actively pursuing institutional reforms and mechanism design to naturally segue into innovation-led growth. Therefore, harmonizing the roles of science policy and technology policy, as well as the positioning of scientific and technological innovators within the national innovation ecosystem, emerges as a critical concern for government, industry, and academia.

Second, since the innovation and growth of "science-based industries" represent a significant gap, and considering that the commercial and social applications of basic scientific research follow distinct rules, it is vital to enhance research into the mechanisms driving innovation in "science-based industries" at this juncture. Additionally, drawing from the practices of early industrialized nations like the United States, where "science-based enterprises" play a pivotal role in the innovation of "science-based industries," increasing focus on these enterprises is warranted.

Third, regarding the methodology of technological innovation research, although China has engaged in this field since the early 1990s, the prevalent methodologies still adhere to the frameworks of Schumpeterian innovation economics, Rendell's national innovation system, Mansfield's descriptive statistical analysis, Porter's logical structure model, and Drucker's expansive logical deduction, yet fall short of effectively uncovering the nuances of the emerging countries' technological innovation environment and the principles of innovation practice. Therefore, attention must be given to developing a research logic for innovation and development that resonates with the special context.

Fundamental Logic of the Book

This book delves into seven key facets of innovation within science-based industries.

Introduction: Classifying Industries and Innovation Based on Science. This opening chapter reevaluates how industries and innovations are categorized, underscoring the imperative to concentrate on science-based industries and their significance. In the realm of science-based industries, newcomers face substantial challenges in catching up with developed nations. Reflecting on China's forty-year journey of reform and opening, while the country has made remarkable strides in various "technology-based industries," catching up in science-based industries remains a daunting challenge. Science-based industries primarily rely on the advancement of science, often embodying exploratory innovations. Investigating these innovations not only augments the theoretical landscape of industrial innovation but also lays the groundwork for refining national science and technology policies and fostering the growth of strategic emerging industries. Furthermore, the chapter highlights that, despite China establishing a solid foundation for exploratory innovation over the past four decades, the innovation and development of science-based industries still lag behind and warrant increased attention and focus.

Chapter 1: Science-Based Industry: The Correlation Index. This chapter begins by delineating the relationship between science and technology, as well as the interaction between science and business. Science primarily tackles the "what" and "why," whereas technology focuses on the "how." With the evolution of science-based industries like biotechnology, the integration of science with business intensifies, blurring the lines between the two domains. Furthermore, this section introduces a classification for SBI and TBI. Unlike TBI, which hinges on new technological advancements or the enhancement, upgrading, and amalgamation of existing technologies, SBI springs from novel scientific discoveries. The chapter proceeds to detail the distinctions between science-based and technology-based industries and introduces an industry-science correlation index (ISCI) to clearly differentiate between the two.

Chapter 2: Science-Based Industry: Technological Catching-Up Perspective. This chapter first elucidates the concept of technological catch-up within industries, followed by an analysis and comparison of technological progression in two emblematic sectors: the pharmaceutical and automobile industries. It further explores the dynamics of technological catch-up in science-based versus technology-based industries, using the pharmaceutical and automobile industries as illustrative examples. The chapter concludes by comparing the technological advancements in these two types of industries, deriving key insights from the comparison.

Chapter 3: Science-Based Industry: Innovation Models. Acknowledging the diverse manifestations of science, this chapter outlines the variability within science-based industries. It initially identifies three SBI models inspired by the commercial success of Nobel Prize-related innovations: the enterprise-led innovation model, the collaborative innovation model between enterprises and universities or public research institutions (PRIs), and the start-up transformation model. Subsequently, the chapter introduces two models of demand-driven innovation, drawing from local Chinese experiences: the scientific discovery-based technology-led model and the scientific discovery-based technology catch-up model. The chapter concludes with a comparative analysis of the Nobel Prize innovation model and the demand-driven model within the context of science-based industries.

Chapter 4: Science-Based Industrial Innovation: Academic Entrepreneurship of Scientists. This chapter delves into the role of academic entrepreneurship in the context of science-based industrial innovation. Initially, it explores the involvement of scientists in entrepreneurial activities linked to science, acknowledging that such entrepreneurship not only advances science itself but also aids in the commercialization of research findings. This acts as a conduit between academia and the business world, propelling science toward practical application. Furthermore, the chapter showcases how scientists' participation in the commercialization process is enhanced through illustrative Nobel Prize examples and cases from China. It concludes by highlighting two pivotal elements of SBI: leadership by scientists and the concept of "transplantation with soil," emphasizing the adaptability and growth of scientific ideas in new commercial environments.

Chapter 5: Science-Based Industrial Innovation: Science-Based Enterprises. This chapter focuses on the significant role of science-based enterprises within science-based industries and their contribution to innovation. It begins by defining what constitutes a science-based enterprise, followed by an examination of how these businesses facilitate the commercialization of scientific discoveries. This exploration is supported by examples from Nobel Prize-winning innovations and Chinese case studies. The chapter wraps up by discussing the developmental and evolutionary traits of science-based entrepreneurial ventures, underscoring their unique position in driving scientific applications in the marketplace.

Chapter 6: Science-Based Industrial Innovation: Industry-University-Research Cooperation. The role of collaboration between industry, universities, and research institutions in science-based industries is the central theme of this chapter. It starts with an investigation into corporate involvement in early scientific discoveries, then shifts focus to corporate participation in application stage R&D. The chapter concludes by comparing these two modes of engagement, highlighting the synergies and distinctions between early discovery and application-focused research collaboration.

Chapter 7: Science-Based Industrial Innovation: China's Path. Focusing on China's strategic direction, this chapter scrutinizes the innovation and development within strategic emerging industries, particularly those identified as science-based. It specifically examines China's innovation journey through the lens of science-based industries, with Huawei serving as a prime example. The discussion extends to strategic approaches for technology catch-up and fostering endogenous innovation within science-based strategic emerging sectors, outlining the nuances of China's path toward technological sovereignty and global competitiveness in science-based fields.

CHAPTER 1

Science-Based Industry: The Correlation Index

1.1 Science and Technology & Science and Business

1.1.1 Science and Technology

Science serves as the foundational bedrock for technology, embodying a distinct significance from technology itself. The encyclopedic dictionary *Ci Hai*, first published in 1915, delineates "science" as a systematic body of knowledge concerning the phenomena, essence, and attributes of various entities in the objective world, along with their laws of motion. The Council for Science and Technology defines "science" as the pursuit of knowledge and understanding of nature and society, derived from everyday phenomena through a systematic approach. Science is typically characterized by its practicality, objectivity, truthfulness, theoretical systematization, and capacity for development (Shi 2007).

Technology encompasses various methods of process operation and skills, rooted in practical production experience and principles of natural science. It can be categorized into empirical technology and scientific technology based on their formation methodologies. Empirical technology evolves from the accumulation of individual experience. In contrast, scientific technology is the technical apparatus developed under the auspices of scientific theory to alter nature.

In essence, science primarily addresses the "what" and "why" questions, whereas technology focuses on solving the "how" issues. Pavitt (1998) argues that technology is not merely the application of science, highlighting several distinctions between scientific research and technological innovations. Qian (1999) further elaborates on the differences between science and technology, noting that they are concepts with entirely divergent connotations and should not be conflated. The key distinctions between science and technology are illustrated in Table 1-1.

Table 1-1 The key distinctions between science and technology

	Science	Technology
Main objectives	Recognize, explain, anticipate natural phenomena; enhance human capacity to understand nature	Apply and transform nature; foster artificial environments; boost human ability to generate material wealth
Main powers	Curiosity and drive to unravel nature's secrets	Motivation for efficiency and creation of greater material wealth
Main methods	Generalization, abstraction, induction, deduction, experimentation, hypothesis, etc.	Analogy, extrapolation, transplantation, experimentation, simulation, etc.
Forms of results	Mental forms: concepts, laws, theorems, formulas, principles, theoretical systems	Material form: new tools, devices, processes, methods, instruments
Relationships to culture module	Deep cultural influences, distinctive cultural traits	Deep cultural influences, less distinct cultural traits

Sources: Qian (1999)

1.1.2 Science and Business

The traditional perspective has long distinguished science and business as separate entities, akin to the division between philosophy and physics. Universities and research institutions were primarily responsible for basic scientific research, while businesses focused on developing practical applications. This division suggested a clear delineation: science explored theories and methodologies, whereas business concentrated on product and process viability for the market (Bolnick et al. 2007; Pisano 2010). However, a paradigm shift occurred in the early 20th century within some American universities, such as MIT, Purdue, and Cornell, which began to equally value applied and basic research. This period also saw the creation of university departments aimed at transitioning scientific discoveries to commercial applications. Concurrently, the late 19th and early 20th centuries witnessed the establishment of in-house R&D laboratories in major corporations like DuPont, General Motors, IBM, and AT&T. These corporate labs not only spearheaded pioneering scientific research but also produced Nobel Prize laureates who conducted pure scientific research and published their findings, similar to their academic counterparts (Shapin 2009; Astebro et al. 2012).

Despite the early 20th century's blending of science and business, three distinct characteristics persisted. First, only a handful of large companies, such as DuPont, Kodak, and IBM, pursued basic scientific research, partially spurred by the Antitrust Act, which encouraged these firms to seek alternatives to growth beyond mergers and acquisitions (Mowery 1990). Second, while new entrepreneurial firms significantly contributed to the commercialization of scientific discoveries, they rarely engaged in basic scientific research themselves. Third, although academic institutions participated in applied research and influenced market demand and the local economy, they were not primary players in the business realm.

These dynamics experienced a profound transformation with the advent of biotechnology (Pisano 2010). The late 20th century marked a quiet revolution in the innovation system, particularly through the integration of science and business, primarily driven by the emergence of bioscience and biotechnology. This shift indicates deeper and more enduring changes, affecting the interplay between science and business more broadly.

A notable transformation was the gradual decline of corporate laboratories. Bell Labs is a prime example; once the world's largest and most esteemed corporate R&D organization, it was disbanded in 1984 following AT&T's breakup under US antitrust policy enforcement. This led to AT&T's reduced capacity to fund expensive basic research, culminating in the closure of Bell Labs. Similar destinies befell other corporate research laboratories, such as Xerox, Kodak, General Motors, and even DuPont, which adjusted their labs' focus toward business needs of ongoing operations, influenced by increased market competition and the imperative to maximize short-term shareholder returns (Hounshell and Smith 1989; Reich 2002).

The second significant shift involved universities aggressively pursuing financial gains from IP. This movement gained momentum with the enactment of the Bayh-Dole Act in 1980, leading to an increase in university patent applications and licensing (Mowery et al. 2004). The trend of universities actively engaging in the commercialization of scientific discoveries through patent licensing, permissions, and even direct investments in startup businesses saw substantial growth in the final decades of the 20th century (Shane 2002; Sampat and Nelson 2002; Thursby and Thursby 2002; Mowery et al. 2009).

The third transformation was the rise of specialized "science-based" enterprises in the late 20th century, particularly in sectors like life sciences, nanotechnology, and new energy. Pisano (2006) describes these enterprises as entities that conduct basic scientific research while aiming to derive financial returns from their efforts. These companies are not mere consumers of scientific knowledge but also its producers. The biotechnology field, with advancements in DNA recombination, monoclonal antibodies, gene technology, stem cells, and ribonucleic acid interference, saw the emergence of science-based businesses. An exemplary case is Genentech, co-founded in 1976 by venture capitalist Swanson and Nobel laureate Boyer, a pioneer in DNA recombination. Genentech not only paved the way for the biotechnology industry but also exemplified the model of integrating basic scientific research with profit-making objectives. Initially, the company secured a $100,000 investment from venture capitalists for R&D startup funding. Unlike past corporate labs, which were funded by revenues from existing products, Genentech had no product revenue at its IPO and introduced its first product two years later. Genentech's successful merger of science and business has set a precedent for the commercialization of scientific findings, inspiring thousands of startups and biotech companies over the subsequent 35 years (Meyer 2002; Pisano 2006).

As evidenced by the evolution of science-based industries like biotechnology, the integration of basic science with business is becoming increasingly seamless. It is now recognized that some basic scientific research not only seeks new knowledge but also addresses practical problems, further blurring the lines between science and business.

1.2 SBI and TBI

The concept of "innovation" was first introduced in 1912 by the economist Schumpeter in his *Theory of Economic Development*. He proposed that innovation involves introducing a "new combination" of factors and conditions of production into the production system. Freeman (1982) defined technological innovation as the first-time transformation of technology into commercialization in the economic sense, manifesting in new products, processes, systems, and equipment. Other scholars, like Frankelius (2009), describe innovation as the market or societal introduction of an original and novel product, process, or service in any field. Therefore, technological innovation is a multifaceted process that begins with new ideas and concepts and culminates in the practical and successful application of a new project with economic and social value, achieved by continuously solving various problems.

The notion of "SBI" stems from Pavitt's research on the industrial classification of innovation. To understand the evolution of certain industries that emerged at the end of the 19th century and underwent rapid changes after World War II, Pavitt surveyed over 4,000 companies in the United Kingdom. His examination of the products, knowledge flows, and organizational structures across sectors revealed that technological innovation varies among different types of industries. In "supplier-led" industries, such as agriculture, construction, mining, forestry, commerce, and traditional manufacturing, innovation is primarily driven by suppliers' equipment and materials, with these firms having minimal involvement in R&D and holding few patents. In "production-intensive" industries, including those that are scale intensive like cement, metal smelting, and transportation equipment, R&D is predominantly conducted by large enterprises, focusing on both product innovation and process innovation. The former is protected by patents, while the latter is guarded by commercial secrecy. "Science-based industries" rely on scientific developments for R&D, with enterprises closely collaborating with universities and PRIs. These industries include fine chemicals, pharmaceuticals and biotechnology, electronics, optical and laser instruments, and advanced materials. Pavitt (1990) also introduced the concept of "Science-Based Technology," emphasizing that the development of science-based technology has been crucial in leveraging scientific discoveries and innovations to spur economic development in the 20th century (Patel and Pavitt 1994).

1.2.1 SBI

The advancement of basic sciences, such as chemistry and physics, alongside the rapid growth of bio-industries, has significantly altered perceptions of technological innovation (Nelson 1996; Malerba 2004; Chen and Cheng

2005). Marsili (2001) delved into the role of scientific research across various industries, uncovering a strong correlation between certain fields—such as biotechnology, pharmaceuticals, aerospace, and chemicals—and scientific advancements, where innovation is deeply reliant on the progress of basic science. Meyer (2002) further differentiated between science and technology-driven innovation, distinguishing SBI from technology-driven innovation and shedding light on the intricate relationship between science and technology. Coriat et al. (2003) define "SBI" as innovation directly propelled by and heavily dependent on scientific research. Lin and Lei (2013) underscored the tight connection between innovation in certain industries and scientific research, particularly in the pharmaceutical industry, where innovation is predominantly grounded in new scientific discoveries.

This type of innovation, which hinges on fresh scientific discoveries, can be termed "innovation based on new scientific discoveries," or "SBI" for short, or "science-driven innovation." This text refers to such innovations as "SBIs."

1.2.2 TBI

The occurrence and realization of TBI primarily rely on the emergence of new technologies or the improvement, upgrading, and combination of existing technologies. Coriat et al. (2003) argue that "TBI," in contrast to "SBI," refers to innovation that stems from process and technology development, which is less dependent on scientific research (Dolata 2009). For instance, current product and process innovations in fields such as machine tools, ships, and automobiles largely originate from technological advances and enhancements in related fields, or even from technological integrations. An example includes the development of computer numerical control machine tools through the integration of computer technology with machine tools, and the creation of "machining centers" by merging various machining technologies with computer technology. This type of innovation can be termed "innovation based on technological progress," "TBI" for short, or "technology-driven innovation." This text refers to such innovations as "TBIs."

In "TBI," innovation results from the evolution of technology itself or from engineering activities. The innovation capability of a company is primarily derived from the cumulative learning process within the organization. The key to successful innovation lies in the integration of various technological knowledge elements and the capabilities of the company.

1.2.3 Importance of Introducing a New Innovation Classification

Freeman (1974) and Böhme et al. (1978) introduced the concept of "science-based technology," highlighting that some technologies have a strong interaction with science, while others do not. For instance, mechanical engineering technology is founded on a set of application-oriented laws and rules, rather than on science. Within this framework, innovation that emerges from "technologies that do not interact strongly with science" is considered, to a certain degree, TBI.

Chinese scholars Chen and Zhao (2013) differentiated between "SBI" and "technology and engineering-based innovation." The former refers to innovation that is directly driven by and heavily relies on scientific research. This approach is characteristic of industries such as the home appliance industry, traditional equipment manufacturing industry, electrical industry, and traditional automobile industry. The latter, innovation based on technology development and process engineering, exhibits a weak dependence on scientific research. Representative industries include the biotechnology industry, fine chemical industry, new material industry, and aerospace industry. The distinctions between TBI and SBI are summarized in Table 1-2.

Table 1-2 The distinctions between TBI and SBI

Comparative dimension	TBI features	SBI features
Innovation participants	Technology suppliers, producers, and customers can innovate	Only producers can innovate; customers do not innovate on technology
Degree of technological change	Continuous improvement in a specific direction	Uncertainty in the direction of change, with jumps in the process
Knowledge base	Innovation based on a similar knowledge base	Based on entirely new technologies, often branching into new scientific areas
Innovation capability	Capable of gradually developing abilities	Must manage complex external relationships
Cost of risk	Lower risk and cost	High risks and costs, not diminishing as R&D advances

The distinction in the triggering mechanisms between "SBI" and "TBI" is profound, primarily because science and technology follow their own unique evolutionary paths. Without a foundational understanding of scientific principles, technological achievements are often the result of "trial and error" (Mowery and Rosenberg 1999; Chuma 2006). For instance, Bessemer, who invented the open-hearth process, lacked an understanding of the metallurgy and smelting principles that Sorby pioneered. Bell, an acoustic physiologist and teacher of deaf language, invented the telephone to amplify sound for the hearing impaired without grasping the electromagnetism principles discovered by Maxwell. Similarly, Edison, who invented the electric light, phonograph, and moving picture projector, had limited knowledge of mathematics. Furthermore, the outcomes of scientific research are not merely basic knowledge; in some cases, the commercialization cycle of scientific results can be quite brief, as seen in the technologies of transistors, plastics, and graphene.

It is important to note that for a long time, academic studies on technological innovation only categorized innovation into "market-pull innovation" and "technology-push innovation," without conducting specialized and systematic in-depth research on "SBI." This has led to numerous misunderstandings of the concept within academia, and even the principles of "technology-driven innovation" are erroneously applied to "SBI." Practically, this misunderstanding has not only misguided activities related to "SBI" but also resulted in a lack of clear demarcation in policy design between government science and technology policies. Often, these two types of policies are conflated, diluting the effectiveness of science and technology policies in promoting "scientific activities" and "SBI" far from their potential impact.

1.3 Science- and Technology-Based Industries

Interest in "SBI and its industries" began to surge in the 1970s, when some scholars identified "a new change and trend." They argued that a category of industries with common evolutionary characteristics had emerged in the late 19th century, leading to significant shifts in the global economy and society after World War II. Efforts to explain these changes and trends resulted in the development of a series of concepts such as "SBI," industry, technology, firm, and paradigm. To distinguish this new paradigm from traditional ones, corresponding classifications were proposed, all emphasizing the differences between the new development paradigm and the traditional one, and highlighting the "science-based" nature of the new paradigm.

Several representative concepts and classifications have been put forward historically. Gibbons and Johnston (1974) distinguished between "science-based industries" and "traditional craft industries," arguing that the development of the former was more reliant on science than the latter. Pavitt later categorized industries into "science-based industries," "production intensive industries," and "supplier dominated industries," positing that the technological trajectory of science-based industries is primarily driven by scientific breakthroughs in the public research sector.

According to Chandler (1992), the time lag between the generation of scientific research results and their industrial application in "science-based industries" is very short. He classified industries such as pharmaceuticals, biotechnology, semiconductors, and fine chemicals as science-based, while placing automobiles, machine tool manufacturing, and household appliance industries in the traditional "craft" category.

Autio (1997) introduced the concepts of a "science-based firm" and an "engineering-based firm." He described the former as more involved in translating scientific knowledge into basic and specific applicable technologies, focusing on converting scientific phenomena and theoretical concepts into commercial applications. In contrast, the latter is more adept at translating basic technologies into specific applications, with an emphasis on technology promotion. Hence, "science-based firms" tend to be at the upstream of the first-generation innovation model (i.e., linear innovation model), while "engineering-based firms" are situated downstream.

Cardinal et al. (2001) differentiated between "SBI" and "TBI." The former is described as the "industry-science" interaction pattern that emerges when both the industry and the related scientific field are nascent, whereas the latter occurs when the industry is immature, but the corresponding scientific field is mature, and there are no significant scientific breakthroughs. He identified industries related to chemistry, physiology, toxicology, and pharmacology as science-based.

Although these perspectives offer varying classifications, they all underscore the development characteristics of "certain industries that rely on science for innovation and development," deeming industries with a high degree of "scientific dependence" as "science-based industries."

1.3.1 Science-Based Industries

Science-based industries rely heavily on scientific research for their growth, with the industry's core technological advancements hinging on new scientific discoveries driven by SBI. The cutting-edge technologies in these sectors often originate from the scientific research departments within companies, but more frequently, they come from public research entities outside the firms. A common trait of such industries is the concurrent immaturity in their development and the sciences they depend on. For instance, the biomedical industry, still in its nascent stages, is based on life sciences and biomedicine, fields that are themselves experiencing rapid evolution with continuous breakthroughs. These sectors are typically the most dynamic segments of the economy, capable of sparking new industrial revolutions and propelling shifts in socioeconomic paradigms. The semiconductor industry post-1960s played a catalytic role in shifting the global economic paradigm, similar to the transformative potential of new materials like graphene and 3D printing in today's economic landscape.

Science-based industries exhibit several distinctive characteristics: innovation is primarily driven by scientific research findings; the innovation source often lies outside the firm, predominantly in the public research sector. Universities and research institutes play a crucial role in innovation, making industry-university collaboration the most characteristic innovation model. The core of such innovations, whether products or processes, lies in the commercialization of new scientific discoveries. Firms maintain strong connections with the public research sector to access external knowledge, crucial for innovation success. These industries are ripe with technological innovation opportunities, as scientific advancements open up possibilities for a variety of potential products. R&D investment levels are high, reflecting the intense industry-science linkage where neither the industry's development nor the science it relies on is fully mature. Similar to the biopharmaceutical industry, which is in its early development phase, the foundational scientific fields of life sciences and biomedicine are also rapidly evolving, continually yielding new research findings.

1.3.2 Technology-Based Industries

Technology-based industries are those whose development is minimally reliant on scientific research. Technological advancement in these sectors primarily unfolds through the evolution of technology itself, with new technologies emerging from breakthroughs, enhancements, combinations, adjustments, and transformations of existing technologies, propelled by TBIs (Basalla 1988; Arthur 2007). The leading technologies in such industries typically arise from within the firms themselves, with minimal external sources of innovation. These industries are usually in their growth or maturity phases, and the related scientific fields are more developed. For instance, in sectors like highway and railroad bridge engineering, shipbuilding, machine tool manufacturing, and furniture making, the corresponding mechanical principles and engineering are relatively mature and stable, having seen no significant new breakthroughs for an extended period. These industries form the backbone of many nations' economies, especially in countries at the early and mid-stages of industrialization, playing a crucial role in national economic development.

Technology-based industries are characterized by several key features: innovation results from the development of technology itself or engineering activities; a firm's innovation capacity largely stems from a cumulative learning process within the organization; the critical factors for innovation success include the firm's technological investment, technological accumulation, and the integration of various technological knowledge and capabilities; the potential for technological innovation growth is relatively stable; R&D investment intensity is comparatively low; in this industry-science relationship, the industry often finds itself in a formative or mature stage, while the related scientific fields are more advanced in their development. For example, in engineering fields such as highway and railroad bridge engineering, shipbuilding, and machine tool manufacturing, the corresponding mechanical principles and engineering are relatively mature and stable, with no significant breakthroughs occurring over a long period.

1.3.3 Importance of Introducing a New Industrial Classification

Unlike traditional industry classifications, this book categorizes industries within the national economy into science-based industries and technology-based industries, due to the marked differences in their formation and developmental patterns. This distinction allows for a more in-depth analysis of each type.

China's economic and social "12th Five-Year Plan" emphasizes the growth of strategic emerging industries, focusing primarily on new energy, energy conservation and environmental protection, electric vehicles, new materials, new medicine, bio-breeding, and the information industry. Among these, several industries are identified as "science-based," including biomass energy, power batteries, nano and superconducting materials preparation, new biological drugs, biomedical engineering, bio-breeding, marine biology, and next-generation information network technology. The majority of the remaining industries are categorized as "technology-based." By separately identifying the development patterns of these two types of industries, the approach offers more nuanced insights, enabling the government to craft more precisely targeted industrial policies.

1.4 Distinctive Differences between the Two Industries

Science-based and technology-based industries exhibit substantial differences in various aspects, including the origins of entrepreneurship, business models, industrial evolution, primary drivers of industrial development, and the contribution of the public research sector to the innovation system.

1.4.1 Developmental Drivers: A Comparative Analysis

Science-based industries rely heavily on scientific research for their development, with technological advances primarily fueled by SBI. The cutting-edge technologies in these sectors may come from the firms' own research departments but are more frequently derived from PRIs outside the companies (Debackere and Veugelers 2005). In such connections between industry and science, it's common for both the industry and its underlying scientific discipline to be in the early stages of development.

Conversely, technology-based industries have a lesser reliance on scientific research for growth, with their technological progress predominantly driven by TBI. The leading technologies in these sectors are typically developed internally within the company, with limited input from external innovation sources. In these "industry-science" relationships, the industry is often at a nascent or mature phase, whereas the associated scientific fields are more advanced.

1.4.2 Innovational Knowledge Sources: A Comparative Analysis

Historically, Nelson and Winter (1982), in their seminal work *An Evolutionary Theory of Economic Change*, categorized firms into two distinct technological paradigms: the "science-based technological regime" and the "cumulative technological regime." They posited that in science-based industries, innovation is often sparked by external changes, such as new discoveries in university research, indicating that the potential for technological development includes exogenous variables, and that innovation is not reliant on the technological capabilities of firms. In contrast, "cumulative" industries do not view the potential for technological development as exogenous, and here, innovation is dependent on the firms' technological capabilities. The "science-based technological regime" aligns with SBI and its industries, while the "cumulative technological regime" aligns with TBI and its industries.

For instance, the biochemical industry exemplifies a science-based industry, where innovation frequently stems from the exogenous public research sector. There is a high degree of interaction between the industry and scientific institutions, with a significant number of patents (about 78%) citing scientific literature. Conversely, the telecommunications industry serves as a typical example of a technology-based industry, with innovations primarily originating from within the industry's R&D efforts (Meyer 2002), and approximately 37% of the cited patents referencing scientific literature. Furthermore, the industrial evolution of the electronics and pharmaceutical industries highlights notable differences: the electronics industry has experienced frequent turnovers of leading and lagging firms over the past thirty years (Hobday 1998), whereas in the pharmaceutical industry, leading firms have generally managed to maintain their advantages over the past century (Achilladelis and Antonakis 2001).

1.4.3 The Distinctive Impact of Science-Based Industries

Science-based industries often catalyze fundamental shifts in the industrial landscape and economic paradigms, serving as engines of economic and social advancement. This impact was notably evident in the rise of the modern electrical and chemical industries in the 19th century. The significance of such industries escalated in the 20th century, exemplified by the semiconductor industry, which revolutionized the economic development paradigm. Presently, these industries represent the most dynamic sectors of the economy, acting as new economic engines and primary forces behind the structural transformation and upgrading of national economies. Their emergence and growth can spark new industrial revolutions and potentially drive shifts in socioeconomic paradigms. Consequently, these industries have emerged as strategic sectors of interest for governments and a new focal point in international industrial competition.

1.5 Identifying Science-Based Industries: ISCI Approach

1.5.1 Introduction to ISCI

In discussions about "science-based industries," many scholars emphasize the "reliance of certain industries on science," often described in terms of "greater dependence," "stronger reliance," and "higher interactivity." However, the question arises: to what extent does an industry qualify as science-based? Qualitative descriptions alone are insufficient; there is a need for a "quantifiable" concept and scale.

Patent analysis is a practical method for examining the "science dependence" and "technology dependence" of an industry. This approach is valid because the "information" cited in a specific patent closely ties the development of the industry to relevant scientific fields. Essentially, patent applications usually require references to other literature, which can be categorized into two types: citations from other patents and non-patent literature (NPL), which includes journal articles, conference papers, dissertations, research disclosures, technical reports, academic books, etc., representing scientific literature.

Based on these considerations, we can define a "science-based industry" as "an industry that consistently cites scientific literature at a high frequency over a prolonged period." Accordingly, the following index can be employed to measure an industry's reliance on scientific research: the ISCI, represented by "P_{NPL}/P_{total}." Here, P_{NPL} is the number of patents with "non-patent citations" within the industry, and P_{total} is the total number of patents in an industry. P_{NPL} counts the NPL cited by an industrial patent; P_{total} encompasses the total number of documents cited by patents in an industry.

The Global Patent Index (GPI) database, provided by the European Patent Office (EPO), is a valuable resource for calculating the "ISCI" for a given industry and determining its "science dependence." The GPI database includes data on over eight hundred million patents across more than ninety countries, featuring patent technology information, legal details, citation information, and more, an example as illustrated in Figure 1-1. It supports searches, statistical analyses, and academic research through the Structured Query Language, and is updated weekly every Friday at 12:00 a.m. (CET). This tool enables a precise measurement of the extent to which industries depend on scientific advancements.

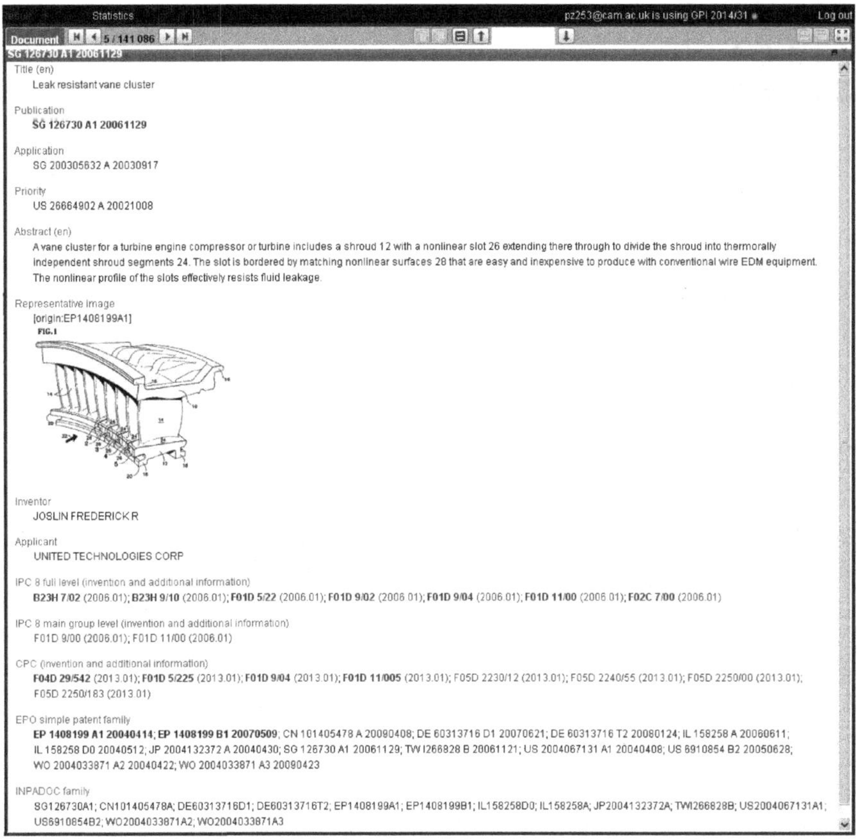
Statistics
pz253@cam.ac.uk is using GPI 2014/31
Log out
Document 5 / 141 086
SG 126730 A1 20061129

Title (en)
Leak resistant vane cluster

Publication
SG 126730 A1 20061129

Application
SG 200305632 A 20030917

Priority
US 26664902 A 20021008

Abstract (en)
A vane cluster for a turbine engine compressor or turbine includes a shroud 12 with a nonlinear slot 26 extending there through to divide the shroud into thermorally independent shroud segments 24. The slot is bordered by matching nonlinear surfaces 28 that are easy and inexpensive to produce with conventional wire EDM equipment. The nonlinear profile of the slots effectively resists fluid leakage.

Representative image
[origin:EP1408199A1]
FIG. 1

Inventor
JOSLIN FREDERICK R

Applicant
UNITED TECHNOLOGIES CORP

IPC 8 full level (invention and additional information)
B23H 7/02 (2006.01); **B23H 9/10** (2006.01); **F01D 5/22** (2006.01); **F01D 9/02** (2006.01); **F01D 9/04** (2006.01); **F01D 11/00** (2006.01); **F02C 7/00** (2006.01)

IPC 8 main group level (invention and additional information)
F01D 9/00 (2006.01); F01D 11/00 (2006.01)

CPC (invention and additional information)
F04D 29/542 (2013.01); **F01D 5/225** (2013.01); **F01D 9/04** (2013.01); **F01D 11/005** (2013.01); F05D 2230/12 (2013.01); F05D 2240/55 (2013.01); F05D 2250/00 (2013.01); F05D 2250/183 (2013.01)

EPO simple patent family
EP 1408199 A1 20040414; **EP 1408199 B1 20070509**; CN 101405478 A 20090408; DE 60313716 D1 20070621; DE 60313716 T2 20080124; IL 158258 A 20060611; IL 158258 D0 20040512; JP 2004132372 A 20040430; SG 126730 A1 20061129; TW I266828 B 20061121; US 2004067131 A1 20040408; US 6910854 B2 20050628; WO 2004033871 A2 20040422; WO 2004033871 A3 20090423

INPADOC family
SG126730A1; CN101405478A; DE60313716D1; DE60313716T2; EP1408199A1; EP1408199B1; IL158258D0; IL158258A; JP2004132372A; TWI266828B; US2004067131A1; US6910854B2; WO2004033871A2; WO2004033871A3

Figure 1-1 Example of EPO patent data

This book utilizes the method of the International Patent Classification (IPC) to classify patents, adhering to the International Patent Classification Agreement, also known as the Strasbourg Agreement. This agreement, rooted in the IPC devised by the 1954 European Convention on the International Classification of Patents for Inventions, took effect on March 24, 1971. The Strasbourg Agreement organizes technology into eight divisions and 69,000 subcategories, with each subcategory assigned a unique symbol by national or regional industrial property offices. The classification system undergoes revisions every five years. Presently, the IPC stands as one of the most extensively adopted patent classification standards by the EPO.

Utilizing the structured and retrievable GPI search system provided by the EPO, we compiled patent data for 59 industries from January 1, 2008, to December 31, 2012, as detailed in Table 1-3.

Table 1-3 Patent citations by industry

Industries	IPC classification number	Total number of patents	Number of patents cited	Number of patents citing other patents but no NPL	Number of patents with NPL citations	Number of patents with NPL citations / number of patents with citations	Number of patents with NPL citations / total number of patents
Biochemistry	C12	455,068	155,843	34,278	121,565	0.780	0.267
Pharmaceutical	A61P	595,110	167,301	50,595	116,706	0.697	0.196
Organic chemistry	C07C08	1,193,740	377,661	152,628	225,033	0.596	0.189
Sugar industry	C13	1,969	308	131	177	0.575	0.0899
Cosmetics	A61Q	87,469	31,665	16,194	15,471	0.489	0.177
Agriculture, forestry, and fisheries	A01	368,214	99,923	52,800	47,123	0.472	0.128
Food engineering	A22–A23	235,681	53,567	28,675	24,892	0.465	0.106
Inorganic chemistry	C01	140,101	42,245	23,110	19,135	0.453	0.137
Medical materials	A61L	105,959	33,257	18,324	14,933	0.449	0.141
Nano-related industries	B82	33,393	13,081	7,248	5,833	0.446	0.175
Electrotherapy, magnetic therapy, radiotherapy, and ultrasound therapy	A61N	68,965	29,092	16,623	12,469	0.429	0.181
Fertilizer and fertilizer manufacturing	C05	21,996	3,485	2,004	1,481	0.425	0.067
Surveying and mapping	G01	1,105,809	382,183	229,277	152,906	0.400	0.138

Petrochemicals	C10	102,942	30,673	18,639	12,034	0.392	0.117
Dyes, coatings, polishes, natural resins, and adhesives	C09	288,650	92,217	56,071	36,146	0.392	0.125
Data processing	G06	1,453,905	657,156	400,596	256,560	0.390	0.176
Calculation	G06	1,453,905	657,156	400,596	256,560	0.39	0.176
Microstructure technology	B81	21,979	8,053	4,956	3,097	0.385	0.141
Cement, concrete, artificial stone, ceramics, and refractory materials	C04	97,859	26,571	16,721	9,850	0.371	0.101
Electric communication	H04	1,651,838	645,467	411,405	234,062	0.363	0.142
Paper making	D21	52,406	14,860	9,517	5,343	0.360	0.102
Implantable medical devices	A61F	194,593	73,640	47,510	26,130	0.355	0.134
Electronic	H03	206,504	84,782	54,720	30,062	0.355	0.146
Basic electronic circuits	H03	206,504	84,782	54,720	30,062	0.355	0.146
Nuclear physics and nuclear engineering	G21	35,496	13,331	8,781	4,550	0.341	0.128
Glass and mineral wool or slag wool	C03	65,406	20,672	13,758	6,914	0.334	0.106
Medicine	A61B–A61N	646,451	238,509	159,594	78,915	0.331	0.122
Metallurgy	C21–C22	150,086	39,416	26,735	12,681	0.322	0.084
Space technology	B64	58,742	22,892	15,644	7,248	0.317	0.123

Industries	IPC classification number	Total number of patents	Number of patents cited	Number of patents citing other patents but no NPL	Number of patents with NPL citations	Number of patents with NPL citations / number of patents with citations	Number of patents with NPL citations / total number of patents
Control technology	G05	161,281	55,197	37,929	17,268	0.313	0.107
Tobacco	A24	24,167	4,683	3,290	1,393	0.297	0.058
Leather	C14	2,098	233	164	69	0.296	0.033
Textile	D01–D07	211,891	54,007	38,654	15,353	0.284	0.072
Drilling of earth or rock and mining	E21	146,990	39,619	28,732	10,887	0.275	0.074
Plastic fabrication and processing	B29	231,774	74,207	54,174	20,033	0.270	0.086
Weapons	F41	31,324	11,697	8,599	3,098	0.265	0.099
Semiconductors	H01L	869,397	331,336	244,886	86,450	0.261	0.099
Processing and preservation of wood or similar materials	B27	34,534	9,003	6,706	2,297	0.255	0.067
Optical	G02	488,084	170,063	129,058	41,005	0.241	0.084
Metal casting and machining	B21–B22	208,929	53,515	40,778	12,737	0.238	0.061
Power	H02	451,945	138,710	107,600	31,110	0.224	0.069
Railroad	B61	43,465	11,302	8,780	2,522	0.223	0.058
Ships	B63	56,816	17,396	13,590	3,806	0.219	0.067

Combustion equipment and methods	F23	66,989	18,206	14,223	3,983	0.219	0.059
Cinematography	G03	332,740	118,824	93,268	25,556	0.215	0.077
Engines and Pumps	F01–F04	549,475	188,684	149,026	39,658	0.210	0.072
Machine tools	B23	268,441	79,626	63,117	16,509	0.207	0.061
Clothing, shoes, and hats	A41–A43	99,396	24,041	19,147	4,894	0.204	0.049
Physical therapy equipment	A61H	46,690	10,121	8,088	2,033	0.201	0.044
Packaging	B65	481,913	141,979	114,922	27,057	0.191	0.056
Mechanical engineering	F15–F17	649,839	205,382	166,503	38,879	0.189	0.060
Printing	B41	212,970	73,755	60,464	13,291	0.180	0.062
Cars	B60	574,728	207,702	170,478	37,224	0.179	0.065
Sports, games, and recreational activities	A63	216,719	81,028	66,758	14,270	0.176	0.066
Furniture	A47	383,478	89,807	74,143	15,664	0.174	0.041
Lighting	F21	186,719	49,150	40,609	8,541	0.174	0.046
Buildings	E04	237,356	64,064	53,387	10,677	0.167	0.045
Road, rail, or bridge construction	E01	79,097	20,843	17,477	3,366	0.161	0.043
Hydraulic engineering and water supply and drainage	E02–E03	153,713	40,927	34,974	5,953	0.145	0.039

In this book, we've selected the second level of the IPC system for industry classification. This level is preferred because the first level, which divides industries into only seven categories, is overly broad, while the third level offers too much granularity. The second level strikes an optimal balance for industry classification. We have refined this second-level classification to identify 59 industries, effectively encompassing the entire range of industries covered by the IPC system.

The previously mentioned "ISCI = Number of patents with NPL citations / Total number of patents with citations" has been mathematically adjusted to fall within a range of [−100, 100]. This ISCI is utilized to distinguish "science-based industries" from others. According to the ISCI, industries with positive indexes are identified as "science-based industries," while those with negative indexes are considered "technology-based industries." Furthermore, a larger positive index value indicates a stronger "science-based tendency" within the industry; conversely, a larger absolute value of a negative index signifies a stronger "technology-based tendency" in the industry.

$$ISCI_j = 100Sgn\left(\frac{P_{NPL,j}}{P_{total,j}} - \frac{\sum_i \frac{P_{NPL,i}}{P_{total,i}}}{i}\right)\sqrt{\left(\frac{P_{NPL,j}}{P_{total,j}} - \frac{\sum_i \frac{P_{NPL,i}}{P_{total,i}}}{i}\right) * Sgn\left(\frac{P_{NPL,j}}{P_{total,j}} - \frac{\sum_i \frac{P_{NPL,i}}{P_{total,i}}}{i}\right)}$$

(P_{NPL}: Number of NPL citations for an industrial patent; P_{total}: Total number of literature citations for patents in an industry; j: Industry)

1.5.2 *Time Stability of the ISCI*

Theoretically, suppose an industry's ISCI value demonstrates instability. In that case, this typically indicates one of two scenarios: either the scientific dependence of certain industries is evolving over time, or some industries exhibit a lower degree of science dependence. Consequently, it becomes imperative to select a few representative industries with high, medium, and low ISCI values to examine the stability of the ISCI over time.

In this book, "stability analysis" is performed every five years, starting from January 1, 1988, and concluding on December 31, 2012. Given that some patents undergo a lengthy filing process and considering the substantial volume of patents in the filing phase post-2012, it's essential to exclude such data to prevent any distortion.

Based on the data mentioned above, we calculated the ISCI indices for typical industries over a 25-year span, from the start of 1988 to the end of 2012. The findings revealed that the ISCI for 59 industries remained relatively stable over time. Despite observable fluctuations in the ISCI values of each industry, as depicted in Figure 1-2, the relative standings of the ISCI indices among industries largely stayed the same, and the fluctuation trends of the ISCI indices for each industry were consistent. Therefore, employing the ISCI to determine the "science dependence of industries" and identify "science-based industries" is deemed appropriate.

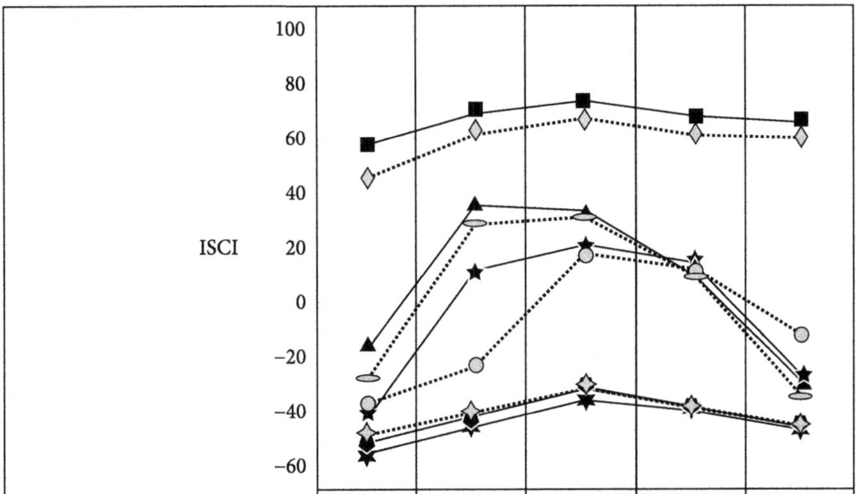

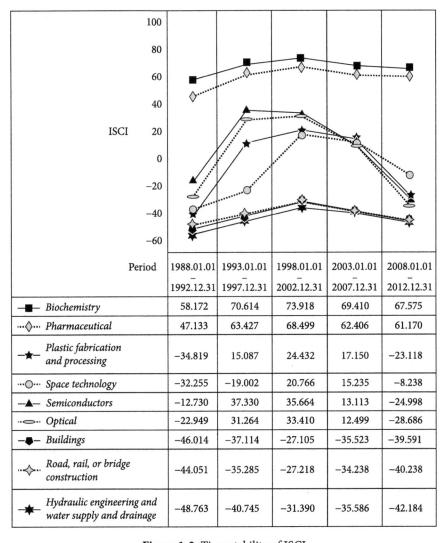

Period	1988.01.01 – 1992.12.31	1993.01.01 – 1997.12.31	1998.01.01 – 2002.12.31	2003.01.01 – 2007.12.31	2008.01.01 – 2012.12.31
Biochemistry	58.172	70.614	73.918	69.410	67.575
Pharmaceutical	47.133	63.427	68.499	62.406	61.170
Plastic fabrication and processing	−34.819	15.087	24.432	17.150	−23.118
Space technology	−32.255	−19.002	20.766	15.235	−8.238
Semiconductors	−12.730	37.330	35.664	13.113	−24.998
Optical	−22.949	31.264	33.410	12.499	−28.686
Buildings	−46.014	−37.114	−27.105	−35.523	−39.591
Road, rail, or bridge construction	−44.051	−35.285	−27.218	−34.238	−40.238
Hydraulic engineering and water supply and drainage	−48.763	−40.745	−31.390	−35.586	−42.184

Figure 1-2 Time stability of ISCI

Biochemistry	67.57541723
Pharmaceutical	61.16999586
Organic chemistry	52.19728074
Sugar industry	50.12695456
Cosmetics	40.64227384
Agriculture, forestry, and fisheries	38.49531911
Food engineering	37.5878855
Inorganic chemistry	35.99289442
Medical materials	35.44207732
Nano related industries	35.00139335
Electrotherapy, magnetic therapy, radiotherapy, and ultrasound therapy	32.43480152
Fertilizer and fertilizer manufacturing	31.86847418
Surveying and mapping	27.69145273
Petrochemicals	26.25411416
Dyes, coatings, polishes, natural resins, and adhesives	26.18446232
Data processing	25.88540434
Calculation	25.88540434
Microstructure technology	24.73317789
Cement, concrete, artificial stone, ceramics, and refractory materials	21.74873249
Electric communication	19.80406603
Paper making	19.01359706
Implantable medical devices	17.72855376
Electronic	17.65667416
Basic electronic circuits	17.65667416
Nuclear physics and nuclear engineering	13.38116656
Glass and mineral or slag wool	10.51565831
Medicine	8.63935774
Metallurgy	−4.10124865
Space technology	−8.23833023
Control technology	−10.27671059
Tobacco	−16.10753658
Leather	−16.51267037
Textile	−19.78034463
Drilling of earth or rock and mining	−22.04807696
Plastic fabrication and processing	−23.11776643
Weapons	−24.19709305
Semiconductors	−24.99815479
Processing and preservation of wood or similar materials	−26.12795263
Optical	−28.68582227
Metal casting and processing	−29.22261662
Power	−31.48385198
Railroad	−31.66351553
Ships	−32.34474293
Combustion equipment and methods	−32.34658201
Cinematography	−32.91348836
Engines and pumps	−33.64848643
Machine tools	−34.06939848
Clothing, shoes, and hats	−34.61723042
Physical therapy equipment	−35.00495508
Packaging	−36.44636208
Mechanical engineering	−36.62011126
Printing	−37.84170126
Cars	−37.97181378
Sports, games, and recreational activities	−38.37866674
Furniture	−38.59866477
Lighting	−38.68203803
Buildings	−39.59074435
Road, rail, or bridge construction	−40.2381784
Hydraulic engineering and water supply and drainage	−42.18412807

Figure 1-3 Axis of industry-science interconnection

1.5.3 Science-Industry Correlation Axis

The ISCI indices of the 59 industries, as detailed in Table 1-4, were ranked to create the "industry-science correlation axis," which reflects the degree of dependence these industries have on science (as illustrated in Figure 1-3). Within this framework, "typical science-based industries" include medicine, biochemistry, the pharmaceutical industry, organic chemistry, and so on, whereas "typical technology-based industries" encompass water engineering and drainage, road, railroad and bridge construction, architecture, and similar fields. Further analysis, based on Figure 1-3 and following suitable industry consolidation, has led to the creation of Table 1-4.

Table 1-4 The ISCI index classification of SBI and TBI

Science-based industries	Technology-based industries
Medicine, biochemistry, pharmaceutical industry, organic and nonorganic chemistry, medical materials, nano-related industries, electromagnetism, surveying and mapping, petrochemical and fuel and new energy, data processing and scientific computing, microstructure technology, electronic communication, implantable medical devices, electronics and basic electronic circuits, nuclear physics and engineering, sugar industry, cosmetics, agriculture, forestry, husbandry and fishery, food engineering, basic building materials, and papermaking and fertilizer	Mining and metallurgy, space technology, control technology, tobacco, leather and textile clothing, weapons and engines, semiconductors, wood processing furniture, optics, metal processing and mechanical engineering, power and lighting, railways and ships, automobiles, combustion equipment, machine tools and physiotherapy instruments, film and television and sports entertainment, packaging and printing, construction, road and bridge construction, and hydraulic engineering

Through the analysis of industries using patent data, it becomes evident that first, here are marked differences in the degree of science dependence (or correlation) for industrial development across various sectors. For instance, the biochemical industry, which demonstrates a strong scientific correlation, has nearly 80% of its patents citing NPL. Conversely, in the field of water engineering, which shows a weak scientific correlation, less than 15% of the industry's patents cite NPL. Second, "science-based industries" typically encompass sectors such as medicine, biochemistry, pharmaceuticals, organic and inorganic chemistry, medical materials, nanotechnology-related industries, electromagnetism, mapping, petrochemicals, fuels and new energy, data processing, scientific computing, microstructure technology, electronic communications, implantable medical devices, electronics and basic electronic circuits, nuclear physics, and engineering, among others. The growth of these industries is heavily reliant on scientific research, with a significant portion of patents within these sectors citing scientific literature. In these fields, frontier technologies often originate from scientific research outcomes in the public research sector, representing an exogenous variable in industry development. Major scientific breakthroughs frequently serve as the foundation for the core innovative products of these industries, potentially sparking a wave of product innovations. Third, industries such as mining and metallurgy, space technology, control technology, tobacco, leather and textile garments, weapons and engines, semiconductors, woodworking and furniture, optics, metalworking and mechanical engineering, electricity and lighting, railroads and ships, automobiles, combustion equipment, machine tools, and physical therapy equipment, as well as film and sports entertainment, packaging and printing, construction of buildings, roads, and bridges, and water engineering, fall into the "technology-based industries" category. Technological innovation in these sectors often reflects the evolution of technology itself, with new technologies emerging from breakthroughs, enhancements, combinations, adjustments, and transformations of existing technologies. The sources of innovation in such industries are typically the accumulation and integration of technologies within the firm.

References

Achilladelis, Basil, and Nicholas Antonakis. 2001. "The Dynamics of Technological Innovation: The Case of the Pharmaceutical Industry." *Research Policy* 30 (4): 535–588.

Arthur, W. Brian. 2007. "The Structure of Invention." *Research Policy* 36 (2): 274–287.

Åstebro, Thomas, Navid Bazzazian, and Serguey Braguinsky. 2012. "Startups by Recent University Graduates and Their Faculty: Implications for University Entrepreneurship Policy." *Research Policy* 41 (4): 663–677.

Autio, Erkko. 1997. "New, Technology-Based Firms in Innovation Networks Symplectic and Generative Impacts." *Research Policy* 26 (3): 263–281.

Basalla, George. 1988. *The Evolution of Technology*. Cambridge: Cambridge University Press.

Böhme, Gernot, Wolfgang Van Den Daele, and Wolfgang Krohn. 1978. "The 'Scientification' of Technology." In *The Dynamics of Science and Technology*, 219–250. Dordrecht: Springer.

Bolnick, Deborah A., Duana Fullwiley, Troy Duster, et al. 2007. "The Science and Business of Genetic Ancestry Testing." *Science* 318 (5849): 399–400.

Cardinal, Laura B., Todd M. Alessandri, and Stephen F. Turner. 2001. "Knowledge Codifiability, Resources, and Science-Based Innovation." *Journal of Knowledge Management.*

Chandler, Alfred D. 1992. "Organizational Capabilities and the Economic History of the Industrial Enterprise." *Journal of Economic Perspectives* 6 (3): 79–100.

Chen, Jin, Zhao Xiaoting, and Liang Liang. 2013. "Science-Based Innovation." *Science and Technology Management* 34 (6): 3–7.

Chen, Yanying, and Cheng Ruiwen. 2005. "A Review of Corporate Collaborative Innovation Research." *Science, Technology, and Industry* 5 (8): 1–5.

Chuma, Hiroyuki. 2006. "Increasing Complexity and Limits of Organization in the Microlithography Industry: Implications for Science-Based Industries." *Research Policy* 35 (3): 394–411.

Coriat, Benjamin, Fabienne Orsi, and Olivier Weinstein. 2003. "Does Biotech Reflect a New Science-Based Innovation Regime?" *Industry and Innovation* 10 (3): 231–253.

Debackere, Koenraad, and Reinhilde Veugelers. 2005. "The Role of Academic Technology Transfer Organizations in Improving Industry Science Links." *Research Policy* 34 (3): 321–342.

Dolata, Ulrich. 2009. "Technological Innovations and Sectoral Change: Transformative Capacity, Adaptability, Patterns of Change: An Analytical Framework." *Research Policy* 38 (6): 1066–1076.

Frankelius, Per. 2009. "Questioning Two Myths in Innovation Literature." *The Journal of High Technology Management Research* 20 (1): 40–51.

Freeman, Christopher, and Luc Soete. 1974. *The Economics of Industrial Innovation.* Harmondsworth: Penguin.

Gibbons, Michael, and Ron Johnston. 1974. "The Roles of Science in Technological Innovation." *Research Policy* 3 (3): 220–242.

Hobday, Mike. 1998. "Product Complexity, Innovation and Industrial Organisation." *Research Policy* 26 (6): 689–710.

Hounshell, David A., and John K. Smith. 1989. *Science and Corporate Strategy.* Cambridge: Cambridge Books.

Lin, Bao, and Lei Jiaxiao. 2013. "Science-Based Innovation Models and Dynamics—a Reanalysis of the Penicillin and Transistor Cases." *Research in Science*, no. 10: 1459–1464.

Malerba, Franco, ed. 2004. *Sectoral Systems of Innovation: Concepts, Issues and Analyses of Six Major Sectors in Europe.* Cambridge: Cambridge University Press.

Marsili, O. 2001. "The Anatomy and Evolution of Industries." *Books.*

Meyer, M. 2002. "Tracing Knowledge Flows in Innovation Systems." *Scientometrics* 54 (2): 193–212.

Mowery, D. C. 1990. "The Development of Industrial Research in US Manufacturing." *The American Economic Review* 80 (2): 345–349.

Mowery, D. C., and N. Rosenberg. 1999. *Paths of Innovation: Technological Change in 20th-Century America.* Cambridge: Cambridge University Press.

Mowery, D. C., and B. N. Sampat. 2004. "The Bayh-Dole Act of 1980 and University–Industry Technology Transfer: A Model for Other OECD Governments?" *The Journal of Technology Transfer* 30 (1): 115–127.

Nelson, R. R., and S. G. Winter. 1982. *An Evolutionary Theory of Economic Change.* Cambridge, Massachusetts, and London, England: The Belknap Press of Harvard University Press.

Nelson, T. O. 1996. "Consciousness and Metacognition." *American Psychologist* 51 (2): 102.

Patel, P., and K. Pavitt. 1994. "National Innovation Systems: Why They Are Important, and How They Might Be Measured and Compared." *Economics of Innovation and New Technology* 3 (1): 77–95.

Pavitt, K. 1990. "What We Know about the Strategic Management of Technology." *California Management Review* 32 (3): 17–26.

———. 1998. "Technologies, Products and Organization in the Innovating Firm: What Adam Smith Tells Us and Joseph Schumpeter Doesn't." *Industrial and Corporate Change* 7 (3): 433–452.

Pisano, G. 2006. "Profiting from Innovation and the Intellectual Property Revolution." *Research Policy* 35 (8): 1122–1130.

Pisano, G. P. 2010. "The Evolution of Science-Based Business: Innovating How We Innovate." *Industrial and Corporate Change* 19 (2): 465–482.

Reich, L. S. 2002. *The Making of American Industrial Research: Science and Business at GE and Bell.* Cambridge: Cambridge University Press.

Qian, Zhaohua. 1999. "Science, Technology, and Experience: A Discussion of the 'Joseph Lee Dilemma.'" *Scientific Research* 3: 14–19.

Sampat, B. N., and R. R. Nelson. 2002. "The Emergence and Standardization of University Technology Transfer Offices: A Case Study of Institutional Change." *The New Institutionalism in Strategic Management* 19.

Shane, S. 2002. "Selling University Technology: Patterns from MIT." *Management Science* 48 (1): 122–137.

Shapin, S. 2009. *The Scientific Life: A Moral History of a Late Modern Vocation.* Chicago: University of Chicago Press.

Thursby, J. G., and M. C. Thursby. 2002. "Who Is Selling the Ivory Tower? Sources of Growth in University Licensing." *Management Science* 48 (1): 90–104.

Shi, Donglu. 2007. "On the Definition of Science." *Science: Shanghai* 59 (3): 4–9.

CHAPTER 2

Science-Based Industry: Technology Catch-Up Perspective

2.1 Industrial Technology Catch-Up

2.1.1 Understanding Technology Catch-Up

The concept of "catching up" was originally proposed by the historical phenomenon of countries catching up with each other. "Catching-up development" is known by several terms, such as "pursue development" and "leaping-over development." Despite the varied terminology, the underlying implications of these phrases are broadly similar.

"Technological leapfrogging" was coined in the mid-1980s by Dutch scholar Luc Soete in his article "International Diffusion of Technology, Industrial Development, and Technological Leapfrogging." He explored the concept of technological leapfrogging by examining the new technological and economic paradigm of newly industrialized countries. Hobday (1995) described "technology catch-up" as the process by which "latecomers" bypass older technologies and substantial investments to catch up with "developed countries." Kim et al. distinguished technological and market catch-up and defined "catching up" as the dual process of "technology catch-up" and "market catch-up" by strategic agents (countries, regions, or enterprises).

Some Chinese scholars introduced the term "technological (capability) catch-up" in response to the potential "catch-up trap" that could arise from repeatedly importing technologies in the 1980s. After 2000, during debates on the "market for technology" policy, the term "technology catch-up" was proposed. According to Lin et al. (1995), "catching up" involves improving resource utilization efficiency and overcoming the development bottlenecks of capital-intensive industries, allowing for rapid progress from a low starting point to reach the level of pioneer countries. Feng (2000) saw "catching up" as the process through which a technologically backward country gains a significant position in the international division of labor through the introduction of advanced technologies from developed countries or through endogenous innovation. Jin and Che (2001) described "catching up" as a "process of economic super development," enabling "latecomer countries" to achieve economic growth by "leapfrogging." Guo (2005) defined "catching up" as the process by which economically and culturally backward countries and regions catch up with advanced countries by prioritizing the development of heavy industries and import substitution.

In summary, the study of "technology catch-up, catching-up, and leapfrogging" has gradually evolved in China. "Technology catch-up" refers to developing countries catching up with or surpassing developed countries in terms of technology; "technological leapfrogging" implies skipping certain stages of technological development to advance alongside developed countries. These terms aim to address China's lag in various industrial and technological fields. Currently, several definitions of "technology catch-up" exist in academia, ranging from adopting emerging technologies at the same stage of industrialization as developed countries to entering higher stages of technological development directly, aiming for rapid technological capability and level upgrades. The definitions in categories (1)–(4) align closely with the concept of "technology catch-up" as discussed in this book, whereas other categories diverge from this focus. The comparisons of definitions in categories (1)–(4) are detailed in Table 2-1.

Table 2-1 The comparison of "technology catch-up" definitions

Categories of definition		Subject	Method	Objective
(1)		Developing countries	Leading the adoption of emerging technologies	Rapid improvement in technical competence
(2)		Developing countries	Adopting new technology paradigms	Enhance technological capabilities, foster innovation
(3)		Developing countries	Bypass stages to enter advanced technological levels	Greatly improve technological level and capability
(4)	Narrow sense	Not country-specific	Skip stages, directly use new tech for new products	Boost enterprise and industry competitiveness
	Broad sense		Accelerate tech development or shorten update cycles	Upgrade technological capabilities, achieve catching up

Table 2-1 reveals commonalities across the four types of "technology catch-up" definitions.

First, regarding the "subject" of technology catch-up, categories (1)–(3) uniformly identify "developing countries" as the primary actors, with only category (4) differing. This suggests that historically, academia has viewed technology catch-up primarily as the pursuit of developing countries to match the technological advancements of developed countries within the same industry. However, catch-up processes also occur among developed countries, such as in the pharmaceutical industry, a topic we will explore further.

Second, concerning the "method" of technology catch-up, all emphasize the "adoption of new technologies," differing only in their phrasing.

Third, in terms of the "objective" of technology catch-up, all four definitions underscore the importance of "enhancing technology." Categories (1) and (3) highlight the aim of "rapidly" or "significantly" improving technology; category (2) focuses on "enhancing technological development capabilities" and thus fostering endogenous innovation; category (4) points out that "upgrading technological capabilities" is crucial for the competitiveness of a company or industry.

Summarizing these definitions, "technology catching-up" as understood by earlier scholars and contemporary peers, refers to the process whereby developing countries bypass certain stages of technological development, embrace emerging technologies or new technological paradigms ahead of others, and directly advance to higher stages of technological development, thereby making substantial technological progress.

Further interpretations of "technology catching-up" exist. For instance, Lee and Lim (2001) argue that it involves latecomers catching up with or surpassing pioneers by following the pioneers' technological trajectory and advancing rapidly. Some domestic scholars view technology catch-up as a super-conventional development process that encompasses both "catching up and surpassing." Initially, latecomers import technology and master it through imitation, digestion, and absorption—the "catch-up stage." This is followed by the "overtaking stage," where latecomers leverage the new economic paradigm to overcome technological backwardness and achieve leapfrogging. According to Chen et al. (2004), technology catch-up is a discontinuous form of technological progress where latecomers catch up with or surpass leaders and gain the capability for sustained endogenous innovation. Nonetheless, these perspectives do not alter the "substantive meaning of the aforementioned definitions."

2.1.2 Theoretical Framework for Technology Catching-Up

The concept of technology catch-up, as outlined by various scholars, suggests that several countries have the potential for success based on specific theories.

1. The Late-Developing Advantage Theory

The Late-Developing Advantage Theory was proposed by American economic historian Alexander Gerschenkron (1962), drawing from the successful economic catch-up experiences of countries like Germany and Italy. By "late-developing advantage," Gerschenkron referred to the ability of latecomer countries to leverage the established knowledge, technology, management, and market experience of developed countries to accelerate their development when they are technologically backward. Using the experiences of developed countries allows latecomers to minimize "trial and error" costs, enabling them to rapidly catch up.

Gerschenkron argued that the late-developing advantage is tied to the "relative backwardness" of latecomer countries' economies, a condition not present in more developed nations. He identified several advantages for latecomer countries over early comers, including in technology, capital, institutions, knowledge, experience, and structural transformation. He emphasized that the economic latecomer advantage primarily stems from a "technological latecomer advantage." This implies that the advanced science and technology developed by developed countries, despite being legally "private goods" with exclusivity, have significant "spillover effects." Latecomer countries, as beneficiaries of these spillover effects, can adopt and locally improve these technologies for their own product development and industrial production without the need for substantial re-investment.

The late-developing advantage also encompasses a "capital late-developing advantage," suggesting that while capital is abundant in developed countries, the law of diminishing marginal returns makes new investments less attractive there. Conversely, although capital is scarcer in latecomer countries, the return on investment is often higher. If latecomer countries liberalize their economies to allow free capital flow, this can attract significant investment from developed countries, funding technology catch-up and promoting economic growth.

Furthermore, the late-developing advantage includes benefits in knowledge and experience. Developed countries not only possess advanced technology but also have superior systems, knowledge, and experience, developed over long periods through trial and error. Latecomer countries can learn from, imitate, and improve the systems, knowledge, and experience of developed countries for their own development, achieving significant gains at a lower cost.

Last, the "late-developing advantage of structural transformation" indicates that latecomer countries, often with unbalanced early development and an inefficient industrial structure, can boost resource allocation efficiency and production efficiency by reallocating capital and labor from agriculture to industry, thus increasing overall economic output.

In summary, Gerschenkron believed that the exploratory efforts of developed countries could offer latecomers a viable development path for successful catch-up. By leveraging the "late-developing advantage" in various domains, latecomers can catch up with developed nations and spur rapid economic development in their own countries.

2. The Technological Gap Theory

The technological gap theory, also known as the technological gap model, delves into the effects of technological disparities or changes on international trade by considering technology as a third factor of production, distinct from labor and capital.

This theory emerged in 1961, with American scholar M.V. Posner as a key proponent. In his seminal article "International Trade and Technique Change," Posner introduced the technological gap theory within the context of international trade. He argued that technology functions as a factor of production and that its level continuously improves, albeit unevenly across different countries. This technological gap can afford technologically advanced countries a comparative advantage, enabling them to export technology-intensive products. However, as the importing country begins to imitate the technology, it may "catch up," diminishing the original country's comparative advantage and potentially ending trade benefits derived from this advantage.

Posner's technological gap theory posits that a significant portion of industrial goods trade between countries is predicated on the existence of a "technology gap." He elucidated the trade possibility between countries through the notion of "imitation lag," suggesting that a new product finds success in the innovating country before the imitating country acquires the corresponding new technology. If the "innovation country" maintains a technological lead, it can export this advantage to the "imitation country." However, as the leading technology disseminates globally through patent transfers, technical cooperation, foreign investment, or international trade, the "imitator country" may begin producing these goods domestically using its cost advantages, thereby reducing imports. Consequently, the "innovation country" may gradually lose its export market for the product, and the trade between the two countries, driven by the technology gap, may decrease; eventually, the "imitation country" masters the new technology, and the "technology gap" closes.

Building on these observations, Posner suggested that developing countries could rapidly enhance their technological capabilities by importing technologies from developed countries or capitalizing on technological diffusion opportunities. Mathews and Cho later used the Korean semiconductor industry as an illustration, demonstrating how it leveraged the technological gap with the US to catch up in the semiconductor industry by exploiting its latecomer advantage. Further examples include the United Kingdom catching up with the Netherlands in technology, and the United States and Germany subsequently catching up with the United Kingdom.

However, based on the "technology gap theory," some scholars have noted that the potential for developing countries to catch up with early industrialized countries in technology can only become a reality under certain conditions.

3. *The "A-U Model" of Technology Catching-Up*

The "A-U model" of technology catch-up explores the intricate relationship between technology-leading and following countries. Vernon (1966, 1979) elucidated this interplay through the lens of "product cycle theory," illustrating how leading nations advance technologically by innovating new products. Once the manufacturing processes for these products become standardized regionally, follower nations begin to adopt these innovations, spurred by technology transfer and diffusion. This dynamic enables developing nations to narrow the technological and economic divide with their developed counterparts by emulating the sophisticated product designs and manufacturing techniques of the latter (Grossman and Helpman 1990; Coe and Helpman 1995; Coe and Helpman 1997; Barro and Sala-i-Martin 1997).

Delving into US production technology innovation, Abemathy (Utterback and Abemathy 1975) and Utterback (Abernathy and Utterback 1978) unveiled that technological advancements usher the innovation process through sequential stages of "flow, transformation, and identity," transitioning from "product innovation" to "process innovation" in the A-U model. This framework has become pivotal not only for analyzing technological innovation and industrial evolution in developed nations but also for strategizing the technological catch-up trajectories for emerging economies.

The 1990s saw a surge in research on technology catching up in developing nations, introducing diverse analytical models. Hobday (1995) dissected the electronics industry's catch-up process in the four Asian tigers, proposing a model emphasizing original equipment manufacturer (OEM)-independent design, manufacturing, and branding. Linsu Kim (1997), after examining over 200 Korean companies over two decades, identified a "reverse A-U model"—a U-A trajectory of "acquisition, digestion, and improvement"—contrasting with the path of developed countries. This finding was corroborated by Qian and Xu (1998) in their study of Chinese firms and further supported by Lee and Lim (2001) in their exploration of Korea's industrial technology catch-up, which advocated a progression through replicative imitation, creative imitation, and innovation.

Entering the new millennium, the focus shifted toward "technological learning" as a lens to understand latecomer countries' catch-up efforts. Mathews (2002) introduced the "3L" framework—linkage, leverage, and learning—to examine Korea and Taiwan's (China) strategies, integrating OEM, in-house branding, and design in their analysis. Bong and Lee (2003) differentiated technological learning into process, design, and R&D stages. Arnold (2003) detailed the evolution from imitation to innovation in these nations' catch-up endeavors. Putranto et al. (2003) segmented the learning process into preparation, production, operation, and evaluation phases. Lee (2005) reinforced Mathews's (2002) insights with further evidence from Korea, while Altenburg (2007) highlighted technological imitation and original innovation as keystones for China's rise as a manufacturing behemoth.

2.1.3 Strategies and Pathways for Technology Catching-Up

Objectively, there are four modes of technology catching-up: independent R&D, introduction of advanced technology, mergers and acquisitions of advanced technology, and collaboration with advanced players. In the first three models, "advanced" refers to "technologically advanced economies (e.g., developed countries)" as opposed to "catching-up countries"; the fourth model pertains to the "advanced" among the "follower countries":

a. Independent R&D: Technology catch-up. This approach enables "follower" countries or enterprises to set new industry standards through the independent R&D of advanced technologies, thereby altering their position in the international technological and economic landscape. This model is characterized by the endogenous nature of technological breakthroughs and pioneering technology and market. Its implementation requires first, sufficient technological accumulation and leading R&D by the follower; second, an objective opportunity for technological and market change; and third, both the follower and the leader pursuing the same "opportunity for change" with concerted effort. When these conditions are met, the follower may successfully "overtake." This model is particularly suited to new industries at the forefront of technology. For instance, in the emerging industry of e-commerce initially developed in the US, Chinese enterprises like Alibaba, accelerated the independent development of e-commerce technology and innovative business models, leading China's e-commerce industry not only to catch up with the US but also to become a global leader.
b. Introduction of advanced technology: Technology catch-up. In this mode, "follower" enterprises introduce advanced technology from "leader" enterprises, digest, absorb, enhance, and innovate upon it to achieve catching up. The essence of this model is transitioning from "imitation innovation" to "endogenous innovation." Key conditions include: first, the

technology introduction aims at long-term technological catch-up, not merely short-term usage; second, the introducer must have the capacity to invest resources in technology for digestion, absorption, enhancement, and innovation. This model is apt for situations where independent R&D is challenging for "follower" enterprises. A potential issue is the "follower" becoming overly reliant on the "technology provider." During the first thirty years of China's reform and opening-up, many Chinese enterprises fell into a cycle of "introduction, use, obsolescence, reintroduction, ..., obsolescence again" without achieving the re-innovation of imported technology. This led to the adoption of an "endogenous innovation strategy" in China post-2005.

c. Merger and acquisition of advanced technology: Technology catch-up. This method involves "follower" enterprises (from developing countries) acquiring advanced technology from "leader" enterprises (from developed countries) to bolster their technological foundations for independent development. This approach allows the technological capabilities of the "followers" to advance rapidly. Research indicates that in this model, the "follower" as the acquirer is typically a large firm from a developing country, targeting the "advanced technology of a leading country's firm," often through acquiring a "technologically advanced small firm" from the leading country. The primary conditions for this model include: first, the target "leading country enterprise" possesses the technology needed by the "follower"; second, the "follower" should navigate or bypass the "merger threshold" set by the government of the leading country, especially any "national security review"; third, the acquiring firm can integrate the advanced technology into its own system, creating a more advanced technological infrastructure. This model is applicable to both emerging and traditional industries. For example, Chinese companies like Tsinghua Unisplendour Corporation Ltd. have acquired American Integrated Circuit Companies, and in traditional sectors, companies like Geely (founded by Li Shufu) have acquired Volvo.

d. Cooperation of advanced players: Technology catch-up. This model emphasizes collaboration among advanced enterprises within the "follower" category. By sharing similar and complementary resources, these enterprises can strategically align technology, capital, and talent to enhance their collective strengths and mitigate weaknesses. The main prerequisites for this approach include: first, all parties face common technological challenges and possess the capability for catch-up; second, the collaborators have closely matched technological capabilities and complementary resources; third, they establish a mutually agreed upon governance mechanism for "cooperative innovation," especially with a willingness to share "common IP" generated from the collaboration. Literature suggests this model is particularly suited to industries with lighter assets and rapid technological advancement, such as electronic information, new materials, and home appliances. Advanced enterprises within the same industry can achieve technological catch-up and even lead with cutting-edge innovations through cooperative endogenous innovation.[1]

Previous studies have characterized "technology catching-up" as the pursuit by "technological laggards" to match or exceed the "technological leaders" through concerted efforts in technology and market strategies. Given the variance in industrial technologies and resource availability for the "laggards," the approach, difficulty, and feasibility of technology catch-up differ across industries. Currently, academia recognizes five types of "technology catching-up paths," outlined as follows:

a. The path of the following: Spiraling forward to catch up. This approach entails following the historical technological trajectory of "leading countries." However, due to initial constraints in the early stages of catching up, laggards need to blend various catch-up modes and progress in a "spiraling" fashion, alternating between rapid and slow advancements. Direct catch-up is often unattainable, necessitating a "spiraling in" method.
b. Creating paths: Detours to catch up. Lee and Lim (2001) describe this as the process where a "follower" forges new technological paradigms and development trajectories to overtake the "leader." This catch-up path diverges from the historical technological evolution of the "leaders" (developed countries).
c. Market catch-up first, then technology catch-up. Here, the "catching-up player" initially adopts technology from developed countries to manufacture products, capture the domestic market, and potentially export. Profits are then reinvested into digesting, absorbing, and enhancing the imported

1. Feng Yanqiu, "The Paradox of Latecomer Advantages and China's Technological Strategy Choices," *World Economy*, no. 7 (2000): 44.

technology for secondary and final innovations, thereby achieving technological leadership (a path proposed by Wang Yi in 2010). Xie et al. (1999) suggest that the evolution of technological capabilities in latecomer countries should transition "from technology introduction to production capacity enhancement and then to innovation capacity improvement."

d. The catching-up path of reverse engineering, R&D early intervention, and reinvention. Shi (1995) identifies these three factors as crucial for gaining a latecomer advantage. For instance, Wu (1995) and Wu et al. (2006) introduced the "secondary innovation" catch-up path of "imitation innovation–creative imitation–improvement innovation–post-secondary innovation," which incorporates "reverse engineering."
e. The catching-up path of accumulation–catching-up–leap. Chen (2006) outlines the technology learning and catching-up process as "introducing–imitating–improving–innovating." Examining the technology catching-up path in three Korean industries, Wu Wei et al. summarized the approach as "technology introduction, capability accumulation, endogenous innovation, and market selection."

These paths offer strategic frameworks for "laggards" aiming to bridge the technological divide with "leaders," highlighting the diverse methodologies available for achieving technological parity or superiority.

2.1.4 Optimal Timing for Technology Catching-Up

1. Identifying the Optimal Timing for Technology Catching-Up

The concept of "right timing" for "catching-up countries" (latecomer countries) to pursue technology catch-up is a significant consideration. Scholars such as Wu (1995) and Kim (1997) suggest that for industries experiencing slow technological changes, the prime time for technology catch-up is during "technological maturity." Lee and Lim (2001), analyzing technology catch-up in sectors like CDMA cell phones, home appliances, personal computers, and DRAMs in Korea, used the technological characteristics of the industry as their analytical framework. This included factors like the fluidity of the technological trajectory, the cumulative nature of technological development, and the availability of external knowledge. They concluded that the "optimal period" for technology catch-up is the "transition period between old and new technological paradigms." They argue that initially, foreign advanced mature technology can be utilized to organize production; following this, through digestion and absorption, the technology gap with developed countries can be rapidly narrowed. As technological capabilities improve, the "follower" may leverage the "transition period of the old and new technological paradigm" to achieve catching-up.

2. Capitalizing on the "Window of Opportunity"

Mathews (2002) and Lee and Lim (2001), in their analysis of DRAMs and CDMAs technology catch-up in Korea, identified that the "rapid innovation period" of product development offers a "window of opportunity" for catching-up players. This "window of opportunity" refers to the period when "laggards" have the "best timing" to undertake technology catching-up efforts.

Soete (1988) examined this "window of opportunity" for technology catch-up, analyzing the shifts in cost factors across the new technology life cycle and different technology entry periods. They discovered that the introduction and maturity phases of the new technology life cycle present the "best windows of opportunity for technology catch-up." However, these optimal windows carry distinct costs and requirements: the "introduction" phase demands significant knowledge of the new technology with minimal capital and experience, while the "maturity" phase necessitates substantial investments and the possibility of purchasing the technology. The outcomes of catching-up during these two windows vary: success in the introduction phase does not guarantee competitive survival, and while catching-up in the "maturity phase" is safer, it can be prohibitively expensive.

Wu Xiaobo and Li Zhengwei applied the chaos principle to the technological evolution process, concluding that the transition period between old and new technological paradigms, the "chaotic period of technological evolution," represents the optimal timing for achieving technology catch-up, termed the "window of opportunity." They argue that during technological paradigm shifts, the pace of change accelerates, and adopting mature technologies not only fails to facilitate catching-up but may also lead to a "catch-up trap." Thus, the strategic timing for technology catch-up should be at the onset of the new paradigm, despite the uncertainties of technological and market conditions, as it presents a significant opportunity for leapfrogging.

Furthermore, the "national technology leadership turnover cycle theory" proposed by Brezis, Krugman, and Tsiddon (1993) also suggests that the emergence of major technological innovations, or the turnover period between old and new technological paradigms, constitutes the "best time" for lagging countries to achieve technology catch-up. This notion aligns with the strategy of "bend and overtake" currently discussed in China.

2.1.5 Role of Government Policies in Technology Catching-Up

1. External Influences on Technology Catching-Up

Government policies are crucial in facilitating technology catch-up, representing a shared objective between the government and industry in lagging countries. While industry initiatives are vital, government support and protection play a pivotal role. Historically, in 1791, the first US Treasury Secretary, Alexander Hamilton, submitted the Report on Manufactures to Congress, advocating for the classic American "Industrialization Forging Ahead Theory." He recommended that the government should increase its economic intervention and implement protective tariffs to nurture the nascent manufacturing industry in the United States. Following this, in 1841, the German economist Friedrich List, reflecting on the United States' catch-up process, published *The National System of Political Economy*, which systematically proposed how backward countries could utilize state power to catch up with advanced nations. In the 1990s, Gover (1993) observed that the US microelectronics industry had regained international leadership through strategic alliances formed with government intervention. In the new century, Vertova (2001) highlighted that the alignment between a country's economic system, institutions, and technological framework is essential for technological development. A mismatch could trap technology at a lower level, while compatibility with the "best technology opportunity" could lead to industry specialization. Mathews (2007) suggested that governments in lagging countries could facilitate "technology catching-up" by establishing "technology leverage institutions" to regulate resources.

The capabilities of "follower" technology, R&D, and human resources are significant for technology catch-up. Mazzoleni and R. Nelson (1998) argued that firms that develop "complementary assets" supporting physical and human capital are more likely to succeed in catching up. Moreover, investment in innovation is crucial, as "latecomers" must invest significantly in R&D to avoid failure. Lee and Lim (2001), examining the "technological capability building process of the follower" and the catch-up process, identified systemic conditions conducive to technology catch-up. Lee (2004) found that R&D plays a catalytic role in developing countries' innovation capacity, particularly in technology-intensive sectors. Lee, Lim, and Song (2005) further demonstrated that innovation frequency in the technology sector correlates positively with the "speed of technology catch-up," though higher innovation frequency complicates predicting technological trajectories, making learning and catching-up more challenging for latecomer enterprises. Barro (1997) emphasized the importance of human capital in technology catch-up. Furman and Hayes (2004) argued that successful technology catch-up requires more than just innovation policies and social institutions; it also necessitates increased investment in financial and human capital. Wu and Chen (2008) stressed the need for an improved national innovation system, government guidance, protection of innovation, attention to human capital, and an open innovation environment. Cao (2009) recommended a biased industrial policy to support technology catch-up, while Cheng and Liu (2011) advocated for the government to foster large, integrated markets to support basic research and technology catch-up.

2. Government Policy and Technology Catching-Up

Literature extensively discusses the pivotal role enterprises play in technology catch-up, yet government policies significantly influence the outcomes and impacts of these efforts, affecting the overall development of industries and nations. Thus, governments need to offer corresponding policy support to facilitate enterprise-led technology catching-up efforts. According to Guo (2004), for enterprises to effectively execute technology catching up, the government should robustly enhance its policy guidance and support. In technology-intensive industries, market mechanisms alone cannot fully regulate technology catching-up; hence, the government must provide correct strategic guidance and efficient support policies. It should selectively concentrate on implementing some "reverse comparative advantage" technology catching-up strategies and enforce "tilted technology catching-up policies" for sectors with conducive conditions, especially in electronics, communication equipment, medicine, computer and communication technology, and biotechnology. However, there are differing opinions on government intervention in technology catch-up. Scholars like Hobday (1994),

Hobday and Cawson (2001), and Kim (1998), who analyzed the government-firm relationship in the electronics industry across four Southeast Asian countries, argue that some studies overemphasize the role of government intervention in firms' technology catch-up. They suggest the government's role should be limited to ensuring macroeconomic stability rather than meddling in firms' specific technology catching-up efforts. Nonetheless, this latter perspective holds a "minor position" in such discussions.

For a long time, academia has generally approached the issue of technology catch-up without considering industry-specific nuances. Such a broad analytical perspective can only offer a superficial analysis of technology catching-up issues and fails to objectively and comprehensively reveal the feasible modes, optional paths, favorable timings, and strategic approaches for technology catch-up. This lack of depth in research hinders its practical application in strategizing and policymaking for technology catch-up. Objectively, it's crucial to categorize industries and examine the technology catching-up challenges distinct to each category. However, some researchers merely divide industries into "traditional" and "new" when studying technology catch-up, a classification that merely reflects "industrial maturity" rather than capturing the "essential differences of industries." We believe that distinguishing between "technology-based industries" and "science-based industries" better reflects these "essential differences," highlighting the "technological sources" and "characteristics" pivotal to industrial innovation and development. Given this book's focus on "technology catch-up," we aim to explore the issue from the standpoint of "technology-based industries," thus enabling a detailed examination of the regularity of technology catch-up across these two distinct industry types.

This book will concentrate on the technology catching-up challenges faced by science-based industries toward fostering endogenous innovation, examining the modes, paths, timings, strategies, and requisite government policies distinct from those applicable to technology-based industries. Specifically, for technology-based industries, the "technology introduction period," the "chaotic period of old and new technology paradigm change," and the "maturity period" might represent the "best times" for technology catch-up. However, for science-based industries, such broad "optimal timing" may not apply, and the viable models, alternative paths, and strategic approaches leading to autonomous innovation are likely to differ fundamentally.

2.2 Re-envisioning Industrial Technology Catching-Up

2.2.1 Reconceptualizing Industrial Technology Catching-Up

1. Core Aspects of Technology Catch-Up among Economies

The endeavor of "lagging countries" to catch up with "leading countries" represents a well-established historical dynamic. In this context, a "lagging country" is one that falls behind in specific industrial areas and aims to catch up with or even surpass the advancements of a leading country. Conversely, a "leading country" is more advanced in certain industries and sets the benchmark for others. It's crucial to clarify that "catching-up countries and lagging countries" does not automatically imply "developing countries." The latter term is rooted in development economics, whereas the former pertains to innovation economics, focusing on the innovation landscape. This means that a developed country can be in a catching-up position in certain sectors. For instance, China currently leads many developed nations in e-commerce, despite its broader classification as a developing country. Therefore, the discussion about "catching-up countries and leading countries" does not directly correlate with "late-developing countries and developed countries."

2. Driving Forces and Catalysts for Technology Catching-Up

Since the inception of academic interest in the dynamic of countries "catching up," the role of technology has been a focal point of research (Gerschenkron 1962; Veblen 1990). The concept of "catching up" is attributed to the "technological gap" between nations, namely, the potential for accelerated development in "catching-up countries" facilitated by innovations pioneered by "leading countries" (Gerschenkron 1962; Veblen 1990). This potential for catching up is made possible by the new knowledge generated by the "leading country" (Abramovitz 1986; Vernon 1992). Initial scholarly discussions centered on the transfer of new technologies from "leading countries" to "catching up countries" and exploring ways to harness the rapid development potential emerging from the "technology gap." In this context, Gerschenkron highlighted the critical role of institutions, particularly emphasizing the influence of banking in Germany's catch-up with the UK, while Abramovitz (1986) introduced the concept of "social capabilities," referring to the capacity to assimilate new knowledge and efficiently deploy existing resources.

Subsequently, several scholars developed a "life cycle theory" to describe how a technology or industry is born in a "leading country" and eventually transitions to a "catching-up country" as it reaches maturity. However, it's important to acknowledge the oversimplification of technology within these theories. One approach characterizes technological change as a "uniform, single-direction" progression (Lee and Lim 2001), while another perceives "catching up" as merely adopting the latest discoveries made by "leading countries," overlooking the innovative contributions made by "catching up" countries in the process (Fagerberg 2005).

3. The Leapfrogging Challenge in Technological Advancements

To address the limitations of previous theories, "technological evolution theory" was developed. This concept gained prominence as the economic catch-up efforts of Asian countries attracted global attention (World Bank 1993), positioning "technological evolution" as a key framework for analyzing the catch-up phenomenon. This approach shifts the focus from mere "technology transfer" to the unique technological development paths of "catching-up countries," which differ from those of "leading countries." Scholars like Lim (1997) and Hobday (1995) have argued that the technological evolution in "catching-up countries" often takes a reverse pattern compared to "leading countries," starting with manufacturing and eventually advancing to product innovation capabilities. Abramovitz and David (1996) observed that the catch-up process for "catching-up countries" can vary, being rapid at certain stages and slower at others, due to its connection with specific states of technology and the economy. Following these insights, researchers began to explore the catch-up phenomenon within the broader context of long-term technological and economic development (Freeman 2001).

4. Existing Research Focus on Technology-Based Industrial Catching-Up

Historically, academic research on "catching up" has predominantly concentrated on successful examples while often overlooking failures. The majority of these studies have been directed at "technology-based industries," with established "catch-up theories" positing that "lagging countries" can acquire "manufacturing capabilities" from "leading countries." Following such acquisitions, the enterprises within "catching-up countries" are expected to evolve these capabilities into "product innovation capabilities." In contrast, the exploration of technology catch-up within "science-based industries"—sectors where "leading countries" have long held technological and innovative supremacy—has been relatively overlooked.

The "technology-based industries" discussed herein rely on "innovation driven by technological advancement" for their creation and growth. These sectors include industries like machine tools, automobiles, ships, aircraft, and machinery. Such industries have historically been central to many nations, particularly during the early and mid-stages of industrialization, and have played a crucial role in the development of their national economies. Currently, China has seen significant advancement in these fields, with many becoming key pillars of the national economy. Since its reform and opening-up, China has made considerable strides in catching up with its counterparts in the United States, Europe, and Japan across various "technology-based industries," providing numerous cases for observation and study. Consequently, the bulk of research has been centered on "technology-based industries." Nevertheless, the insights derived from these studies do not adequately account for the dynamics within "science-based industries."

2.2.2 Case Studies: Pharmaceutical and Automobile Industries

1. Pharmaceutical Industry: A Science-Based Industry Perspective

As detailed in the earlier section "Science-Based Industry Identification" (refer to chapter 1), the pharmaceutical industry is identified as a prime example of a "science-based industry." The Nobel Prize case study further underscores the pharmaceutical industry's high reliance on scientific advancements for innovation and development. Historically, Germany managed to achieve technology catch-up with the British pharmaceutical industry in the latter half of the 19th century. In the first half of the 20th century, the United States accomplished technology catch-up with the German pharmaceutical industry. Japan attempted to catch up with the United States in the pharmaceutical sector during the latter half of the 20th century, although it has not yet succeeded. This sequence presents a highly instructive case study, offering insights into the overarching characteristics of technology catch-up within "science-based industries."

2. Japanese and Korean Automobile Industries: A Technology-Based Industry Perspective

As previously outlined in the "Science-Based Industry Identification" section (refer to chapter 1), the automobile industry exemplifies a "technology-based industry." Globally, the development of the automobile industry has historically unfolded in two distinct patterns: the "originator" (leading countries) and the "latecomer" (catching-up countries). Europe and the United States, as the originators, pioneered the global development of the automobile industry. The latecomer countries, notably Japan, South Korea, and Brazil, followed in their footsteps. Despite all being latecomers, Japan initially surpassed Europe and the United States in this sector, followed by South Korea, which appeared to overtake both the United States and Japan. Analyzing the technology catching-up experiences of Japan and Korea's automobile industry provides valuable insights into the dynamics of technology-based industries and sets a foundation for contrasting the catching-up processes between different industry types.

3. Comparative Insights from Science-Based and Technology-Based Industries

The concepts of the technology gap and technological evolution have led the academic community to the understanding that examining technology catch-up from an industry-specific perspective is crucial. Since its reform and opening-up, China has vigorously pursued technology catch-up with leading countries across both industry types. However, the "stage effect" observed in the technology catching-up efforts between these two industries significantly differs, indicating distinct underlying principles governing the catching-up processes in science-based versus technology-based industries. Therefore, a detailed analysis and comparison of the pharmaceutical and automobile industries, focusing on their respective catching-up characteristics, will enhance our understanding of the nuances in science-based industries' technology catch-up. This analysis also aims to shed light on the historical challenges faced by science-based industries in catching up with leading countries.

2.2.3 Analytical Framework for Technology Catch-Up across Industries

1. Science-Based Industries: The Pharmaceutical Industry Case

When examining technology catch-up in the pharmaceutical industry, an initial step involves analyzing the "history of technology catching-up" in Germany and the United States to delineate a catch-up model for "science-based industries." Subsequently, leveraging this model, we can scrutinize Japan's shortcomings in pharmaceutical industry catch-up efforts to understand its failure. Key considerations in this analysis include: (1) given the reliance of pharmaceutical industry innovation on new scientific discoveries, is scientific "leadership" essential for successful catching-up? (2) while innovation stems from scientific research, it ultimately involves a commercialization process. Thus, how do other capabilities (such as production and marketing) impact the success of catching-up efforts? (3) how can catching-up countries cultivate "industrial competitiveness" within the pharmaceutical sector?

2. Technology-Based Industries: The Automobile Industry Case

The automobile industry, a quintessential technology-based sector, exhibits distinct phases of industrial development, technological advancement, and the interplay between industry and national growth. This backdrop, or "reference system," provides a foundation for analyzing the consistent characteristics of technology catch-up across various developmental stages. Specifically, this involves identifying the regular features of the technology catching-up model at different phases of industrial and technological evolution, the "catch-up path" formed by linking these models across stages, and the requisite government policies to support this progression.

2.3 Technology Catch-Up in Science-Based Industries: The Pharmaceutical Industry

2.3.1 Germany's Catch-Up in Organic Chemical / Pharmaceutical Industry

1. Background Overview

Germany's effort to catch up with Britain, the industrial world leader at the time, took place in the latter half of the 19th century, marking one of the earliest instances of one country catching up with another globally. Despite initially lagging behind Britain, Germany swiftly advanced past Britain in the nascent chemical and electrical industries, securing a dominant position in the international market by the century's end. This section focuses specifically on Germany's catch-up in the organic chemical/pharmaceutical industry.

The organic chemical industry emerged as the first modern era science-based industry, spurred by the laboratory discovery of new substances by scientists, with early significant breakthroughs including dyes. Many pivotal scientific discoveries in this field were made by British scientists, such as the isolation of benzene and the introduction of organic substance isomerism in 1825, followed by coal tar decomposition and distillation, and the unveiling of benzene's molecular structure in 1865. British scientists recognized the commercial potential of their discoveries; for instance, Perkin, who discovered the first aniline dye in 1856, promptly established a company to manufacture his discovery. Given England's status as the home to the largest textile industry at the time, which had a high demand for dyes, Britain initially led the new aniline dye industry. However, within just a decade, Germany managed to catch up and surpass Britain's leading position in the aniline dye industry (Murmann and Landau 1998).

2. Two Phases of Germany's Catch-Up

Germany's journey to catch up with Britain in the organic chemical and pharmaceutical industry can be segmented into two distinct phases.

(1) First phase (primarily before the 1870s)

a. Technology transfer and knowledge flow. Germany facilitated the flow of new knowledge from England by welcoming German chemists who had worked in England back home. As the German chemical industry began to offer better job opportunities, many, notably Hoffmann, whose return marked a significant turning point, moved back to Germany, bringing a wealth of new knowledge.
b. Establishment of intra-company R&D. The world's first corporate R&D organizations appeared in the German chemical industry during this period. By 1886, all major dye companies had set up corporate laboratories to conduct R&D.
c. University-industry collaboration. Germany pioneered the world's first research universities in the early 19th century, developed technical colleges, and produced graduates tailored to industrial needs, laying the groundwork for robust university-industry linkages. This influx of high-quality professionals significantly propelled the German chemical industry forward. Conversely, British university research in the 19th century retained a more "collegiate" character.

d. Investment in production and marketing. Improvements in production methods allowed the German chemical industry to increase its market reach through scale. In terms of sales, the practice of deploying salespeople to engage directly with professional users became standard in the pharmaceutical industry, setting the stage for Germany's subsequent product innovation leap over the UK. Despite the UK's initial lead in product innovation, it lagged in production and marketing innovation and investment.

(2) Second phase (primarily from the 1870s to the early 20th century)

a. Focus on basic research. With increasing competitiveness and a desire for new products, more German companies began collaborating with universities on basic research. Notably, three chemical research institutes were founded with private funding between 1911 and 1914, establishing Germany as a global scientific hub.
b. Accelerated product innovation. Germany's leadership in basic research fueled a continuous stream of new products. Merck, for example, was producing up to 10,000 products at the time (Sturchio and Galambos 2011), cementing Germany's dominance in the organic chemical and pharmaceutical industries into the early 20th century until disrupted by the world wars.
c. International market expansion. During this period, the German chemical and pharmaceutical industries not only dominated the European market but also targeted the burgeoning US market. By the late 19th to early 20th century, the German pharmaceutical industry had achieved a leading position globally, with investments in the US market facilitating knowledge transfer.

In summary, Germany's successful catch-up with the UK in the pharmaceutical sector was marked by a strategic division into stages, each with specific focuses. Initially, the emphasis was on receiving technology transfers and knowledge flows from the UK, developing enterprise R&D capabilities, and investing in production and marketing to build market competitiveness. In the latter stage, Germany concentrated on emphasizing basic research, strengthening product innovation, and expanding into international markets, which endowed the German chemical industry with the technological prowess and market presence to surpass its British counterparts.

3. Typical Cases

(1) 1901 Nobel Prize in Physiology and Medicine: Diphtheria vaccine

German scientist Emil Adolf von Behring (1854–1917) was awarded the inaugural Nobel Prize in Physiology or Medicine in 1901 for his pioneering work on serotherapy in treating diphtheria.

Infectious diseases have long posed a significant threat to human life. The inception of immunology, the study of the body's defense against pathogenic microorganisms, began with the exploration of the immune system's role in combating infections. Immunology investigates how the body wards off epidemics and resists disease onset, with its research findings directly applicable to clinical medicine, including vaccines, transplants, and immune tolerance, for diagnosing, treating, and preventing diseases. The *History of Immunology* delineates the evolution of immunology into three eras: the era of flourishing bacteriology, the era of silent chemical immunity, and the resurgence of biological immunology.

By the early 19th century, chemists had already begun extracting and concentrating active plant ingredients for therapeutic use. In the laboratory of Robert Koch, a contemporary of Louis Pasteur, Behring and Kitasato Shibasaburo each discovered antibodies in the serum of animals immunized with Corynebacterium diphtheriae, the bacterium responsible for the acute respiratory disease diphtheria. Prompted by Koch, Behring and Kitasato collaborated, publishing a joint article, with Behring additionally describing the discovery of "antitoxin" in a separate publication. Paul Ehrlich, also working in Koch's lab, transitioned from chemical to immunological research, immunizing animals with plant toxins to produce "antitoxins" in their serum.

In 1889, Behring became Koch's assistant, dedicating his research to diphtheria. Initially experimenting on mice and later on sheep, Behring and Kitasato achieved success in extracting diphtheria serum, which not only prevented diphtheria in mice but also cured infected ones. Their first human trial occurred in 1891, during Christmas, to save a child dying from diphtheria. The trial's success marked the beginning of serotherapy.

Behring confirmed the serum's efficacy in an infant in 1891, but industrial production had yet to be developed. He enlisted Ehrlich, who utilized his expertise in immunization against plant toxins and chemistry, to produce immune horse serum. Ehrlich later devised a method to quantify the diphtheria antitoxin, paving the way for its development as an injectable drug. In 1892, the Frankfurt Chemical and Pharmaceutical Company partnered with Behring to develop this new medication, which saw remarkable success during the subsequent diphtheria epidemic. Behring, awarded the first Nobel Prize in Medicine in 1901, gained wealth through contracts with pharmaceutical companies. Regrettably, Ehrlich, also nominated for the Nobel Prize alongside Behring, did not receive the same recognition.

Behring's discovery of antitoxin, his groundbreaking work in diphtheria treatment with animal serum, and his status as the first Nobel laureate in Physiology or Medicine epitomize advances in passive immunity and serotherapy. His contributions, particularly in diphtheria prevention, have significantly influenced medical science, symbolizing the inception of immunology.

(2) 1939 Nobel Prize in Physiology and Medicine: Antibacterial action of sulfa

The 1939 Nobel Prize in Physiology or Medicine was awarded to the German pathologist Gerhard Domagk (1895–1964) for his groundbreaking discovery of the antibacterial effects of sulfonamides.

Before the dawn of the 20th century, while chemical treatment for diseases caused by trypanosomes and protozoa had shown promise, successful chemical treatment for infections by true bacteria, such as cocci and bacilli, remained elusive. It was a common belief that serum was the only effective treatment available.

In 1908, German chemist Gelmo first synthesized sulfanilamide, but its potential uses went unrecognized. In 1917, Heidelberg and Jakob prepared sulfanilamide using Gelmo's method, proposing that it was produced in tissues by the breakdown of sulfonamide. However, due to its weak bactericidal effect, further exploration was halted. In 1929, I.G. Farbenindustrie AG founded a new institute for pathological anatomy and bacteriology, appointing Domagk, who had left the University of Munster, as its director. There, Domagk was tasked with investigating the chemotherapeutic effects of synthetic azo compounds, leading him to study a substance known as "Prontosil."

Domagk's discovery in 1932 that injections of Prontosil effectively combated streptococcal infections in mice was a significant breakthrough. This finding led to the application of Prontosil to humans, notably demonstrated when Domagk's daughter, Elisa, suffering from sepsis caused by a streptococcal infection, recovered dramatically after receiving a large dose of Prontosil. Despite this success, Domagk initially hesitated to publish his findings.

Domagk later found that Prontosil was effective against other bacteria, including pneumococci and staphylococci, and developed a water-soluble version, marketed under the name Soluble Prontosil. His publication in February 1932 spurred global research into Prontosil, confirming its efficacy against a broad range of microorganisms. The active ingredient was eventually identified as sulfanilamide, which competes with p-aminobenzoic acid (PABA), a nutrient essential for bacterial growth, thus inhibiting bacterial reproduction.

Prontosil's success story reached its peak when it saved the life of President Franklin D. Roosevelt's son, who was suffering from a severe streptococcal infection. This event catapulted Prontosil into the spotlight, leading to a surge in the development of sulfa drugs. A series of sulfonamides were synthesized in the following years, marking a fiercely competitive era in drug development across various countries.

The production and use of sulfonamides skyrocketed, with US soldiers carrying sulfonamide powders during World War II to prevent infection in open wounds. Domagk's discovery of Prontosil revolutionized the treatment of infectious diseases and marked a significant milestone in medical history.

2.3.2 US Pharmaceutical Industry's Catch-Up with Germany

1. Background Overview

Contrary to the German pharmaceutical industry, which evolved from the chemical sector, the US pharmaceutical industry emerged from specialized pharmaceutical firms. At the start of the 20th century, the US pharmaceutical landscape was dominated by companies focused on the production and distribution of existing medications, heavily reliant on German expertise and technology for drug development, and largely incapable of independent drug innovation (Liebenau 1987). The catch-up process of the US pharmaceutical industry with Germany unfolded in two phases, mirroring the catch-up strategies employed by Germany in its pursuit of the UK, yet differentiated by the unique dynamics of the US domestic market and institutional frameworks (universities, government roles, etc.).

2. Two Phases of US Catching-Up

During its quest to catch up with Germany, the US pharmaceutical industry underwent two distinct stages.

(1) First stage (late 19th century to early mid-20th century)

a. Export of knowledge and technology transfer from Germany. The main conduit for the flow of pharmaceutical knowledge from Germany to the US was through German investment in US companies. For instance, Merck KgaA, established in 1668 in Darmstadt, Germany, ventured into the US market before World War I by founding a subsidiary in New York in 1891 (Merck US / Merck & Co.) to domestically produce its developments. This led to significant equipment and personnel transfer from Germany and the training of American graduates in Germany, equipping Americans with Merck's pharmaceutical knowledge and technology. World War I, turning the US and Germany into adversaries, saw the US confiscating Merck's patents.

b. Establishment of corporate R&D organizations in the US. Pre-World War I, the US pharmaceutical industry's R&D was minimal, attributed to underdeveloped basic science and a focus on sales due to a large domestic market. However, World War I's outbreak and subsequent US-Germany hostility compelled US pharmaceutical firms to bolster R&D, notably illustrated by the development of penicillin production techniques.

c. Developing university-industry relationships. American universities have historically emphasized practical application, particularly in engineering disciplines. This trend toward the scientification of technology led to closer ties between the pharmaceutical industry and universities, especially as breakthroughs in fields like microbiology emerged.

d. Cultivating production and marketing capabilities. Originating from domestic drug manufacturers and wholesalers, the US pharmaceutical industry quickly established production capacities and sales networks, particularly around Philadelphia and New York.

(2) Second stage (1950s to present)

a. Increased investment in basic research. Post-World War II, the US government amplified support for basic research at universities, especially in health-related fields, propelling the US to the forefront of new industries like semiconductors, computers, and biotechnology.

b. Extensive development of university-industry relationships. The growth of science, particularly microbiology in the 1890s, the "medical revolution" in the 1950s, and the molecular biology revolution in the 1970s, encouraged deeper university-industry collaborations. Some companies even conducted basic research to keep pace with scientific advancements.

c. Innovation leadership and international market dominance. Post-World War II, the US pharmaceutical industry embarked on extensive R&D, with American companies holding most drug patents globally, indicating strong innovation leadership and market dominance.
d. Proliferation of entrepreneurial ventures. The molecular biology revolution in the 1970s transformed drug discovery from randomized trials to design-oriented approaches, establishing a significant gap between the US and other countries, including Germany. This era saw a surge in innovation-driven entrepreneurial activity.

In summary, the US pharmaceutical industry's catch-up with Germany is characterized by a clear division into stages, with specific actions taken in each phase. The initial stage focused on importing German technology and knowledge, establishing R&D organizations, fostering university-industry relationships, and enhancing production and marketing capabilities. The subsequent stage concentrated on boosting basic research, expanding university-industry ties, leading innovation, and encouraging entrepreneurial ventures, enabling the US pharmaceutical industry to surpass its German counterparts in capability and market effectiveness.

3. Typical Cases

(1) 1951 Nobel Prize in Physiology and Medicine: Yellow fever vaccine

The 1951 Nobel Prize in Physiology or Medicine was awarded to American microbiologist Max Theiler (1899–1972) for his development of a vaccine against yellow fever. This breakthrough not only provided a method for effectively preventing the disease but also significantly advanced the understanding of its epidemiology.

Yellow fever, a disease transmitted by mosquitoes, puzzled scientists for centuries. Despite observations dating back to the 18th century of the prevalence of mosquitoes in affected areas, the true nature of yellow fever and its transmission mechanisms remained elusive. In 1881, Cuban doctors posited that the disease was mosquito-borne, but their assertions received little attention. It was not until 1900 that the US-appointed Walter Reed Commission substantiated the mosquito transmission theory and identified the virus as the causative agent. Further investigations in the early 20th century revealed that yellow fever could also spread in jungle environments among wild monkeys and from these animals to humans, highlighting the existence of a "jungle-type" yellow fever.

Max Theiler's work was pivotal in demystifying yellow fever. After moving to the US in 1922 to join Harvard University's Department of Tropical Medicine, Theiler was part of a 1925 scientific expedition to West Africa to study the disease. His team's groundbreaking discovery in 1927 that yellow fever was caused by a filterable virus, transmissible to mice, significantly lowered research costs by enabling mice, rather than monkeys, to serve as experimental subjects.

Recognizing the impracticality of relying solely on mosquito control in rural areas of Southwest Africa and South America, Theiler focused on developing a vaccine. Initial personal experiments were unsuccessful, but in 1930, at the Rockefeller Foundation's Virus Laboratory, he made crucial discoveries about the virus's behavior in white rats and its mutation patterns. By 1936, Theiler had developed the safe, standardized YFV-17D vaccine strain. Following successful large-scale clinical trials funded by the Rockefeller Foundation in 1937, mass production of the YFV-17D vaccine commenced.

Theiler's nearly four-decade-long engagement with the Rockefeller Foundation's International Health Division significantly expanded the scientific community's knowledge of yellow fever. His work led to a deeper understanding of the disease's epidemiology and laid the groundwork for its effective prevention, marking a monumental achievement in the battle against infectious diseases.

(2) 1954 Nobel Prize in Physiology and Medicine: Polio vaccine

The 1954 Nobel Prize in Physiology or Medicine was awarded to American scientists John Franklin Enders (1897–1985), Thomas Huckle Weller (1915–2008), and Frederick Chapman Robbins (1916–2003) for their groundbreaking discovery that the poliovirus can be cultured in various types of tissue cultures. This advancement paved the way for the development of vaccines against poliomyelitis, a debilitating disease caused by the poliovirus, which can lead to paralysis and sometimes death.

In the early 20th century, poliomyelitis was a sporadic and relatively rare occurrence worldwide. However, by the time of World War II, pandemics of the disease had occurred on all continents between 1940 and 1950. The 1950s saw an annual average of 28,500 children affected by polio in Europe alone, with the United States witnessing its peak in 1953, reporting 1,450 deaths and more than 7,000 cases of posterior paralysis. The disease was poised to become the second infectious disease eradicated by the World Health Organization (WHO), following smallpox.

Efforts to develop a vaccine encountered numerous challenges. Early attempts by Maurice Brodie and John Kollmer in the 1930s were unsuccessful, leading to allergic reactions and even deaths among vaccinated individuals. A significant breakthrough came in 1948 when a team led by John Franklin Enders at Boston Children's Hospital managed to culture poliovirus in human tissue. This, along with the discovery of three serotypes of the virus and the presence of the virus in blood before paralysis, provided a crucial foundation for vaccine development.

Jonas Salk of the University of Pittsburgh developed the first effective polio vaccine, known as the inactivated poliovirus vaccine or Salk vaccine, in 1952. The vaccine, developed using three serotypes of the pathogenic virus strain, was cultured in monkey kidney tissue (Vero cells) and then inactivated with formalin. Subsequent human trials demonstrated strong antibody responses, laying the groundwork for large-scale clinical trials.

The pivotal trial, known as the "Francis Test," began in 1954 and involved approximately 1.8 million children across 44 states. The results, published in 1955, showed the Salk vaccine to be 60% to 70% effective against PV1 and over 90% effective against PV2 and PV3. Following the successful trials, the vaccine was licensed for use in 1955, leading to a rapid decrease in polio cases in the United States.

By the summer of 1957, over 100 million doses of the vaccine had been administered, reducing the annual number of polio cases to 5,600. The inactivated poliovirus vaccine, further improved in potency, was licensed in the United States in 1987 and continues to be one of the vaccines used today.

The development and success of the polio vaccine marked a monumental achievement in medical science, effectively controlling a disease that had once caused widespread fear and disability.

(3) 1976 Nobel Prize in Physiology and Medicine: Hepatitis B vaccine

The 1976 Nobel Prize in Physiology or Medicine recognized significant advancements in medical science, awarding American scientists Daniel Carleton Gajdusek for his pioneering work on the etiology of Kuru disease, and

Baruch Blumberg for discovering the hepatitis B virus (HBV) and elucidating its pathogenesis mechanism.

Hepatitis, characterized by inflammatory liver damage, can result from viral infections, drugs, alcohol, metabolic issues, or autoimmunity, with symptoms ranging from anorexia and malaise to jaundice and fever. The medical community's quest to identify the causative agent of hepatitis B began in earnest in the 1940s when it was established that the disease could be transmitted through blood. Despite isolating numerous pathogens, their specific role in viral hepatitis remained unconfirmed until the 1960s.

Baruch Blumberg's groundbreaking research in the early 1960s identified what was initially termed the "Australian antigen" in 1969, linking it conclusively to hepatitis B. His subsequent publication proposed a strong association between this antigen and the transmission of acute viral hepatitis through blood transfusions, effectively mapping the HBV's transmission route.

Blumberg's discovery catalyzed global research into HBV, leading to the visualization of the virus's internal structure and the confirmation that subunits (antigens) of the virus were immunogenic but not infectious. These findings laid the groundwork for vaccine development.

Merck, seizing on Blumberg's insights, licensed his technology from the Fox Chase Cancer Center in Philadelphia in 1971 to develop a hepatitis B vaccine from the virus's subunit. Under the leadership of Hilleman, Merck's research team developed a vaccine by purifying the hepatitis B surface antigen from blood, which showed over 90% efficacy in providing immunity against HBV in high-risk populations. This vaccine, derived from human plasma and chemically inactivated, was approved in the United States in 1982, marking the advent of the first-generation hepatitis B vaccine.

This pioneering vaccine was pivotal in combatting hepatitis B, significantly impacting public health and paving the way for the development of a second-generation vaccine in 1986. The success of the hepatitis B vaccine represents a landmark achievement in the fight against viral hepatitis, underscoring the profound significance of Blumberg's discovery for global health.

(4) 1985 Nobel Prize in Physiology and Medicine: Lipid-lowering drugs

The 1985 Nobel Prize in Physiology or Medicine was awarded to Professors Michael S. Brown and Joseph L. Goldstein of the Department of Molecular Genetics, Southwestern Medical School, University of Texas at Dallas, for their pioneering work on cholesterol metabolism and the development of treatments for cholesterol-related diseases.

In 1972, Brown and Goldstein embarked on a collaboration at the Southwestern Medical Center at the University of Texas at Dallas. By 1973, they had made a significant discovery: normal surface cells could internalize low-lipid proteins through a protein receptor mechanism. Their continued research unveiled the pathogenesis of cardiovascular diseases in patients with high cholesterol, leading to the purification of the low-density lipoprotein (LDL) receptor from bovine adrenal cells and the cloning of the LDL receptor gene. A crucial breakthrough was their discovery that the enzyme hydroxymethylglutaryl coenzyme A (HMG-CoA) reductase could effectively inhibit cholesterol synthesis, laying the groundwork for the development of statin drugs.

Parallel to Brown and Goldstein's research, Japanese scientists had been exploring cholesterol-lowering compounds, leading to the discovery of compactin, the world's first lipid-regulating compound, by Sankyo Japan in 1976. However, its potential was not fully recognized until the launch of pravastatin in 1989, an improved version of compactin.

Brown, also a consultant for Merck, played a pivotal role in the pharmaceutical giant's pursuit of compounds that inhibit HMG-CoA reductase, culminating in the discovery of lovastatin in 1978. Merck's lovastatin, approved by the Food and Drug Administration (FDA) in 1987, marked the beginning of a new era in lipid-lowering medications.

Simultaneously, Warner-Lambert embarked on the development of atorvastatin, leading to the launch of Lipitor in partnership with Pfizer in 1997. Despite entering the market after the first-generation statins, Lipitor's sales skyrocketed, capturing a significant market share and eventually becoming Pfizer's flagship product following a monumental acquisition in 2000.

The groundbreaking discoveries by Brown and Goldstein not only elucidated the mechanisms underlying high cholesterol's role in cardiovascular disease but also demonstrated that cholesterol levels could be effectively managed through dietary adjustments and pharmacological interventions. Their work has had a profound impact on the treatment of cholesterol-related conditions, leading to the development of a range of cholesterol-lowering drugs that continue to save millions of lives worldwide.

(5) 1998 Nobel Prize in Physiology and Medicine: Mechanism of nitric oxide function

In 1998, the Nobel Prize in Physiology or Medicine was awarded to American scientists Robert F. Furchgott, Louis J. Ignarro, and Ferid Murad for their groundbreaking discovery that nitroglycerin and other organic nitrates release nitric oxide gas, which causes vasodilation by relaxing vascular smooth muscles.

Professor Murad and his team at the University of Virginia conducted systematic studies on the pharmacological effects of nitroglycerin and other vasodilating organic nitrates from the 1970s. In 1977, Murad demonstrated that nitroglycerin and similar nitrates must be metabolized into nitric oxide to exert their vasodilatory pharmacological effects, proposing nitric oxide as a "messenger molecule" regulating blood flow, though lacking direct experimental proof at that time.

Meanwhile, Professor Furchgott's research at the State University of New York on substances like acetylcholine's effects on blood vessels revealed inconsistent outcomes based on the vascular endothelium's integrity. His discovery in 1980 that acetylcholine-induced vasodilation required an intact endothelium led to the hypothesis of an endothelium-derived relaxing factor (EDRF), later identified as nitric oxide.

Ignarro, focusing on the pharmacological impacts of nitroso compounds, collaborated with Furchgott to elucidate EDRF's pharmacological and chemical nature. They discovered that EDRF activates soluble guanylate cyclase, like nitric oxide, primarily facilitating vasodilation through the cGMP pathway.

This foundational work led to Pfizer's development of Sildenafil, or "Viagra," initially aimed at treating heart failure and hypertension. Clinical trials unexpectedly revealed its effectiveness in treating erectile dysfunction in men, leading to Viagra's FDA approval in 1998. Within three months of its launch, Viagra received 2.9 million prescriptions in the US, with sales exceeding $1 billion in its first year, establishing a long-term trend of rising sales.

Beyond their physiological functions, Furchgott, Ignarro, and Murad's discovery of nitric oxide as a significant "messenger molecule" has profoundly influenced research directions, drawing in pharmacologists, biochemists, and neurobiologists. This has led to the development of effective drugs based on nitric oxide's mechanism, marking a significant advance in medical science and therapy.

2.3.3 Japan's Pharmaceutical Industry Catch-Up Efforts

1. Background Overview

Since the 1960s, Japan has aimed to match or surpass the global leaders in various industries, including heavy machinery, automobiles, consumer electronics, and pharmaceuticals. While Japan has seen considerable success in catching up within the fields of heavy machinery, automobiles, and consumer electronics, its efforts in the pharmaceutical sector have not yielded similar results (Chandler 2009). The Japanese pharmaceutical industry has remained relatively inconspicuous on the international stage. Throughout the latter half of the 20th century, the forefront of the global pharmaceutical industry was dominated by companies from the United States, which had previously surpassed Germany. Japan's role in this industry was markedly minor. Data from the early 21st century reinforces this observation. For instance, among the top twenty global pharmaceutical companies by sales up to 2009, only two Japanese firms—Takeda and Daiichi Sankyo—made the list, ranking 16th and 19th, respectively, as per the IMS report. Moreover, in terms of innovation, Japanese pharmaceutical companies lag significantly behind their US counterparts, introducing new active substances to the market at a rate only one-third that of the US, as illustrated in Figure 2-1, and securing patents at merely a quarter of the US rate, as illustrated in Figure 2-2.

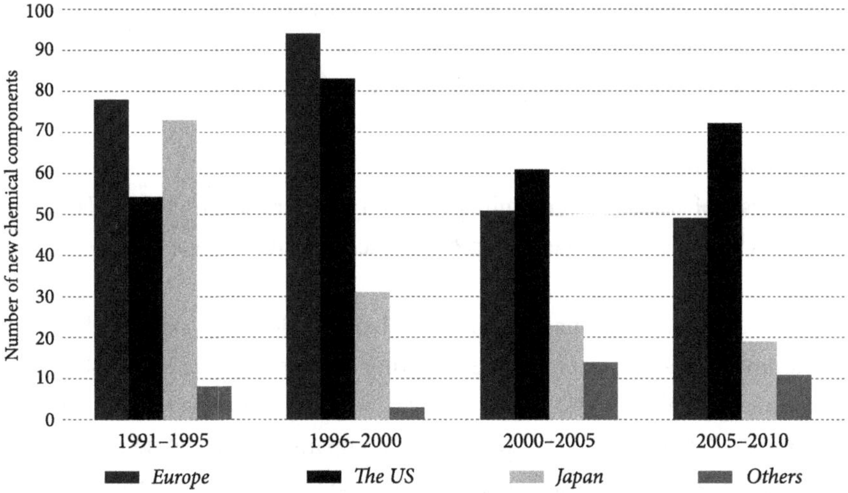

Figure 2-1 New chemical and biological components introduced on the global market

Source: EFPIA (2010)

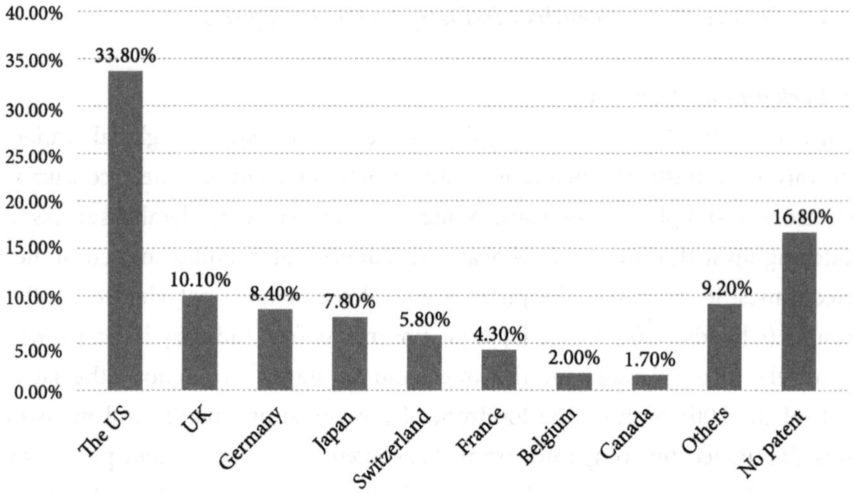

Figure 2-2 US drug approval classification by patent owner's country, 1992–2004

Source: Keyhani et al. (2010)

Although the Japanese pharmaceutical industry has made strides forward, it continues to struggle with competitiveness on the international stage. Economist Chandler attributes this to the developmental stage of the industry at the time Japan began its efforts to catch up with Europe and the United States. Other researchers have focused on the impact of policy, suggesting that healthcare policies, in particular, have encouraged Japanese pharmaceutical firms to prioritize cost reduction over innovation. This perspective is highlighted in Reich's 1990 analysis, which underscores how regulatory environments can shape industry priorities and innovation trajectories.

2. Challenges in Catching-Up

An analysis of the literature highlights several key reasons why the Japanese pharmaceutical industry has struggled to catch up with Europe and the United States.

First, Japanese pharmaceutical firms have applied the same technology development strategy as companies in other sectors, such as automotive and electronics (Kneller 2003). This involves refining existing technologies to accumulate "tacit knowledge" within the company, which, while effective in other industries, does not suffice in science-based sectors like pharmaceuticals. In these fields, cutting-edge technology relies on fresh scientific breakthroughs, and without leading-edge technology, Japan has found it challenging to catch up with Western counterparts.

Second, Japanese universities have historically focused little on basic research. With a tradition of distancing themselves from industry collaboration and a tendency to pursue basic scientific research through state funding, Japanese universities have not adequately prepared the high-level human resources needed by the industry. Their collaborations with industry, especially in the biopharmaceutical field, have been minimal, and university-driven entrepreneurial ventures are scarce (Probert 2006). Despite recent attention to this issue from both the government and universities, and increased efforts by pharmaceutical companies to bolster basic research, these measures have yet to enable Japan to catch up in the pharmaceutical sector (Kneller 2003).

Third, Japan's success in catching up in "technology-based industries" such as home appliances, electronics, automobiles, and engineering machinery has been largely attributed to its industrial policy (Funaba 1988). This policy, which involves prioritizing specific industries and technological directions (Arora 1998), works well in sectors where the path of technological development is predictable. However, in a science-based industry like pharmaceuticals, where technological progress depends on unpredictable scientific breakthroughs, such policies may not be effective. This has hindered the Japanese pharmaceutical industry's ability to innovate and catch up with European and American leaders.

In summary, the Japanese pharmaceutical industry's attempts to catch up with Europe and the United States in the latter half of the 20th century were marked by a lack of clear developmental stages, the application of inappropriate catch-up strategies from technology-based industries, insufficient emphasis on basic research by universities, and the misapplication of industrial policies suited to more predictable sectors. These factors have collectively impeded the industry's capacity for innovation.

2.3.4 Comparative Analysis and Insights

When comparing the outcomes of the preceding analyses, we can summarize the findings in the table below, designated as Table 2-2.

Table 2-2 The comparison of three typical cases

Cases	Germany overtook Britain in pharmaceuticals	America overtook Germany in pharmaceuticals	Japan overtook Europe and America in pharmaceuticals
Catching-up stages	Distinct stages of development with specific goals and actions	Distinct stages of development with specific goals and actions	No clear catching-up stages identified
The first stage: Catch up and strive	Adopted technology transfer from the UK; developed R&D capabilities within enterprises; fostered industry-university interactions; invested in production and marketing to build market competitiveness	Sought knowledge export and technology transfer from Germany; established R&D organizations; enhanced university-industry relationships; built production and marketing capacities to achieve market competitiveness	Utilized similar catch-up methods as in technology-based industries
The second stage: Catch up and strive	Valued basic research; enhanced product innovation; expanded into international markets, achieving greater capability and market impact than British counterparts	Increased investment in basic research; improved university-industry relations; innovated and gained an international market advantage, catching up with German market impact	Limited focus on basic research in universities; challenges in fostering pharmaceutical innovation

From the analysis of previous cases and the summary in Table 2-2, we can observe that the pharmaceutical industries in three countries aimed to catch up with their international counterparts, with Germany and the United States achieving success, but Japan not. The successful countries shared similar approaches, while Japan's approach appeared uniquely individual. From these observations, we can draw several conclusions.

First, in science-based industries, it's beneficial for a country aiming to catch up in a particular industry to have distinct "stages" of development. Different goals and actions are appropriate at each stage. Initially, the focus should be on acquiring knowledge and technology, expanding production, enhancing marketing capabilities, and fostering the market competitiveness and innovation potential of domestic enterprises. For example, both Germany, in catching up with the British pharmaceutical industry, and the United States, in catching up with the German pharmaceutical industry, made efforts at this stage to accept technology transfer or knowledge flow from leading countries, cultivate R&D capabilities within local enterprises, and invest in building the production and marketing capabilities of enterprises. In the subsequent stage, the emphasis shifts toward forming the innovation capability and international market development capability of local enterprises by strengthening basic research, product innovation, and expansion to international markets. Japan's attempt to catch up in the pharmaceutical industry without clear stage differentiation and without decomposing the goal into phases resulted in efforts to "reach the top in one step," which inevitably led to inefficiency.

Second, the formation of industrial innovation capacity inherently has its stages, necessitating phased efforts by catching-up countries. SBI is crucial for the establishment and development of science-based industries. A country must first introduce and learn from the knowledge and technology of leading countries before it can develop its SBI.

Third, the "catch-up model" for science-based industries might resemble a "double helix," as illustrated in Figure 2-3, where in the first stage, catch-up efforts focus on building production and sales capabilities, while in the second stage, efforts shift toward training, R&D, and leading in basic research. The intersection of these stages involves developing a close relationship between universities and industry, which is crucial for transitioning from market competitiveness to SBI capabilities.

In conclusion, catching up in science-based industries requires innovation-oriented companies, universities that value industrial linkages and basic research, and government policies that facilitate the formation of effective

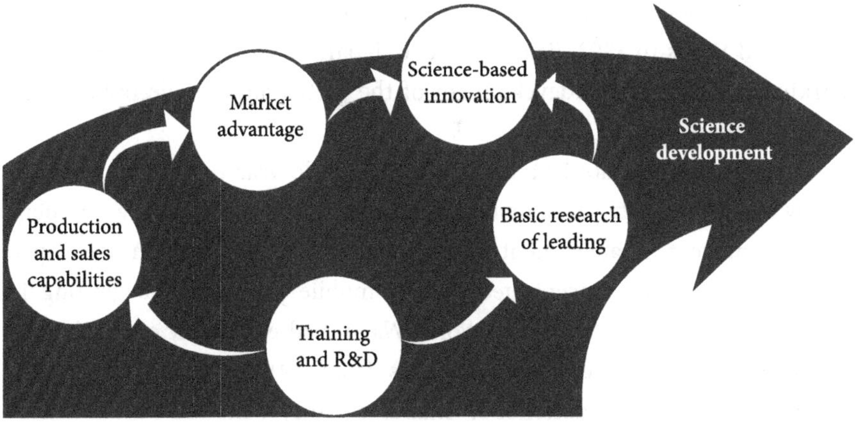

Figure 2-3 Catching-up in science-based industries

industry-university relationships. Without these elements, catching up in industries that depend heavily on scientific advancements will be challenging.

2.4 Technology-Based Industrial Catching-Up: The Automobile Industry

Globally, the evolution of the automobile industry is distinguished by two distinct developmental archetypes: the "originator" paradigm, represented by Europe and the United States, which pioneered automotive industry development, and the "latecomer" paradigm, exemplified by Japan, South Korea, and Brazil. These "latecomer" nations embarked on their automotive industry development after the "originators." Despite all being classified as "latecomer countries," their trajectories in the automotive sector have varied significantly due to different approaches to innovation and strategies for catching up.

2.4.1 Evolution of the Global Automotive Industry

1. Inception and Inventor Era

At the turn of the 19th to the 20th century, as the major capitalist nations in Europe and the United States concluded the first Industrial Revolution, there was a significant surge in productive forces, necessitating the parallel evolution of transportation means. The invention of the world's first automobile by Germans Mercedes-Benz and Daimler in 1886 sparked a global race in automobile manufacturing. France followed with its first car in 1890, the United States in 1893, Britain in 1896, Japan in 1907, and Russia in 1910, marking the continuous development of the global automobile industry for about 130 years.

The era from the late 19th century up to World War I, spanning approximately twenty to thirty years, represented the inventor phase of the automobile and the nascent establishment of the automobile industry in developed countries. Germany concentrated on automobile production beginning in 1886, and by 1913, on the eve of World War I, had essentially established an independent automotive sector. Statistics from 1914 indicate over 50,000 workers in Germany's automobile manufacturing, with an annual output of 20,000 vehicles and a national inventory reaching 100,000 cars. In the

United States, the Duryea brothers crafted the nation's first car in 1893. By the following three years, the number of individuals involved in car manufacturing had increased, with Henry Ford and Rae Oz emerging as notable figures. Ford, the founder of the Ford Motor Company, constructed his initial car in 1896, achieving an annual production of 600 units. By 1902, US car production had escalated to 9,000 units per year.

2. Product Innovation Evolution

The journey of product innovation within the automotive industry has seen remarkable milestones. The advent of off-road vehicles was marked by Mercedes-Benz in Germany, launching the G1 off-road vehicle in 1926, capable of traversing rugged terrains. However, the concept truly came to fruition in the United States. On November 11, 1940, the Willis Group presented two prototypes named "QUAD" to the US military, featuring both four-wheel and two-wheel drive capabilities. The Jeep emerged as a significant innovation during World War II, with US factories inventing numerous new products, including the Jeep, which was developed in response to the US Army's call in July 1940 for a light reconnaissance vehicle. Bantam Car Company responded by creating the first prototype on September 21, 1940, dubbed the Bantam Scout Car, the Jeep's precursor. From 1941 to 1945, approximately 640,000 Jeeps were produced in the US, accounting for 18% of the total military vehicle production, with Willis and Ford being the main manufacturers.

The evolution of car design witnessed the introduction of the wedge-shaped "Steamboat Abendi" in 1963, a design later adopted and evolved by Oldsmobile and Cadillac in 1966 and 1968, respectively. The wedge shape became a preferred design, paving the way for the Ford V8 type car in 1949, known for its boat-like silhouette. The design evolution continued with the introduction of the "fish-type car," characterized by a slant-back rear window, as seen in the 1964 Chrysler Plymouth and the 1965 Ford Mustang.

The engine, the automobile's "heart," has undergone significant developments since the invention of the steam engine by Watt in the mid-18th century. The first application of a steam engine in a vehicle was by France's N. J. Cugnot in 1770. The gas engine was later invented by Lenoir in 1858, and in 1867, Nicolaus August Otto of Germany made groundbreaking contributions with his research on gas engines, introducing the four-stroke theory foundational to the internal combustion engine. This theory inspired the development of modern gasoline engines by Aumueller and Karl Benz. In 1892, Rudolf Diesel of

Germany innovated further with the development of the compression ignition engine.

The rotary piston engine, invented by the German Wankle in 1957, represented a significant branch in gasoline engine development. Wankle's engine was later adopted by Japan's Mazda, indicating a product born in Germany but matured in Japan.

The automotive industry's evolution can be segmented into distinct phases: pre-steam engine invention, the inception of steam cars, and the onset of mass production, each marking pivotal developments in automotive history.

3. Management Innovation History

The 20th century marked the era when humanity fully transitioned into an industrialized society, with the manufacturing sector leading this industrial revolution. Within this landscape, the automobile industry held a unique and pivotal position in the development of manufacturing. Not only did the automobile industry represent a significant portion of the manufacturing sector in terms of scale and market presence, but it also played a crucial role in propelling the entire sector forward. More critically, the production methods and management innovations within the automobile industry had a profound and lasting impact on the broader manufacturing industry.

In the early 20th century, Frederick Taylor introduced the principles of "scientific management," laying the groundwork for efficiency and productivity improvements in industrial operations. Building upon this foundation, Henry Ford revolutionized the automobile manufacturing process with the development of the assembly line for the Model T. This innovation drastically reduced the production cycle and costs, enabling Ford to significantly lower the selling price of automobiles. By October 1925, Ford's assembly line allowed for the production of over 9,000 cars daily. This shift to an assembly line-based "mass production method" not only cemented Ford Motor Company's status as one of the world's largest corporations but also set a new standard for manufacturing efficiency and effectiveness across industries.

By the 1970s, the "Toyota Production System" developed by Toyota Motor Corporation in Japan had distinguished itself significantly.[2] Toyota managed

---

2. The Toyota Production System (TPS) embodies a holistic approach to invigorating a company, established as Toyota's hallmark manufacturing strategy. This system, fundamentally aimed at the complete eradication of waste, advocates for efficiency in manufacturing and places

to halve the time, engineering hours, and inventory on hand, while producing much less waste compared to other automakers, to develop new products. Moreover, Toyota was capable of producing a wider and better range of variants. In the mid-1980s, a group of professors from the Massachusetts Institute of Technology encapsulated the principles of the "Toyota production system" and dubbed it "lean production." Lean production drastically reduced all inputs compared to traditional mass production methods.

By the late 1980s, the United States recognized the necessity of reclaiming its manufacturing supremacy to sustain its global leadership. The Iacocca Institute, under the commission of the US Congress, brought together representatives from the Departments of Defense, industry, and academia to form a collaborative research group involving more than 100 companies. This group analyzed and studied over 400 reports from the US industry and introduced the concept of "agile manufacturing." This concept was swiftly implemented in the US automobile industry, aiming to enhance flexibility, efficiency, and responsiveness in manufacturing processes.[3]

The concept of "product structure modularity" found its initial application within the automobile industry. The technical prowess of the auto parts manufacturer Delphi Systems gave rise to the development of cockpit, interface disc brakes, doors, front ends, integrated air/fuel modules, and more, introducing a fresh perspective to the modern automobile assembly line. These advancements make it evident that management innovation in the

---

a premium on quality as a means to achieve cost savings by streamlining production processes. In 1979, Taiichi Ohno, the former Vice President of Toyota Motor Corporation, published *Toyota Production System*, a seminal work that methodically reveals the principles underpinning Toyota's success. The book delves into various facets of production management, including just-in-time (JIT), automation, the Kanban system, standardized operations, and lean production. Recognized as the "Father of the Japanese Revival" and the "Godfather of Production Management," Taiichi Ohno's contributions through the Toyota Production System marked a pivotal advancement beyond the traditional "Ford Production Method," exerting a significant influence on the global industrial landscape. This book is heralded as the definitive guide to Toyota's competitive edge and a cornerstone text in the realm of global production management, earning its place as a universally revered manual for business practitioners.

3. Agile manufacturing is not confined to a specific production process or operational mode. Rather, it embodies an integration of organizational structures, a workforce endowed with high skills and knowledge, and cutting-edge technology, all aimed at fostering collaboration and innovation. This approach enables rapid and effective adjustments across all facets of a business, facilitating swift responses to the dynamic and highly competitive global market.

automobile industry has led the way for the entire manufacturing sector. The transformative journey of business management within the automobile industry is monumental. Indeed, the history of the automobile industry's development mirrors the history of business management innovation.

2.4.2 Japan's Automobile Industry Development and Catching-Up

To recover and revitalize its economy after World War II, the Japanese government prioritized the development of heavy chemical industries, among which the automobile industry was identified as a key focus. However, in the early 1950s, Japan's automobile industry was characterized by its small scale, numerous companies, and limited R&D capabilities, rendering it non-competitive with the United States. In response, Japan embarked on an effort to catch up with the US auto industry. This initiative propelled the Japanese automobile industry from a position of weakness to a place of strength, securing a competitive advantage in the global automobile market.

1. Industry Development Trajectory

The first car was manufactured in France in 1890, followed by the United States in 1893, Britain in 1896, and Japan in 1907. Entering the 20th century, Japan's automobile production was notably slow, with only 200 cars produced by 1923. However, by the early 1960s, the Japanese Ministry of International Trade and Industry significantly promoted the development of the automotive industry. In November 1963, the Industrial Structure Review Council formally recognized the automobile industry as a strategic sector for Japan. The evolution of Japan's automobile industry can be segmented into four stages.

The initial stage occurred during the 1950s, a period marked by Japan's economic recovery. During this time, the automobile industry was relatively weak and focused on resuming production. The technology primarily relied on imports, with a focus on manufacturing trucks.

The second stage unfolded in the 1960s, as Japan experienced a phase of economic liberalization and significant growth in the automobile sector. Japan imported 488 advanced technologies from the US, UK, Italy, and other nations, utilizing these as a foundation for derivative innovation. This period saw extensive innovative efforts in adapting a multitude of non-proprietary technologies from these countries. Often, Japanese automobile companies were able to enhance these technologies significantly. For instance, Toyo's derivative innovation of rotary engine technology, initially acquired from German automakers, resolved the issue of vibration caused by the piston's contact with the cylinder, resulting in a rotary engine that surpassed the original German design in performance and quality. After years of importing technology and assimilating knowledge, Japan's capability for indigenous innovation advanced. Japanese automobile manufacturers began designing and producing new models independently, with companies like Toyota and Nissan establishing factories for production.

The latter part of the second stage marked a pivotal moment when the Japanese automobile industry developed its own innovative capabilities and essentially reached parity with its European and American counterparts.

The third stage encompassed the 1970s and 1980s, marking a period of rapid development for the Japanese automobile industry. During this time, the pace of development, production efficiency, and export growth all saw significant acceleration, enabling Japan to surpass the European and American automobile industries in various respects. At this juncture, the Japanese automobile industry had essentially "outpaced" the US automobile industry in certain areas.

The fourth stage, spanning from the 1990s to the present, coincides with a phase of market saturation in the global automobile industry. It represents a period during which the Japanese automobile sector sought new directions for development. Competing on the global stage in automobile production and new product development, Japan focused especially on creating new environmentally friendly vehicles. This effort aimed at pioneering innovation and capturing technological leadership to lay a foundation for the sustainable development of Japanese automobile brands. Concurrently, major Japanese automobile manufacturers commonly established joint ventures in emerging markets overseas, marking this era as the "global market expansion stage through innovation."

Overall, after navigating through these four developmental stages, the Japanese automobile industry has firmly established a path toward endogenous innovation. This is evident from the shift in Japan's international standing in automobile production, particularly highlighted by changes in the global comparison of car production.

From World War II until the early 1990s, the production volume of the Japanese automobile industry saw consistent growth. In 1946, Japan produced

15,000 automobiles, a number that doubled to 32,000 by 1950. By 1955, production had increased to 69,000 automobiles, and by 1960, it had surged to 482,000—a nearly sevenfold increase from 1955. The growth continued with 1.9 million automobiles produced in 1965, which was 3.94 times the number produced in 1960. The upward trend persisted, with 5.29 million automobiles produced in 1970, 7.08 million in 1973, 11.04 million in 1980, 12.27 million in 1985, and reaching a historical peak of 13.49 million in 1990. After the 1990s, the absolute number of cars produced in Japan began to decline, but the transfer of production capacity overseas, especially to China, was notably active. Compared to other countries, Japan surpassed Italy in 1960, France in 1964, the United Kingdom in 1966, and Germany in 1967 to become the world's second-largest automobile producer, trailing only the United States.

The car represents the core technology of the automobile industry. By 1970, Japan's car production exceeded 50% of its total automobile production, and the proportion of cars in the production mix continued to increase, reaching 66% by 1975. From 1980 to 1985, this ratio remained stable, and in 1991, car production accounted for 73.8% of total automobile production. When compared to the car production of other major car-producing countries, Japan produced only 20,000 cars in 1955, approximately 1/400 of the United States, 1/45 of the United Kingdom, 1/38 of the Federal Republic of Germany, 1/28 of France, and 1/11 of Italy. However, by 1990, Japan's car production (9.95 million units) was 1.64 times that of the US, 2.15 times that of Germany, 3.02 times that of France, 7.64 times that of the United Kingdom, and 5.32 times that of Italy.

2. Technological Catching-Up Strategies

As a newcomer to the automobile industry, Japan has evolved from a position of "follower" and "imitator" to become an "innovator." This transformation occurred over four stages of development, during which Japan navigated the technological catch-up process involving "technology introduction, learning and absorption, imitation and innovation, and indigenous innovation" (refer to Table 2-3).

The technology catch-up process in the Japanese automobile industry, particularly its adoption of advanced international technology from the post-war period to the late 1960s, is especially noteworthy.

Table 2-3 Japanese automotive industry's technological catch-up and the embedding of innovation in overall economic development

Period	Automobile industry development	Technology catching-up	Government policy background	Economic development
The 1950s	Production resumed, mainly trucks	Introduced technology on a small scale	Subsidized Korean car manufacturers and consumers; raised tariffs on imported cars, implemented an industrial entry licensing system, restricted foreign car company entry, imposed high tariff protection on components like engines, etc.	Economy recovered, implemented import substitution strategies
The 1960s	Scaling-up development; became the world's second-largest car producer	Large-scale introduction; innovation from imitating introduced technologies	Fostered the introduction of automatic production lines by car manufacturers in terms of capital, taxation, and foreign exchange, and severely restricted car imports through tariff and non-tariff barriers	Entered a period of economic freedom, implemented an export-oriented strategy
The 1970s–1980s	Rapid development, catching up with Europe and the US	Large-scale improved imitation; initiation of endogenous innovation	Encouraged the automobile industry to internationalize	
The 1990s–present	Global market expansion through innovation	Autonomous innovation to seize technological leadership; self-developed for the host market	Encouraged the automobile industry to internationalize while simultaneously upgrading technology for domestic demand	Years of trade surpluses with Europe and the US; increased trade frictions, demands for market opening

First, the introduction of technology was both extensive and systematic. From 1961 to 1974, Japan imported 274 automobile production technologies from the United States, 72 from the Federal Republic of Germany, 64 from the United Kingdom, 23 from France, and 55 from other countries, totaling 488 items. Through the initial introduction and subsequent digestion and absorption of these technologies, by the mid-1970s, Japan had essentially mastered the world's most advanced automobile manufacturing technologies.

Second, there was significant improvement and upgrading following the technology introduction. For example, in response to environmental pollution and the impacts of the two international oil crises, Japan's major automobile companies invested substantial human and material resources. Building upon the introduced technologies, they researched, developed, and produced cars that were fuel-efficient, had exhaust gas purification capabilities, and were safe. By the latter half of the 1970s, the exhaust gas purification technology of Japanese cars reached a world-class level, and the overall production costs of cars significantly decreased.

Third, Japan introduced and utilized non-patented technologies from leading countries in the automobile industry, encompassing both expired patents and technical secrets. In particular, for the latter, many Japanese automobile companies acquired the desired technology by sending personnel to study at companies in leading countries, visiting these companies, and networking with their R&D staff.

Fourth, there was a vigorous introduction of automobile production machinery, equipment, and advanced production technology, including process, flow, and management technologies. This approach allowed the domestic automobile industry ample time to digest and absorb advanced technologies and innovate upon them, without the interference of foreign automobile companies. Notably, in 1965, spurred by the National Income Doubling Plan and the challenges of automobile import liberalization, Japanese automobile factories made large-scale investments in equipment to enhance the industry's production technology and management, resulting in the establishment of several world-class car production plants. From 1953 to 1977, the total investment in the Japanese automobile industry amounted to JPY 4,729.39 billion.

3. Policy Background and Innovation Integration

The Japanese automobile industry successfully achieved technological catch-up through extensive technology introduction, followed by digestion, absorption, improvement, upgrading, and ultimately, indigenous innovation. The timely support of government policies and adaptive adjustments over time created a favorable policy environment for businesses.

First, the Japanese government implemented a systematic industrial policy, elevating some policies to the level of law to reflect the national will. Before World War II, Japan's automobile industry policy was primarily defined by three legal documents: the Automobile Subsidy Law, the Ministry of Commerce and Industry's Automobile Localization Policy, and the Japan Automobile Manufacturing Business Law. These laws significantly contributed to the protection and early development of the Japanese automobile industry, laying a solid domestic foundation for its post-war growth.

The Automobile Subsidy Law offered subsidies to both manufacturers and consumers, stimulating automobile production and purchase. From 1951 to 1959, the Japanese government provided JPY 369 million in entrusted business fees as subsidies to the Automobile Technology Association and the Car Industry Association. The Ministry of Commerce and Industry enacted a series of protective measures, such as increasing tariffs on imported automobiles, restricting foreign auto company entry, implementing a licensing system for industry entry, and imposing high tariffs on parts like engines. The Japan Automobile Manufacturing Business Law was particularly influential; under its regime, the presence of foreign companies like General Motors and Ford declined in Japan, leading to the cessation of all foreign automobile production in Japan by 1961.

After World War II, in an effort to restore and rejuvenate the severely damaged automobile industry, the Japanese government introduced a series of revitalization policies building on the existing laws. These measures included government subsidies to auto companies, preferential loan and tax policies, and exemption of import duties on essential manufacturing equipment. Notably, the Foreign Investment Law, enacted in 1950, legally guided and protected the introduction of foreign investment and technology, marking an expansion in technology introduction. To address the quality and price disadvantages of Japanese cars, manufacturers were permitted to collaborate with foreign companies for a period, importing loose parts for assembly under strict foreign exchange controls. In 1959, the Technologist Law concerning overseas technology transfer was established, introducing a "qualification system" for the export of complete equipment. In the 1960s, the Japanese government integrated technology introduction policies directly into its broader industrial policies, which were previously centered on finance and taxation.

Second, the Japanese government's policy toward the automobile industry was comprehensive, covering all aspects of the sector and the entire production and marketing process. Post-war, Japan identified the automobile industry as a key industry. At this time, the Japanese government recognized that free trade and an open economy could negatively impact the Japanese automobile industry, hindering its ability to compete internationally. Consequently, the government implemented specific industrial policies in areas such as international trade, direct investment, and technology transfer, along with domestic institutional arrangements. These measures aimed to revitalize the automobile industry and enhance its global competitiveness. Policies included trade protection for automobiles, buying valuable time for the industry's catch-up development, and promoting automobile technology, along with stringent exhaust and safety standards. These efforts prepared Japanese automobiles for entry into European and American markets, especially after Japan's first oil crisis.

In terms of trade policy, during the 1950s and 1960s, the Japanese government strictly limited automobile imports through tariffs and non-tariff barriers. From April 1949 to March 1962, the tariff rate was 50% for luxury cars, 40% for standard cars, and 20% for small cars. The new tariff rates implemented after March 1962 were 40% for small-wheelbase cars, 35% for large-wheelbase cars, and 30% and 27% for trucks, respectively. These tariffs significantly shielded the domestic car industry from competitive pressures.

Regarding foreign exchange policy, the foreign exchange quota system was crucial in limiting automobile imports. From 1952 to 1953, there was a significant increase in the number of small cars from European countries entering the Japanese market with a "low-cost advantage." In response, Japan introduced the "foreign exchange quota system" and "foreign exchange restrictions" in 1954 to curb automobile imports. Upon joining the General Agreement on Tariffs and Trade (GATT) in 1955, Japan's automobile industry was "protected by tariffs" under GATT Article 18, with import tariffs reaching as high as 35%–40% until 1978 when the tariffs were lifted. In 1964, with Japan's accession to the Organization for Economic Cooperation and Development (OECD), the "quota restriction" shifted from a monetary amount to a quantity basis, with an expanded scope for the quantity restriction.[4]

---

4. In Japan, import restrictions on passenger cars were lifted in 1965, and restrictions on car engine imports were removed in 1972. Compared to the deregulation of other goods, the relaxation of automobile import restrictions occurred relatively late.

In terms of restricting foreign direct investment, the Japanese government prohibited foreign direct investment in the Japanese automobile industry to nurture domestic enterprises. In 1950, the Law on Foreign Investment was enacted, establishing "approval criteria" and "disapproval criteria" for foreign direct investment. While the criteria appeared reasonable, detailed conditions for approval were never disclosed in the implementation process, allowing the government discretion to strictly regulate foreign direct investment. Throughout the 1950s, almost no foreign companies received authorization to invest in the automobile industry. In 1951, it was further specified that "foreign automobile manufacturers were restricted from investing in and importing into Japan, while domestic automobile manufacturers were encouraged to adopt advanced technology from abroad."

Regarding technological advancement in automobiles, companies were urged to accelerate equipment updates. The Special Depreciation System, outlined in Japan's post-war Rent and Tax Special Measures Act, allowed for half of the depreciation in the first year for rationalized machinery and a special 50% depreciation over three years for critical machinery. This system was applied to the automobile manufacturing industry in 1951 and extended to the automobile parts manufacturing industry in 1956, granting the Japanese automobile sector substantial tax benefits. In 1955, the Five-Year Plan for Economic Self-Reliance was announced, providing further support to automobile manufacturers in terms of capital, taxation, and foreign exchange to import high-volume automatic production lines from Detroit, US, and to facilitate large-scale equipment investments.

4. Technology Catch-Up in the Japanese Automobile Industry and the Integration of Innovation in Economic Development

In a country's economy, the innovation and catch-up of an industry are embedded within the broader development process of the country's economy. The innovation and catch-up of the Japanese automobile industry are closely linked to at least two stages of the overall strategic evolution of Japan's economy in the post-war period.

After the war, Japan faced a recession. Being a small, resource-scarce country with a large population, Japan needed to effectively utilize international markets and resources to develop its economy and maintain a high standard of living. The "import–export–import" cycle became a crucial component of Japan's economic development. During the post-war development of its economy, Japan implemented policies transitioning from "import substitution" to "export orientation," and then to "boosting domestic demand," based on this cyclical chain. This approach has shaped a unique economic development strategy model in Japan, creating a favorable domestic and international economic environment for the automobile industry to innovate and catch up.

First, during the import substitution stage, Japan implemented measures such as import restrictions, high tariffs, restrictions on foreign direct investment, and technology introduction. In less than thirty years, this policy fostered an automobile industry with enhanced survival and innovation capabilities. The Japanese automobile industry not only reached an international leading level in technology but also achieved lower manufacturing costs than those of leading automobile countries. This revitalization of the domestic economy also fostered industrial competitiveness for the Japanese automobile industry's global expansion.

Second, in the export-oriented strategy stage, as the Japanese automobile industry grew more competitive, the government shifted its policy focus to providing enterprises access to international markets. This was achieved by promoting trade and financial liberalization through participation in international organizations and agreements. In 1960, Japan proposed the Outline of Trade and Foreign Exchange Liberalization, followed by the Trade and Foreign Exchange Liberalization Plan in 1961 to accelerate the liberalization process. Crucial amendments were made to the Foreign Exchange and Foreign Trade Control Act in 1964, abolishing the foreign exchange quota system central to import substitution. As the automobile industry sought greater foreign expansion, the pace of trade liberalization quickened, with liberalization rates increasing dramatically from 1960 through 1971, and a fully open economic system was essentially established by 1980 following fundamental changes to the Foreign Exchange and Foreign Trade Control Law.

Third, in the stage of enhancing domestic demand, following the success of its export-oriented strategy, Japan experienced trade surpluses with Europe and the United States, leading to intensified trade frictions. The demand from these regions for Japan to open its domestic market grew, especially after the yen appreciated in 1985, increasing export pressures. The Japanese government then guided the industry to accelerate the development of high-tech industries and modernize traditional industries with technology, spurring another period of high economic growth. From 1987 to 1991, Japan's GDP grew at an average annual rate of 5%, marking the longest post-war economic boom. Although the overall Japanese economy did not see significant improvement after the 1990s, the Japanese automobile industry largely maintained its competitiveness domestically, responding to rising demands for quality and new consumption trends both domestically and internationally. Additionally, as emerging countries like China sped up the development of their automobile industries, Japanese automobile companies established joint ventures or wholly owned factories in these countries, securing a competitive edge in the global market.

2.4.3 Korean Automobile Industry Development and Catching-Up

1. Industry Development Trajectory

Kia Motors was founded in December 1944, marking the beginning of the South Korean automobile industry. However, due to the immediate post-World War II challenges and the turbulent domestic and international situation, Kia experienced a prolonged period of stagnation. The real momentum for the South Korean automobile industry began in the early 1960s, following the Korean War in the early 1950s. The development of this industry can be segmented into five stages.

The initial stage was the foundational period of automobile industry development. In the 1960s, specifically in 1962, South Korea's 1st Five-Year Economic Development Plan outlined a strategy to promote the development of the automobile industry through the "parts assembly method" over the next five years. Consequently, Korean automobile companies started by assembling complete vehicles from imported parts.

The second stage involved transitioning from assembly to independent production. In the 1970s, the South Korean government established the Basic Development Plan for the Automobile Industry, identifying automobiles, steel, and shipbuilding as "pillar industries" and offering tax exemptions for importing raw materials to encourage localization. As a result, Korean automobile companies began to introduce foreign production technologies extensively. Hyundai Motor Company, established in 1967, developed its R&D capabilities through imitation and innovation until the mid-1990s. The company's new models evolved from simple imitation of foreign cars to innovative imitation and eventually independent R&D.

During this process, Hyundai Motor Company assimilated and enhanced patented automobile chassis technology acquired from abroad, independently developing models like the Excel mini car, Stella compact car, and Sonata medium-sized car. Such imitation and innovation enabled Hyundai to produce models that could compete with European and American cars. In 1973, the company also acquired engine, drivetrain, and chassis technologies from Mitsubishi Corporation of Japan and by 1975 began developing and producing its own cars, exporting them in large quantities to Africa. Meanwhile, Daewoo Motor Company formed a joint venture with General Motors in 1972 and later started technical cooperation with Nissan of Japan.

Simultaneously, South Korea's Basic Development Plan for the Automobile Industry set a goal for the industry to achieve localization, with companies focusing on "technology catch-up and independent development." Following this, the South Korean government led the consolidation of automobile companies in response to the rapidly deteriorating domestic and international market conditions and the emergence of overcapacity spurred by the oil crisis. This led to the formation of several core automobile production enterprises and numerous specialized auto parts supporting enterprises. The government also introduced the Long-Term Automobile Industry Revitalization Plan, supporting large conglomerates, with Kia and Daewoo emerging as automotive manufacturers during this period. Additionally, the South Korean government initiated the Unification Measures for the Automobile Industry to further centralize automobile production and ensure profitability for each manufacturer in certain areas, resulting in the establishment of four major automobile companies: Hyundai, Kia, Daewoo, and Ssangyong.

The third stage was the period of automobile localization. After entering the 1980s, South Korea accelerated the localization of automobiles and made significant efforts to promote automobile exports. The government mandated that each automobile company must have its own engine and body plants, encouraged the development of the parts industry, and ensured that a plant primarily produced a large category of parts. Consequently, the self-production rate for small-displacement cars reached 93.5%, 69.4% for mid-range cars, 90.4% for general buses, 67.7% for high-speed buses, and 79.5% for trucks. By 1986, the self-production capacities of Kia and Hyundai were 67.7% and 67.4%, respectively.

The fourth stage was characterized by self-research, self-production, and mass exportation. By the 1990s, Korean automobile companies had developed sufficient self-research and self-production capabilities, leading to a significant increase in the production and sales of domestic automobiles. However, given the limited capacity of Korea's local market, the industry turned toward the international market. Concurrently, the government promoted an "export-oriented" strategy, significantly increasing Korea's automobile exports and rapidly positioning the country as an important player in the global automobile trade.

The fifth stage was the globalization of Korean automobile production and marketing. After 2000, the Korean automobile industry essentially achieved globalization in production and marketing. Korean automobile companies established manufacturing plants in Western Europe, North America, Eastern Europe, central Asia, and Oceania, creating a relatively complete overseas production system and a globalized marketing network. From the initial phase of establishing a vehicle manufacturing industry based primarily on assembling parts, through the vigorous promotion of localization and restrictions on automobile imports, to the current export-oriented development model, South Korea has fundamentally achieved its original goal of developing the automobile industry.

2. Technological Catching-Up Strategies

The Korean automobile industry has undergone four distinct stages of technological catch-up.

The first stage was introduction and learning. In the nascent phase of its development, the industry primarily focused on introducing technology. It initially utilized the semi-knocked down (SKD) method, where finished products were disassembled by foreign automobile companies, shipped to Korea as semi-finished products or parts, and then reassembled into complete vehicles by Korean companies for sale domestically. Subsequently, through collaboration with Toyota of Japan, Korean automobile companies adopted the completely knocked down (CKD) method, importing entire vehicles in the form of full part sets for assembly in Korea and selling them at reduced retail prices.

The second stage involved absorption, imitation, and improvement. During the 1970s, Korean automobile companies concentrated on absorbing, imitating, and enhancing the introduced technologies. Notably, from its establishment in 1968 until the mid-1990s, Hyundai Motor Company worked on absorbing, imitating, and improving upon foreign product designs. This led to the evolution of new models from simple imitation of foreign automobiles to innovative imitation. Hyundai, in particular, developed models such as the Excel minicar, StellaJ compact car, and Sonata medium-sized car, leveraging patented chassis technology acquired from abroad.

The third stage was parts and vehicle localization. By the mid-to-late 1970s, the Korean government mandated each automobile company to select a model and begin developing a fully localized vehicle. By 1976, the localization rate for Korea's major automobiles exceeded 85%, and the production capacity for both complete automobiles and parts expanded significantly. Hyundai Motor Company, focusing on cars and commercial vehicles, began incorporating engine assembly, transmission, and rear axle production technologies from Japan's Mitsubishi in 1974, while also engaging Italian design firms for styling and bodywork, establishing a robust foundation for future growth. As the localization rate increased, so did the R&D capabilities of the Korean automobile industry, which began establishing its own brands in 1973.

The fourth stage was independent development. Starting in the early 1980s, the Korean automobile industry entered a phase of independent development, prioritizing product development and the creation of cars unique to Korea. Companies established specialized R&D institutions, significantly invested in development, enhanced efforts to train R&D personnel, and pursued active collaborations with foreign entities. Notably, both Hyundai and Daewoo allocated about 4% of their sales to R&D in 1986, aligning with the 3%–5% investment level of leading automotive nations. Hyundai employed approximately 2,000 R&D staff, while Daewoo had about 500. Through these efforts, Hyundai and Daewoo developed a range of models, including innovations in body, chassis, engine, and other systems and parts, allowing the Korean automobile industry to evolve into a comprehensive industrial system and achieve a significant technological breakthrough.

3. Policy Background and Innovation Integration

In the technological catch-up of the Korean automobile industry, government policies have been instrumental in several key areas.

First, the government provided protection to domestic automobile companies. To shield domestic companies from foreign competition, the Korean government enacted the Automobile Industry Protection Act, which prohibited the import of complete vehicles and parts (except for loose parts for assembly), and the Special Consumption Tax Act, which limited automobile imports. As a result, in the 1960s, Korea imported only about 1,000 cars per year. Even after 1980, to support the development of the domestic automobile industry and encourage national consumption of domestic cars, the government maintained "high tariffs" on imported cars and imposed various taxes, such as special consumption taxes and special indirect taxes, fostering a sense of pride in using domestic cars.

Second, the government aimed to reduce the cost of car production domestically through subsidies and concessions. From 1962 to 1990, Korea implemented a series of regulations and policies to bolster the automobile industry. The First Five-Year Economic Development Plan in 1962 outlined a strategy to promote the development of the domestic automobile industry through parts assembly. In the 1970s, the Basic Development Plan for the Automobile Industry identified automobiles, along with steel and shipbuilding, as pillar industries, offering tax exemptions for importing raw materials to facilitate automobile localization.

Third, the government encouraged the conglomeration of automobile companies. In the 1960s and 1970s, Korea increased automobile production concentration through strict market access and labor division. It enacted measures to abolish assembly permits for small and medium-sized enterprises, focusing production on four major manufacturers like Hyundai. Additional measures were introduced to promote production concentration and ensure profitability for manufacturers in specific sectors. Hyundai was designated to produce small cars, small and medium-sized trucks, and special vehicles. After establishing the policy of "independent development," the government actively led the consolidation of automobile companies, supporting large conglomerates through the Long-Term Plan for the Revitalization of the Automobile Industry. This period saw Kia and Daewoo joining the ranks, leading to the formation of four major companies: Hyundai, Kia, Daewoo, and Ssangyong. By 1992, these companies accounted for 98.7% of Korea's automobile production.

Last, the government enhanced localization and promoted timely exports. In the 1980s, Korea accelerated automobile localization and export promotion. Each automobile company was required to have its own engine and body plants and to focus on parts industry development. The government mandated that components meeting state-set price and quality standards should cease to be imported, encouraging companies to master core technologies and enhance R&D and production capacities. This led to significant self-production rates for various vehicle types by 1986. With increased localization, the government shifted toward an "export-oriented" strategy, making Korea a significant automobile exporter. After the 1990s, the industry saw a major boost in exports, achieving its first significant export to the US in 1992, with 360,000 units sold, marking the largest volume of cars sold in the US by any country at that time.

4. Technology Catch-Up in the Korean Automobile Industry and the Integration of Innovation in Economic Development

Table 2-4 clearly demonstrates that the technological catch-up and innovation within the Korean automobile industry are highly aligned with the overall development of the country's economy, meaning they are deeply integrated into the economic development process.

Table 2-4 Korean automotive industry's technological catch-up and the embedding of innovation in overall economic development

Period	Automobile industry	Technology catchinging up	Government policy	Economic development
The 1960s	Primary stage	Introduced technologies; SKD and CKD production	Provided protection to domestic automobile enterprises	Began industrialization and automobile industry development
The 1960s	Transition from assembly to self-production	Absorption, imitation, and enhancement of imported technologies	Implemented the Basic Nurturing Plan for the Automobile Industry; increased localization and	Invested in heavy industry; increased car localization rate
The 1980s	Car localization period	Localization of components; focus on complete vehicles then independent development	promoted enterprise conglomeration; offered subsidies and concessions to reduce production costs; timely promoted exports	Promoted economic liberalization; focused on automotive industry centralization and accelerated localization
The 1990s	Development of self-research, production, and mass exports	Enhanced self-research and self-production capabilities	Continued to promote automobile exports	Rapid integration into the global market with a continual rise in automobile export rates
2000 and onwards	Globalization of production and sales	Advanced self-research and self-production to boost innovation capacity in the industry		

First, in the 1960s, Korea embarked on industrialization and accordingly began to develop its automobile industry. With the initiation of the 1st Five-Year Economic Development Plan, Korea aimed to industrialize. To boost exports, the Korean won was devalued by 100%, transitioning from a multiple exchange rate system to a single exchange rate system. The Foreign Capital Promotion Act was enacted to encourage foreign investment inflow. Statistics show that in 1962, foreign investment constituted 83% of Korea's investment. At this time, Korea had low labor costs, its exports were primarily light industrial products, and a significant portion of its imports were food. Against this backdrop, Korea started developing its automobile industry.

Second, the 1970s saw Korea promoting the development of heavy industries and the localization of the automobile industry. In 1973, Korea announced and implemented the Heavy Chemical Industry Development Plan, shifting investment toward heavy chemical industries. This period marked the beginning of rapid development in industries such as shipbuilding, steel, automobile, electronics, and petrochemicals and initiated an accelerated urbanization process. The impact of heavy chemical industry development on Korea's economy was significant, with GDP growing at an average annual rate of 10.8% from 1972 to 1978, and the share of heavy chemical products in exports increasing from 21% in 1972 to 35% in 1978. The government also launched the "New Rural Movement," significantly enhancing production and living standards in rural areas and expanding the market for the automobile industry. By the late 1970s, in 1977, the Korean government designated the automobile industry as a strategic export industry and established the Comprehensive Export Promotion Policy, providing various incentives and subsidies for automobile exports.

Third, in the 1980s, Korea began to liberalize its economy, further increasing the concentration and localization rate of the automobile industry and actively promoting automobile exports. Addressing issues from previous industrialization efforts, the government mandated industrial enterprises to merge and reorganize, focusing on industries such as automobile, heavy machinery manufacturing, smelting, shipbuilding, and overseas engineering and construction, promoting large enterprise market monopolies. Korea also started privatizing the banking sector and lowered barriers to private capital in the financial sector. Additionally, restrictions on foreign direct investment were eased, with the Foreign Investment Attraction Act amended in 1984 to eliminate foreign shareholding ratio restrictions and profit remittance limitations, moving to a negative system for foreign investment approval. This led to a significant increase in the automobile industry's concentration. By the late 1980s, in 1987, Korea's automobile exports surpassed 500,000 units.

Fourth, in the 1990s, Korea accelerated its integration into the global market, with a corresponding increase in the automotive product export rate. The global international trading system was refined in the 1990s. Korea actively engaged in the Uruguay Round negotiations and became a founding member of the WTO. In 1995, its per capita income exceeded $10,000, and it joined the OECD in 1996, achieving "official" developed country status. Korea also became a member of APEC, ASEM, and other international organizations, opening further development opportunities. Consequently, Korea expanded its automobile industry's production capacity to increase exports. By the mid-1990s, in 1995, Korea's automobile exports exceeded one million units.

2.4.4 Comparative Analysis of Japan and Korea's Automobile Industries

1. Technology Catching-Up Comparison

Based on the described development of the automobile industries in Japan and Korea, their technological catch-up and innovation can be compared, as illustrated in Table 2-5.

Table 2-5 Comparison of technology catch-up and innovation in the Japanese and Korean automobile industries

Development and catching-up	**Country**	**Stage 1**	**Stage 2**	**Stage 3**	**Stage 4**
Automobile industry development	Japan	Production resumed, mainly trucks (1950s)	Scaling-up (1960s)	Rapid development, catching up with Europe and the US (1970s–1980s)	Global market expansion through innovation (1990s–present)
	Korea	Started up (1960s)	Transition to in-house production, car localization (1970s–1980s)	Self-developed, self-produced, mass exports (1990s)	Globalization of production and sales (2000 and onwards)

Development and catching-up	Country	Stage 1	Stage 2	Stage 3	Stage 4
Technology catch-up in the automobile industry	Japan	Small-scale technology importation (1950s)	Large-scale introduction and imitation (1960s)	Improved imitation, initiation of endogenous innovation (1970s–1980s)	Self-innovation for technological leadership (1990s–present)
	Korea	Technology introduction, SKD and CKD production (1960s)	Large-scale absorption, imitation, and improvement (1970s)	First domestic production, then self-development (1980s–1990s)	Continuous self-research and innovation (2000 and onwards)

2. Analysis and Summary

When setting aside the chronological development of the automobile industry in Japan and Korea to compare their technological catch-up, several common features emerge.

First, regarding development stages, the Japanese automobile industry went through "resumption of production (the 1950s) → scale development stage (the 1960s) → high-speed development and catch-up with Europe and the United States (the 1970s–1980s) → innovation to expand the global market (the 1990s to present)." Korea's automobile industry experienced "the initial stage (the 1960s) → transition from assembly to independent production (the 1970s) and domestic production (the 1980s) → self-research, self-production, and extensive exports (the 1990s) → globalization of automobile production and sales (after 2000)." Considering Japan's "resumption of production" stage post-war as the "start-up stage" and Korea's "transition from assembled cars to in-house production and localization" as the "scale development stage," the development stages of the automobile industries in both Japan and Korea are strikingly similar, following a "start-up → scale development → rapid development → global market entry" trajectory.

Second, from the perspective of technological catch-up, the patterns in both countries are also remarkably similar. In Japan, it was "small-scale technology introduction (the 1950s) → large-scale introduction and imitation innovation based on imported technology (the 1960s) → extensive improvement, imitation, and the start of endogenous innovation (the 1970s–1980s) → endogenous innovation and seizing the technological lead (the 1990s to present)." In South Korea, it progressed from "technology introduction and SKD/CKD assembly production (the 1960s) → large-scale absorption, imitation, improvement (the 1970s) → initial parts, components and vehicle localization, then independent development (the 1980s), forming self-research and self-production capabilities (the 1990s) → self-research, self-production, and continued enhancement of endogenous innovation capability (after 2000)." Generally, the technological catch-up in Japan and South Korea can be summarized as "technology introduction production → digestion and imitation, absorption, and improvement → localized production, improved imitation → enhancing endogenous innovation capacity in practice."

Third, from the perspective of internal mechanisms, both the Japanese and Korean automobile industries achieved technological catch-up with leading countries through the process of "introducing technology production → digesting and imitating, absorbing, and improving → localizing production, improving imitation → enhancing endogenous innovation capacity in practice." This success is primarily due to two factors. First, the automobile industry is largely technology-based, and the explicitness of automobile design and production technology is high. Explicit technology can be transmitted through "drawings, technical specifications, and technical documents" (applicable to both patented and non-proprietary technologies). Second, automobile design is increasingly "componentized" (i.e., modularized), and automobile production is increasingly "assembly line," allowing for technology to be understood by analogy. Based on this, latecomer countries in the automobile industry may achieve technological catch-up with leading countries through the described process.

2.5 Cross-Industry Insights on Technology Catching-Up

The concept of "technology-based industry" cannot be straightforwardly applied to catch-up strategies in "science-based industries."

In "technology-based industries," such as the automobile sector, and "science-based industries," like the pharmaceutical field, catch-ups begin with knowledge and technology gaps. Their approach to innovation relies on transferring knowledge and technology from leading countries. Initially, followers innovate mainly in production, market development, and marketing. Catch-up involves cultivating and enhancing innovation capabilities. However, significant differences exist between these two types of industries. For instance, in "technology-based industries," due to the cumulative and codifiable nature of technological development and the diverse sources of innovation, catching-up entities can gain innovative capabilities through patent licensing or transfer, as well as through accumulating production and marketing knowledge. They can leverage structural changes in the industrial chain to achieve catch-up. In contrast, "science-based industries" depend on new scientific discoveries for technological advancement. Catching-up countries mainly rely on the diffusion, dissemination, and importation of scientific discoveries from leading countries, which may pose challenges for companies in these countries to complete "applied research, product development or engineering development, and commercialization" based on the scientific discoveries of leading countries, despite having a solid foundation in production and marketing knowledge.

Therefore, the catch-up strategy effective in "technology-based industries" cannot be directly applied to "science-based industries." Recognizing this distinction at the enterprise level and adopting different strategies for each industry type is crucial. Additionally, governments should implement distinct policies for supporting catch-up efforts in these two industry types. For example, in science-based industries, where innovation hinges on new scientific discoveries, government policies should first encourage and support knowledge creation catch-up, guiding and supporting large enterprises to focus on basic research and fostering collaboration between enterprises, universities, and public research institutes. Second, government policies should also promote the "intermediate stages" of innovation in science-based industries, including "applied research, product development or engineering, and commercial product development."

2.5.1 Cross-Industry Comparative Analysis

If Table 2-2 and Table 2-5 are combined, Table 2-6 can be obtained.

As illustrated in Table 2-6, the process of technological catch-up in the pharmaceutical industry (a science-based industry) and the automobile industry (a technology-based industry) showcases both similarities and differences.

Table 2-6 Comparative analysis of technological catch-up across two industry sectors

Science-based technology catch-up in the pharmaceutical industry		Technology-based catch-up in the automobile industry	
Stages of catching up: Clear division of stages, distinct actions at each stage		Stages of catching up: Clear division of stages, distinct actions at each stage	
1st-stage catch-up	Received technology transfers; fostered R&D and industry-university interaction; nurtured production and marketing; developed market competitiveness	Introduced technology, organized production, and developed manufacturing capacity	1st-stage catch-up
		Large-scale technology introduction, assimilation, imitation, and enhancement	2nd-stage catch-up
2nd-stage catch-up	Focused on basic research; developed university-industry relationships; increased start-ups; enhanced product innovation; expanded internationally; aimed for innovation leadership and market dominance	Improved domestic production and imitation	3rd-stage catch-up
		Enhancing indigenous innovation capabilities within autonomous innovation	4th-stage catch-up

First, in both industries, "technological catch-up" unfolds in multiple, sequential stages. However, the pharmaceutical industry's catch-up process is divided into two main stages, whereas the automobile industry's process spans four stages.

Second, combining the first two stages of technological catch-up in the automobile industry corresponds to the first major stage of catch-up in the pharmaceutical industry; similarly, merging the third and fourth stages in the automobile industry equates to the second major stage in the pharmaceutical industry.

Third, across both industries, the initial major stage of technological catch-up involves "acquiring industry knowledge and production technology, establishing production capacity, and fostering market competitiveness; concurrently, digesting, absorbing the acquired production technology, and developing R&D capability." In the pharmaceutical industry, this entails "receiving technology transfers or knowledge exports from leading countries, actively developing enterprises' production and marketing capabilities to build their own market competitiveness, and enhancing enterprises' R&D capabilities (including setting up in-house R&D organizations and promoting university-industry interactions)." In the automobile industry, it involves "introducing technology, organizing production to establish manufacturing capacity, and on a large scale, digesting, imitating, absorbing, and improving introduced technology."

Fourth, in both sectors, the second major stage of technological catch-up focuses on "developing endogenous innovation capabilities and external value networks, engaging in improved imitation, initiating endogenous innovation, and aiming to secure competitive market advantages." For the pharmaceutical industry, this is manifested through "emphasizing basic research, increasing basic research investment, fostering extensive university-industry relationships, enhancing product innovation, expanding into international markets, and developing innovative leadership with international market advantages." In the automobile industry, it's demonstrated by "localizing production, engaging in improved imitation, and bolstering endogenous innovation capabilities through practical application."

Fifth, a unique aspect of the pharmaceutical industry is the phenomenon of scientists directly contributing to "SBI ventures" to achieve "rapid catch-up" by "accelerating progress," as evidenced by several Nobel Prize cases in Germany and the United States.

2.5.2 Key Insights and Takeaways

1. Distinguishing Elements of Catching-Up in Different Industries

In "technology-based industries" such as the automobile industry, the key element of innovation primarily revolves around technology—whether it's new technology, improvements, or novel combinations of existing technologies. This technology is highly visible, facilitating easier dissemination and transfer from leaders to followers. It can readily be protected by IP rights, which can be legally licensed or transferred. Additionally, the technology's codifiable nature makes it simpler for followers to understand, learn, and assimilate. Furthermore, as technology becomes increasingly "modular," altering a few modules can lead to significant product innovations. This modularity also enables specialization within the industry, allowing companies to focus on different modules, which simplifies the cultivation and enhancement of each following enterprise's differentiated innovation capability (or "core capability"), thereby bolstering the collective innovation capacity of the industry.

Conversely, "science-based industries" like the pharmaceutical sector rely primarily on new scientific discoveries for innovation. Some of this knowledge can be easily codified, while other parts may not, making it challenging to spread and transfer knowledge from leaders to followers. Certain knowledge that is hard to codify can pose difficulties in patent application, and knowledge transfer often encounters legal barriers. Furthermore, the path from scientific discovery to commercial products involves multiple intermediary steps, including applied research, product development or engineering, and commercial development, requiring followers to not only grasp the knowledge but also complete these "intermediate steps." Due to the challenges in modularizing these innovations, implementation often needs to occur within an organization that maintains tight integration among its various components. Therefore, the development and enhancement of a catching-up enterprise's innovation capability must be managed in a coordinated and systematic manner within the organization.

2. The Interplay between Technology Catch-Up and Endogenous Innovation

From the case study provided, it's evident that in the realm of science-based industries, once technological catch-up reaches a certain level and innovation capacity improves to at least match that of the leader, the follower can embark on independent innovation. This development is inevitable in the short term. However, looking at the long-term perspective, or over a "longer time period," in the competition between the follower and the leader, there will undoubtedly be intense rivalry, with the leader and follower roles frequently exchanging. This dynamic leads to a cyclical pattern within any given industry: Country A, initially lagging, commits to technological catch-up and stages endogenous innovation, only for Country B to then become the lagging country, embarking on its own technological catch-up and staged endogenous innovation. This cycle repeats, with each country alternating between leader and follower roles, driven by their continuous efforts in technological catch-up and autonomous innovation. Thus, for the "laggard," its journey of technological catch-up and independent innovation exhibits a "double helix" of push-pull interactions, symbolizing an interactive relationship.

The "double helix" push-pull dynamic between technological catch-up and endogenous innovation for the laggards offers several insights. First, in practical terms, these processes are intertwined, each being a part of the other, where innovation is embedded in catch-up efforts, and catch-up is a form of innovation. Second, from a short-term viewpoint, it might seem appropriate to distinguish between the two, analyzing them as separate stages and phenomena.

However, from a long-term perspective, they should be considered collectively as a single phenomenon, or "innovation/catch-up." Crucially, the essence of moving from technological catch-up to endogenous innovation lies in the "catch-up in knowledge acquisition," with the acquisition of new knowledge itself constituting "innovation." This implies that in long-term analyses of "catching up" and "innovation," these elements cannot be dissected separately. Consequently, the "perspective distance" of the issue under study at any given time dictates whether to "analyze both as two distinct phenomena" or "consider both as an integrated whole."

References

Abernathy, William J., and James M. Utterback. 1978. "Patterns of Industrial Innovation." *Technology Review* 80 (7): 40–47.

Abramovitz, Moses. 1986. "Catching Up, Forging Ahead, and Falling Behind." *Journal of Economic History*: 385–406.

Abramovitz, Moses, and Paul A. David. 1996. "Convergence and Deferred Catch-Up." *The Mosaic of Economic Growth*: 21–62.

Altenburg, Tilman. 2007. "Donor Approaches to Supporting Pro-poor Value Chains." *Donor Committee for Enterprise Development.*

Arnold, Lutz G. 2003. "Growth in Stages." *Structural Change and Economic Dynamics* 14 (1): 55–74.

Arora, Ashish, Ralph Landau, and Nathan Rosenberg, eds. 1998. Chemicals and Long-Term Economic Growth: Insights from the Chemical Industry. *Wiley-Interscience.*

Barro, Robert J., and Xavier Sala-i-Martin. 1997. "Technological Diffusion, Convergence, and Growth." *Journal of Economic Growth* 2 (1): 26.

Birdsall, Nancy, and John Page. 1993. *East Asian Miracle: Economic Growth and Public Policy*. World Bank, Policy Research Department.

Brezis, Elise S., Paul R. Krugman, and Daniel Tsiddon. 1993. "Leapfrogging in International Competition: A Theory of Cycles in National Technological Leadership." *The American Economic Review*: 1211–1219.

Cao, Ping. 2009. "Technology Catch-Up Strategies of Firms in Late-Developing Regions of East Asia and the Role of China." *Reform*, no. 12: 106–112.

Chandler, Alfred D. 2009. *Shaping the Industrial Century: The Remarkable Story of the Evolution of the Modern Chemical and Pharmaceutical Industries*. Massachusetts: Harvard University Press.

Chen, Dezhi. 2006. "A Study on the Definition of Technology Leapfrogging Concept and Sign." *Scientific Research* 24 (3): 364–367.

Cheng, Peng, Liu Xielin, Chen Ao, et al. 2011. "Basic Research and Technology Catch-Up in Chinese Industries: The Case of High-Speed Rail Industry." *Management Review* (12): 48–57.

Coe, David T., and Elhanan Helpman. 1995. "International R&D Spillovers." *European Economic Review* 39 (5): 859–887.

Coe, David T., Elhanan Helpman, and Alexander W. Hoffmaister. 1997. "North-South R&D Spillovers." *The Economic Journal* 107 (440): 134–149.

Engerman, Stanley L., and Robert E. Gallman, eds. 1996. Vol. 3 of *The Cambridge Economic History of the United States*. Cambridge: Cambridge University Press.

Fagerberg, Jan, David C. Mowery, and Richard R. Nelson, eds. 2005. *The Oxford Handbook of Innovation*. Oxford: Oxford University Press.

Feng, Yanqiu. 2000. "The Paradox of Latecomer Advantage and China's Technological Strategy Choice." *World Economy* (7): 44–49.

Freeman, Chris, and Francisco Luzan. 2007. *From the Industrial Revolution to the Information Revolution*. Beijing: People's University of China Press.

Freeman, Christopher, Francisco Louçã, et al. 2001. *As Time Goes By: From the Industrial Revolutions to the Information Revolution*. Oxford: Oxford University Press.

Funaba, Mitsuyo. 1988. "Technology Policy and Economic Performance: Lessons from Japan by Christopher Freeman and Evaluating Applied Research: Lessons from Japan by John Irvine (Book Review)." *Japan Quarterly* 35 (3): 326.

Furman, Jeffrey L., and Richard Hayes. 2004. "Catching Up or Standing Still?: National Innovative Productivity Among 'Follower' Countries, 1978–1999." *Research Policy* 33 (9): 1329–1354.

Gambardella, Alfonso. 1995. *Science and Innovation: The US Pharmaceutical Industry during the 1980s*. Cambridge: Cambridge University Press.

Gerschenkron, Alexander. 1962. "Economic Backwardness in Historical Perspective." *The Political Economy Reader: Markets as Institutions*: 211–228.

Gil, Youngsoo, Sung Bong, and Lee Jin. 2003. "Integration Model of Technology Internalization Modes and Learning Strategy: Globally Late Starter Samsung's Successful Practices in South Korea." *Technovation* 23 (4): 333–347.

Gover, John E. 1993. "Analysis of US Semiconductor Collaboration." *IEEE Transactions on Engineering Management* 40 (2): 104–113.

Grossman, Gene M., and Elhanan Helpman. 1990. "Trade, Innovation, and Growth." *The American Economic Review* 80 (2): 86–91.

Guo, Genshan. 2005. "On the Nature of Catch-Up Strategy and the Lessons of China's Implementation of Catch-Up Strategy." *Journal of Henan Normal University: Philosophy and Social Science Edition* (1): 64–67.

Guo, Kesha. 2004. "China's Industrial Development Strategy and Policy Choices." *China Social Science* (1): 30–41.

Hamilton, Alexander. 1904. *The Works of Alexander Hamilton*. New York: GP Putnam's Sons.

Henderson, Rebecca, Gary P. Pisano, and Luigi Orsenigo. 1999. "The Pharmaceutical Industry and the Revolution in Molecular Biology: Interactions among Scientific, Institutional, and Organizational Change."

Hobday, Michael. 1994. "Export-Led Technology Development in the Four Dragons: The Case of Electronics." *Development and Change* 25 (2): 333–361.

———. 1995. "East Asian Latecomer Firms: Learning the Technology of Electronics." *World Development* 23 (7): 1171–1193.

———. 1995. "Innovation in East Asia: Diversity and Development." *Technovation* 15 (2): 55–63.

Hobday, Michael, Alan Cawson, and Kim Sang-Ryong. 2001. "Governance of Technology in the Electronics Industries of East and South-East Asia." *Technovation* 21 (4): 209–226.

International Federation of Pharmaceutical Manufacturers & Associations (IFPMA). 2017. "The Pharmaceutical Industry and Global Health: Facts and Figures."

Jin, Mingshan, and Che Weihan. 2001. *The Theory of Catching Up Economy*. Beijing: People's Publishing House.

Keyhani, Soheil, Wang Siyi, Herbert Hebert, et al. 2010. "US Pharmaceutical Innovation in an International Context." *American Journal of Public Health* 100 (6): 1075–1080.

Kim, Linsu. 1997. "The Dynamics of Samsung's Technological Learning in Semiconductors." *California Management Review* 39 (3): 86–100.

Kim, Sang-Ryong. 1998. "The Korean System of Innovation and the Semiconductor Industry: A Governance Perspective." *Industrial and Corporate Change* 7 (2): 275–309.

Kneller, Robert. 2003. "Autarkic Drug Discovery in Japanese Pharmaceutical Companies: Insights into National Differences in Industrial Innovation." *Research Policy* 32 (10): 1805–1827.

———. 2003. "University-Industry Cooperation and Technology Transfer in Japan Compared with the United States: Another Reason for Japan's Economic Malaise." *University of Pennsylvania Journal of International Economic Law* 24: 329.

Landes, David S. 2003. *The Unbound Prometheus: Technological Change and Industrial Development in Western Europe from 1750 to the Present*. Cambridge: Cambridge University Press.

Lee, Jeong. 2005. "Effects of Leadership and Leader-Member Exchange on Commitment." *Leadership & Organization Development Journal*.

Lee, Keun. 2005. "Making a Technological Catch-Up: Barriers and Opportunities." *Asian Journal of Technology Innovation* 13 (2): 97–131.

Lee, Keun, and Lim Chaisung. 2001. "Technological Regimes, Catching-Up and Leapfrogging: Findings from the Korean Industries." *Research Policy* 30 (3): 459–483.

Lee, Keun, Lim Chaisung, and Song Wang. 2005. "Emerging Digital Technology as a Window of Opportunity and Technological Leapfrogging: Catch-Up in Digital TV by the Korean Firms." *International Journal of Technology Management* 29 (1–2): 40–63.

Lee, Tae Joon. 2004. "Technological Learning by National R&D: The Case of Korea in CANDU-Type Nuclear Fuel." *Technovation* 24 (4): 287–297.

Liebenau, Jonathan. 1987. *Medical Science and Medical Industry: The Formation of the American Pharmaceutical Industry*. Springer.

Lim, Tai-Chee. 1997. "Innovation in East Asia: The Challenge to Japan." *Korean Studies* 21 (1): 138–142.

Lin, Yifu, Cai Fang, and Li Zhou. 1995. "Rethinking Catch-Up Strategies and Alternative Comparative Advantage Strategies." *Strategy and Management* (3): 1–10.

Mathews, John A. 2002. "Competitive Advantages of the Latecomer Firm: A Resource-Based Account of Industrial Catch-Up Strategies." *Asia Pacific Journal of Management* 19 (4): 467–488.

Murmann, Johann Peter, and Ralph Landau. 1998. "On the Making of Competitive Advantage: The Development of the Chemical Industries in Britain and Germany Since 1850."

Mazzoleni, Roberto, and Richard R. Nelson. 1998. "The Benefits and Costs of Strong Patent Protection: A Contribution to the Current Debate." *Research Policy* 27 (3): 273–284.

Nakayama, Shigeru, and Michael F. Low. 1997. "The Research Function of Universities in Japan." *Higher Education* 34 (2): 245–258.

Posner, Michael V. 1961. "International Trade and Technical Change." *Oxford Economic Papers* 13 (3): 323–341.

Probert, Jocelyn. 2006. "Global Value Chains in the Pharmaceutical Industry." *Recovering from Success: Innovation and Technology Management in Japan*: 87–105.

Putranto, Kusno, David Stewart, and Geoffrey Moore. 2003. "International Technology Transfer and Distribution of Technology Capabilities: The Case of Railway Development in Indonesia." *Technology in Society* 25 (1): 43–53.

Qian, Yingyi, and Chenggang Xu. 1998. "Innovation and Bureaucracy Under Soft and Hard Budget Constraints." *The Review of Economic Studies* 65 (1): 151–164.

Reich, Michael R. 1990. "Why the Japanese Don't Export More Pharmaceuticals: Health Policy as Industrial Policy." *California Management Review* 32 (2): 124–150.

Rosenberg, Nathan, and Richard R. Nelson. 1994. "American Universities and Technical Advance in Industry." *Research Policy* 23 (3): 323–348.

Rosenberg, Nathan. 2009. "Technological Change in Chemicals: The Role of University–Industry Relations." *World Scientific Book Chapters*: 329–366.

Shi, Peigong. 1995. "Imitation Innovation and the Choice of Innovation Strategy of Chinese Enterprises." *Science and Technology Herald* 13 (004): 49–51.

Soete, Luc. 1985. "International Diffusion of Technology, Industrial Development and Technological Leapfrogging." *World Development* 13 (3): 409–422.

———. 1988. "Catching Up in Technology: Entry Barriers and Windows of Opportunity."

Sturchio, Jeffrey L., and Louis Galambos. 2011. "The German Connection: Merck and the Flow of Knowledge from Germany to the United States, 1880–1930." In *Business History Conference*. Business and Economic History On-Line: Papers Presented at the BHC Annual Meeting. Business History Conference 9: 1.

Utterback, James M., and William J. Abernathy. 1975. "A Dynamic Model of Process and Product Innovation." *Omega* 3 (6): 639–656.

Veblen, Thorstein. 1990. *Imperial Germany and the Industrial Revolution*. New Jersey: Transaction Publishers.

Vernon, Raymond. 1966. "International Investment and International Trade in the Product Cycle." *The Quarterly Journal of Economics* 80 (2): 190–207.

———. 1979. "The Product Cycle Hypothesis in a New International Environment." *Oxford Bulletin of Economics & Statistics* 41: 255–267.

———. 1992. "International Investment and International Trade in the Product Cycle." In *International Economic Policies and Their Theoretical Foundations*. Massachusetts: Academic Press: 415–435.

Vertova, Giovanna. 2001. "National Technological Specialisation and the Highest Technological Opportunities Historically." *Technovation* 21 (9): 605–612.

Wu, Xiaobo. 1995. "The Evolutionary Process of Secondary Innovation." *Science Research Management* (2): 29–37.

Wu, Xiaobo, Hu Baoliang, and Cai Quan. 2006. "Research on the Framework and Path of Using Information Technology Capabilities to Gain Competitive Advantage." *Research Management* 27 (5): 53–58.

Wu, Xiaodan, and Chen Dezhi. 2008. "Research Progress on Technology Catch-Up." *Science and Technology Progress and Countermeasures* 25 (11): 236–240.

Xie, Wei. 1999. "The Origin and Development of National Innovation System Theory." *China Science and Technology Forum* 3: 20–21.

CHAPTER 3

Science-Based Industry: Innovation Models

In most industries, innovation primarily stems from technological evolution, with a wide array of sources fueling this innovation. Technology progresses through enhancement, adaptation, and amalgamation. Conversely, in SBI, new scientific discoveries serve as the principal source of innovation. This is followed by the development of processes for mass production or product design tailored to customer needs, accomplished chiefly through the improvement, adaptation, and integration of existing technologies.

3.1 Analyzing Innovation Models through Nobel Prize Cases

By examining the commercialization process of Nobel Prize achievements, innovation can be categorized into three stages: the scientific discovery stage, the application-oriented research stage, and finally, the market stage, as illustrated in Figure 3-1. This new model distinctly categorizes the "output" of new scientific discoveries into theoretical and applied value. At the discovery stage, new scientific theories might be formulated, or scientific findings with practical application potential could emerge, enhancing the cumulative effect of knowledge through the contributions of both. This framework maintains the characteristic that innovation is propelled by scientific discovery, and

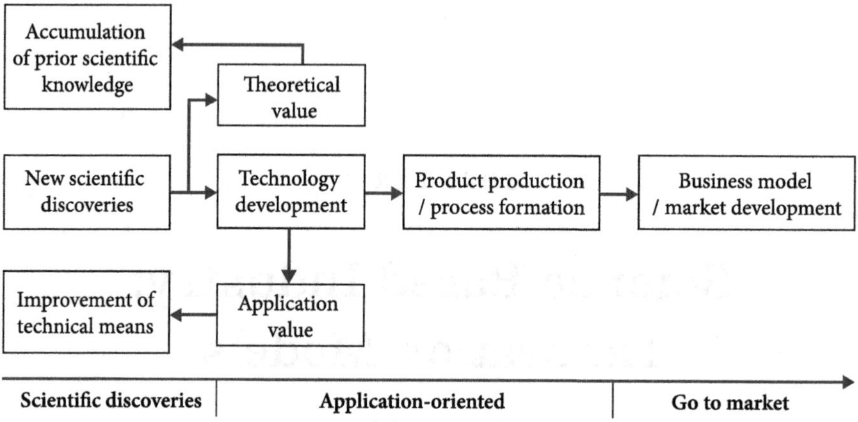

Figure 3-1 Basic model of SBI

it accurately represents the critical sequence from scientific discovery to marketable products or processes, through application-oriented technology development (Zhang and Lei 2015).

The analysis in this chapter will build upon the foundational innovation model shown in Figure 3-1. It introduces the two primary participants, R&D institutions and companies, differentiates them based on the timing and nature of their cooperation, and establishes three SBI models: a. the firm-led innovation model, where companies undertake basic scientific research that is directly converted into marketable products; b. the innovation model involving cooperation between companies and universities or public institutions, where enterprises collaborate with these entities, engage in applied R&D, and bring products to market through patent licenses and transfers; c. the innovation model in which start-up companies convert their achievements, with universities or public institutions conducting scientific research and then developing market products through these start-ups. The evolution of innovation outcomes exhibits distinct characteristics under each model and context, which this study further elucidates through the example of transforming Nobel Prize scientific achievements into commercial successes.

3.1.1 Model 1: Enterprise-Led Innovation

Enterprise-led scientific research involves the direct conversion of scientific discoveries into marketable products via technological development. The innovation originates from scientific discoveries made within companies, rather than universities or public institutions. This encompasses new scientific findings produced by companies engaged in independent basic science research, as well as discoveries made through collaborative basic science research between companies.

In the late 19th and early 20th centuries, several large corporations established their own in-house research institutes or laboratories. Notable examples include DuPont, General Motors, IBM, and AT&T, which all founded research departments focused on pioneering scientific endeavors. Researchers in these industrial labs conducted pure scientific research and disseminated their findings in the same manner as their academic peers. However, corporate participation in basic science research has generally been confined to these large entities. Table 3-1 provides typical examples of enterprise-led scientific research.

Table 3-1 Examples of business-led scientific research initiatives

Year	Award	Product/ technology	Scientific research	Companies involved in commerciali-zation	Scientific discovery	Applica-tion
1956	Physics	Transistors	Bell Laboratories	Bell Laboratories	1947	1957
1971	Physics	Holography	BTH	BTH	1948	1965
1973	Physics	Tunnel diodes	Sony Corporation of Japan, IBM	Sony Corporation of Japan, IBM	1956	1963
1986	Physics	Scanning tunneling microscope	IBM	IBM	1979	1982
2000	Physics	Integrated circuits	Texas Instruments	Texas Instruments / IBM	1958	1962
2009	Physics	Fiber optic communica-tion	STL	Corning	1966	1975
1991	Physics	Nuclear magnetic resonance spectroscopy	Varian Associates	Bruker	1966	1972
2001	Chemistry	Chiral catalysts	Monsanto Company	Monsanto Company	1968	1972
1979	Biomedical	CT scanner	Electric and Music Industries	Electric and Music Industries	1963	1972

This type of SBI primarily relies on basic scientific research conducted by companies, which is subsequently turned into marketable products through applied R&D. Innovations, driven by scientific discoveries, originate mainly within firms rather than universities or public institutions. Such innovation was predominantly seen in the 1950s to 1970s, spearheaded by large corporations with their own independent laboratories, including AT&T's Bell Labs, IBM, Texas Instruments, among others, where the initial scientific research was aimed at practical applications.

In the scientific discovery phase, the primary actors in this innovation model are the enterprises themselves. New scientific discoveries create application value, leading to the formation of relevant patents and the production of products or processes. These are then introduced to the market to facilitate application. Patents are directly held by the enterprises engaged in the initial R&D or are transferred to other companies through patent licensing, enabling joint participation in the application-oriented R&D and the creation of marketable products. This innovation model is depicted in Figure 3-2.

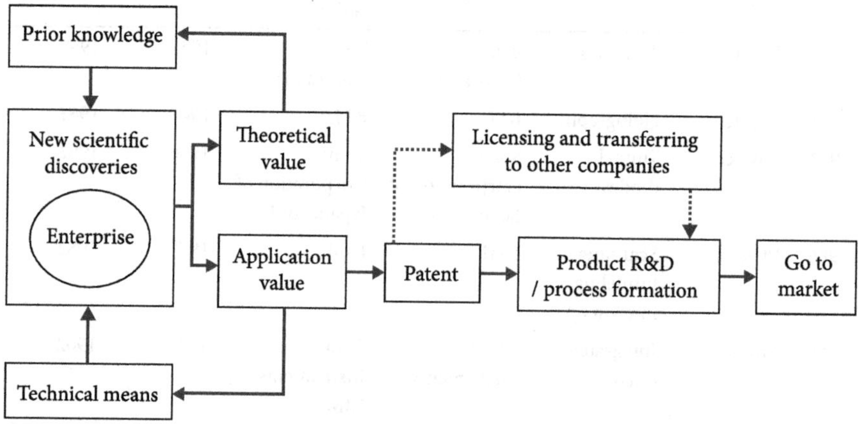

Figure 3-2 Model of business-led innovation

3.1.2 Model 2: Collaborative Innovation between Enterprises and Academic or Public Institutions

Companies engage in innovation through partnerships with universities or public institutions, with two primary modes of involvement.

One approach is early participation, where companies either participate in or fund basic scientific research during the research stage. Subsequently, they generate patents and secure patent licenses to carry out applied R&D, leading to the development of marketable products. Notable instances include the 1931 Nobel Prize in Chemistry for the "synthetic ammonia industry" and the 1952 Nobel Prize in Physiology or Medicine for "The Discovery and Application of Streptomycin." Table 3-2 provides examples of companies that were involved early in scientific discoveries.

Table 3-2 Early corporate contributions to scientific research discoveries

Year	Award	Product/ technology	Scientific research	Early participating companies	Scientific discovery	Application
2000	Physics	GMR	Université Paris-Saclay	Thomson CSF	1988	1997
1931	Chemistry	Synthetic ammonia industry	Karlsruhe Institute of Engineering	Baden Aniline and Soda Factory	1909	1913
1939	Chemistry	Sex hormones	Kaiser Wilhelm Research Institute	Schering Company	1929	1940
1965	Chemistry	Natural organic compound synthesis	Harvard University	Polaroid	1942	1945
1952	Biochemical	Streptomycin	Rutgers University	Merck	1943	1947

Another mode of participation occurs at a later stage, specifically after a university or PRI has produced scientific research results with significant application potential and has applied for the corresponding patent. At this point, a company obtains the patent license to engage in the subsequent development of market-oriented products. Notable examples include the discovery and application of insulin, the discovery and application of penicillin, and the discovery and application of the giant magnetoresistance (GMR) effect, which earned the Nobel Prize in Physics in 2007. Table 3-3 presents typical cases of companies involved in application-oriented stage R&D.

Table 3-3 Examples of business involvement in the application-oriented phase

Year	Award	Product/technology	Scientific research	Companies involved in application development	Scientific discovery	Application
1953	Physics	Phase contrast microscopy	University of Groningen	Zeiss AG, Germany	1930	1941
1905	Chemistry	Synthetic dyes	University of Strasbourg	BASF Corporation	1870	1897
1938	Chemistry	Carotene	University of Heidelberg and Wilhelm Kaiser Institute for Medical Research	Winthrop Chemical Co.	1931	1938
1923	Biochemical	Insulin	University of Toronto	Eli Lilly/Novo	1869	1923
1924	Biochemical	Electrocardiogram	Faculty of Medicine, Leiden University, the Netherlands	Cambridge Scientific Instruments, UK	1842	1911
1945	Biochemical	Penicillin	University of Oxford	Pharmaceutical companies such as Pfizer	1928	1943
1977	Biochemical	Trappistrellein	New Orleans Laboratory, Tulane University School of Medicine	Debiopharm	1971	1986
2008	Biochemical	Cervical cancer vaccine	University of Nuremberg, Germany	Merck	1983	2006

In this context, determining whether an enterprise is an early or late participant hinges on the timing of the patent application. An enterprise is considered an early participant if it engages in research before the corresponding patent is filed; conversely, if its involvement in R&D occurs after the patent has been filed, it is deemed a late participant.

In this innovation paradigm, enterprises are drawn to the scientific research outcomes or application results from universities or PRIs. They embark on the journey of converting new scientific discoveries into products or processes by securing patent licenses and acquiring and transferring patents. Typically, the process of acquiring patents is also accompanied by the hiring of scientists as R&D consultants by the enterprises, especially for patents that are somewhat removed from market application. This approach can effectively ensure the continuity and quality of R&D efforts. The corresponding innovation model is illustrated in Figure 3-3.

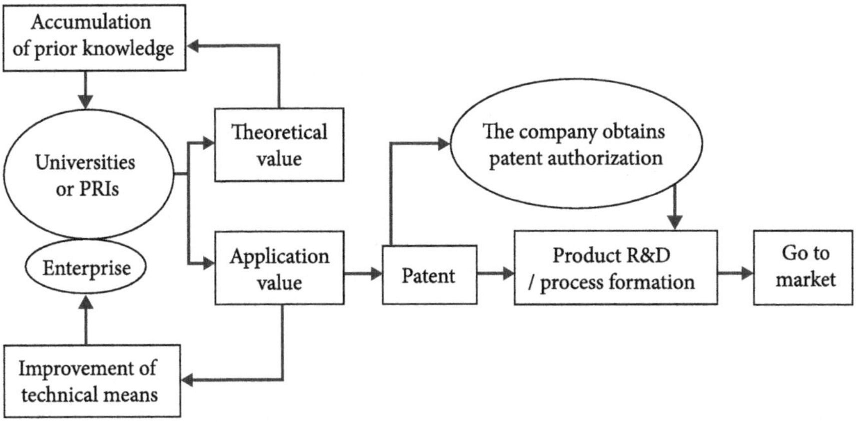

Figure 3-3 Innovation models for collaborative research between companies and universities or PRIs

3.1.3 Model 3: Start-Up Led Transformation of Innovations

In the 1980s, with the advent of biotechnology, a significant number of science-based start-ups emerged, playing a crucial role in SBI. Notable examples include the 2005 Nobel Prize laureate in Physiology or Medicine, Marshall, who established Tri-Med Distributor, a firm specializing in the research of diagnostic devices and treatments for Helicobacter pylori. Another example is the 2008 Nobel Prize winner in Chemistry, Roger Yonchien Tsien, who founded Aurora Biosciences and Senomyx, companies focused on the commercialization of

GFPs. Table 3-4 lists typical cases of such start-ups engaged in the translation of research outcomes.

Table 3-4 Start-ups transforming Nobel Prize discoveries into commercial success

Nobel Prize achievements	Start-up case summaries
Chemistry award 2002 (Mass Spectrometer)	In 1988, Finn pioneered the electrospray ionization method, expanding mass spectrometry to biological macromolecules analysis. He established Analytica of Branford in 1987, leveraging patented technology and its licensing.
Chemistry award 2008 (Green fluorescent egg)	Qian, unveiling the crystal structure of GFP and designing variants, holds 132 patents. He founded Aurora in 1996 and Senomyx in 1999, with Aurora later acquired by Vertex Pharmaceuticals in 2001.
Physiology or Medicine award 2003 (MRI scanner)	Damadian, inventing the FONAR imaging method in 1972 and building the first whole-body MRI unit in 1977, founded FONAR company in 1978, launching the first commercial whole-body MRI machine in 1980.
Physiology or Medicine award 2005 (Role of Helicobacter pylori)	Marshall, patenting a diagnostic method for gastrointestinal diseases in 1985, founded Tri-Med Distributor in 1996 for diagnostics and treatments, which was acquired by Kimberley Clark in 1999.
Physiology or Medicine award 2010 (Vitro fertilization)	Phil and Mello's 1998 discovery of RNA interference, published in *Nature*, marked a significant advancement, although the case does not detail the formation of a start-up.

In this innovation paradigm, start-ups founded on scientific discoveries play a pivotal role in the innovation process. These enterprises are not merely consumers of scientific findings but also contributors to them. Their knowledge base predominantly originates from the research outcomes of universities or PRIs. Through licensing or transferring patents, these companies further develop and apply these scientific discoveries to introduce products to the market. Funding for such enterprises often comes from venture capital, stock market financing, and the licensing and transfer of patents. A distinctive feature of the SBI model compared to other companies is that the entrepreneurial teams behind these firms are largely composed of scientists from universities or research institutions. The corresponding innovation model is depicted in Figure 3-4.

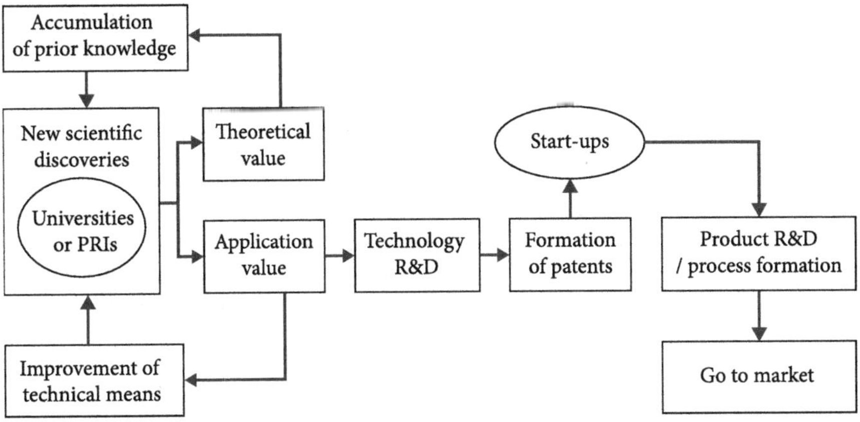

Figure 3-4 Start-up innovation models for result transformation

3.1.4 Nobel Prize Innovation Model Comparison

Regarding R&D characteristics, innovation mode 1 typically involves large enterprises with independent research departments focused on basic scientific research that has strong application potential. Mode 2 is primarily led by universities and PRIs conducting basic scientific research. Upon identifying the application potential of scientific research outcomes, market-oriented applied R&D is undertaken by enterprises. Mode 3 features start-up companies actively engaging in basic scientific research and maintaining a leading position in foundational research through entrepreneurship by scientists or by hiring scientists as consultants for the enterprise.

In terms of IP rights, large enterprises in mode 1 achieve breakthroughs in applied R&D and then file for patents owned by the enterprise. Companies in mode 2 secure patent licenses through collaboration with universities or PRIs and proceed with applied R&D. Start-ups in mode 3, on the one hand, obtain patent licenses from universities or PRIs and, on the other hand, conduct their own basic research and file for their patents.

From a funding source perspective, R&D funding in mode 1 mainly come from the enterprises' own finances but may also include public R&D funding, especially for projects aligned with specific national interests (such as defense). In mode 2, initial basic research funding predominantly comes from public sources, while applied R&D funding mainly derives from the enterprises' private funds. For mode 3, early basic research funding primarily originates from public sources, with subsequent funding heavily reliant on venture capital,

IPO financing, and patent licensing. A comparison of these three innovation models is presented in Table 3-5.

Table 3-5 Comparison of three innovation models

Aspect	Model 1	Model 2	Model 3
R&D features	Large firms with in-house research focus on applied basic science	Universities and PRIs focus on basic research; firms focus on applied R&D	Companies engage in basic research, lead with start-ups, or hire scientist consultants
IP rights	Patents filed post-applied R&D breakthroughs within firms	Patent licenses or assignments obtained through academia-industry collaborations	Patents from universities or PRIs; firms also file their own patents
Funding source	Primarily internal funds; possibly public funds for national needs	Basic research funded publicly; applied R&D funded by companies	Basic research funded publicly, later stages backed by venture capital, stock financing, or licensing

Drawing from the Nobel Prize case study on SBI, this chapter outlines three distinct types of SBI models:

a. Firm-led innovation model. In this model, companies spearhead basic scientific research, with scientific discoveries originating within the company itself. During the late 19th and early 20th centuries, several large companies set up their own R&D facilities and laboratories. These in-house researchers conducted pure scientific research and disseminated their findings just as their academic peers would. Such corporate involvement in basic scientific research was typically restricted to large corporations.
b. Innovation model involving cooperation between enterprises and public institutions. Depending on the stage of enterprise involvement, there are two forms of participation. One is the enterprise's involvement in basic research during the scientific discovery phase (early participation), and the other is enterprise engagement during the application-oriented phase (late participation). In this innovation approach, companies convert new scientific discoveries into products or processes by acquiring patent licenses from universities or public institutions. This method often includes hiring scientists as R&D consultants for the corporation, particularly for patents

far from market application, to effectively ensure R&D continuity and quality.

c. Innovative model of start-ups transforming results. Research indicates that start-ups have emerged as a significant mechanism for scientists to commercialize research outcomes. Typically, once scientific research results are established, scientists or their research institutions create their own start-up companies dedicated to the commercial development and operation of these outcomes, facilitating the commercialization of scientific discoveries.

3.2 Insights from the Chinese Context

There are two primary models of industrial innovation based on Chinese cases: first, technology leadership grounded in scientific discovery, achieved through the concentration of resources; second, technology catch-up inspired by science, propelled by the force of attraction.

3.2.1 Model 1: Technology-Led Model Based on Scientific Discovery

The 2015 Nobel Prize in Physiology or Medicine was awarded to Chinese pharmacologist Tu Youyou, alongside Irish scientist William C. Campbell and Japanese scientist Satoshi Ōmura for their groundbreaking work in the treatment of parasitic diseases. Parasitic diseases have afflicted humanity for millennia, posing a significant global health challenge. Tu Youyou's discovery of artemisinin has led to a dramatic decrease in the mortality rates of malaria patients, while Campbell and Ōmura's invention of avermectin has significantly lowered the incidence of river blindness and lymphatic filariasis. The introduction of artemisinin and avermectin has revolutionized the treatment of parasitic diseases.

This recognition marks the first occasion a Chinese scientist has received the Nobel Prize in Natural Sciences for research conducted within China. It represents the most prestigious accolade awarded to traditional Chinese medicine to date, highlighting remarkable achievements within the field.

1. Malaria and Artemisinin Case

Humanity's struggle against malaria has been both tragic and valiant, with five scientists receiving Nobel Prizes in Chemistry and Physiology or Medicine for their malaria-related research in the 20th century.

Malaria is an ancient disease, recognized over 2,000 years ago. The *Medical Classic of the Yellow Emperor* detailed symptoms of malaria, and ancient Rome documented the disease as well. In folklore, malaria was known as the "cold-heat mixed disease" or "pendulum," causing sufferers to alternate between feeling intensely cold, as if in an ice cellar, and unbearably hot, as if in an oven. This debilitating condition, termed "malaria," has been a persistent challenge throughout history. In the 17th century, Spaniards discovered that local South American Indians used cinchona tree bark, ground into powder, as a remedy for malaria. In 1820, French chemists Pelletier and Caventou first isolated quinine, an antimalarial compound, from cinchona bark, referred to as "cinchona cream" due to the unknown chemical structure at the time.

The cause of malaria remained a mystery to scientists worldwide until 1880 when Alphonse Laveran (1845–1922), a French army doctor, identified the culprit. He observed melanin in the organs of malaria victims, particularly the spleen and liver, leading to the disease's association with "melanemia." Through diligent research, Laveran discovered these granules were parasites, varying in size and capable of free movement. By 1882, he confirmed the same pathogen in Italian malaria patients, identifying these "little black things" as the cause of malaria. His seminal work, "The Treatment of Febrile Malaria," published in 1884, introduced the world to Plasmodium. For his groundbreaking discovery, Laveran was awarded the 1907 Nobel Prize in Physiology or Medicine.

Although Laveran identified the malaria pathogen, the transmission mechanism remained unknown until Ronald Ross (1857–1932), a British physician, discovered Plasmodium in the stomach of Anopheles mosquitoes while serving as a British military doctor in India in 1897. Ross's experiments with Anopheles mosquitoes feeding on malaria patients led to the discovery of Plasmodium in the mosquitoes' stomachs, proving Anopheles as the vector for malaria. This discovery earned him the 1902 Nobel Prize in Physiology or Medicine.

Despite the purification of the antimalarial compound quinine from cinchona bark in 1820, its artificial synthesis was challenging until American organic chemists Woodward and William Dowling achieved the total synthesis of quinine in 1944. Woodward was honored with the 1965 Nobel Prize in Chemistry for his work on synthesizing natural compounds.

Even with the understanding of malaria's cause and mosquito vector, by 1930, malaria was still devastating, infecting ten million people and causing three million deaths annually. Swiss chemist Paul Hermann Muller was awarded the 1948 Nobel Prize in Physiology or Medicine for inventing DDT to kill malaria-carrying mosquitoes. Additionally, Austrian psychiatrist Julius Wagner-Jauregg received the 1927 Nobel Prize in Physiology or Medicine for using malaria inoculation to treat paralytic dementia. To date, five scientists have been recognized with Nobel Prizes for their contributions to malaria research.

2. Discovery of Artemisinin

Since the purification of quinine from cinchona bark in 1820, cinchona cream has been heralded as a miraculous remedy against malaria. However, with quinine constituting only about 5% of cinchona bark and its sources being limited, it fell short of meeting the global demand from malaria patients. This shortfall prompted scientists to explore the artificial synthesis of quinine. In 1944, American chemists Robert Woodward and William Dorn achieved a landmark synthesis of quinine, marking a significant milestone in the history of organic compound synthesis.

In 1934, Dr. Hans Andrzejczyk of the German pharmaceutical company Bayer developed chloroquine, a structurally simplified yet highly effective alternative to quinine. Chloroquine soon became a powerful weapon in the fight against malaria. Over time, however, the malaria parasite developed significant resistance to the drug, rendering it less effective. The resurgence of falciparum malaria in the 1960s, particularly during the Vietnam War, saw both US and Vietnamese forces combating malaria in the Asian rainforests alongside their military engagements. Despite escaping the gunfire, thousands of soldiers were incapacitated by malaria. The US, centering efforts around the Army Research Institute, conducted extensive research, screening over 200,000 compounds without finding an ideal new antimalarial drug. Seeking assistance, the Vietnamese turned to China, highlighting the urgent need for new antimalarial drugs.

On May 23, 1967, under the direct interest of contemporary leaders, China held a special planning meeting to develop an effective new medicine, initiating the 523 Project. In January 1969, at 39 years old, Tu Youyou joined the 523 Project team as the head of the scientific research group at the Institute of Chinese Materia Medica. Prior to her involvement, other research institutions in China had screened over 40,000 compounds and herbs without significant breakthroughs. Tu Youyou decided to first systematically review ancient medical texts, compiling a *Collection of Anti-malaria Single Prescriptions* with over 640 types of herbs, including Artemisia annua, which later led to the discovery of artemisinin. However, in the initial drug screening and experiments, the inhibition rate of artemisinin extracts against malaria was only 68%, and the results were inconsistent. Reports from other research entities in the "523" Office also did not highlight Artemisia annua as particularly effective. In a subsequent round of drug screening, the anti-malarial efficacy of Artemisia dropped to just 12%. For a considerable period, Artemisia annua did not receive much attention.

Artemisia annua, also known as herba Artemisia hedinii and all-grass of Creeping Acroptilon, is an annual herb belonging to the Asteraceae family, widespread across both northern and southern China. Ancient Chinese medical texts document Artemisia annua's ability to treat malaria, with many local populations using it effectively in traditional remedies. However, the extract's efficacy in suppressing malaria in the laboratory was initially not very significant. Prompted by this discrepancy, Tu Youyou revisited ancient literature, scrutinizing it meticulously. A passage from *A Handbook of Prescriptions for Emergencies · Prescription for Cold and Fever Malaria* by Ge Hong caught her attention, describing the use of fresh Artemisia annua juice for treating malaria.

Motivated by this discovery, Tu Youyou devised a low-temperature extraction process, keeping the temperature below 60°C and using various solvents such as water, alcohol, and ethanol for extraction, while also separating the stems from the leaves. Experimental studies revealed that the ethyl-oxide extract of Artemisia annua showed high potency in a rat malaria model but contained impurities and exhibited some toxicity. Therefore, the extract was divided into neutral and acidic types. The acidic part was found to be highly toxic and ineffective, whereas the neutral part contained potent antimalarial efficacy. After numerous experiments, a breakthrough came on October 4, 1971, with Artemisia extract sample No. 191 showing a 100% inhibition rate of Plasmodium vivax, marking a significant advancement in the screening process.

Continuing to refine the extraction and purification methods, Tu Youyou presented the promising antimalarial effects of Artemisia annua and its extracts at an internal anti-malarial research conference in Nanjing on March 8, 1972. Following the conference, the National "523" Office commissioned the Institute of Chinese Materia Medica to conduct clinical trials to observe the antimalarial efficacy of the effective Artemisia annua extract.

Subsequent safety trials and clinical tests in Changjiang, Hainan, confirmed the extract's ability to reduce fever in patients and significantly eliminate Plasmodium, outperforming chloroquine. Further validation in Beijing's 302 Hospital reinforced the extract's efficacy. By November 1972, Tu Youyou had reported the comprehensive effectiveness of Artemisia extract in thirty cases. A professional meeting convened by the National "523" Office in November 1973 focused on "malaria prevention and control drugs (including chemical synthesis)" and emphasized the importance of Artemisia as a key drug. Following this meeting, the effective compound was named artemisinin and was developed into a new drug, marking a pivotal moment in the fight against malaria.

3. Artemisinin's Chemical Structure and Synthesis

After isolating the effective monomer of Artemisia annua against malaria, Tu Youyou's research team embarked on identifying its chemical structure. Given the limited research capabilities and instrumentation at the Academy of Chinese Medical Sciences, they found it challenging to carry out the structural identification study on their own. Consequently, they decided to collaborate with the Shanghai Institute of Organic Chemistry at the CAS (SIOM) for this endeavor. In 1974, SIOM agreed to the collaboration, and its staff, led by Zhou Weishan, joined forces with the researchers from the Academy of Chinese Medical Sciences to determine the structure of artemisinin.

To elucidate the structure of a compound, its molecular formula and molecular weight must first be established to identify its type. The collaborative team employed a high-resolution mass spectrometer to ascertain artemisinin's molecular weight. They then integrated this with carbon-hydrogen analysis data to deduce artemisinin's molecular formula as a compound comprising 15 carbon atoms, 22 hydrogen atoms, and 5 oxygen atoms. The challenge lay in determining the correct structure from the myriad of possibilities for these 42 atoms.

At this juncture, Wu Yulin and his wife Li Ying from SIOM became part of the collaborative effort. During a meeting in Chengdu in April 1975, Yu Dequan from the Beijing Institute of Pharmaceutical Sciences presented findings that suggested hawk's claw was a peroxide compound. Li Ying relayed this information to the research group upon her return. Motivated by this insight, the group executed a series of intricate oxidation and reduction reactions. By December 1975, they had determined artemisinin's relative configuration and subsequently ascertained its absolute configuration. They discovered it possessed a unique sesquiterpene lactone structure with a peroxide group, notably lacking nitrogen in its molecule. This finding challenged the long-standing medical assumption held by Western scholars for over 60 years that an antimalarial chemical structure would be ineffective without nitrogen (Li et al. 1979).

The chemical structure of artemisinin was essentially determined by 1976. The China Academy of Chinese Medical Sciences communicated its findings to the Party Group of the Ministry of Health and, upon receiving approval, submitted an article to the *Chinese Science Bulletin* on February 20, 1976. The article was published in 1977, revealing the chemical structure of artemisinin (Artemisinin Structure Research Collaborative Group 1977). The collaboration between the China Academy of Chinese Medical Sciences and the Shanghai Institute of Organic Chemistry (SIOM) continued to explore the "structure and reaction" of artemisinin, resulting in the publication of the paper "Structure and Reaction of Artemisinin" in *Acta Chimica Sinica* in 1979 (Liu et al. 1979).

In 1978, the total synthesis of artemisinin was included in the science and technology plan set forth by the National Science and Technology Conference. As the leading institution for structure determination, SIOM was tasked with this challenge. Early in 1979, Zhou Weishan, Xu Xinxiang, and their team initiated the synthesis process. Concurrently, as China embarked on its reform and opening-up policy, representatives from Swiss Novartis Pharmaceuticals visited SIOM. Zhou Weishan detailed the structure of artemisinin to them during their visit. Shortly thereafter, SIOM learned that Switzerland had also commenced work on the total synthesis of artemisinin, sparking a race, albeit a challenging one (Wang Danhong 2008).

The pivotal step in synthesizing artemisinin was the addition of the peroxy group. After several attempts with different methods, Xu Xinxiang suggested using artemisinic acid, rather than vanillin, as the starting material. On January 6, 1983, through the meticulous efforts of Xu Xinxiang and Zhu Jie, the synthesis of artemisinin was successfully achieved, producing a compound identical to natural artemisinin (Xu Xingxiang 1983; Xu Xingxiang 1984). Yet, the task was not complete; the total synthesis of dihydroartemisinic acid still needed to be finalized, culminating in what was termed the total synthesis of artemisinin. By early 1984, Zhou Weishan's group accomplished the total synthesis of artemisinin, with their findings published in *SCIENTIA SINICA*, no. 02, 1984.

4. Development of Artemisinin-Based Medications

The successful determination of artemisinin's structure and its total synthesis have established the groundwork for developing artemisinin-derived drugs. Research into artemisinin derivatives has been conducted by the China Academy of Chinese Medical Sciences, the CAS Shanghai Institute of Materia Medica (SIMM), and Guilin Pharmaceutical Factory, among others. Scientists have modified artemisinin's chemical structure and synthesized derivatives like dihydroartemisinin (China Academy of Chinese Medical Sciences), artemether (SIMM), and artesunate (Guilin Pharmaceutical Factory) by introducing different groups to artemisinin's carbon-oxygen double bond.

Following the enactment of the Pharmaceutical Administration Law in 1986, several institutions declared new drugs based on artemisinin: the Institute of Chinese Materia Medica declared artemisinin (1986), the Shanghai Institute of Pharmaceutical Sciences of the CAS and Kunming Pharmaceutical Factory declared artemether (1987), and Guilin Pharmaceutical Factory declared artesunate (1987). Post-1986, Tu Youyou's research group delved deeper into dihydroartemisinin for seven years, leading to its market introduction as a new Class I drug in 1992. Dihydroartemisinin, artemether, artesunate, and other artemisinin-based monotherapies have significantly impacted the antimalarial market.

These derivatives maintain the original peroxy-bridge structure, offering improved stability, more effective Plasmodium eradication, and therapeutic benefits against drug-resistant strains. However, these single formulations are not without flaws, having short action durations and high recurrence rates. In July 1982, the former Steering Committee for Research on Artemisinin and its Derivatives in China initiated a project at the Academy of Military Medical Sciences titled "Exploratory Research on Combining Drugs to Delay Artemisinin Resistance," starting preliminary research in 1983 to mitigate resistance to artemisinin-based drugs. The Academy of Military Medical Sciences explored combining artemisinin with the chemical benzoyle, leading to the development of Compound Artemether with an RMB 350,000 venture capital investment from Kunming Pharmaceutical Factory in 1987. In 1992, Compound Artemether received a new drug certificate in China and became a crucial weapon against drug-resistant malaria.[1]

The Chinese Academy of Military Medical Sciences then partnered with Novartis, the Swiss company holding the patent for Compound Artemether's production, exclusively managing its global sales. On April 22, 2002, Compound Artemether was added to the 12th edition of the WHO's Essential Medicines List, marking it as the sole artemisinin-based compound antimalarial drug on the list and one of only three patented drugs included over the list's 25-year history.

5. Global Expansion of Artemisinin-Based Treatments

The discovery of artemisinin-based drugs occurred under specific historical conditions, at a time when China had not yet established patent laws[2] or adopted international standards for drug management. Consequently, the results of Chinese artemisinin research were published in Chinese academic journals in both English and Chinese from 1977 to 1980, disclosing molecular structures that could not be registered for patents. As a result, a drug with significant economic value lacked effective patent protection in China, where a patent system was not yet in place. The artemisinin drug, which could have enjoyed fully independent IP rights and had a promising market, became a generic drug.

Once artemisinin was classified as a generic drug, many countries began to replicate it, conduct follow-up research, and introduce similar foreign products. These products, protected by applied patents, captured a substantial portion of the international antimalarial drug market. To promote Compound Artemether globally as quickly as possible, Chinese government departments, along with experts and scholars, began seeking partners.

In April 1991, the "Chinese Science, Industry, and Trade Consortium," comprising the Academy of Military Medical Sciences, Kunming Pharmaceutical Factory, and CITIC Technology, signed a preliminary agreement with Novartis, Switzerland. A cooperation project was initiated to establish a Compound Artemether industrial chain that met international standards. The project's shared goal was to secure world patents for China's new antimalarial drug and

---

1. In 2009, Professor Zhou Yiqing and his team from the Institute of Microbiology and Epidemiology at the Academy of Military Medical Sciences were awarded the "European Inventor Award for Non-European Countries" for inventing the highly effective antimalarial drug "Artemisinin-Based Combination Therapy."
2. China's first patent law was implemented from April 1, 1985.

introduce it to the international market.

The patent application became a crucial foundation for cooperation and a test for both parties involved. To preserve the decades of hard work by scientists, a PCT international application, WO9202217A, was submitted to the World Intellectual Property Organization (WIPO) on June 5, 1991, citing CN90106722 and CN91102575 as priority documents. This application requested protection for the antimalarial combination of Compound Artemether in 49 countries worldwide, securing the successful patent filing for Compound Artemether. In 1994, the Academy of Military Medical Sciences entered into a patent development license agreement with Novartis. Under the agreement, Novartis was tasked with the research, development, and international sales of Compound Artemether, while research entities like the Academy of Military Medical Sciences were to receive 4% of the sales as royalties.

After signing the cooperation agreement, Novartis assembled a research team, including internationally renowned scientists and Chinese collaborators, to conduct central clinical trials of Compound Artemether in over twenty countries globally. Following international clinical trials involving more than 5,000 patients, artemisinin was first registered under the trade name "Coartem" in Gabon, Africa, in October 1998 and introduced to the Swiss market in January 1999. By 2004, Compound Artemether had been patented in 49 countries and regions and successfully registered in 79 countries and regions worldwide. In April 2009, Coartem received approval from the US FDA and secured marketing rights in the US. After over a decade of effort, Coartem gained access to the international market. Novartis secured the WHO order, dominating the international market with twenty years of exclusive patent protection. However, China's patent revenue was less than 1% of the global market for artemisinin-based drugs, which amounts to $1.5 billion.

In 2002, WHO and the WTO conducted assessments and tests on manufacturers producing artemisinin and its derivatives, as well as the quality of their products, according to international standards. The results highlighted that Chinese pharmaceutical companies primarily served as raw material production bases, with only two qualified raw material production bases: Guangxi Guilin Nan Pharmaceutical Co. Ltd. (the production base of artesunate for Sanofi) and Beijing Novartis (the production base of Compound Artemether for Novartis Switzerland).

Since the 1990s, Western pharmaceutical companies have sourced artemisinin raw materials from Chinese firms or produced them directly on an OEM basis, capitalizing on China's raw material products and process technology to secure high profits. This is due to the disparity between China's pharmaceutical product development standards and international norms. The Compound Artemether tablets developed by Kunming Pharmaceutical Company and Novartis Switzerland utilize raw materials supplied by Kunming Pharmaceutical, including artemisinin and benzyl alcohol. Additionally, Kunming Pharmaceutical collaborates with the French company Aventis to provide large packages of artemisinin solutions, which Aventis distributes in France and registers for global sales under the brand name Pahither. Similarly, Guilin Pharmaceutical Factory partners with French company Sanofi, relegating China to the role of a low-cost raw material supplier for artemisinin.

This situation underscores China's challenges in converting scientific and technological achievements into marketable products, particularly in the realm of SBI. The journey from patent to market for such companies is arduous, requiring substantial financial, human, and material resources, and entails considerable risk. For instance, the top ten global pharmaceutical companies allocate 18% of their profits to new drug R&D, which is characterized by lengthy timelines, high costs, and uncertain cost recovery. In the United States, only 1 out of every 250 new drugs entering preclinical trials receives FDA approval, and merely 3 out of 10 new drugs on the market can recoup their initial investments. Moreover, it typically takes 10 to 15 years to advance a drug from concept to market. Chinese pharmaceutical companies primarily focus on sales, with minimal engagement and investment in drug development, registration, and academic promotion, as vividly illustrated by the case of artemisinin.

6. Case Summary

The discovery of artemisinin stands as one of the most significant accomplishments in natural product chemistry in the latter half of the 20th century and represents the first Nobel Prize awarded for scientific research conducted entirely by Chinese scientists. Following the identification of the artemisinin molecule, the 523 Project swiftly directed its drug synthesis laboratory to develop artemisinin derivatives, leading to a new generation of antimalarial drugs. This represented a major advancement in antimalarial drug research both within China and globally.

The successful discovery of artemisinin and the development of artemisinin-based drugs are testament to the collaboration of multidisciplinary teams. Given the research conditions in China at the time, including a weak foundation and inadequate equipment, reliance on multidisciplinary and multi-institutional collaboration was essential.

From R&D to its global introduction, with the support of Novartis, the renowned pharmaceutical group, Compound Artemether has emerged as the only innovative drug with Chinese IP rights and international patents that is registered and sold on a global scale. However, in the context of the global industry chain, China's artemisinin industry remains at the lowest end of the value chain. There are still numerous challenges to overcome in transforming scientific and technological achievements into tangible products.

The journey of artemisinin's discovery and the commercialization process of artemisinin-based drugs are depicted in Figure 3-5.

Scientific discovery

- **1967** China initiates "523" project for new anti-malarial drugs. Tu Youyou joins in 1969 to lead drug screening.
- **1971** Tu discovers artemether extract from Artemisia annua, showing 100% Plasmodium inhibition.
- **1972** Tu presents Artemisia annua's anti-malarial benefits, prompting "523" to focus on artemisinin development.

Application R&D

- **1973–1975** BITCM and SIOM identify artemisinin's structure.
- **1976–1981** Shanghai Institute of Pharmaceuticals develops artemisinin derivatives, with artemether proving most effective.
- **1983** The Chinese Academy of Military Medical Sciences starts preliminary studies on compounded artemether to counter resistance to artemisinin-based drugs.
- **1983** Artemisinin synthesis achieved; CAMS studies compounded artemether.
- **Funding** 1983 grant for RMB 15,000 and 1987 venture capital of RMB 350,000 from Kunming Pharmaceutical Factory.

Go to market

- **1992** China issues new drug certificate for compound artemether.
- **1994** Patent license agreement with Novartis.
- **1998–2009** Coartem registers in Gabon, launches in Switzerland, and receives US FDA approval.

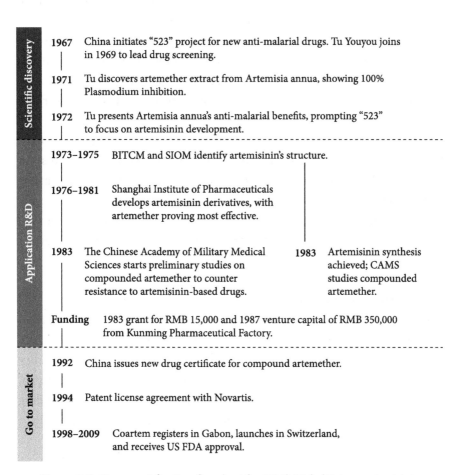

Figure 3-5 Commercialization flowchart for 2015's Nobel Prize—artemisinin

3.2.2 *Model 2: Technology Catching-Up Model Based on Scientific Discovery*

We will explore the scientific discoveries of the Beijing Genomics Institute (BGI) and their commercialization.

1. Genes

Genes are segments of DNA that exert genetic effects and serve as the fundamental genetic units governing biological traits. They underpin the basic structure and characteristics of life, encoding all information for life processes such as ethnicity, blood type, conception, growth, and apoptosis. Every phenomenon of life, including birth, growth, decline, illness, aging, and the death of living organisms, is linked to genes. Genes are also an intrinsic factor determining health. Thus, genes possess a dual nature: materiality (mode of existence) and informativeness (fundamental property).

"The Human Genome Project" is essentially a "map" detailing the precise arrangement of the three billion base pairs constituting the deoxyribonucleic acid (DNA) in each human cell. By decoding each base, scientists can discover new methods to treat and prevent numerous diseases, including cancer and heart disease.

The understanding of genes has evolved since the 1860s when geneticist Mendel proposed that "biological traits are controlled by genetic factors." In the early 20th century, geneticist Morgan demonstrated through experiments on fruit flies that genes are located on chromosomes and are linearly arranged, leading to the recognition that chromosomes are carriers of genes. From the time of Mendel's discoveries to the present, our comprehension of genes has continuously deepened over more than a century.

2. Entrepreneurial Innovation

The Chinese part of the Human Genome Project, that is, the 1% International Human Genome Project, was launched in 1997, and in 1999, a few researchers founded the BGI to complete the project. BGI China became the sixth country to join the international sequencing organization after the US, UK, Japan, Germany, and France. Since its establishment, BGI has made outstanding contributions to the development of genomic science in China and the world.

(1) Inception

On September 9, 1999, coinciding with the official commencement of the International Human Genome Project's 1%, the BGI Research Center was formally established in Beijing by Wang Jian and his two partners. In 2007, BGI relocated to Shenzhen, establishing "Shenzhen BGI," a national public welfare research institution, and completed the first Chinese genome sequence map that October. Subsequently, BGI transitioned into "BGI Genomics Co."

Since its inception, BGI has adhered to the "law of genome science and industry development," leveraging a technology platform that combines "biotechnology, exemplified by high-throughput sequencing, with information technology powered by high-performance computing." This approach has propelled BGI to the forefront of genome science while also spawning several industrial projects with promising market prospects in fields such as "medicine and health," "modern agriculture," and "new bioenergy." BGI has undertaken significant "forward-looking, original, and strategic" initiatives for the advancement of China's biological industry.

In January 2008, BGI, in collaboration with British and American scientists, initiated the International 1,000 Genomes Project. This was followed by the launch of the Giant Panda Genome Project in March 2008, the completion of the giant panda genome framework map and development of hand-cloned pigs in October 2008, and the inauguration of the Technology Catch-Up and Endogenous Innovation of the World's Tripolar Animal Genome: Typical Practice Chapter 9 Project in April 2009. August 2009 saw the launch of the Ten Thousand Microorganisms Genome Project. In December 2009, the "Key Laboratory of Genomics of the Ministry of Agriculture" was established jointly with the Ministry of Agriculture and the Shenzhen Municipal People's Government, and in January 2010, the 1,000 Plant and Animal Genomes Project commenced.

Beyond gene sequencing and analysis, BGI has also engaged in functional genome and applied genome research to expedite the growth of the gene industry. In agricultural breeding, BGI has harnessed genomic technology to develop crop and transgenic varieties of cereals, rice, and trees, which have entered field trials. In medical health, BGI's non-invasive fetal chromosomal disease detection technology has received clinical testing licenses in multiple locations and has been promoted in Japan and Korea. In 2013, BGI was recognized by MIT Technology Review as one of the world's most innovative technology companies.

BGI has established laboratories and clinical centers in Beijing, Tianjin, Shanghai, Hong Kong, Guangzhou, Hangzhou, Xi'an, and other locations. Through international collaborations, BGI has initiated projects such as the China-Denmark Collaboration on Diabetes, the China-EU Collaboration on Gut Microbiology, the Symbiosis Genome Project with American scientists, the "China-Denmark Cancer Research Center" with Danish scientists, and the "Chinese Genome Research Center" with the Chinese University of Hong Kong. BGI has emerged as the R&D institution with the largest number of researchers, the most extensive platform, the highest sequencing capacity, and the greatest data generation in the field of genomics globally, with its sequencing capacity surpassing the combined output of the Broad Institute (US) and the Sanger Centre (UK), the second and third highest in the world, respectively.

(2) Global leadership in gene sequencing and big data analysis

Since its inception, BGI has successively established extensive technical platforms for large-scale sequencing, bioinformatics, cloning, health, and agricultural genomes, with integrated multi-omics forming the core of its integrated platform. This innovation has transformed the research paradigm of life sciences. BGI's sequencing and bioinformatics analysis capabilities are world-class, positioning it as a global leader in genome research. In academic circles, BGI has conducted significant genomic studies on plants, animals, human health, and bioenergy, publishing over a hundred papers in prestigious international journals like *Nature* and *Science*.

BGI has developed a range of internationally renowned software, databases, and service platforms, training a multitude of professionals in bioinformatics and related experimental technologies. It possesses robust research capabilities and extensive experience across all levels of genomic research, having established a comprehensive suite of data generation and analysis platforms for second-generation sequencers. BGI has honed its skills in everything from data acquisition and processing to the development of bioinformatics algorithms and software.

Following the completion of the Human Genome Project, BGI embarked on constructing its "Biotechnology + Information Technology" (BT + IT) big data empire. Each of the 900 academic papers it has published is backed by up to terabytes of data. BGI manages, computes, and analyzes all life science data, achieving a peak gene computing capacity of 236.5 Tops, with a storage capacity of 24 PB and a daily data output of 20 TB, contributing to 47% of the global DNA data volume.

Moving beyond the traditional "hypothesis research model," the "BT + IT" model shifts scientific research from experimental, theoretical, and computational science to intensive data analysis, integrating multilevel biological information and analyzing multi-omics to uncover scientific discoveries while generating immense industrial value. In health care, this model promises to revolutionize medical treatment. Resource collection, preservation, and utilization also represent strategic priorities for BGI's sustainable growth. In 2010, BGI proposed creating the "National Gene Bank," and the "Shenzhen National Gene Bank" now collaborates with over 50 domestic and international institutions and organizations, storing thirty million biological samples by the end of 2015.

With the accumulation of massive data, the demand for data mining, analysis, and interpretation is growing. From its foundation, BGI has prioritized computing resources, transitioning from early supercomputers like Dawning 2000 and Dawning 3000 to Tianhe-1 and Tianhe-2. These supercomputers have become BGI's mainstay in computational support, enabling the development of advanced bioinformatics tools for massive data storage and processing. For instance, what took a year to analyze with previous computers now takes just three hours with Tianhe-2, significantly enhancing productivity.

BGI's high-performance computing primarily supports scientific research projects and the growth of related industries. Since 2011, BGI has offered the "BioCloud Computing" service, innovating products to fulfill the informational needs of major research institutions and the life science industry.

(3) High-level positioning and innovation depth and breadth

BGI has positioned itself to maintain a high standard, consistently aiming to achieve international first-class status and prioritizing filling scientific gaps through innovation rather than duplicating existing work. For instance, during the E. coli outbreak in Germany in May 2011, BGI received a sample of the bacteria on May 27. In collaboration with the University Medical Center Hamburg-Eppendorf, Germany, BGI sequenced the genome, successfully developed a diagnostic kit, and made the testing method available worldwide for free. BGI has also earned national recognition by responding to crises such as the Indian Ocean tsunami and tackling diseases like thalassemia, emphasizing the importance of deepening technological innovation's depth and breadth. The innovation depth has yielded more practical innovations and original innovations, such as the use of gene measurement technology for the early screening of diseases. A notable example is the "non-invasive Down's syndrome screening," which predicts the fetus's risk of Down's syndrome through maternal blood testing, offering a safer alternative to traditional amniocentesis. Moreover, BGI has ventured into original sequencing methods and functional omics research.

To expand the scope of innovation, BGI has sought to make significant strides in the commercial sector since 2009, extending its services from scientific and technological to health, agricultural, and information services.

As a result, BGI has established a comprehensive innovation ecosystem, encompassing a "research-production-medical" system that spans from basic and applied research to clinical studies, clinical products, collaboration with hospitals, and ultimately reaching individual consumers. This ecosystem, comprising the BGI research institute, Gene Technology Company, partner hospitals, and tens of thousands of consumers, facilitates the continuous development and introduction of new products and services by BGI.

(4) Capital-driven and cross-border M&A expansion

BGI operates in various sectors, including technology services, healthcare, and agriculture, employing over 1,500 people. In 2012, private equity firms such as Everbright Holdings and Sequoia Capital made substantial investments in BGI Technology Services, a subsidiary of BGI. From 2007 to 2010, the revenue of BGI Technology Services surged threefold at an annual rate, with the genomic science and gene industry evolving concurrently. In 2011, the output value of UWGS reached approximately RMB 8.6 billion, and nearly RMB 1.2 billion in 2012.

In early 2013, BGI acquired Complete Genomics (CG), a US-based sequencing company. Prior to the acquisition, CG was focused on upstream gene sequencing services, whereas BGI excelled in downstream product and equipment development, presenting a clear complementarity. Following the acquisition of CG, BGI first gained access to CG's advanced gene sequencing technology. Among these, the "key technology of combined probe anchor point ligation reading" stood out as a crucial asset BGI sought from CG. Second, this move diminished BGI's reliance on importing cutting-edge technology and equipment from abroad, reducing its dependency on upstream providers like Illumina and significantly cutting the cost of sequencing services. Third, it ensured the retention of the acquired company's R&D resources, including engineer teams, plants, and machinery, thereby effectively mitigating the risk of losing these resources. Last, the acquisition expanded BGI's entire sequencing research and application industrial chain, facilitating a strategic vision for the interactive development of life sciences and the biotech industry.

(5) Achievements in science, public welfare, and business

BGI has developed industrial and incubation platforms across various sectors, including science and technology services, healthcare, molecular breeding, cloning, and protein research. It has established branches like Wuhan BGI, Hong Kong BGI, Americas BGI, and Europe BGI. These branches are committed to genomic research and the application of IP-intensive domains such as human health, large-scale important species, and economically significant plants and animals, as illustrated in Table 3-6.

Table 3-6 Selected completed or initiated projects by BGI Genomics

Genome classes	Specific jobs	
Human Genome Project	International Human Genome Project's China Part (1%)	Human Pan-genome Sequence Atlas
	International HapMap Project (10%)	International Thousand Genomes Project
	Chinese Human Genome Atlas (Yanhuang Project No. 1)	Dutch Genome Project
	Sino-British Monozygotic Twins Epigenetics Study	Ancient Human Genome
Animal Genome Project	Global Extreme Environment Animal Genome Project	Chicken Genome Project
	Giant Panda Genome Atlas	Silkworm Genome Project
	A Thousand Plant and Animal Genome Project	Drosophila and Indian Ant Genome
	Ten Thousand Vertebrate Genomes Project	Hand-Cloned Pig Development
Biological Genome Project	Ten Thousand Microbial Genomes Project	Sino-European Cooperation on Gut Microbiome Project
Plant Genome Project	Major World Crop Genome Sequencing	International Potato Genome Project
	Rice Genome Project	—
Disease Genome Project	Human Gut Microbiome Metagenomics Study	Anti-SARS Research
	Sino-Danish Diabetes Project	—

BGI has marked numerous significant achievements in the annals of Chinese biotechnology. In 2002, it achieved the 100% sequencing of the rice genome, setting a landmark in China's life sciences. In the same year, BGI represented China in the Human Haplotype Map Project, completing 10% of the project's workload in collaboration with the National Center for Southern and Northern Genomes. By 2008, BGI independently finalized the first Chinese human genome map, marking a monumental leap from 1% to 100% completion. In 2010, BGI co-led the Thousand Human Genome Project with the UK and the US, transitioning from a follower and participant to a co-leader in genome research. By 2012, BGI was responsible for sequencing over 50% of the world's major crop genomes. Its sequencing data output grew from 0.2 PB in 2007 to 20 PB in 2012, with the 500 TB of data produced in 2010 equating to ten times the twenty-year data output of the National Center for Biotechnology Information as of 2009. The Nature Publishing Index 2010 China ranked BGI 4th, trailing only the CAS, Tsinghua University, and the University of Science and Technology of China.

In the realm of patent applications, BGI's filings for invention patents surged from 6 in 2007 to 201 in 2012. Over five years, BGI applied for a total of 342 invention patents, 65 of which were granted. Concurrently, it maintained an annual economic growth rate of threefold, with an output value nearing RMB 1 billion in 2010. Its sales revenue in 2011 reached nearly RMB 8.2 billion, half of which originated from international customers.

In January 2011, the "National Gene Bank" was established in Shenzhen, based on the UWGRI, positioning it as the fourth national gene bank globally, following those in the United States, Japan, and Europe. Leveraging extensive, high-quality, and standardized biological sample resources, alongside nucleic acid and protein sequencing technologies, a high-performance computing platform, and leading genomic science research, the Shenzhen BGI Bank Research Institute has mastered the process from "sample collection and data acquisition to whole-omics analysis and the industrialization of research findings." It aims to establish Chinese standards in biological cloud computing, genetic data storage and analysis, and biological sample preservation.

3. Innovative Development Model of BGI

(1) "Three developments and three leads" model

BGI has pioneered the "three developments and three leads" model, encompassing the "three joint developments" of genome-based scientific discovery, technological invention, and industrial development, alongside the "three leads model" that focuses on being driven by internationally competitive and comprehensive large-scale scientific projects, and spearheading disciplines, industries, and talents with mission-driven leadership.

Since initiating the "three joint developments," BGI has achieved global firsts in crucial research areas such as the mass discovery of genetic resources, complex genome assembly of higher organisms, and genetic background research of complex diseases. It has completed numerous internationally advanced scientific projects including the "Chinese portion" of the International Human Genome Project (1%), the International Human Haplotype Project (10%), the Rice Genome Project, and the Genomes Project for Silkworm and Chicken, among others. Additionally, BGI established the "National Key Laboratory of Agricultural Genomics," creating a technological platform for large-scale sequencing, bioinformatics, cloning, health, and agricultural genomes, advancing toward a world-leading position in sequencing capacity and genome analysis capability.

Under the "three joint developments" model, BGI is dedicated to conducting IP-intensive genomic research and applications on human health, significant species, and economically vital plants and animals, while also vigorously advancing the science and technology service industry, healthcare industry, and modern agriculture industry. In 2010, BGI's acquisition of 128 HiSeq2000 sequencers marked the formal establishment of its business model, combining technical services for researchers with applied research in functional genomics directly related to human health.

Embracing the "three leads" model, BGI has been at the forefront of genomic science and industry development. During the SARS outbreak, BGI was the first to sequence the genomes of four SARS viruses, leading to the development of diagnostic antigens, antibodies, and markers, and launching the world's first SARS diagnostic kit. BGI has also made significant contributions to the China Marrow Donor Program and post-disaster epidemic control following the Wenchuan earthquake.

Transitioning from pure scientific research to a dual focus on research and service, BGI leverages advanced sequencing and detection technologies, robust information analysis capabilities, and rich biological resources. It is committed to building platforms for nucleic acid research, protein research, bioinformatics, and participating in the establishment of national gene banks, thus providing innovative biological research services worldwide and fostering progress in genomics research, molecular breeding, healthcare, environmental energy, and more.

Furthermore, BGI has developed a unique education and training system, including innovative student training models and joint master's and doctoral training programs, swiftly cultivating talent to meet the diverse needs of science, technology, and industry fields. By the end of December 2011, BGI had graduated 139 doctoral, 994 master's, and 1,939 bachelor's degree holders, comprising 87% of its workforce. With 15 foreign employees, 103 returned scholars, and an average technical team age of just 25 years, BGI's young researchers have made "milestone contributions" to human genome research, including the introduction of the "human pan-genome" concept.

Guided by the "three developments and three leads" model and an integrated platform of cutting-edge biotechnology and computing technology, BGI orchestrates, designs, and services sequencing-based scientific and technological projects. This model fosters innovation in key product and technology R&D and services, effectively bringing R&D achievements to market, enabling a virtuous cycle of "driving technological inventions with scientific discoveries, propelling industrial development with technological inventions, and supporting scientific discoveries with industrial development."

(2) Organizational evolution and BGI's vitality boost

BGI has navigated transitions from state-owned to private, from private back to state-owned, and then from state-owned to private again. In 1999, Yang Huanming, Yu Jun, Liu Siqi, and Wang Jian departed the state-owned system to establish the BGI. After being tasked with 1% of the International Human Genome Project, they secured RMB 15 million in funding and additionally received support from relevant state departments, bringing the total funding to RMB 50 million. The completion of significant projects like the Human Genome Project and the Rice Genome Project garnered acclaim from both the domestic and international scientific communities. In 2002, the CAS decided to create the Beijing Genome Institute on the foundation of the UWGRI, integrating the original entrepreneurs and core team into the CAS system, thus transitioning from "outside the system" to "inside the system." In 2007, the advent of a new generation of sequencers presented a unique opportunity for "genomics," prompting Wang Jian and others to once again leave the state-owned system and establish "Genomics" with the backing of the Shenzhen government. Consequently, BGI was formed, transforming into a "public welfare institution."

BGI's management adheres to two principles. First, granting the president full autonomy in scientific research, allowing for independent determination of research directions and tasks, independent deployment of scientific and technological resources, and focusing nearly 4,000 people and over RMB 800 million solely on gene sequencing and analysis. Second, it employs a flexible approach to talent utilization, eschewing title evaluations and paper quantity assessments, and entrusting talented young individuals with significant responsibilities. Wang Junquan, the executive director of BGI, only 37 years old, has spent over a decade at BGI, contributing to more than forty papers in prestigious international journals. Zhao Bowen, who joined BGI at the age of 17 after opting out of high school and foregoing the college entrance examination, now leads a research team comprising nearly ten foreign professors and PhD holders.

4. Conclusions and Inspirations

Based on the preceding discussion and analysis, comprehensive insights have been gained into the subject matter.

With its strategic focus on gene sequencing and its role as a private research institution, BGI has set high standards for itself, fostering innovation in both depth and breadth. It has pursued rapid expansion through capital infusion and international mergers and acquisitions, achieving global leadership in gene sequencing and big data analysis. This strategy has yielded significant accomplishments across science, public welfare, and commerce.

The swift growth of BGI underscores its novel "three developments and three leads" innovation model and its adaptive approach to organizational changes in line with business evolution. Leveraging the "three developments and three leads" framework, BGI spearheads, orchestrates, and supports sequencing-based scientific and technological initiatives, underpinned by an integrated platform combining cutting-edge biotechnology and computational technology. This approach facilitates innovation in the R&D and services of pivotal products and technologies, effectively transitioning R&D achievements into the marketplace. This establishes a beneficial cycle of fueling technological innovation through scientific discovery, spurring industrial growth through technological innovation, and enhancing scientific discovery through industrial progress. Institutional transformations have infused BGI with dynamism, transitioning from state-owned to private, then back to state-owned, and once again to private. These shifts have empowered BGI to autonomously define research agendas and tasks, employ talent without constraints, and independently manage scientific and technological resources, thereby ensuring the effective execution of its "three developments and three leads" innovation model.

3.3 Comparative Analysis and Insights

3.3.1 Science-Based Innovation in Nobel Laureates

1. Existing Perspectives

In the discourse on "technology innovation models" by international scholars, various models are identified, including technology-driven innovation, market demand-driven model, linear innovation model, feedback innovation model, networked model, matrix innovation model, cluster model, and open innovation model. These are categorized based on the "original driving force of innovation," the "innovation process," and the "organization of innovation."

From the perspective of "original drivers of innovation," the "technology-driven innovation model" encompasses the "SBI model." This inclusion arises because the distinction between SBI and TBI is not always clear in international studies, with many scholars equating SBI with TBI, as evidenced by the prevalent view that R&D is the sole source of innovation. Historical figures like Von Siemens (1883) highlighted advanced science as a key driver of industrial innovation and development, laying the groundwork for the "linear innovation model." Similarly, Vannevar Bush (1944) emphasized that basic research acts as a precursor and significant driver of technological progress, with applied R&D transforming basic research into technological innovations.

From the "innovation process" standpoint, models such as the linear, feedback, and networked innovation models are applicable to SBI, acknowledging the presence of "feedback" within the SBI process. According to

Rothwell (1992), innovation is a process interlinking sectors and institutions; R&D activities and production organizations evolve alongside the innovation process. In a "pan-innovation team," the innovation process becomes networked, connecting customers, suppliers, and strategic partners both vertically and horizontally. Chen (2014) delineated a "three-generation evolutionary model" of corporate technological innovation, encompassing "internal R&D-centered innovation" (first generation), "synergy/integration-based innovation" (second generation), and "innovation heavily based on corporate strategic orientation" (third generation), which outlines the trajectory of TBI. These models offer valuable perspectives for contemplating related issues in innovation.

2. Nobel Case-Based Analysis: Linear Feedback Model

In their analysis of numerous Nobel Prize cases, Lin and Lei (2013) introduced a "foundational model" of SBI, which they characterize as a "linear model derived from science," as illustrated in Figure 3-6. This model is fundamentally driven by scientific discovery, distinguishing SBI from technology-driven innovation.

According to Lin, the "linear model derived from science" sets SBI apart from innovation in "technology-based industries," where innovation primarily results from technological evolution with diverse sources. These sources can involve technological improvements, adaptations, and integrations. In contrast, "SBI" relies solely on "new scientific discoveries" as the genesis of innovation. Following a scientific discovery, the process involves designing products to meet customer needs, developing processes to meet production demands, and improving and integrating technologies to meet these process requirements, culminating in a manufacturing process. This foundational approach to SBI is referred to as the "first generation: purely linear model."

Further investigation by Lin and Wang (2017) revealed that the model depicted in Figure 3-6 overlooked the "cumulative effect of scientific knowledge." They suggested that the SBI model required refinement and integration based on this insight. They segmented SBI into three distinct stages: the scientific discovery stage, the application-oriented research stage, and the commercialization and marketing stage, as demonstrated in Figure 3-7.

The revised model distinctly categorizes the outcomes of new scientific discoveries into two types: theoretical value and applied value. It posits that the discovery phase can yield new scientific theories or produce scientific

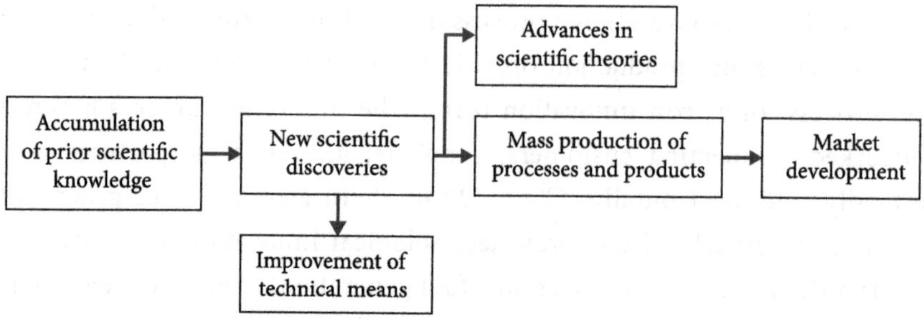

Figure 3-6 Foundational model for SBI (first generation: purely linear model)

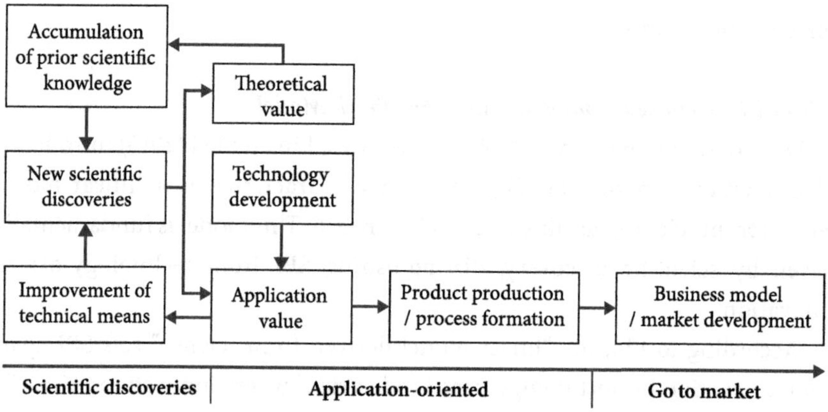

Figure 3-7 Foundational model for SBI (second generation: linear feedback model)

outcomes with practical applications, thereby enhancing the accumulation of knowledge through the feedback of both aspects. Concurrently, the model upholds the innovation-driving essence of scientific discovery, illustrating how such discoveries can evolve into commercially viable prototype products or processes through application-oriented technological development. These then transform into widely accepted commercial products or processes through further commercial development, ultimately reaching the marketplace. This refined approach to SBI is aptly described as the "second generation: linear feedback model."

3.3.2 *The SBI/Catch-Up Model*

Through a comparative analysis of the two cases and the abstraction of characteristics of relevant elements and activities, it is evident that these cases share common features:

a. Their core achievement lies in effectively transforming scientific progress into products needed by the market. This is characterized by product innovation in science-based industries, which successfully develops and meets market demands.
b. Regarding the initiation of innovation/catching up, a common feature of the five cases is their origin from "national major needs." Specifically, the artemisinin case was driven by the need to treat diseases among soldiers. The Nuctech case stemmed from the demand for security inspection equipment at customs and airports, especially to combat smuggling. The BGI case was due to China's need to participate in the International Human Genome Project. The Dawning computer case was about addressing China's lack of international standing in large parallel computers and meeting domestic demands. The Huawei case began when the telecommunications equipment industry, dominated by international corporations, needed a shift in the national context.
c. In terms of positioning for innovation or catching up, they all focus on advancing their disciplines' scientific progress and its transformation to serve national and market needs. For instance, artemisinin was about developing drugs to utilize its benefits for humanity. Nuctech translated university research to meet national needs. BGI led in global gene sequencing and big data analysis. Dawning aimed to create the world's best parallel computers and servers. Huawei developed the capacity for continuous innovation as market demands evolved.
d. The innovation/catching up model involved early research by scientific teams, followed by scientists' involvement in commercial development, with ongoing support from basic scientific findings for frontline innovation. The artemisinin case, for example, moved from basic research to application and then to international market development in collaboration with Novartis. Nuctech began with university research "transplantation," followed by the integration of product-oriented and manufacturing technologies, with ongoing input from academic findings into product innovation.
e. The pathway of innovation/catching up generally starts with foundational and applied research, closely aligns with market needs for product development, and culminates in effectively serving especially the leading customers. For instance, artemisinin evolved from identifying optimal extraction conditions to discovering its molecular structure, developing synthetic methods, and finally creating new clinical drugs.

f. In market development, innovators proactively adapt to existing market demands and, after winning initial (leading) customers, continue to develop commercial clientele. The artemisinin case initially targeted military clients, then expanded through commercial product development and international market outreach with Novartis. Nuctech's growth was supported by government-created customers, leading to a chain of client development. BGI focused on serving scientific research and commercial clients. Dawning primarily targeted the domestic market, expanding through competitive bidding. Huawei started with serving rural China, then expanded internationally through collaborative and independent innovation.

It should be noted that the above points on positioning, mode, pathway, and market development of innovation/catching up collectively form the strategy for innovation/catching up.

a. In the innovation/catch-up process, pivotal events lead innovators to make strategic decisions at crucial junctures concerning technology selection, product development, and market development. For instance, in the artemisinin case, Tu Youyou opted to develop an anti-malarial drug using artemisinin; Wu Yulin from the SIOM delved into artemisinin's molecular structure; and the national science and technology plan advocated for the full synthesis of artemisinin. BGI's case illustrates decisions to transform the institutional system thrice, aiming for rapid expansion through capital infusion and cross-border acquisitions.
b. Regarding the innovation mechanism, the key individual, team, and organization form the internal mechanism, while external support constitutes the environmental mechanism. A common trait across the cases is the key individual—a scientist or entrepreneur with a scientific mindset—leading innovation and catch-up efforts. The innovation team's cohesion is driven by goals and values, necessitating the establishment of appropriate organizational and operational mechanisms tailored to the resource needs of innovation and catch-up. Key figures, such as Tu Youyou in the artemisinin case and Wang Jian in BGI, play pivotal roles, with external support from government policies, industry collaboration, or other forms of backing providing an essential environmental mechanism.

Table 3-7 Preliminary inductive theoretical model of innovation/catching-up in science-based industries

Innovation/ catching-up	Strategies of catching-up and innovation				Processes of catching-up and innovation		Mechanisms of catching-up and innovation				Commercial-ized effects
	Position	Model	Path	Market develop-ments	Great decisions	Important events	Key figures	Team	Organiza-tion	External supports	
The traction of major national needs	Based on scientific advancements in the field and their transforma-tion to serve national and market needs	Early research by scientific teams followed by scientists' participation in the commercial development of the team, continuing to support frontline innovation with basic scientific findings	Building foundational and applied research outcomes → closely aligning with market demands for product development → effectively engaging particularly the initial leading customers	Proactively adapting to existing market demands; after securing leading customers, continually developing commercial clientele	Making appropriate decisions at crucial junctures in market selection, product develop-ment, and market expansion	Encouraging innovators to make suitable choices and adjustments	Scientists or entrepre-neurially minded scientists as key leaders in innovation and catching up	Driven by goal orientation and value motivation	Establishing organizations and operational mechanisms based on the resource allocation needs of innovation and catching up	Receiving encourage-ment and support from government policies; industry collaboration or complemen-tary support	Often cultivating a domestic industry, thereby elevating related sectors and contributing to national development in specific areas

c. In terms of the commercial impact of innovation and catch-up, the commonality across the two cases is their contribution to fostering domestic industries, thereby enhancing related sectors or making significant national development contributions. The artemisinin case introduced a new generation of anti-malarial drugs benefiting humanity.
d. Collectively, these observations can be integrated into the theoretical model depicted in Table 3-7. It illustrates that the innovator's "innovation behavior" and "catch-up behavior" are intricately interwoven, making them practically indistinguishable. Catch-up inherently depends on innovation, and the innovation process concurrently serves as the catch-up process. Thus, there's no need to strictly differentiate between the two in theoretical models.

References

Artemisinin Structure Research Collaborative Group. 1977. "A New Type of Sesquiterpene Mushroom Lactone, Artemisinin." *Science Bulletin* 3 (3).

Cheeseman, I. H., B. A. Miller, S. Nair, et al. 2012. "A Major Genome Region Underlying Artemisinin Resistance in Malaria." *Science* 336 (6077): 79–82.

Dondorp, A. M., C. I. Fanello, I. C. E. Hendriksen, et al. 2010. "Artesunate Versus Quinine in the Treatment of Severe Falciparum Malaria in African Children (AQUAMAT): An Open-Label, Randomised Trial." *The Lancet* 376 (9753): 1647–1657.

Klayman, D. L. 1985. "Qinghaosu (Artemisinin): An Antimalarial Drug from China." *Science* 228 (4703): 1049–1055.

Lai, R. H., Y. Rao, and D. Q. Zhang. 2013. "Historical Exploration of 'Mission 523' and the Discovery of Artemisinin." *Nature Dialectics Letters* 35 (1).

Li, Ying, Yu Peilin, Chen Yixin, et al. 1979. "Synthesis of Artemisinin Derivatives." *Science Bulletin* 14 (14): 667–669.

Liu, Jingming, Ni Muyun, Fan Jufen, et al. 1979. "The Structure and Reactions of Artemisinin." *Journal of Chemistry* 37 (2): 129–143.

Luo, X. D., and C. C. Shen. 1987. "The Chemistry, Pharmacology, and Clinical Applications of Qinghaosu (Artemisinin) and Its Derivatives." *Medicinal Research Reviews* 7 (1): 29–52.

Miller, L. H., and Su X. Artemisinin. 2011. "Artemisinin: Discovery from the Chinese Herbal Garden." *Cell* 146 (6): 855–858.

Qingzhi, Z., Yacheng Y., Yaoyuan Q., et al. 2018. "Science-Based Innovation in China: A Case Study of Artemisinin from Laboratory to the Market." *Journal of Industrial Integration and Management* 3 (2): 1850011.

Tu, Youyou. 2009. *Artemisinin and Artemisinin-Like Drugs*. Beijing: Beijing Chemical Industry Press.

Wang, Danhong. 2008. "Zhou Weishan, Member of the Chinese Academy of Sciences: Determination of the Structure of Artemisinin and Total Synthesis After." *Science Times*, December 2.

Wu, Yulin. 2009. "Artemisinin: One-by-One Historical and Practical Insights." *Advances in Chemistry* (11): 2365–2371.

Xu, Xinxiang, Zhu Jie, and Huang Dazhong. 1983. "Studies on the Structure and Synthesis of Artemisinin and Its Analogues X. Stereocontrolled Synthesis of Artemisinin and Deoxynivalenol from Artemisinic Acid." *Journal of Chemistry* (6): 96–98.

———. 1984. "Structure and Synthesis of Artemisinin and Its Analogues XVII: Stereocontrolled Total Synthesis of Methyl Dihydroartemisinin-Artemisinin." *Organic Chemistry of Natural Products* 42 (9).

Zhang, Qingzhi, Duan Yongqian, and Lei Jiaxiao. 2015. "Science-Based Innovation Research—an Example of Nobel Prize Scientific Achievement." *Studies in Science* 33(12): 1770–1778.

Zhou, Weishan, Shen Jiming, Chen Zhaohuan, et al. 1984. "Studies on the Structure and Synthesis of Artemisinin and Its Analogs—Total Synthesis of Isodeoxyartemisinin." *Chinese Science* 2 (2): 150–156.

CHAPTER 4

Science-Based Industrial Innovation: Academic Entrepreneurship of Scientists

4.1 Scientists' Participation in Science-Based Entrepreneurial Activities

4.1.1 Entrepreneurship as a Pathway to Innovation

In recent years, "academic entrepreneurship," encompassing scientists' patent applications, risk cooperation, and spin-off creation, has emerged as a focal point in innovation studies. This concept broadly refers to all commercial endeavors beyond the traditional educational and research duties at universities. It encompasses the establishment of new ventures for exploiting academic research outcomes and the commercial development process, including the derivation of technology and knowledge from universities (Meyer 2003; Franklin 2001; O'Shea 2004). Drawing on this research, this book defines scientists' involvement in science-based entrepreneurial activities as the actions of university academics or researchers in PRIs commercializing their findings through patent applications, enterprise collaborations, enterprise service, or enterprise creation.

With biotechnology and life sciences advancing, scientists' participation in science-based entrepreneurial activities is increasingly common. The research primarily explores the following parts:

a. The feasibility of scholars engaging in commercialization. Initially, there might have been skepticism about scholars' involvement in commercialization, with concerns that it could detract from the purity of scientific research. However, the evolution of biological sciences has seen scholars successfully engage in commercial endeavors. Research indicates that these scientists have not seen a dip in their academic output. Instead, they have outperformed their peers in publications, citations, and funding, aiding their basic scientific research pursuits (Grimaldi et al. 2011; Astebro 2013).
b. The factors motivating scholars to engage in commercial activities. Studies from both supply and demand perspectives highlight personal attributes, experiences, attitudes, motivations, research areas, and educational levels. Factors such as a desire for practical application, wealth, and further research motivate scholars (Lam 2011). The demand side examines the work environment, national policies, and cultural influences. For example, Stanford University professors receive ample support for commercialization efforts; the Bayh-Dole Act of 1980 in the US significantly encouraged academic commercialization; the commercial activities of peers also inspire scholars to participate.
c. The pathways through which scholars can commercialize their research. Scholars typically use channels like patent applications through University Technology Transfer Offices, industry collaborations, patent licensing, contract-based research for enterprises, direct employment in businesses as researchers or consultants, and engaging in start-ups to commercialize their findings (Zhang 2015; Dottore and Kassicieh 2014).

Existing literature, often constrained by data limitations, tends to rely on individual cases, small-scale studies, or specific fields like biology, medicine, or life sciences. This chapter focuses on natural science field scientists, including Nobel Prize laureates, covering a broad range of industries. Given that these scholars are among the most esteemed in basic science research globally, their involvement in science-based entrepreneurial activities provides compelling insights into the commercialization of foundational achievements. Moreover, there is scant research examining scholars' commercialization involvement from the basic scientific research achievements' commercialization process perspective. We aim to fill this gap by assessing the impact of scientists' participation in science-based entrepreneurial activities on the commercialization of basic scientific research achievements, exploring dimensions such as patent applications, enterprise collaborations, and start-up engagement.

4.1.2 Methodology and Data Selection

Over the 114 years from 1901 to 2015, this study selects 123 Nobel Prize laureates in Physics, Chemistry, and Physiology or Medicine from the years 2000 to 2015 as research subjects. The rationale for focusing on Nobel laureates in these natural science fields is multifaceted: Nobel laureates are among the world's most esteemed scientists and represent the pinnacle of achievement in their respective disciplines, making them highly representative and authoritative research subjects; the majority of Nobel laureates are affiliated with universities or PRIs and are engaged in fundamental scientific research; selecting laureates awarded after 2000 aligns with contemporary trends and developments.

The investigation into the extent of these 123 scientists' involvement in science-based entrepreneurial activities and their impact on the commercialization of fundamental scientific research is conducted across three dimensions: patent application, enterprise collaboration, and participation in new enterprise creation. The research first involves querying the databases of the United States Patent and Trademark Office and the WIPO to ascertain if these laureates have applied for patents related to their Nobel-recognized discoveries. Second, it evaluates whether the scientists have engaged with the industry, including employment or serving as scientific consultants for enterprises. Third, it examines whether the scientists have contributed to founding new companies to commercialize their Nobel-winning work. Last, the study identifies Nobel Prize achievements that have been commercially utilized and further explores the scientists' roles in the commercialization process of these innovations. Sources for this data include the laureates' profiles on the Nobel Prize official website, their institutions' websites, autobiographies, and Google searches. The methodology is outlined in Figure 4-1.

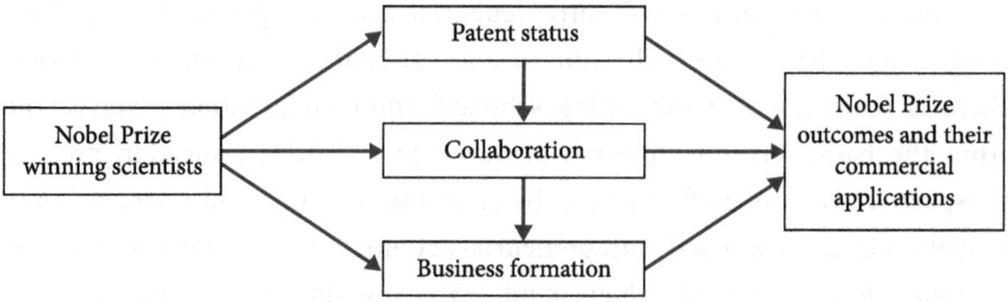

Figure 4-1 Nobel laureates' routes to commercializing their discoveries

4.1.3 Scientists' Involvement in Science-Based Entrepreneurial Activities

To assess the involvement of the 123 Nobel laureates in science-based entrepreneurial activities and their influence on the commercialization of fundamental scientific discoveries, this study examines three key dimensions: their engagement in patent applications, their collaboration with businesses, and their participation in founding new enterprises.

1. Scientists Applying for Patents

When scientists' scientific discoveries have potential commercial applications, they often opt to secure patents to protect their innovations. This study tallied all patents granted to the 123 laureates by 2015. As indicated in Table 4-1, there are 2,809 patents across physics, chemistry, physiology, and medicine, averaging 22.84 patents per individual. Of these, 83 laureates possess at least one patent linked to their Nobel-recognized work, representing 67.48% of the total awardees. Specifically, 17 physics laureates hold patents, making up 40.48% of winners in this field; 35 laureates in chemistry have patents, constituting 87.5% of the chemistry awardees; and 31 laureates in physiology or medicine have patents, accounting for 75.61% of winners in their category. Previous research indicated that about one-third of professors at top US universities hold patents. However, this study reveals that Nobel laureates are significantly more engaged in patent applications than their counterparts, highlighting their keen interest in applying research outcomes and their active participation in the patenting process.

Table 4-1 Patent statistics for Nobel laureates, 2000–2015

Fields	Relevant patents	Number of people with patents	Maximum number of individual patents
Physics	392	17 (40.48%)	303
Chemistry	1,273	35 (87.5%)	258
Physiological Medicine	1,144	31 (75.61%)	202
Total	2,809	83 (67.48%)	

The 2007 Nobel Prize in Physics was jointly awarded to Albert Fert from France and Peter Grunberg from Germany for their independent discovery of GMR. Grunberg's team quickly recognized the significance of this discovery for the development of hard disk reading heads and promptly filed for a patent on hard disk technology based on GMR. This decision proved to be astute as the technology's potential was recognized by numerous major corporations, leading to the Forschungszentrum Juelich, where Grunberg was based, earning tens of millions of euros from patent licensing fees. IBM became the pioneer in applying this breakthrough to practical use.

The active involvement of Nobel Prize-winning scientists in patent applications can be significantly attributed to the Bayh-Dole Act enacted in the United States in 1980. This legislation allows institutions to retain patent rights for federally funded research outcomes, granting them the liberty to license or transfer patents to businesses. The enactment of this law has fostered collaborations between the government, academia, research institutions, and the industrial sector, alleviated corporate concerns regarding patent rights, hastened the commercialization process of innovations, and spurred scientists' interest in pursuing patent applications.

2. Cooperation between Scientists and Businesses

Beyond patent applications, Nobel Prize-winning scientists actively engage in collaborations with businesses to commercialize their scientific discoveries. Some have even established close partnerships with corporations during the basic scientific research phase, receiving research funding from these entities. Beyond early-stage collaborations, other scientists have worked with companies to further commercialize their scientific breakthroughs after achieving significant progress in basic research. According to Table 4-2, from 2000 to 2015, 31 Nobel Prize-winning scientists collaborated with enterprises, representing 25.2% of the total. Among these, ten Nobel Prize winners worked with companies to develop and commercialize their scientific findings, twelve served as scientific consultants to facilitate commercialization, and seven were directly employed by businesses to conduct basic scientific research and translate their discoveries into practical applications.

Table 4-2 Nobel scientists cooperated with enterprises, 2000–2015

Years	Award	Nobel Prize laureates	Cooperative company	Position	Product/technology
2014	Physics	Isamu Akasaki	Toyoda Gosei	Collaborative R&D	Blue light diode
2014	Physics	Hiroshi Amano	Toyoda Gosei	Collaborative R&D	Blue light diode
2014	Physics	Shuji Nakamura	Nichia Chemical Industries	Corporate appointments	Blue light diode
2009	Physics	Charles K. Kao	British Standard Telecom	Corporate appointments	Fiber optics
2009	Physics	Willard S. Boyle	Bell Labs	Corporate appointments	Charge-Coupled Devices
2009	Physics	George E. Smith	Bell Labs	Bell Labs	Charge-Coupled Devices
2007	Physics	Albert Fert	Thomson—CSF, Philips, Siemens	Collaborative R&D	Frontiers in spintronics
2000	Physics	Jack S. Kilby	Texas Instruments	Corporate appointments	Integrated circuit
2014	Chemistry	Stefan Hell	Leica Microsystems	Collaborative R&D	Ultra-high resolution Microscope
2014	Chemistry	Eric Betzig	Carl Zeiss	Collaborative R&D	Optical microscopes
2013	Chemistry	Michael Levitt	Oplon, Cocrystal Discovery, etc.	Scientific advisers	Computer simulation experiments
2010	Chemistry	Richard F. Heck	Hercules Corporation	Collaborative R&D	Palladium-catalyzed coupling reactions
2010	Chemistry	Ei-ichi Negishi	Teijin, Sony	Scientific advisors	Palladium-catalyzed cross-coupling reaction technology

Years	Award	Nobel Prize laureates	Cooperative company	Position	Product/technology
2006	Chemistry	Roger Kornberg	Oplon, Prize4Life, StemRad	Scientific advisors	Eukaryotic transcription techniques
2005	Chemistry	Robert Grubbs	ORFID, Materia Inc., Novomer	Scientific advisors	Olefin decomposition reaction
2004	Chemistry	Aaron Ciechanover	BioLineRx, StemRad	Scientific advisors	Ubiquitin-regulated protein degradation
2003	Chemistry	Peter Agre	Ferring	Collaborative R&D	Development of urologic drugs
2002	Chemistry	Koichi Tanaka	Shimadzu Manufacturing	Corporate appointments	Mass spectrometer unit
2002	Chemistry	Kurt. Wuthrich	Spectrospin AG, Bruker	Collaborative R&D	Nuclear magnetic resonance technique
2001	Chemistry	Ryoji Noyori	Takasago Spice Industries of Japan	Collaborative R&D	Synthetic menthol
2001	Chemistry	K. Barry Sharpless	Baker	Collaborative R&D	Toxic moth attractant dextro
2001	Chemistry	William Knowles	Monsanto	Corporate appointments	Industrial synthesis of levodopa
2000	Chemistry	Alan J. Heeger	BioSolar	Scientific advisors	New energy Development
2013	Biomedical	James E. Rothman	ARIAD Pharmaceuticals	Scientific advisors	Mechanisms regulating intracellular vesicle transport
2009	Biomedical	Jack W. Szostak	Ra Pharmaceuticals	Scientific advisors	Mechanism of chromosome protection by telomerase
2007	Biomedical	Mario R. Capecchi	Q Therapeutics, Inc	Scientific advisors	Gene targeting technology
2006	Biomedical	Craig Mello	Invitrogen Corp	Scientific advisors	Ribonucleic acid interference mechanism
2004	Biomedical	Richard Axel	Genentech	Scientific advisors	Mechanism of olfactory production
2002	Biomedical	Sydney Brenner	Lynx Therapeutics, Xcovery	Scientific advisors	Programmed cell death
2001	Biomedical	Leland Hartwell	Arrowhead Research Corporation	Scientific advisors	Genes regulating the cell cycle
2000	Biomedical	Arvid Carlsson	ACADIA Pharmaceuticals	Scientific advisors	Signal transduction in the nervous system

Moreover, Nobel Prize-winning scientists also act as scientific consultants for companies, contributing to the commercialization of scientific discoveries. For instance, James Rothman, the 2013 Physiology or Medicine Laureate, has been a scientific consultant for ARIAD Pharmaceuticals since 2002, working on pioneering drug research and the regulation of cellular small molecule signals. In another case, Oplon, an Israeli start-up, has enlisted two Nobel laureates as its scientific advisors simultaneously: Michael Levitt, the 2013 Chemistry Laureate, and Roger Kornberg, the 2006 Chemistry Laureate.

Furthermore, seven Nobel Prize-winning scientists within the sample are employed by companies, forming stable employment relationships, which is also considered a form of enterprise collaboration. These scientists are primarily affiliated with institutions like Bell Laboratories, Texas Instruments, Monsanto Company, British Telecommunications Laboratories, and two Japanese companies.

3. Scientists Engaging in Start-Ups

Beyond the previously mentioned modes of engagement, Nobel Prize-winning scientists are also keen on founding new enterprises to commercialize their research findings. Data collected on scientists who have utilized this approach for their Nobel-recognized work from 2000 to 2015 reveals that 21 Nobel laureates have initiated companies, encompassing three laureates in Physics, nine in Chemistry, and nine in Physiology or Medicine (Table 4-3). Overall, 17.07% of the Nobel laureates investigated have ventured into start-ups, with the share of Chemistry and Physiology or Medicine laureates involved being higher, at 22.5% and 21.95% respectively. This participation rate significantly exceeds that of their counterparts in similar disciplines.

Table 4-3 Nobel laureates co-founded companies, 2000–2015

Year	Award	Nobel Prize laureates	Founded companies	Year of foundation	Product applications
2014	Physics	Shuji Nakamura	Soraa	2008	LED light
2009	Physics	Charles K. Kao	ITX Services Limited	1999	
2005	Physics	Theodor Hänsch	Menlo Systems	2001	Lasers

Year	Award	Nobel Prize laureates	Founded companies	Year of foundation	Product applications
2012	Chemistry	Brian K Kobilka	ConfometRx		Providing a technology platform for basic drug discovery and development
2009	Chemistry	Thomas A Steitz	Rib-X Pharmaceuticals	2000	New broad-spectrum antibiotics (clinical)
2008	Chemistry	Roger Y. Tsien	Aurora Biosciences	1995	Fluorescent protein screening technology
			Senomyx	1999	New flavor materials
			Avelas Biosciences	2009	Development of luminescent maps of cancerous tissues
2006	Chemistry	Roger Kornberg	Cocrystal Discovery	2008	Genetic interventions in clinical trials
2005	Chemistry	Richard Schrock	XiMo AG	2010	Providing decomposition catalyst solutions
2005	Chemistry	Robert Grubbs	Materia	1997	Development and production of catalysts
2002	Chemistry	John B. Fenn	Analytica of Branford	1987	Mass spectrometer
2001	Chemistry	Barry Sharpless	Coelecanth	1996	Creation of new combinatorial chemical libraries
2000	Chemistry	Alan Heeger	Uniax Corporation	1990	Conductive polymer development
			Konarka	2001	Developing organic solar cells
2010	Biomedical	Robert Edwards	Bourn Hall Clinic	1980	test tube baby
2007	Biomedical	SirMartin Evans	Celixir	2009	Dedicated to breakthrough drug development
2006	Biomedical	Craig C. Mello	RXi Pharmaceuticals	2006	Developing innovative therapies using RNA technology
2005	Biomedical	Barry J.Marshall	ONDEK	2005	Helicobacter pylori diagnosis and treatment
			TRI-MED	1996	Helicobacter pylori diagnosis and treatment

Year	Award	Nobel Prize laureates	Founded companies	Year of foundation	Product applications
2002	Biomedical	Sydney Brenner	CombiChem	1994	Accelerating drug discovery through medicinal chemistry
2002	Biomedical	Robert Horvitz	NemaPharm	1990	Targeted drug development
		Robert Horvitz	Idun Pharmaceuticals	1993	Targeted drug development for cancer treatment
2001	Biomedical	Leland Hartwell	Rosetta Inpharmatics	1996	Analysis of genetically diseased tissue
2000	Biomedical	Paul Greengard	Intra-Cellular Therapies	2002	Development of innovative small molecule drugs
2000	Biomedical	Eric Kandel	Memory Pharmaceuticals	1998	Central nervous system innovative drug development

The Nobel laureates are often co-founders of these enterprises, typically acquiring a stake in the company through technology transfer. Their primary role within the company is to further research and develop scientific achievements, while the day-to-day business operations are managed by a professional team. Involving scientists in start-ups not only keeps them at the forefront of scientific research, enabling timely updates on the latest scientific advancements, but also facilitates collaboration with top research institutions. Furthermore, start-ups can attract the attention of venture investors through the involvement of distinguished scientists in the field. This, in turn, allows scientists to expedite the commercialization process of their scientific discoveries by leveraging the focus and resources of the start-ups.

4.1.4 Impact of Scientists' Involvement on Achievement Commercialization

The research meticulously examines the commercial application of scientific discoveries in the three natural science fields from 2000 to 2015, revealing that 15 Nobel Prize-winning achievements have found widespread business applications. Specifically, four achievements are from the field of physics, six from chemistry, and five from physiology or medicine. The detailed findings are presented in Table 4-4.

Table 4-4 Market commercialization of Nobel Prizes, 2000–2015

Year	Award	Achievement	Commercial application	Participation
2014	Physics	Blue LEDs change lighting	Blue light diode, LED light	Patent applications, employment in companies
2009	Physics	Fiber optic and semiconductor imaging devices	Fiber optic communication and charge coupled devices	Patent applications, employment in companies
2007	Physics	Discovery of the GMR effect	Computer hard disk drives, etc.	Patent application
2000	Physics	Invented circuit	Integrated circuits, digital integrated circuits, etc.	Patent applications, employment in companies
2014	Chemistry	Super-resolution fluorescence microscopy	Super-resolution fluorescence microscopy	Patent applications, employment in companies
2008	Chemistry	Discovery of GFP	For drug screening, molecular labeling, etc.	Patent applications, start-ups
2003	Chemistry	Discovery of cell membrane water channels	Treatment of central urolithiasis	Patent applications, employment in companies
2002	Chemistry	Mass spectrometric methods for the analysis of macromolecules	Mass spectrometer, medical diagnostics, etc.	Patent applications, start-ups
2001	Chemistry	Chiral catalyzed hydrogenation	For the development of chiral drugs	Patent applications, employment in companies
2000	Chemistry	Discovery of conductive polymers	LED liquid crystal display	Patent applications, start-ups
2015	Biomedical	Discovery of artemisinin	Artemisinin derivatives for the treatment of malaria	Patent applications, employment in companies
2010	Biomedical	Discovery of in vitro fertilization	Test tube baby	Patent applications, start-ups
2008	Biomedical	cervical cancer vaccine	Developed a cervical cancer vaccine	Patent applications
2005	Biomedical	Discovering Helicobacter pylori	Diagnosis and treatment of gastritis and gastric ulcers	Patent applications, start-ups
2003	Biomedical	Nuclear magnetic resonance imaging	Applications in medical clinical diagnostics	Patent applications

In an in-depth analysis of the commercialization process of these discoveries, it has been observed that all Nobel Prize-winning scientists played various roles in the commercialization of their achievements. The 15 achievements that have been commercialized all have relevant patents filed by the award-winning scientists. Among these, four achievements involved Nobel laureates directly applying their research within enterprises to foster commercialization. These four achievements include the Nobel Prize-winning discoveries in physics for the years 2014, 2009, and 2000, and in chemistry for 2001. Additionally, three achievements were developed and commercialized through close cooperation between enterprises and Nobel Prize-winning scientists via patent licensing. These include the Nobel Prizes in chemistry for 2014 and 2003, and in physiology or medicine for 2015. Five achievements were commercialized by Nobel laureates creating new enterprises, including chemistry awards for 2008, 2002, and 2000, and physiology or medicine for 2010 and 2005. These 12 achievements were commercialized with significant involvement from scientists, whether through employment in enterprises, close cooperation with enterprises, or by founding new enterprises for commercialization. However, there are three Nobel Prize achievements where scientists did not deeply engage in commercialization after patent applications. These include the 2007 Nobel Prize in Physics and the 2008 and 2003 Nobel Prizes in Physiology or Medicine. For instance, after the GMR discovery, IBM licensed the patent from Professor Grünberg, and corporate scientist Parkin led the R&D, swiftly bringing the application of GMR to fruition. Following Professor Hausen's discovery that human papillomavirus causes cervical cancer, researchers Frazer and Zhou Jian began developing a cervical cancer vaccine, which was later commercialized by Merck and the University of Queensland. In 2003, despite Nobel laureates applying for relevant patents, direct promotion of product development was undertaken by academic entrepreneurs, facilitating the achievement's commercialization.

Out of the 39 scientists associated with these 15 commercially applied Nobel Prize achievements, including 11 in physics, 17 in chemistry, and 11 in physiology or medicine, 33 scientists have at least one patent related to their discoveries, representing 86.62% with patents. Regarding enterprise collaboration, seven Nobel laureates were employed by enterprises for their Nobel-winning research, and 11 scientists from universities or PRIs worked closely with enterprises, constituting 43.59%. In terms of founding start-ups, eight scientists participated in establishing enterprises to apply their Nobel Prize-winning research, accounting for 20.51%.

4.1.5 Overview

This chapter analyzes the involvement of Nobel Prize-winning scientists in academic entrepreneurship and the impact on the commercialization of their discoveries, focusing on 123 laureates in natural sciences from 2000 to 2015. The findings reveal that among these laureates, 83 scientists, or 67.48%, have filed at least one patent related to their Nobel-recognized work, averaging 22.84 patents per person. Furthermore, 31 scientists, representing 25.2% of the total, have engaged closely with enterprises through research collaborations, serving as scientific advisors, or employment within these companies. Additionally, 21 Nobel laureates have participated in founding start-ups, accounting for 17.07% of the total, with a notably higher participation rate among winners in Chemistry and Physiology or Medicine.

The research highlights that of the 15 Nobel Prize-recognized achievements that have been widely commercialized, the associated laureates have significantly participated in their commercialization. In particular, 12 of these achievements were commercialized with the deep involvement of the Nobel laureates, demonstrating the necessity for scientists to engage actively in translating basic scientific research into market applications. This involvement is crucial due to the tacit nature of new knowledge generated from basic research, requiring scholars' active participation to bridge academic findings with market applications. Through patent applications, enterprise collaborations, or establishing start-ups, scholars not only further scientific progress but also drive the commercialization of research findings, thus serving as a vital link between academia and industry and fostering the application of scientific discoveries.

4.2 Nobel Prize Case Studies

4.2.1 Case Study 1: Blue LED Invention and Commercialization

The 2014 Nobel Prize in Physics was awarded to Isamu Akasaki, Hiroshi Amano of Nagoya University in Japan, and Shuji Nakamura of the University of California, Santa Barbara, US, for their groundbreaking work in inventing a new energy-efficient light source: the blue light-emitting diode (LED).

While red and green LEDs had been in existence for over half a century, the development of blue LEDs completed the primary color spectrum necessary for creating white light sources. This innovation was a significant technological challenge that the industry and academia had struggled with for more than three decades.

Working at Nagoya University, Akasaki and Amano, along with Nakamura who was then affiliated with a small company named NICHIA in Tokushima City on Shikoku Island, Japan, overcame the persistent challenge of producing blue light through semiconductors. Their achievement not only filled a critical gap in the light spectrum but also laid the foundation for the widespread use of LED-based white lighting and full-color displays. This groundbreaking work enabled the development of all subsequent LED lights, LED backlit LCDs, and LED full-color display matrices.

1. Semiconductor Light Emitting

On October 21, 1879, an American inventor illuminated the world with the first practical electric light after extensive experimentation. This inventor was Thomas Edison, later hailed as the "king of invention." Edison's light bulb revolutionized human life, enabling cities to thrive around the clock. Similarly, the advent of LED technology ushered in a new era of lighting, emphasizing energy conservation, environmental protection, and intelligent applications. The invention of the blue LED, in particular, has enriched our world with vibrant colors, from the dazzling arrays of street lights to the vivid displays of smartphones. Blue LED technology has also laid the groundwork for blue lasers, making the recording of high-definition content a reality. The LED represents a monumental leap in lighting technology since Edison's iconic invention.

The first historical account of using semiconductors for light emission was reported by Henry Rode, a colleague of Guglielmo Marconi, the 1909 Nobel Prize laureate and pioneer of radio and telegraphy. In the 1920s, Soviet scientist Oleg Losev conducted extensive research into the luminescence principle, although both Rode and Losev lacked the comprehensive understanding needed for practical application. It wasn't until the principle of electroluminescence was proposed decades later that significant progress was made.

The theoretical foundation for electroluminescence was laid in the early 1950s with the advancement of semiconductor physics. LEDs, similar to conventional diodes, consist of a PN junction and exhibit unidirectional conductivity.

Atoms, molecules, and certain semiconductor materials can emit or absorb light or electromagnetic waves of specific wavelengths. Solid-state band theory divides electron energy states in semiconductors into valence and conduction bands. Electron transitions between bands result in the emission or absorption of light at certain frequencies, with photon energy correlating to wavelength. Shorter wavelengths indicate higher energy and a purple hue, while longer wavelengths show lower energy and a redder color.

In 1955, Rubin Braunstein of the Radio Corporation of America discovered that gallium arsenide semiconductors could emit infrared light, although commercial applications were not pursued. In 1961, Americans James Biad and Gary Pittman observed infrared light emission from gallium arsenide when electrically stimulated. By 1968, this discovery led to a patent and, subsequently, practical applications in electronic watches, calculators, and as indicators for various electronic devices. The early 1970s saw the introduction of green LEDs made from gallium phosphide and yellow LEDs from silicon carbide, improving LED efficiency and expanding the spectrum to include orange, yellow, and green. Initially, LEDs had low luminous efficiency and were primarily used as indicator lights. As efficiency improved, LEDs found broader applications in digital and textual displays.

2. Blue Light Diode Invention

In scientific and industrial circles, the quest to create blue LED persisted as a formidable challenge for researchers over decades. While red and green LEDs had become staples in electronic devices and instruments for over half a century, the development of a blue diode, which possesses a shorter wavelength and higher photon energy, was crucial for achieving a white light source based on the principle of the three primary colors. Despite concerted efforts, success remained elusive for many years.

In 1971, Jacques Pankove and Ea Miller, two Soviet scientists, demonstrated the potential for creating a blue LED using zinc-doped nitride. However, their initial LED made with gallium nitride emitted green light instead. A year later, Herb Maruska and Wally Rhines of Stanford University, along with doctoral students in materials science and engineering, developed the first LED capable of emitting blue-violet light using magnesium-doped gallium nitride. In 1974, the United States Patent and Trademark Office awarded Maruska, Rhines, and Stanford professor David Stevenson patent rights for their work. Despite this milestone, the blue LED's emitted light was too faint for practical applications, leading to a hiatus in gallium nitride research and no subsequent breakthroughs. In 1989, Cree launched the first commercial blue LED, opting for silicon carbide, an indirect bandgap semiconductor, instead of gallium nitride, due to its extremely low efficiency.

Meanwhile, in 1973, Isamu Akasaki, then at Panasonic Corporation's Tokyo Research Institute, embarked on a long-term project to develop blue light diodes. Collaborating with his student Hiroshi Amano, a doctoral candidate at Nagoya University, they focused on nitride materials despite the challenges of obtaining high-quality light sources from nitride crystals. By 1986, they had succeeded in creating high-quality hybridized nitride crystals and made significant progress in developing P layers. Their discovery that electron flow from a scanning electron microscope could enhance the efficiency of the P layer led to the world's first nitride PN junction blue LED by the end of 1989.

Shuji Nakamura began his work on blue light diodes in 1988. After joining NICHIA, a small company, post-graduation in 1979, Nakamura dedicated himself to the blue LED project, choosing the MOCVD method for its cost-effectiveness compared to the molecular beam epitaxy (MBE) method. Despite initial setbacks due to the corrosive nature of nitride's raw gas, Nakamura eventually engineered a durable heater. By September 1990, he had successfully produced a nitride film, laying the groundwork for the diode's development. In 1992, Nakamura's team achieved the trial production of a GaN LED, though its initial output was too dim. By adding impurities to the emission layer and improving film crystallinity, they significantly enhanced the LED's brightness. By October 1993, Nakamura had increased the blue LED's brightness a hundredfold, marking a new era in lighting technology. This breakthrough paved the way for LED lighting, heralding the fourth-generation of lighting in human history.

3. *Blue LED Commercialization*

The foundational research conducted by Akasaki and Amano at Nagoya University initially received funding from Toyota Synthesis Company. However, as Toyota Synthesis redirected its focus toward traditional LED research, it ceased funding Akasaki's innovative endeavors, inadvertently paving the way for Nakamura's groundbreaking work at NICHIA.

NICHIA, established in 1956, initially specialized in manufacturing high-purity calcium salt products. By 1966, it had expanded into producing phosphors for fluorescent lamps, securing a patent license from GE for phosphor production and venturing into the lighting industry. Despite its efforts, NICHIA remained a minor player, lacking the capability to pioneer advanced lighting technologies.

In September 1992, Nakamura's team celebrated a milestone with the successful trial production of the double heterostructure GaN LED. Though the initial light output was dim, NICHIA's commitment to GaN LED research was unwavering. The following year, NICHIA invested $3.3 million in R&D—a substantial sum for a small company. This investment bore fruit in October 1993 when Nakamura's blue diode, enhanced by a phosphor coating, marked a breakthrough in solid-state lighting, achieving a hundredfold increase in brightness. This advancement shattered the long-standing belief that high-brightness blue LEDs were a distant future prospect, ushering them into practical use.

By 1994, NICHIA had commenced mass production of its blue LED, successfully introducing it to the market. Toyota Synthetic, having previously withdrawn support for Akasaki and Amano's research, later expressed regret over its premature exit from the blue LED development race. In 1995, Toyota Synthetic and HITACHI collectively reignited their GaN LED project, investing JPY 700 million over seven years. Although they had relinquished their lead, Toyota Synthetic remained optimistic about its position in the market.

Nakamura's introduction of the high-brightness blue LED was swiftly followed by the development of white LEDs. Contrary to expectations, the prevalent method for producing white light was not by combining LEDs of three primary colors but by coating a blue LED with light-yellow phosphor. Compared to incandescent lamps, LEDs offer several advantages: they are significantly more efficient, converting up to 60% of electrical energy into light (compared to the 10% efficiency of incandescent lamps), operate on low voltages of just a few volts, and boast long lifespans of up to 100,000 hours, surpassing the typical 1,000-hour lifespan of incandescent lamps by a decade.

4. Nakamura's Patent Litigation

Following Nakamura's 1993 invention of the blue LED, NICHIA capitalized on the technology, bringing LED lighting products to market and generating substantial profits. Despite his pivotal role, Nakamura received a meager bonus of JPY 20,000 (approximately $200 at the time) from the company, covering both the patent application and registration. Recognizing Nakamura's talent, Henry T. Yang, the Chinese American chancellor of the University of California,

Santa Barbara, set out to recruit him. Despite Nakamura's modest position as a technician conducting experiments in a basement, Yang personally visited Japan, offering Nakamura a research team and a culturally accommodating environment at the university. This personalized approach led Nakamura to choose Santa Barbara over offers from Stanford University and Hewlett-Packard.

In 2000, Nakamura moved to the United States. During his resignation process, NICHIA sought to prevent him from conducting basic research on blue LEDs for three years, which Nakamura declined, resulting in NICHIA suing him, the American Kerry Company, and the University of North Carolina, where Nakamura consulted, for alleged corporate espionage.

In 2004, Nakamura countered with a lawsuit against NICHIA in the Tokyo District Court, claiming compensation for his invention. The court initially ordered NICHIA to pay Nakamura JPY 20 billion, recognizing his invention's valuation at a minimum of JPY 60 billion. Unsettled by the verdict, NICHIA appealed, but in 2005, under the Tokyo High Court's mediation, both parties settled with NICHIA compensating Nakamura JPY 843.91 million.

This landmark case spurred many inventors to pursue legal recognition of their contributions, with Nakamura vs. NICHIA becoming a pivotal reference in patent litigation. Despite the lawsuit, NICHIA maintained its industry dominance, securing fundamental patents across the LED spectrum and engaging in patent litigation to safeguard its market position. Between 1996 and 2010, NICHIA was involved in 62 patent lawsuits, significantly more than any competitor.

However, a 2001 Tokyo District Court ruling in a case against Sumitomo Commercial, concerning blue LEDs manufactured by American Cree, challenged NICHIA's monopolistic stance. Subsequently, NICHIA adjusted its strategy, entering into cross-licensing agreements with major LED manufacturers like Lumileds Lighting (now Philips Lighting), Cree, and others, fostering collaborative relationships within the industry.

5. Nakamura's Founding of Soraa Company

In 2008, Shuji Nakamura, alongside Professors Stephen DenBaars, a semi-conductor expert, and James Speck, a materials expert at the University of California, Santa Barbara, founded Soraa in Fremont, California. This start-up focuses on developing high-end LEDs based on Nakamura's research, aiming to reduce energy consumption and address societal energy challenges through the advancement of violet LEDs.

Khosla Ventures, one of Soraa's earliest investors, recognized the potential in clean energy technology a decade ago. Vinod Khosla, the founder, approached Nakamura, who had recently left NICHIA for a teaching position at the University of California, Santa Barbara. Despite initially declining Khosla's offer due to workload, Nakamura was eventually persuaded to establish Soraa in 2008, with Khosla Ventures among the early investors looking to make inroads in the clean energy sector.

Soraa secured venture capital from Khosla Ventures, NEA, NGEN Partners, Angeleno Group, and others, providing it with more funding than its peers. Despite this, Soraa faced financial challenges due to its commitment to developing high-end LED products using exclusively gallium nitride, avoiding other impurity materials like sapphire chips or silicon carbide. This approach, while yielding light quality comparable to natural sunlight, presented cost barriers that deterred most companies.

Navigating through financial hurdles required additional venture capital, with Soraa also spinning off discoveries to reduce operating expenses. In 2010, Avogy was spun off to focus on new energy systems for mobile communication devices. SoraaLaserDiode was established in 2013 to specialize in laser technology development. Avogy secured approximately $40 million in funding from Intel in 2014.

By the end of 2014, Soraa had raised over $100 million in venture capital and received $7.95 million in research funds from the US Department of Energy's Advanced Research Projects Agency-Energy (ARPA-E) for power electronic substrate projects related to the development of bulk gallium nitride.

Soraa's focus on violet LEDs offers energy savings compared to blue LEDs for similar brightness levels. In 2012, the company introduced "GaN on GaN" solid-state lighting technology with its MR16 LED lamp, featuring a full spectrum of visible light and unique violet emission 3-phosphor (VP3) technology for enhanced color and white representation. In 2014, Soraa launched the GU10 LED spotlight, utilizing third-generation GaN-based LED chips and hybrid technology to significantly improve color rendition and white light performance, achieving a color rendering index greater than 95.

Soraa's market presence is primarily in commercial settings like restaurants, shops, high-end residences, and office environments. The company aims to lower manufacturing costs, reduce product prices, and expand its product appeal in the general lighting market within the next 2-3 years.

6. Government Support for LED Development

Due to its significant advantages in energy efficiency and environmental sustainability, LED technology is increasingly adopted, with governments worldwide bolstering their support.

Since 2014, the United States has been phasing out 40–60 W incandescent bulbs, granting LED lighting products greater application opportunities and urging manufacturers to ramp up production and enhance LED lighting's market penetration. By offering subsidies for lighting products certified with the "Energy Star,"[1] the US government has contributed to the reduction of LED lamp prices.

The European Union, known for setting the global benchmark in environmental standards, outlined a timeline as early as March 2007 for gradually discontinuing incandescent bulbs. It prohibited the sale of 100 W traditional bulbs from September 2009 and banned all traditional bulbs by 2012. Following his 2007 inauguration, UK Prime Minister Brown announced that the United Kingdom would adhere to EU regulations. Despite the absence of large-scale LED industry subsidies in Europe, the high cost of electricity propels a continuous demand for LED lighting in commercial and outdoor architectural lighting. The ban on incandescent lamps will further ensure a steady growth in the LED market.

Japan, facing a notable energy crisis, has seen a remarkable growth rate in the LED sector. Launching the "21st Century Light Plan" industrialization project in 1998, Japan was among the pioneers in implementing policies to foster LED development and became the world's first nation to prohibit incandescent lamps.

South Korea, also heavily dependent on energy imports, prioritizes energy conservation as a key strategic initiative, thus emphasizing the LED industry's development. The "Fourth Basic Plan for Rationalization of Energy Utilization" in South Korea aimed to periodically increase the minimum energy efficiency

---

1. Since its inception in 1992, the US "Energy Star" program has aimed to steer consumers toward selecting products with high energy efficiency. Those who purchase products bearing the "Energy Star" label can enjoy benefits such as tax deductions or direct subsidies offered by the program.

standards for incandescent lamps, targeting their complete phase-out by the end of 2013.

With the expedited phase-out of incandescent lamps, LED lighting products are set to gain widespread popularity and comprehensively supplant traditional lighting solutions.

7. Case Overview

Incandescent lamps illuminated the entire 20th century, but the 21st century will be dominated by LED lamps. Although blue LED technology has only been developed over the last twenty years, its impact on humanity is growing, transforming our lighting experiences. LED lights, known for their high efficiency and energy-saving attributes, will also enable the 1.5 billion people worldwide without access to power grids to leave behind an era devoid of lighting.

In both scientific and industrial circles, red and green LEDs had long been developed, with many materials available for producing them. However, blue LEDs presented a significant challenge for researchers for decades. Akasaki and Amano from Nagoya University commenced their collaboration in 1973, undertaking foundational R&D into blue light diodes. The breakthrough in blue LED research began in 1989 when Nakamura, with NICHIA's support, embarked on his quest to develop a blue light diode. Within a mere four years, Nakamura overcame two major material preparation challenges through relentless experimentation: creating high-quality nitride films and managing the hole conduction of nitrides. By 1993, Nakamura had increased the brightness of blue LEDs to one hundred times their original intensity. Nakamura's technology, in comparison to that of the Nagoya University team, was simpler and more cost-effective. In 1994, NICHIA's blue LEDs went into production and were introduced to the market, generating significant profits.

After achieving a breakthrough with blue LEDs, Nakamura, under the encouragement of venture capital firms, co-founded Soraa in 2008. The company focuses on the R&D of high-end LEDs, aiming to reduce energy consumption and address societal energy issues through the development of purple LEDs. Soraa has received investments from several venture capital firms, including Kosra, and has secured R&D funding from the US Department of Energy's ARPA-E to advance the development of gallium nitride. By 2012, Soraa had successively launched premium products, marking another instance where Nakamura seamlessly integrated basic scientific research with commercial applications.

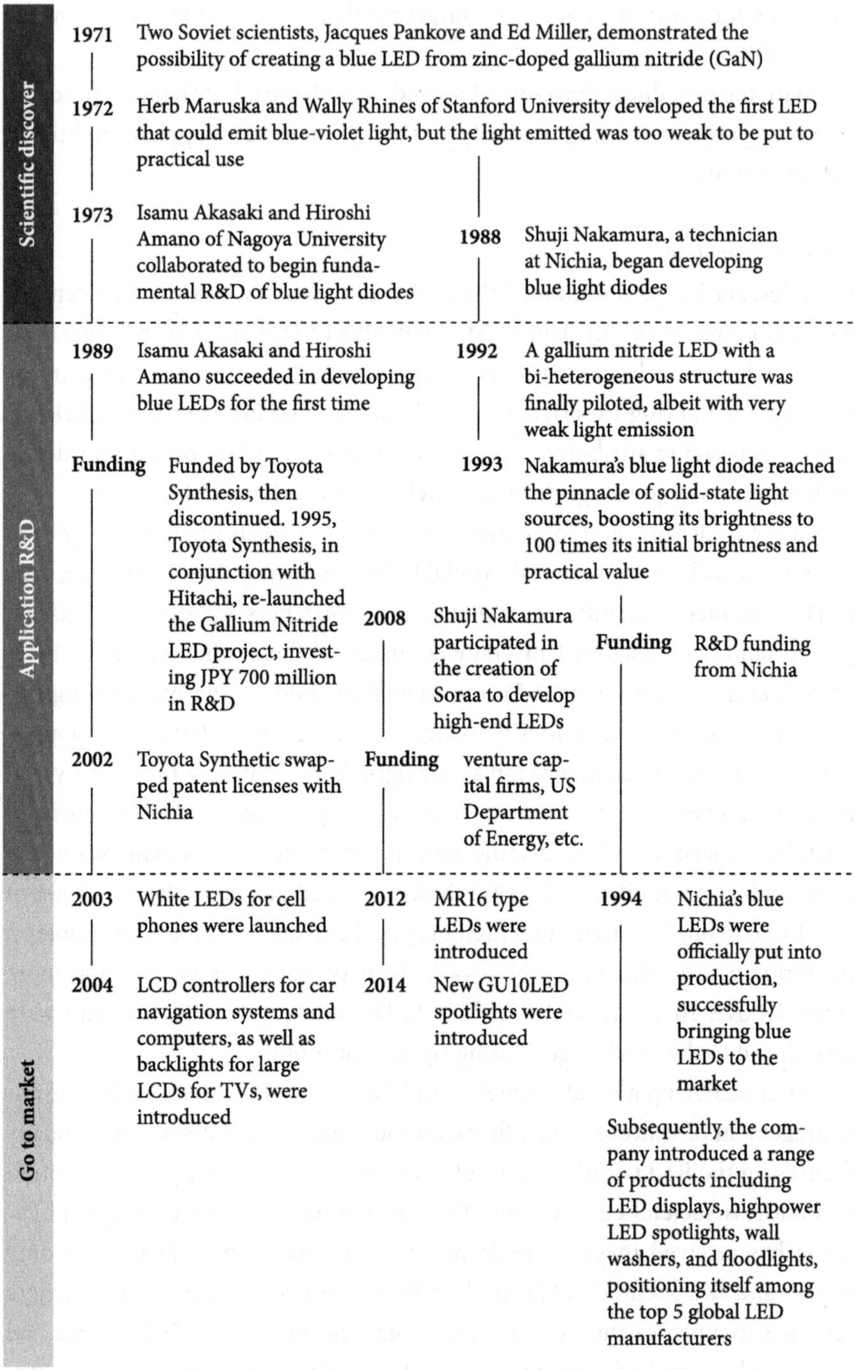
Scientific discover
1971 Two Soviet scientists, Jacques Pankove and Ed Miller, demonstrated the possibility of creating a blue LED from zinc-doped gallium nitride (GaN)
1972 Herb Maruska and Wally Rhines of Stanford University developed the first LED that could emit blue-violet light, but the light emitted was too weak to be put to practical use
1973 Isamu Akasaki and Hiroshi Amano of Nagoya University collaborated to begin fundamental R&D of blue light diodes
1988 Shuji Nakamura, a technician at Nichia, began developing blue light diodes
Application R&D
1989 Isamu Akasaki and Hiroshi Amano succeeded in developing blue LEDs for the first time
1992 A gallium nitride LED with a bi-heterogeneous structure was finally piloted, albeit with very weak light emission
Funding Funded by Toyota Synthesis, then discontinued. 1995, Toyota Synthesis, in conjunction with Hitachi, re-launched the Gallium Nitride LED project, investing JPY 700 million in R&D
1993 Nakamura's blue light diode reached the pinnacle of solid-state light sources, boosting its brightness to 100 times its initial brightness and practical value
2008 Shuji Nakamura participated in the creation of Soraa to develop high-end LEDs
Funding R&D funding from Nichia
2002 Toyota Synthetic swapped patent licenses with Nichia
Funding venture capital firms, US Department of Energy, etc.
Go to market
2003 White LEDs for cell phones were launched
2012 MR16 type LEDs were introduced
1994 Nichia's blue LEDs were officially put into production, successfully bringing blue LEDs to the market
2004 LCD controllers for car navigation systems and computers, as well as backlights for large LCDs for TVs, were introduced
2014 New GU10LED spotlights were introduced
Subsequently, the company introduced a range of products including LED displays, highpower LED spotlights, wall washers, and floodlights, positioning itself among the top 5 global LED manufacturers

Figure 4-2 Commercialization flowchart for the 2014's Nobel Prize in Physics—blue LED

The government played a crucial role in the commercialization process of LED lighting, from supporting basic scientific research with funding to establishing specific policies that facilitated LED development, spurring rapid growth in the LED industry. The invention and commercialization journey of the blue LED is depicted in Figure 4-2.

4.2.2 Case 2: GFP Discovery and Use

In 2008, the Nobel Prize in Chemistry was awarded to three American scientists: Osamu Shimomura of the Woods Hole Oceanographic Institution, Martin Chalfie of Columbia University, and Roger Y. Tsien of the University of California, San Diego, for their pioneering work on the green fluorescent protein (GFP). Osamu Shimomura was the first to isolate GFP from jellyfish, discovering its luminescence in ultraviolet light. Martin Chalfie demonstrated GFP's utility as a fluorescent marker for tracking biological processes. Roger Y. Tsien further innovated by diversifying the color palette beyond green, enabling the distinction of various proteins and cells with different hues. GFP has become an indispensable tool in life sciences and medical research, revolutionizing experimental methodologies. The advent of optical imaging technology utilizing GFP allows for the direct observation of vibrant biological phenomena across scales. The Swedish Royal Academy of Sciences likened the discovery and application of GFP to the invention of the microscope, marking it as a cornerstone in contemporary biological research.

1. Discovery of GFP

Shimomura, a Japanese scientist, spent his youth living with his traditional grandparents. After World War II, he embarked on his academic journey at a local medical college, graduating with outstanding results in 1951. He then joined Professor Ernst & Young's laboratory to delve into substance purification and chromatography analysis. Four years later, on Professor Ernst & Young's recommendation, Shimomura sought to join Professor Jiang Shangxiu's molecular biology lab at Nagoya University. In an unforeseen twist, Professor Jiang was unavailable, leading Shimomura to accept an invitation from Professor Yoshimasa Hirata. It was in Hirata's lab that Shimomura's path to discovering GFP began.

Tasked by Professor Hirata with the daunting challenge of fluorescein purification and crystallization, Shimomura encountered numerous setbacks. One night, opting to temporarily shift focus, he left his samples with preliminary reagents and went home. To his astonishment, he discovered upon his return that the fluorescein had crystallized, marking a pivotal moment in his research journey.

Shimomura's prowess led to an invitation from Professor Johnson at Princeton University to explore the luminous mechanisms of jellyfish. The prevailing belief was that biological fluorescence stemmed from substances akin to fluorescein rather than proteins, steering initial research away from proteins. However, persistent failures prompted Shimomura to consider proteins in his experiments. A serendipitous observation one night—when waste samples mixed with seawater in a washbasin emitted fluorescence—revealed the protein's calcium sensitivity, leading to the discovery of the photoprotein Aequorin.

After isolating Aequorin and examining its properties, Shimomura noticed its blue light emission differed from the jellyfish's natural green fluorescence. He hypothesized the presence of another protein, GFP, which converted Aequorin's blue light to green. Subsequent experiments confirmed this theory, leading to the successful isolation of GFP. His groundbreaking work, including the elucidation of GFP's luminescence mechanism and its calcium dependence, was detailed in prominent journals, laying the groundwork for the extensive application, and understanding of GFP in scientific research.

2. Cloning of GFP

During a time when biological research heavily relied on collecting extensive experimental materials for the observation and quantification of biological molecules through chemical analysis, a process that often stripped these molecules of their spatial and temporal characteristics, turning "living" specimens into "dead" ones and imposing a significant workload, the advent of GFP marked a revolutionary shift. Shimomura, who initially isolated GFP, did not pursue its application potential upon moving to the Woods Hole Oceanographic Institution. In contrast, his colleague Douglas Prasher, recognizing the groundbreaking implications of GFP, dedicated himself to the study of biological fluorescence, envisioning GFP as a versatile marker for tracking cellular molecules and processes through genetic engineering—a concept revolutionary at the time.

Prasher's ambition to clone the GFP gene, supported by a grant from the American Cancer Society, was successful, yet the lack of subsequent funding and institutional support forced him to abandon his laboratory and seek alternative employment. Despite these professional setbacks, Prasher generously shared his GFP gene clone with researchers including Martin Chalfie and Roger Y. Tsien, laying the groundwork for the widespread application of GFP in scientific research. Although Prasher's contributions were not formally recognized by the Nobel Committee, his role was pivotal, acknowledged by his invitation to the Nobel Prize ceremony by Chalfie and Tsien. Prasher's story underscores the vital, yet often underappreciated, contributions of scientists in the advancement of research and the transformative power of collaboration in the scientific community.

Following the successful cloning of the GFP gene, the scientific community pondered the practical applications of such a fluorescent marker. A pressing question emerged: Did GFP's fluorescence require special jellyfish substances to activate? Without these substances in other species, GFP expression might not produce fluorescence, rendering the innovative labeling technique ineffective. Prasher, acknowledging this uncertainty, termed the cloned GFP a "precursor," implying it needed unknown substances for fluorescence activation.

In the midst of this speculation, Martin Chalfie, a biology professor at Columbia University, embarked on a pioneering venture. Inspired by a bioluminescence seminar in 1988, Chalfie recognized GFP's potential as a cellular marker for observing biological phenomena, such as gene expression in transparent nematodes. Despite Prasher's incomplete cloning of the GFP gene, Chalfie remained determined. By 1992, Prasher had successfully cloned the complete GFP gene, and although initially unsuccessful in expressing fluorescence in E. coli, a subsequent attempt by Chalfie's team led to a breakthrough: E. coli expressing GFP emitted green fluorescence, proving GFP did not require jellyfish-specific substances to fluoresce. Chalfie's further experiments expressing GFP in nematodes confirmed its versatility as a fluorescent marker. This landmark discovery, published in Science, heralded a new era in molecular biology and genetics, with GFP revolutionizing the field by enabling direct observation of biological processes in living organisms.

3. Modification of GFP

The burgeoning biological revolution initiated by GFP was on the cusp of transformation, awaiting further refinement. GFP, akin to a raw gemstone, required the ingenuity of visionary artisans for its full potential to be realized. Roger Y. Tsien, a Chinese American scientist, emerged as one such master craftsman.

As an interdisciplinary chemist with a keen interest in molecular dynamics, Tsien's fascination with biological phenomena through microscopy predates his engagement with GFP. During his doctoral studies in the 1970s, Tsien devised Bapta, a compound for visualizing cellular calcium ion concentrations via optical imaging, a method still prevalent today. Following Prasher's successful cloning of GFP, Tsien addressed lingering questions about GFP's universal fluorescence capability. Through experimentation, he identified oxygen molecules as the previously speculated processing agents, explaining GFP's ability to fluoresce in a broad range of organisms. His team's subsequent elucidation of GFP's luminescent principle and crystal structure paved the way for transformative work.

In 1994, leveraging the foundational GFP alongside insights into its maturation and molecular architecture, Tsien embarked on a comprehensive alteration of GFP. By inducing mutations within the protein sequence, he enhanced GFP's properties—accelerating maturation, boosting brightness, and ensuring stability for live organism applications. His innovations yielded cyan and yellow fluorescent proteins. Additionally, following Sergey A. Lukyanov's discovery of a red fluorescent protein, Tsien refined it for better utility in biological marking. This ushered in an era of multicolored fluorescent proteins, enabling the intricate labeling and observation of life processes across the spectrum. Tsien's adept manipulation birthed a biological rainbow, heralding a new chapter in the biological revolution with his meticulous craftsmanship (Tsien 1998).

4. Commercial Application of GFP

Roger Y. Tsien and his colleagues not only deciphered and refined GFP but also laid the foundation for its successful implementation in biological sciences through entrepreneurial ventures. Between 1996 and 2009, Tsien co-founded three companies dedicated to the R&D of GFP technology, broadening its applications in molecular markers, drug screening, signaling, and beyond.

In 1996, with backing from the University of California, San Diego, Roger Y. Tsien, along with Charles Zuker, a professor of biology and neurology, and Michael Geoffrey Rosenfeld, a medical school professor, established Aurora Biosciences. Aurora centered its efforts on developing and commercializing fluorescent protein screening technologies to expedite drug R&D. Additionally, Aurora licensed patents to other biopharmaceutical firms in exchange for research funding, facilitating the advancement of innovative drug discoveries. In its initial round of private financing, Aurora raised $13.6 million. The following year, Aurora went public on NASDAQ, with shares priced at $10 each. By around 2000, Aurora had introduced several fluorescence technologies such as Geneblazer™, Genomescreentmx Vivid™, and Phosphorylight™, alongside screening platforms like the ultra-high throughput screening system UHTSSR platform and the ion channel technology screening platform Viprtm. Moreover, Aurora offered assay development and screening services to drug R&D enterprises. Aurora's fluorescence technologies and screening platforms gained global usage across leading life science corporations and research entities through patent licensing, collaborating with companies such as American Home Products Corporation, Squibb, Ceres, Eli Lilly, GlaxoSmithKline, Genentech, Johnson & Johnson, Merck, Pfizer, and others. In October 2001, Vertex Pharmaceuticals acquired Aurora for $592 million. Post-acquisition, Aurora maintained its focus on the development of fluorescent protein-related technologies.

In 1999, Roger Y. Tsien, a foundational figure in science, along with renowned biochemist Lubert Stryer from Stanford University, co-founded Senomyx. This company primarily employs fluorescent protein technology to develop innovative flavoring agents. Human preference for sweet, umami, and salty tastes is deeply ingrained, as these flavors provide essential energy, proteins, and electrolytes. However, the high sugar and salt content in such foods poses a significant risk for obesity, heart disease, and type II diabetes, some of the most challenging health issues today. Senomyx, leveraging breakthroughs in taste biology, has pioneered the application of this novel technology. By analyzing human genome sequences, Senomyx has identified hundreds of taste receptors. The compounds they've developed are tasteless but can activate receptors related to the taste of sugar, salt, and other seasonings in the human mouth, enhancing the perception of sweetness, saltiness, and umami. This innovation allows food manufacturers to reduce the use of sugar, salt, and monosodium glutamate in traditional foods, making them healthier. Initially, Senomyx received venture capital from Rho Ventures. In 2004, Senomyx went public on NASDAQ with shares priced at $6 each. By 2013, Senomyx had launched Complimyx®, Sweetmyx™, and Savorymyx™, offering materials that enhance various flavors. The company also collaborates with several leading global food, beverage, and ingredient supply firms, including Kraft Foods, Nestlé, Coca-Cola, Campbell Soup, and Pepsi. Notable collaborations include Nestlé's introduction of flavor-enhanced broths in 2007, Coca-Cola and Cadbury Schweppes' adoption of Senomyx's sweeteners in 2009, and Pepsi's partnership in 2014 to develop a salt-enhancing agent. In these partnerships, Senomyx focuses on developing new flavors and achieving regulatory approval, while partners handle product sales and marketing. In March 2014, Sweetmyx, one of Senomyx's food ingredients, was granted Generally Recognized as Safe status.[2] This marks a successful application of fluorescent protein technology in the realm of flavor enhancement.

In 2009, Roger Y. Tsien, as one of the co-founders, participated in establishing Avelas Biosciences, becoming the company's research partner (as shown in Table 4-5). Avelas secured authorization for fluorescence technology from the University of California, San Diego, to develop products aimed at molecularly coloring tumors. This innovation assists surgeons in distinguishing between cancerous and healthy tissues during surgeries. Currently, surgeons lack the means to verify in real-time if a tumor has been entirely removed during surgery; MRI scans post-surgery are the only method to check for residual tumor tissue. Avelas is developing AVB-620, a product comprising genetically engineered peptides that bind to various tumor types. These peptides are linked to a fluorescent label via a chemical bond. When injected into the surgical site, this compound allows surgeons to identify tumor tissue, which lights up under a fluorescent imaging device, while healthy tissue remains dark. From 2009 to 2012, Avelas received a Series A investment of $7.65 million from Avalon Ventures to advance the clinical research of the Avelas Cancer Illuminator (ACI). Between 2013 and 2014, with Avalon Ventures leading the funding, Avelas garnered an additional $6.8 million in venture capital for further development of ACI technology. Currently, Avelas's product, AVB-620, is still undergoing commercialization efforts. Hisataka Kobayashi, the chief scientist of the Molecular Imaging Program at the US National Cancer Institute, commented, "There is no doubt that this is a groundbreaking technology that will be a significant aid to surgeons."

2. The Flavor and Extract Manufacturers Association of the United States established the Generally Recognized as Safe program in 1960 under the auspices of the US FDA. The program aims to oversee the safety evaluations of flavoring substances utilized in minimal quantities. Given their limited use, these compounds are exempt from the FDA's more rigorous food additive safety assessment procedures.

Table 4-5 Enterprises founded by Roger Y. Tsien

Enterprise	Year	Position	Goal
Aurora Biosciences	1996	Co-founder and scientific adviser	Developing and commercializing fluorescent protein screening technologies while providing technical services to other biological companies
Senomyx	1999	Co-founder and scientific adviser	Creating new flavor ingredients for food and beverages using fluorescent protein technology
Avelas Biosciences	2009	Co-founder and research collaborator	Advancing cancer surgery for surgeons through development of luminescent maps of cancerous tissue

Roger Y. Tsien and his team not only unraveled and refined GFP, but more critically, they facilitated the widespread application of GFP in the biological sciences through innovative enterprises. Today, GFP and its derivatives, serving as gene markers, have become indispensable tools and a "universal toolbox" for scientific research across all life systems.

5. *Case Overview*

GFP has evolved through four stages: discovery, cloning, modification, and application. In 1962, Shimomura first isolated GFP from jellyfish and discovered that the protein emitted a bright green light under ultraviolet light. In 1992, Martin Chalfie utilized the cloned GFP to construct an expression vector, transforming it into various organisms, which established the foundation for GFP as a bioluminescent marker. By 1996, Roger Y. Tsien and his team had analyzed the crystal structure of GFP, creating multiple GFP variants with different fluorescence properties through mutation. Subsequently, with backing from the University of California, San Diego, Tsien founded three companies dedicated to the research and application of GFP technology, widely employing it in molecular markers, drug screening, signal transduction, and more. His contributions extended beyond elucidating GFP's fluorescence mechanism and introducing other usable colors for tagging besides green. Crucially, he also spearheaded the successful commercialization of this technology. The specific commercialization process of GFP is illustrated in Figure 4-3.

Scientific discover

1962 Shu Shimomura of Japan discovered the GFP from a jellyfish

1985 Douglas Prescher cloned the gene for jellyfish

1992 Douglas Prescher cloned the complete gene for the GFP encoded by 238 amino acids

Application R&D

1992 Martin Chalfie utilized clones of GFP to construct expression vectors and transformed them into different organisms, laying the foundation of GFP as a biofluorescent indicator, and applied for a patent

1996 Tsien and his team at the University of California, San Diego, resolved the crystal structure of GFP and obtained many GFPs with different fluorescent properties by mutation

1995 Tsien founded Aurora Biosciences Biologicals, Inc. to focus on the development and commercialization of fluorescent protein screening technologies and to provide technical services to other biological companies

Funding $13.6 million in private financing was raised in the first round by Abingworth, with seed funding from several investment firms such as Avalon Ventures. Startup team: Tsien and colleagues at the University of California

1997 Aurora Biosciences went public on the NASDAQ at $10 per share

1999 Tsien founded Corporation Senomyx, a company that develops foods and beverages with novel flavor components using GFP technology

Funding Received venture capital from Rho Ventures. Venture Team: Tsien and Lubert Stryer, a renowned biochemist from Stanford University, among others

2004 Corporation Senomyx went public on the NASDAQ at a price of $6 per share

Go to market

2000 Aurora Biosciences filed applications for Big Biology™, CellSensor™, GeneBLAzer™, GenomeScreen™, PhosphoryLIGHT™, UHTSS®, VIPR™, Vivid™ and other trademarks for technologies such as drug screening. Vivid™ and other trademarks for drug screening and other technologies;

2001 Aurora and Hyseq entered a technology collaboration and licensed fluorescent protein technology to Hyseq, and in September 2001, partnered with Amersham Biomedical to accelerate drug discovery and development using GFP technology

2001 Aurora Biosciences was acquired by Vertex Pharmaceuticals, Inc.

2013 Trademark applications were filed for Complimyx®, Sweetmyx™, Savorymyx™, and other trademarks for the marketing of the Company's different flavored products

2014 The first product with the partnership with Pepsi using the sweetener S617 will be available

Figure 4-3 Commercialization flowchart for the Nobel Prize in Chemistry—GFP

4.3 Analysis of Chinese Case Studies

4.3.1 Case 1: Laser Scanning Phototypesetting System Research and Commercialization

In the 1970s, China was still employing the traditional "hot metal typesetting" method, which involved melting lead to cast individual types—a process that was labor-intensive, energy-consuming, and time-consuming. At that time, the West had already advanced to "computer typesetting technology," which utilized computer control for phototypesetting. To keep pace with the global development of information technology, it was crucial for Chinese characters to be integrated with computers. Without this integration, China's entry into the information age would have been significantly hindered. To address this technological gap, in 1974, China initiated the "Chinese Character Information Processing System," known as the 748 Project, marking the start of the second revolution in China's printing industry.

1. Initiation of Laser Scanning Phototypesetting System

The 748 Project comprised three sub-projects: a high-precision Chinese character phototypesetting system, a Chinese character information processing system, and a Chinese character news communication system. When the project was initiated, Wang Xuan, a faculty member in the Radio Department at Peking University, showed a keen interest in the high-precision Chinese character phototypesetting system component. Wang Xuan believed that the adoption of "paperless editing and phototypesetting" through computers would significantly enhance the typesetting speed of newspapers and books in China, thereby playing a crucial role in propelling the country into the information age and accelerating the development of Chinese civilization. At that time, the second- and third-generation phototypesetters were prevalent internationally, but upon thorough analysis and comparison, Wang Xuan concluded that they lacked future potential and faced insurmountable technical challenges within China. Consequently, he opted to directly pursue the development of a fourth-generation laser scanning phototypesetting system—a technology not yet realized globally. This system, under computer control, would allow digitally stored fonts to be photo-imprinted onto negative film for character formation, plate making, and printing.

Peking University designated research on the Chinese character phototypesetting system as a self-initiated campus project, aiming to secure this component within the 748 Project. With a clear objective, Wang Xuan immersed himself in the feasibility study of the digital Chinese character pattern scheme. By the end of October 1975, he successfully demonstrated the practicality of this scheme by simulating the character "义" (*yi*) using dots, apostrophes, and letters within the computer. The 748 Project Office ultimately adopted the digital Chinese character pattern scheme, officially selecting Peking University in September 1976 as the lead design and development entity for the system. This pivotal decision positioned China's printing industry to leap directly into the era of laser phototypesetting, bypassing four decades of development that foreign phototypesetters underwent.

2. Development and Reconstruction of the Prototype

When the Chinese character phototypesetting system project was initiated, China had not yet embarked on its reform and opening-up policies, presenting significant challenges in acquiring imported components and equipment. The team had to rely solely on domestically produced components and equipment. At that time, the domestically developed and produced computer memory was limited to 64 KB, with external storage equipment having a maximum capacity of only 500 KB. Wang Xuan's team was confronted with the daunting challenge of the storage capacity being insufficient for Chinese characters. Without access to disk storage, the team ingeniously utilized tape and a magnetic drum to address the issue of storing and retrieving Chinese characters.

The next hurdle Wang Xuan faced was the development of a precise Chinese character output device. The newspaper fax machine developed by the Hangzhou Communication Equipment Factory, which was already in use, had a resolution of only 24 lines/mm. By replacing the video lamp light source with a laser light source, the resolution could be enhanced to 29 lines/mm. However, the volume of information in a newspaper approached 20 MB, far exceeding the capacity of existing memory solutions. Wang Xuan devised a strategy to generate font grids section by section, effectively tackling the challenge posed by the continuous output limitations of laser scanning equipment. Furthermore, the team at Peking University innovated by shifting from one-way to four-way simultaneous laser scanning, boosting the text output speed to sixty characters per second.

As the Peking University project team was diligently working on the development of the Chinese character laser scanning typesetting system, the Western language laser typesetting system developed by the British company

Monotype went into production in 1976. Monotype then set its sights on developing a Chinese character laser scanning typesetting system. In early 1979, the company expressed interest in showcasing its Chinese laser scanning phototypesetting system in Beijing and Shanghai and discussed equipment transfer, personnel training, joint venture establishment, and other matters. Encouraged by the State Publication Bureau, the Chinese government consented to a two-week exhibition in Beijing and Shanghai scheduled for October 1979. It was apparent that there was an intention to introduce Monotype's Chinese laser scanning typesetting system into the Chinese market. Faced with this international competition, the Peking University project team was under pressure to develop a principle prototype before Monotype's exhibition in China, to demonstrate China's capability to independently solve the Chinese character laser scanning typesetting challenge without resorting to imports.

As time was pressing, the project team swiftly identified the Shandong Weifang Telecommunication Instrument Factory as the production unit for the system, the Wuxi Electric Meter Factory as the R&D collaborator for the Chinese character terminal, and the Xinhua Printing House as the user. To ensure the rapid and effective completion of this endeavor, the collaborating units were highly motivated to participate in the prototype's development, and the researchers involved in the project were deeply committed. In the spring of 1979, the principle prototype was assembled and commenced its trial phase. After three months of diligent effort, the hardware part's debugging was completed. On July 27, 1979, in the computer room of Peking University's "Research Room of Chinese Character Information Processing Technology," the first sample of an eight-page newspaper produced by China's laser scanning typesetting system was successfully generated.

Although the principle prototype met basic practical standards, it had several shortcomings: the system's large size and suboptimal performance; the Chinese character terminal's display capacity was too limited; the drum typesetter's usage was inconvenient; the phototypesetting process struggled with complex table layouts; and the typesetting software was ill-suited for scientific and technical books with complex symbols and formulas. Clearly, without addressing these issues, the laser scanning phototypesetting system would struggle to transition from the laboratory to the market.

Despite the principle prototype being developed before Monotype's domestic exhibition, it remained a laboratory prototype and was not ready for regular use. However, Monotype's exhibition in China in October 1979 was a significant success. The debate between the printing and publishing sectors and the scientific and technological communities regarding whether to introduce the Monotype system or continue developing a domestic Chinese character laser scanning phototypesetting system became pronounced. The former advocated for importing the Monotype system to meet the immediate needs of domestic publishing, while the latter pushed for more substantial support for the independent development of a Chinese character laser scanning typesetting system.

In February 1980, the Chinese character laser scanning typesetting system underwent a series of enhancements to address the principle prototype's many shortcomings, improving system stability and reducing the imagesetter's size. A critical and urgent task was enhancing the typesetting and printing software, a responsibility that fell to Wang Xuan's wife, Chen Kunqiu, who was gravely ill at the time. Without access to a monitor or disk, relying solely on tape for input, she led her team to write 140,000 lines of assembly language programs that passed testing. In September 1980, the first laser scanning phototypeset book, *Sword of Wu Hao*, produced by Peking University's project team, emerged as the first experimental book printed by the Chinese using a self-developed laser phototypesetting system. The practical research of the Chinese character laser typesetting system began to enter into a period of rapid development.

In early 1980, Peking University signed technical cooperation agreements with HITACHI and Panasonic with the Japanese side supplying terminals, small computers, and large-scale integrated circuit equipment, and Peking University was tasked with developing a practical Chinese character laser typesetting system. This collaboration not only enhanced the software development environment but also system stability. Additionally, a partnership with Wuxi Computer Factory was established to develop a microprocessor-based Chinese character terminal, leading to the introduction of a new type of terminal in 1982 that addressed the issue of limited character display.

The Peking University team sought to safeguard core IP rights through patent applications. However, with no established patent system in China, they initially considered seeking patent protection overseas. Ultimately, European patent applications were filed in Hong Kong in 1982 for "compressed representation of glyphs on computers."

By early 1984, the "computer laser Chinese character editing and typesetting system" was trialed by Xinhua News Agency, marking a significant milestone. After rigorous testing and enhancements, the system's performance stabilized.

In May 1985, the system, now dubbed "Huaguang II," passed national appraisal, and Xinhua News Agency's laser typesetting pilot project also met national acceptance standards. This achievement signified a monumental leap from a principle prototype to a practical prototype for China's Chinese character laser phototypesetting system.

3. Overcoming the "Valley of Death"

In 1984, as China accelerated its reform and opening-up policies, foreign brands, including phototypesetting systems, began to enter the Chinese market. During this period, dozens of newspapers, publishing houses, and printing enterprises inked deals with overseas companies to procure phototypesetting systems. Against this backdrop, the domestically developed Huaguang II system was still nascent and struggled to compete with established foreign brands. To prevent the nascent market for Chinese character laser phototypesetting systems from being dominated by multinational corporations, it was imperative for the system to undergo significant upgrades to reduce both its price and operational costs.

In response to this challenge, the Ministry of Electronic Industry spearheaded the development of a new iteration of the system, dubbed Huaguang III, in October 1984. This advanced system utilized a desktop computer from the American company DG as its main server, while new front-end typesetting software was developed for use on PCs. The Huaguang III system addressed compatibility issues with laser typesetters and sample laser printers, significantly bolstering its competitiveness in the market. Additionally, it could be integrated with the flat plate rotating mirror imagesetter developed by the Changchun Institute of Optics and Fine Mechanics, making it particularly well-suited for book and periodical typesetting. By November 1985, the Huaguang III system was officially introduced to the market.

At the end of September 1986, the first Huaguang III system was introduced to the *Economic Daily*. By October, the fourth edition of *Machine China*, printed by the *Economic Daily*'s printing plant, began utilizing the laser phototypesetter. By December, the system was adopted for every edition. Despite initial plans to use a laser phototypesetter for the entire daily from May 22, 1987, operational challenges led to a unanimous request from the deputy chief editors to revert to lead typesetting just seven days later. The laser phototypesetting system encountered issues such as duplicating characters and lines, missing characters and lines, poor anti-interference performance, scanning jitter, and uneven paper feeding.

Faced with the potential failure of the Huaguang III system test for technological upgrades in the printing and publishing industry, Xia Tianjun, director of the *Economic Daily*'s printing plant, committed to resolving these issues within 15 days. A team of core technical personnel, including Shen Zhongkang, Wang Changmao, Wang Xuan, Xiang Yang, and Kong Zhaoyuan, embarked on a concerted effort to address the system's challenges. By December 1987, after overcoming significant hurdles, the Huaguang III system, and its technological transformation project at the *Economic Daily* became a success, indicating that China's Chinese character laser phototypesetting system had essentially surmounted its major obstacles and was on the path to commercialization. The finalized Huaguang III system was acclaimed internationally for its cost-effectiveness, priced at only RMB 680,000, significantly lower than comparable international products.

4. International Market Entry of Laser Typesetting System

In 1987, the World Bank decided to grant millions of dollars in loans to over twenty colleges and universities in China to support their printing plants in purchasing laser phototypesetting systems. This decision necessitated an international bidding process for the procurement of these systems, attracting major global laser phototypesetter manufacturers to participate. Amid this competitive landscape, five domestic companies in China also prepared to enter the bidding, which emphasized the need for enhanced system stability and reliability. This competitive environment paved the way for the development of the Huaguang IV system, which represented a significant leap in terms of stability and reliability, incorporating the latest equipment and components.

Key advancements of the Huaguang IV system included the use of PCs to ensure on-screen and print output consistency, the introduction of high-resolution displays from the US, and the development of new software and memory technologies to enhance typesetting capabilities. Particularly notable was the TC86 imagesetter controller, which supported a wide range of fonts and advanced typesetting features, achieving a then-unprecedented font restoration speed. Despite its technological prowess, the Huaguang IV system faced challenges in matching the quality of foreign laser printers and typesetters, impacting its global competitiveness.

To address this, the decision was made to incorporate high-quality foreign equipment, such as Canon laser printers and ECRM laser typesetters, significantly enhancing the system's market appeal. This strategic move allowed the

Huaguang IV system to outperform international competitors in the World Bank's bidding process, marking a significant success in both domestic and international markets. This victory led to the retreat of several international companies from the Chinese market.

The success of China's independently developed phototypesetting system under Wang Xuan's leadership did not mark the end of innovation. The team continued to advance the technology, achieving milestones such as the development of a remote newspaper version transmission system, the first satellite transmission of newspaper pages by the *People's Daily*, and the integration of text and color photos in the *Macao Daily News*. These innovations facilitated the computerized management of news acquisition and editing, propelling the domestic Chinese character laser phototypesetting systems into overseas markets, including the Japanese and Korean publishing industries. This journey underscored the potential of China's core technological innovations to compete globally, leveraging independent IP rights to enter developed markets successfully.

5. Establishment of Peking University New Technology Company

In 1985, the Chinese government issued pivotal reforms encouraging educational and research institutions to develop industry-oriented enterprises, aimed at fast-tracking the application of scientific and technological advancements to civilian uses. Against this backdrop, Ding Shisun, the President of Peking University, advocated for establishing a university-run industry. This led to the formation of the Peking University New Technology Company in 1986, initially focused on developing and selling Chinese character laser typesetting systems, particularly excelling in the creation of the typesetting controller. Wang Xuan, a key technical leader and one of the founders, played a pivotal role in the company's direction. In 1989, the production and sales responsibilities of the Huaguang System transitioned from Weifang to a collaborative effort between Peking University New Technology Company and Weifang.

By March 1991, Peking University and Weifang Huaguang concluded their partnership, marking a new chapter where the Peking University New Technology Company, under Wang Xuan's guidance, took sole charge of the laser phototypesetting initiative, rebranding it as the "Peking University Founder Electronic Publishing System." Wang Xuan emerged as the driving force behind Founder, propelling the laser typesetting system into a phase of rapid development. From 1991 to 1994, under Wang's leadership, the team at Peking University catalyzed three major technological revolutions within the newspaper and printing sectors. In 1991, they introduced remote publishing technology based on page description language, significantly enhancing the quality and distribution of newspapers across China; in 1992, they revolutionized color publishing with the development of an open color desktop publishing system, moving away from traditional electronic color separators; and in 1994, they modernized news gathering and editing with a computer-integrated management solution, abandoning the outdated paper and pen methods.

The Founder Electronic Publishing System from Peking University quickly dominated the market, capturing 99% of China's newspaper industry and over 95% of the black-and-white book printing market. This monumental success established Founder as a legendary entity in the realm of electronic publishing.

6. Wang Xuan: Key Figure in Laser Phototypesetting System

In 1975, upon learning about the "Precision Phototypesetting of Chinese Characters" sub-project of the 748 Project from his wife, Chen Kunqiu, Wang Xuan was captivated by its potential for sparking a technological revolution. At that time, China had five research teams working on the Chinese character phototypesetting system, employing analog storage for Chinese character information and considering second or third-generation computers for output. Curious about the international state of phototypesetting, Wang Xuan consulted English literature at the Institute of Scientific and Technical Information of China. His thorough review led him to a groundbreaking decision: to digitally store Chinese character information and leapfrog to developing a fourth-generation laser phototypesetting system, bypassing the prevalent second and third-generation systems. Despite skepticism, Wang Xuan steadfastly pursued his vision.

Wang Xuan was not only an enthusiast for new technologies but also dedicated to turning research into practical, marketable solutions. He believed in the imperative of making applied research outcomes "usable" for them to contribute meaningfully to societal advancement, seeing "academic ambition" and "market dominance" as complementary forces. In 1979, just after producing the first report sample with the principal prototype of laser phototypesetting, Wang Xuan was already planning the Huaguang II system for practical application. By 1985, with the Huaguang II system operational at Xinhua News Agency, he foresaw limitations in its broader adoption and quickly moved to develop a next-generation system. Despite the successful deployment of the Huaguang III system at the *Economic Daily* in 1987, critics deemed it technologically advanced but operationally deficient due to its high cost compared to manual typesetting. With foreign systems entering China, Wang Xuan set a decisive target: by 1988, the new system must display clear technological superiority and capture the Chinese market before 1991 to seize a fleeting opportunity. This led to the successive introduction of the Huaguang IV, Founder 91, and other systems, quickly dominating the Chinese printing and publishing market with their technological and competitive edge.

In addition to his distinctive personal traits, Wang Xuan placed a high priority on team building and talent development. At 56, in 1993, he recognized the swift pace of computer technology advancements and the clear edge young individuals had in this field. Observing that those of middle age or older often struggled to keep pace, potentially leading to critical errors in technical or market strategy, he experienced a pivotal moment. This came when Liu Zhihong, a graduate student, ingeniously challenged Wang Xuan's design for the fifth-generation RIP chip, reinforcing Wang Xuan's belief in the dynamism of youth in the tech domain. Consequently, he chose to step back from active research to champion the growth of young talents, dedicating himself to nurturing a cadre of exceptional young tech minds.

In the mid-1980s, he tasked Xiao Jianguo, a fresh graduate student, with developing a large-screen newspaper typesetting software. He set forth ambitious goals: the software had to gain nationwide adoption, operate with impeccable reliability, and incorporate key technological innovations to enhance typesetting efficiency, such as the ability to tweak lifelike details directly on the computer screen. These rigorous standards propelled Xiao Jianguo and his team into years of focused R&D, culminating in the creation of the world's first practical large-screen, full-page composition and output Chinese newspaper typesetting system, which saw widespread adoption across China.

In 1989, Wang Xuan presented Xiao Jianguo with another challenging project: to pioneer a color publishing technology that seamlessly integrated text and graphics. Motivated by Wang Xuan's guidance and vision, Xiao Jianguo's team, after nearly two years of dedicated effort, developed the world's inaugural color publishing system capable of blending color images with Chinese text.

This innovation sparked a color publishing revolution in the global Chinese newspaper industry, further cementing Wang Xuan's legacy as a mentor who significantly advanced the field through his commitment to empowering the next generation.

In 1990, Wang Xuan anticipated that the advent of an international industrial standard for page description language would eliminate Chinese characters as a "natural barrier" for the West. Recognizing the necessity to align with this standard to break into Hong Kong, Macao, Taiwan, and international markets, Wang Xuan embarked on developing the world's first PostScript Level 2 Chinese interpreter, which would be pivotal for the sixth generation of RIP in laser typesetting. He entrusted this significant task to the younger generation, including doctoral student Yang Zhenkun. The students felt a deep sense of motivation, understanding that success would not only rewrite but also surpass the achievements of the first five generations of RIPs developed under Wang Xuan's guidance. By 1993, they successfully completed the system, prompting Wang Xuan to jubilantly declare, "My European patented technology has been updated by half!" Subsequently, he supported Yang Zhenkun in replacing the original chip with a software algorithm to restore Chinese character font information, leading to the development of the seventh-generation RIP solely through software. This advancement enabled the laser typesetting system to not only dominate the Chinese market but also to successfully penetrate overseas markets.

Reflecting on the journey of laser typesetting R&D, Wang Xuan distilled two key insights. First, the true essence of scientific research lies in "curiosity, the allure of research problems and challenges, and the potentially significant impact on science or industry following a breakthrough. This driving force can engross individuals, fostering dedication and willingness to forsake the pleasures accessible to the average person, and sustain their passionate endeavor for over a decade." Second, allowing young people to freely choose their research topics based on their interests can significantly enhance their creative drive. Wang Xuan's leadership and passion led his team to surmount technical challenges, introduce successive new products, and establish a new electronic publishing industry, ultimately displacing foreign competitors from the Chinese market. This achievement serves as a paradigm of how endogenous innovation technology can transform traditional industries in China.

4.3.2 Case 2: Development and Commercialization of a Container Inspection System

1. Introduction to Tongfang Nuctech's Container Inspection System

"Tongfang Nuctech," also known as Tongfang Nuctech Technology Co., Ltd., originated from Tsinghua University. In November 1998, the inaugural "Tongfang Nuctech container inspection system" was established at Tianlu East Port Customs, commencing trial operations in December 1999. Prior to this, only a few global companies, such as British Aerospace, Germany's Heimann, and France's Schlumberger, had the capability to produce similar products.

The development of the container inspection system marks the most successful and significant project in Tsinghua University's history concerning the transformation of scientific and technological achievements. The "Container Inspection System" is a sophisticated product designed for "rapid, non-intrusive scanning and fluoroscopic inspection" of large freight containers and their transport vehicles. It is essential for monitoring activities at seaports, airports, and inland ports.

The adoption of containers for transporting goods has become a crucial practice within the modern transportation industry, predominantly for the import and export of cargo through ports. Industry insiders have noted that containerization has historically revitalized the waning shipping sector. Since China's economic reform and opening-up policy, the nation's burgeoning foreign trade has increasingly relied on container transport. This method has significantly contributed to the advancement of China's logistics industry and overall economic growth. However, it also presents challenges, notably the increased activity of domestic and international illegal traders exploiting containers for smuggling purposes. Given the substantial size of containers (standard containers measure twenty meters in length and four meters in height) and their capacity to carry large quantities of goods, traditional customs inspections have become increasingly insufficient. Before the advent of the container inspection system, domestic manual inspection rates lingered at a mere 3%, a figure far too low to curb the illegal smuggling of contraband via containers effectively.

Developed during China's 8th Five-Year Plan period, Tsinghua University's container inspection system aims to address these challenges. Its successful implementation has significantly increased the sampling rate and inspection speed at customs (with the installation of this system, the sampling rate has surged from 3% to 50%, and a four-meter tall, twenty-meter long container transport vehicle can now be inspected every two minutes, providing a detailed image of the contents within the container). This advancement poses a substantial deterrent to those considering container-based smuggling operations. Moreover, the system overcomes the limitations of traditional manual unpacking inspections, such as their complexity, time-consuming nature, high labor intensity, and the risk of damaging goods, thereby facilitating faster goods turnover. Table 4-6 outlines the advantages and disadvantages of traditional manual unpacking inspections compared to the container inspection system, highlighting the transformative impact of this technology on customs operations.

Table 4-6 Traditional manual unpacking versus container inspection systems: Pros and cons

	Manual unpacking	Container inspection system
Containers inspected per day (number)	1–2	480/16 hours
Time required to inspect a container	> 120 minutes	2 minutes
Impact on the containers	Frequently damaged	No impact
Labor intensity of testing personnel	High	Low

Source: General Administration of Customs of China, "Modernization and Innovation in Chinese Customs Inspection" (2000).

The operational principle of the container inspection system hinges on the material's absorption rate of X-rays, utilizing radiation imaging technology to facilitate real-time, non-intrusive inspections of contents within containers. This technology was first introduced internationally. In 1991, the world's inaugural container inspection system became operational at Charles de Gaulle Airport in France. Capable of discerning objects as diminutive as cigarette boxes within containers through high-energy X-ray fluoroscopic scanning, this innovation boosted the airport's inspection efficiency by a hundredfold. Its application extended beyond air freight, accommodating "substantially

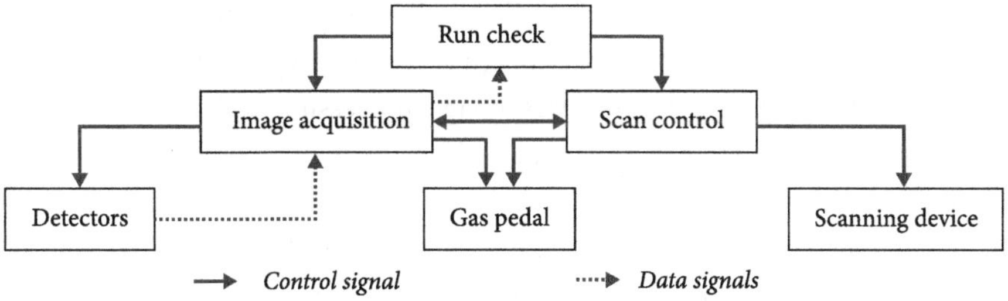

Figure 4-4 Basic composition of the container inspection system

smaller" containers compared to the standard maritime containers. The large container inspection system developed by Tsinghua University, branded as Tongfang Nuctech, represents a sophisticated high-tech system (refer to Figure 4-4 for details).

The Tongfang Nuctech container inspection system is composed of three primary components: the accelerator subsystem, the detector subsystem, and the image processing subsystem, along with a crucial auxiliary device, the container intelligent transmission device (as depicted in Figure 4-5). Its development spanned multiple disciplines and research areas, encompassing accelerator physics, materials science, particle physics, particle technology, nuclear electronics and detection technology, biomedicine, electronic technology and information technology, computer technology, networking, control systems, radiation protection, and mechanical engineering.

The working principles of each part of the Tongfang Nuctech container inspection system are as follows:

a. Accelerator subsystem. This subsystem forms the foundation for imaging. It uses microwave power to excite an accelerating electric field within the accelerator tube, linearly accelerating the electron beam emitted from the electron gun to the energy level required by the system. The accelerated electron beam then bombards a heavy metal target to generate X-rays with strong penetration power.
b. Detector subsystem. This subsystem is tasked with capturing the pulsed X-rays (radiation information) that have passed through the object under inspection and converting them into electrical signals.
c. Image processing subsystem. Its role involves performing high-precision transformation processing of large-scale array detector signals in a strong

interference environment. It handles high-speed projection data acquisition, processing, and real-time imaging synchronized with the radiation pulse. Additionally, it comprises image processing and comprehensive cooperative operation software that fulfills the requirements for container inspection.

d. Container conveyor. Through intelligent control, this device transports the inspected container and its carrier vehicle to the inspection channel for examination. Since the inspection channel is exposed to high doses of X-rays, drivers cannot enter it with their vehicles.

These components work in concert to enable the system to perform "fast non-unpacking scanning and fluoroscopy inspection" on large freight containers, ensuring a highly efficient and effective inspection process.

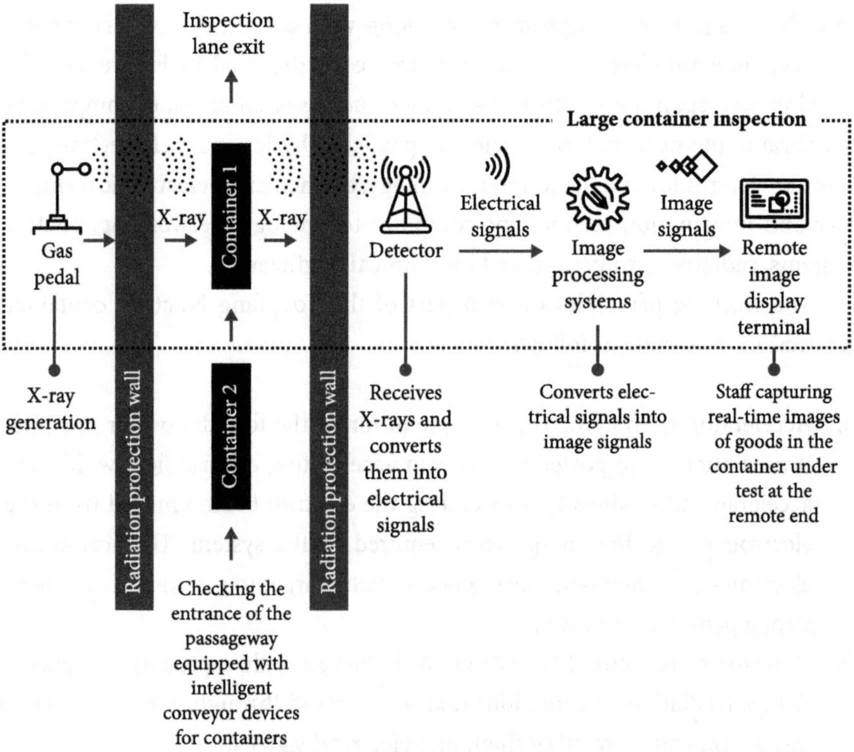

Figure 4-5 Schematic diagram of container inspection system

2. Widespread Usage of Tongfang Nuctech's Container Inspection System

The container inspection system developed by Nuctech employs a 9MeV accelerator and a tri-vehicle cycle transmission mechanism, boasting rapid scanning speeds, high throughput, advanced image processing software, and comprehensive radiation safety measures. According to evaluations by customs after implementation, the system is priced at less than half of its international counterparts yet outperforms similar foreign systems in overall functionality and image clarity.

By 2006, Nuctech's container inspection systems were categorized into three types: fixed, vehicle-mounted mobile, and modular mobile systems, all based on the same principles and components. The fixed systems are permanently installed at customs ports, offering a stable work environment and facilities but requiring significant investment and longer setup times, making them ideal for high-traffic ports.

The vehicle-mounted variant integrates system components onto specialized vehicles, allowing operation on standard roads and flexible site transfers via rail or water, with minimal location constraints. This mobility enables rapid deployment and is suitable for sporadic inspections or ports with varied and lower volumes of traffic.

The modular mobile system combines the best features of fixed and vehicle-mounted systems. It can be disassembled, transported, and reassembled at new locations within approximately four weeks, offering moderate throughput without the need for permanent installations. This versatility makes it suitable for various port types.

Nuctech's dominance in the domestic market is evident as its systems are installed across Chinese customs, spanning over forty maritime, land, and rail ports in more than twenty coastal cities including Dalian, Qingdao, Fuzhou, Shanghai, Tianjin, Shenzhen, and Xiamen. Internationally, Nuctech has carved out a significant market share alongside German, French, and American competitors, with systems purchased by customs in Australia, Turkey, Iran, South Korea, the UAE, and beyond. The adoption of Nuctech systems by these countries has led to increased inspection efficiency, reduced customs workload, lower costs for goods owners, and higher national tariff revenues.

The success of Nuctech's container inspection system in both development and commercial production can largely be attributed to effective technology integration, showcasing an exemplary model of technical innovation (Hu 2010).

3. Technical Integration in the Development of Tongfang Nuctech's Container Inspection System

(1) Innovative idea proposal in the system's development

The theoretical framework for integrating technology into product development is encapsulated by the three-stage model of "technology research, technology integration, and physical development," also known as the "flexible product development model." This model was proposed by Professor Marco Iansiti, who posited that the stages of technological research, technological integration, and physical development could overlap and interact throughout the process.

In the technology research stage, the objective is to search for and evaluate existing technologies, conducting in-depth research into the enterprise's current technological assets to formulate a "product concept." During the physical development stage, the focus shifts to refining and enhancing the technical concept of the product, culminating in the creation of a product prototype. Technological integration serves as the crucial "link" between the R&D phases.

Proposing "product innovation ideas" marks the initial step in innovation, determining the nature of the innovation through new technologies or technical solutions. Mowery and Rosenberg (1979) emphasized the importance of "technology supply promotion," highlighting the interplay between the availability of scientific and technological knowledge, market demand, and innovation. This concept is exemplified by the product innovation behind the Tongfang Nuctech container monitoring system.

In the late 1980s, nuclear technology experts from Tsinghua University and other institutions, after learning that container inspection systems were already under development abroad, undertook overseas visits. In 1989, in response to the use of containers by "illegal enterprises" for smuggling, and amid rising instances of tax evasion and fraud, China Customs initiated discussions with British Aerospace and German Heimann to acquire two large-scale container inspection systems for installation at the Huanggang and Wenjindu customs supervision sites in Shenzhen, areas heavily afflicted by smuggling.[3] During

3. In 1991, Chinese customs officially purchased two sets of fixed, large-scale container inspection systems from the British Aerospace company and the German Heimann company. Construction began in September 1992 at the Huanggang and Wenjindu customs stations in Shenzhen, with the systems becoming operational in August 1994 and June 1994, respectively. The deployment of these systems resulted in significant economic and social benefits.

these negotiations, an expert from Tsinghua University was invited to serve as a technical consultant.

The expert discovered that the three primary technologies encompassed within the container inspection system offered to customs by foreign companies—accelerator, detector, and radiation imaging technology—were all based on "fundamental research and the application of existing technological achievements" at Tsinghua University. This revelation indicated that a similar container inspection system could potentially be developed in China using Tsinghua University's existing technological advancements, leaving a significant impression on the Tsinghua expert.

Furthermore, several Tsinghua University professors, specialists in accelerator, detector, and radiation imaging technology, gathered information from international reports. They convened to discuss the possibility of Tsinghua developing its own container inspection system. Their preliminary findings were that (1) with the growth of China's foreign trade, smuggling issues were expected to worsen, underscoring a strong market demand for such a system, aligning with national interests; (2) Tsinghua possessed all the critical technologies necessary for developing the container inspection system. Though the transport mechanism for container vehicles was outside their area of expertise, the Department of Machinery at Tsinghua University could undertake its development, enabling Tsinghua to create the complete system; (3) developing a container inspection system also held academic value, representing a novel technical application of accelerator, detector, and image processing technologies; (4) foreign-made systems were costly, and their maintenance was expensive. Given China's numerous lands and seaports, a domestically developed system by Tsinghua could significantly address the nation's pressing needs. Consequently, the professors unanimously recommended the rapid development of a container inspection system by Tsinghua.

Acting on this consensus, they promptly wrote to the university's leadership, advocating for the immediate commencement of system development. Their proposal received the leadership's endorsement. In March 1992, the development of the container inspection system officially began.

From this narrative, it's evident that the innovative drive behind the container inspection system's development stemmed from three main factors. First, the inspiration from international counterparts (such as BAE and German Hyman's development of a large-scale container detection system); second,

Tsinghua University's departments holding the essential technologies needed for the system's development (accelerator, detector, and image processing); and third, the alignment with domestic market demands (with China's extensive network of land and sea ports, Tsinghua's development of such a product would significantly meet the country's urgent requirements). In this context, the combination of international developmental trends, internal technological expertise, national interests, and domestic market demand collectively fueled the innovative vision of Tsinghua University's container inspection system innovation team.

(2) Nuctech's 1351 organizational structure development

The commercialization of academic scientific and technological advancements often faces a challenge: the necessary technologies for a single product's development are dispersed across various schools and departments within a university. To address this issue, Tsinghua University mobilized three colleges and departments to collaborate on the development of the container inspection system technology. To facilitate the coordination of this R&D effort, the university adopted a "1/3/5/1" team organization structure.

The "1" at the beginning signifies a vice president responsible for overall management. The "3" represents the collaboration among three schools or departments which brought together essential capabilities for the project.

The "5" in the organization structure represents five specialized working groups, each tasked with a distinct segment of the R&D process, divided as follows:

a. Physics group. This group's primary responsibility is the system's overall design, focusing on defining the physical parameters of the entire system. Key considerations include image clarity, detection speed, and the performance testing of the developed system.
b. Detector and front-end circuit group. The main objective of this team is to develop detectors that can convert radiation signals into electrical signals, forming the foundation for the system's detection capabilities.
c. Signal and image processing group. This group is charged with tasks related to nuclear electronics, radiation imaging, data acquisition, image processing, and nuclear radiation protection. It handles the digitalization of electrical signals, converting them using computers into image signals, and then performing image processing to produce usable outputs.

d. Accelerator group. Tasked with developing a new accelerator specifically for the system, this team works in collaboration with external entities to achieve its objectives, ensuring the system has the necessary power and precision for detection.
e. Mechanical and drag control group. This group's mission is to design and realize the mechanical intelligent transport device for containers, enabling intelligent transportation within the system.

Another "1" refers to a core group comprised of the leaders from each of the five groups. This core group convenes weekly meetings to share progress updates, address any research challenges encountered, and discuss solutions to problems arising within or between the groups. This setup ensures that timely coordination and problem-solving mechanisms are in place, allowing the teams to swiftly adapt to any changes or challenges that may emerge during the development process.

(3) Generation and selection of specific technical solutions

The core group serves as the key decision-maker for the overall technical direction of the container inspection system. Each group, responsible for a different subsystem, submits its technical proposal to the core group for review and decision-making.

Technical selection for the accelerator subsystem. For the development of accelerators, the options included electrostatic accelerators (as used in the container inspection system at Charles de Gaulle International Airport in France in 1991) and linear accelerators. Linear accelerators can be categorized by the type of particles they accelerate (protons or electrons) and by the acceleration method (standing wave or traveling wave). Since the 1970s, the Accelerator Research Center has specialized in the research of electron linear accelerators, holding significant expertise and technological reserves in this area. The electron linear accelerator was also internationally recognized as the superior option. Thus, following the principle of "ensuring reliable performance and development speed," the core group accepted the accelerator group's recommendation and selected the electron linear accelerator approach.

Among electron linear accelerators, there are two types: traveling waves and standing waves. After comparing both, the traveling wave was found to be more reliable, with a longer service life and greater durability. In terms of domestic accelerator component production technology, the traveling wave was deemed more stable. Despite its larger size, its high dose capacity could better ensure the system's overall performance. Ultimately, the core group selected the traveling wave electron linear accelerator, guided by the "principle of reliability and economy."

Technical selection for the image processing subsystem. The selection of technology for the signal and image processing subsystem centered on the choice of computer for image processing. The debate was between developing a specialized computer for the system or using a general-purpose computer. Some argued for a specialized image processor, noting that the processing speed of general-purpose computers at the time might not meet the system's requirements, as evidenced by some foreign products. Conversely, the image processing research group contended that developing a specialized processor would be costly, time-consuming, and risky. They believed that with predicted advancements in computer technology, general-purpose computers would soon offer significantly improved data and image processing speeds. Therefore, using general-purpose computer platforms for developing compatible image processing hardware and software would meet the system's needs, reducing development costs and aligning with international standards. The core group, prioritizing "reliable performance and development speed," opted for the general computer approach.

Following the selection of a general-purpose computer, the next decision was whether to use a workstation or a microcomputer. One perspective was that workstations, being technologically advanced with fast processing speeds and significant development potential, justified their higher cost compared to microcomputers, especially when considering the overall system cost. Others argued that microcomputers, with their lower costs, could sufficiently meet the system's reliability requirements, making workstations unnecessary. In the end, the core group chose the workstation option, adhering to the principle of "prioritizing performance and ensuring reliability."

Technical selection of the detector subsystem. The selection process for the detector subsystem encountered diverging opinions. Some advocated for the development of solid-state detectors, highlighting their compact size, high detection efficiency, and reliability. However, the detector team assessed that their expertise and technological base in solid-state detector research were not sufficiently developed, requiring significant additional funding for further research. Conversely, the laboratory had extensive experience with gas detectors, which offered low costs, stable performance, and longevity. Despite gas detectors' drawbacks, such as their larger size and lower sensitivity for detecting small objects, these issues could be addressed with minimal additional research investment. Ultimately, the core group opted for the gas detector approach, guided by the principle of "ensuring performance while conserving funds."

Post-discussion on technology selection. From the discussions on technical scheme selection for the subsystem development, it's evident that the decision-makers (core group) adhered to three main principles (as shown in Table 4-7): reliable performance, cost-saving, and development speed. "Reliable performance" implies that the chosen technical approach must guarantee the achievement of the set technical standards. "Cost-saving" refers to minimizing R&D expenditures, while "development speed" emphasizes selecting options that expedite the completion of the development task.

A crucial strategy was to leverage as much of the existing technological base of the R&D unit as possible. Utilizing proven and established technological resources not only ensures reliable performance but also reduces subsequent R&D costs, facilitating faster progress. However, this approach introduces potential challenges, such as "path dependence" on the existing knowledge and technological base and a "bias" among developers toward familiar technologies. These factors can influence the objectivity of technology selection, potentially compromising the decision-making process in favor of "speeding up development" at the expense of exploring more innovative or suitable options.

Table 4-7 Guidelines for choosing technical solutions for container inspection system subsystems

Technical solutions to be selected		Selection principle	Selection results
Technology selection for gas pedal subsystems	Use of electrostatic or linear gas pedal	Reliability and speed of development	Use of an electron linear accelerator
	Use of traveling wave or standing wave linear gas pedal	Reliability and economy	Use of traveling wave electron linear gas pedal
Technical choice of image processing subsystem	Specialized or general-purpose machine	Reliability and speed of development	Use of general-purpose computers
	Workstation or microcomputer	Prioritize performance and ensure reliability	Use of workstations
Labor intensity of testing personnel	Fixed or gas detectors	Ensure performance, save money	Use gas detectors

(4) Verification of subsystem technology selection and integration of complete system

Selecting the appropriate technical scheme for the subsystems was a crucial initial step for the Tongfang Nuctech container inspection system. However, to validate the suitability of these technology choices, relevant experiments were necessary, particularly to verify the functionality of the overall system and to confirm the efficacy of the technology selection and development efforts.

In 1993, Tongfang Nuctech achieved a significant milestone by developing a small prototype of the container inspection system in the lab, which was a quarter the size of the original design. This prototype was the Tsinghua team's first integrated product of three key technologies. The successful development of this small prototype, especially the detector and image processing subsystems, validated the technology selection made during the earlier experimental phase.

By August 1995, the development of each subsystem was complete, and the five subsystem development teams came together to construct a 1:1 scale large experimental prototype. This prototype comprised four main components: an X-ray radiation source powered by a traveling wave electron linear accelerator with 9 MeV energy and a 4,000 rad per minute dose rate; a high-energy X-ray array detector and front-end circuit standing 6 meters tall with 1,024 detection channels; a 16-bit analog-digital conversion system, multi-layer pipeline transmission system, and image processing workstation; and a radiation-protected inspection channel measuring 20 meters in length to accommodate a vehicle carrying the container, with dimensions of 4 meters in height and 3 meters in width. Shortly after, the large-scale prototype was successfully developed, and when tested separately, the accelerator, detector, and image processing subsystems all met the expected criteria.

After the successful development of the 1:1 scale experimental prototype, the core group organized comprehensive tests. During these tests, several issues emerged. For example, when the system's main switch was engaged, the accelerator failed to emit X-rays, rendering the image processing unit unable to detect images. This issue was traced back to a discrepancy in the principle of the switch used in the accelerator's development and testing phases, which prevented interchangeability. The problem was rectified by making slight modifications to the accelerator. Initially, the comprehensive indicators of the system prototype did not meet expectations. However, after two months of continuous testing and improvements, the prototype achieved the anticipated performance by October 1995. In January of the following year, the prototype passed national appraisal.

The extensive debugging of the large-scale prototype offered valuable insights to the developers. First, achieving functional realization and cost efficiency in the subsystems is foundational for the overall system's "functional realization and economic saving." Second, solving the coordination issues between subsystems is crucial for the ultimate functionality of the entire system. While the first objective can be attained through leveraging existing technologies and further R&D, the second requires system integration post the successful development of all subsystems, a process through which the necessary insights can only be acquired.

4. Manufacturing-Oriented Technology Integration of Tongfang Nuctech's Container Inspection System

(1) The transition of two-stage technology integration

Transitioning from prototype to commercial manufacturing involves a significant shift: technology integration, initially focused on development, must pivot toward integration aimed at commercial mass production. This was also true for the container inspection system's commercialization. A key aspect of this transition was the need to "transplant with soil" the technological achievements generated during the product development stage by establishing corresponding systems and mechanisms, as discussed by Li and Zhang (2013) and Zhang et al. (2019).

In response, Tsinghua University modified its personnel recruitment system to support the commercial mass production of the container inspection system, encouraging its scientific researchers to contribute to the system's commercial production efforts. Under this policy, doctoral advisors Kang Kejun and Cheng Jianping led additional research teams to participate in the commercial mass production of the container inspection system. Following the founding of Tongfang Nuclear Technology Co., Ltd. in July 1997, the university further motivated researchers from relevant departments to engage with the company as part-time employees. This strategy facilitated the "transplanting with soil (personnel)" of the technical achievements developed during the system's development phase.

Specifically, with subsequent adjustments to the company's organizational structure, the scientific researchers who had joined the company or worked there part-time were integrated into the company's "product system group," "administrative system group," and "engineering system group." This integration significantly enhanced the extent to which the technical achievements from the development phase of the container inspection system were "transplanted with soil (personnel)," ensuring a smooth transition from development to commercial mass production.

(2) Funding sources for prototype commercialization

The commercialization of scientific and technological achievements at universities often faces financial challenges. This was certainly the case for the development and commercial mass production of Tongfang Nuctech's container inspection system. By January 1996, after completing the prototype development, all developers agreed on the urgency of commercializing mass production to capture the market. However, transitioning from prototype to commercial mass production proved more challenging than anticipated, not just technically, but also in securing necessary follow-up funding, as universities typically lack such financial resources.

In November 1996, an agreement was reached between the Customs General Administration and Tsinghua University on the commercial mass production of the container inspection system. The administration agreed to provide an "advance payment" of RMB 2 million in engineering commercialization fees. This financial injection revived the stalled commercialized manufacturing process. Subsequently, Tongfang Company, a university-run enterprise, covered all manufacturing costs and established Tongfang Nuclear Technology Company in July 1997, specializing in manufacturing the system.

Thanks to the development team's efforts, the fixed container inspection system received national product certification in January 1998. The customs noted that the Tsinghua system's overall performance surpassed similar foreign products, particularly in image quality, while costing less than half of those products. Amid an intensified crackdown on smuggling, Tongfang Nuctech's container inspection systems were installed at numerous critical ports. In May 1998, customs expressed a need for a mobile container inspection system. The Customs General Administration initiated the H986 Project in June 1998, ordering ten sets of fixed systems in the first batch and advancing RMB 10 million to Tongfang Nuctech to support the development of a mobile system. In December 1998, a second-phase contract was signed for an additional ten systems.

Tongfang Nuctech's resolution of its initial financial challenges in commercial manufacturing was significantly aided by the system's alignment with the national customs administration's needs, the attention of senior government officials, active cooperation from customs as a user, and the university's strategic coordination, particularly through timely interventions by existing university-run enterprises. This collective effort created a commercial platform for the system's mass production, namely Tongfang Nuclear Technology Company, later renamed Tongfang Nuctech Company.

(3) Establishment of an organizational system for manufacturing

After resolving the financial challenges, the commercial manufacturing of the Tongfang Nuctech container inspection system necessitated the creation of an organization system oriented toward manufacturing. This system included essential components such as a technical organization system, production organization system, and marketing system, all critical for "mass production-oriented technology integration."

Tongfang's establishment of a nuclear technology company in July 1997 served as a commercial platform for developing this mass production organizational system. To facilitate the smooth transition to commercial mass production of the container inspection system, the company organized seven departments: Engineering Marketing, Production, Finance, Quality Assurance, Accelerator, Detector, and Control System. In 1998, a Development Department was formed, primarily focusing on the development of vehicle-mounted systems, which later split into development department I and II, alongside the creation of a technical office.

By July 1999, Tongfang Nuclear Technology Co., Ltd. had integrated its "technical organization system" and "production organization system" into a "product system group," led by the chief engineer (also the vice-general manager). Concurrently, an "administrative system group" was established, encompassing financial and administrative departments, and an "engineering system group," including market and engineering departments.

Under the chief engineer's direction, the product system group featured a technical director, who oversaw the technical organization system, including departments such as Accelerator Technology, Detector, Nuclear Electronics, Software, Radiation Protection, and Control. These departments aligned closely with the Nuclear Technology Research Institute's various research divisions within the Department of Engineering Physics, ensuring ongoing technical support. Additionally, a Machinery Department focused on product aesthetic and structural design improvements, mainly handling structural design and product processing. The production director managed the production organization system, setting up workshops for accelerators, electronics, assembly, an outsourcing manufacturing department, and a production office.

By the end of 2001, to enhance product design comprehensiveness, the Nuclear Technology Company merged the mechanical department, which focused on structural design, with the control department, which concentrated on electrical control design, to form a design center. In late 2003, Tongfang Nuclear Technology Co., Ltd. was restructured into Tongfang Nuctech Technology Co., Ltd. (referred to as "Tongfang Nuctech"), dividing the design center into an overall department and a design department. Meanwhile, the technical organization system was separated into a technical system and a joint research institute. The technical system included the software department, overall department, design department, radiation protection department, and technical office. The joint research institute, created in partnership with the Department of Engineering Physics, focused on new product development and technology planning, adding a mathematics department and a new product department to its structure. This institute primarily dedicated to new product innovation and technological strategy.

(4) Cultivation of complementary assets for commercial mass production

Transitioning from prototype to commercial mass production necessitates the development of "complementary assets"—capabilities crucial for product manufacturing, marketing, and after-sales service. For the commercial mass production of the Tongfang Nuctech container inspection system, establishing these assets was essential within the framework of "mass production-oriented technology integration."

Initially, it was critical to establish the production capacity needed for the commercial mass production of the container inspection system. Upon receiving orders in 1998 and in the absence of national and industry standards for this product in China, Tongfang Nuctech set its own enterprise standards and quality assurance system, modeled after ISO9000. The procurement of parts and accessories, the production of complete machines, and their acceptance were all conducted following this system. Through OEM partnerships, Tongfang Nuctech selected over one hundred domestic and international parts and support suppliers, outsourcing the production of components such as trailers, racks, and casings, and managing these suppliers according to the stipulated quality system requirements. Concurrently, the company expedited the establishment of production bases, including purchasing 17,000 square meters of production space to set up final assembly facilities.

By January 1999, Tongfang Nuctech's integrated manufacturing capacity for the container inspection system had reached 20 sets annually. By 2000, this capacity expanded to 18 sets of fixed inspection systems, 24 sets of vehicle-mounted systems, and 40 sets of combined mobile systems per year. By 2002, the company was launching 2–4 new products annually, customizable to user needs, with standard products delivered within 6–9 months, customized products within 12–15 months, and new products within 15–18 months.

Simultaneously, while enhancing production capacity, Tongfang Nuctech also focused on training customs operators and developing after-sales service capabilities for the use and maintenance of the detection systems. In 1998, the company dispatched personnel to customs offices for on-site consultations and training. By January 1999, the Technical Support Department was established to handle user training, on-site engineering support, and spare parts management. To better serve users in East and South China, the East China Maintenance Service Center and South China Maintenance Service Center were founded in Shanghai and Shenzhen, respectively, in May of the same year. This initiated a three-tier after-sales service system: Tongfang Nuctech headquarters providing technical guidance, spare parts, training, and emergency support to regional centers; regional centers in North, East, and South China offering spare parts and technical support to maintenance stations; and maintenance stations at inspection system sites, staffed with engineers experienced in installation, commissioning, and maintenance. Additionally, Tongfang Nuctech established several overseas maintenance centers responsible for the operation and maintenance of international equipment. These comprehensive efforts have earned the recognition of users.

5. *Summary and Insights*

From the detailed description and analysis provided, several key observations emerge regarding the development and commercial mass production of the container inspection system by Tsinghua University's Tongfang Nuctech Co., Ltd.

First, the project's success in developing and commercially mass-producing the container inspection system can be attributed significantly to effective technology integration, particularly in terms of innovative technology methods. This integration facilitated the blend of novel ideas with practical application leading to groundbreaking advancements.

Second, the development-oriented technology integration played a crucial role in the system's development. The innovation was spurred by international trends, leveraging key technologies already within Tsinghua University's departments, with the motivation further amplified by domestic market demands. These elements synergistically inspired the research team's innovative approaches. The university organized the related departments, each holding a key technology for the container inspection system, to coordinate efforts effectively. The adoption of a "1/3/5/1" team organization structure proved instrumental in advancing the R&D endeavors. The core group's role as the primary decision-maker in technology selection, guided by the principles of "reliable performance, cost efficiency, and development speed," was pivotal in achieving the desired outcomes. Verifying the appropriateness of subsystem technology choices and integrating the entire system were also critical steps. Addressing the subsystems' "function realization" and "cost-saving," followed by solving the "coordination" challenges between subsystems, were achieved through existing technology utilization and comprehensive system integration post all subsystems' successful development.

Third, the transition from prototype to commercial mass production necessitated the implementation of technology integration tailored for commercial scalability. The journey from prototype to commercial production involved strategically "transplanting with soil" the technical achievements from the development stage, facilitated by the establishment of systems and mechanisms at the university level. This transition garnered the attention of senior government officials, secured active user cooperation, and received timely support from existing university-affiliated enterprises, establishing a robust commercial platform for the system's manufacturing. The commercial platform company promptly developed an organizational system for mass production, encompassing technical, production, and marketing systems. Additionally, the company adeptly cultivated "complementary assets," such as production capacity and after-sales service capabilities, for the container inspection system. The strategic development and timely enhancement of these assets significantly propelled the commercial manufacturing process forward.

4.4 Crucial Factors: Scientist Leadership and Contextual Adaptation

4.4.1 Scientist-Led

The genesis of new scientific knowledge marks the beginning of its transformation into business opportunities. Theoretically, anyone with a novel business concept based on this knowledge can bring the concept to fruition by utilizing labor and other resources. However, in the realm of SBI, the intricate nature of knowledge composition means that the researchers behind this knowledge often become catalysts for its commercialization. Their involvement plays a crucial role in bringing new technologies to the market.

Among Nobel Prize-winning scientists from 2000 to 2015, a significant 67.48% have obtained at least one patent. Moreover, 25.2% of these laureates have engaged in collaborative research with companies, served as scientific consultants for corporations, or have been directly employed by these entities. Additionally, 17.07% of Nobel Prize-winning scientists have been involved in founding companies. Looking at the 15 Nobel Prize-winning discoveries that have been commercialized, the corresponding laureates have shown a higher degree of involvement in the commercialization process. Specifically, 12 of these achievements were commercialized with substantial participation from Nobel Prize-winning scientists, and the commercialization of the remaining three also benefited from the scientists' involvement.

4.4.2 Contextual Adaptation in Scientific Ventures

Local Chinese examples also underscore the significance of scientists and original R&D teams in driving innovation. In the laser phototypesetting case, Wang Xuan and his team were pioneers, leading efforts in R&D. Their work with the laser phototypesetting system resulted in significant technological advances in the press and publication field, enabling the industry to "bid farewell to lead and fire," "paper and pen," "newspaper fax machines," "electronic color separators," and "film."

In the case of Tongfang Nuctech, the development of the entire container inspection system involved key technologies across multiple subsystems, including the accelerator, detector, and image processing subsystems, along with crucial auxiliary devices. The development process spanned multidisciplinary fields, engaging in over ten areas and research topics such as accelerators, material science, particle physics, particle technology, nuclear electronics, detection technology, biomedicine, electronic technology and information technology, computer technology, networking, control, and radiation protection. The original core project development team's investment in the industry and their participation in the commercialization of foundational achievements ensured that the university's scientific research seamlessly transitioned into subsequent industrial research, laying a solid foundation for the technology's industrialization.

This discussion highlights the critical role that scientists and original scientific research teams play in the commercialization of scientific achievements, as evidenced by Nobel Prize cases and local Chinese instances. In SBI, given the uncertainty surrounding basic scientific research outcomes, inventors are compelled to continue refining and advancing their work. The involvement of scientists and research teams in the technology commercialization process and their close collaboration with enterprises are essential for successfully bringing scientific discoveries to market.

References

Akasaki, I., H. Amano, Y. Koide, et al. 1989. "Effects of Ain Buffer Layer on Crystallographic Structure and on Electrical and Optical Properties of GaN and Ga1− xAlxN (0 < x ≤ 0.4) Films Grown on Sapphire Substrate by MOVPE." *Journal of Crystal Growth* 98 (1–2): 209–219.

Amano, H., M. Kito, K. Hiramatsu, et al. 1989. "P-type Conduction in Mg-doped GaN Treated with Low-Energy Electron Beam Irradiation (LEEBI)." *Japanese Journal of Applied Physics* 28 (12A): L2112.

Åstebro, T., P. Braunerhjelm, and A. Broström. 2013. "Does Academic Entrepreneurship Pay?" *Industrial and Corporate Change* 22 (1): 281–311.

Braunstein, R. 1955. "Radiative Transitions in Semiconductors." *Physical Review* 99 (6): 1892.

Dottore, A., and S. K. Kassicieh. 2014. "University Patent Holders as Entrepreneurs: Factors That Influence Spinout Activity." *Journal of the Knowledge Economy* 5 (4): 863–891.

Franklin, S. J., M. Wright, and A. Lockett. 2001. "Academic and Surrogate Entrepreneurs in University Spin-Out Companies." *The Journal of Technology Transfer* 26 (1): 127–141.

Grimaldi, R., M. Kenney, D. S. Siegel, et al. 2011. "30 Years after Bayh–Dole: Reassessing Academic Entrepreneurship." *Research Policy* 40 (8): 1045–1057.

Hu, Haifeng. 2010. "Incubation, Transfer, Feedback, and Alliance: The Innovation Development Path of University-Derived Enterprises: The Case of Nuctech Corporation." *China Soft Science*, no. 7: 58–63.

Lam, A. 2011. "What Motivates Academic Scientists to Engage in Research Commercialization: 'Gold,' 'Ribbon' or 'Puzzle'?" *Research Policy* 40 (10): 1354–1368.

Li, Zhengfeng, and Zhang Han. 2013. "Shaping the Social Network of University Technology Transfer 'with Soil Transplantation'—a Case Study of Tongfang Nuctech." *Science and Society* 3 (003): 121–135.

Meyer, M. 2003. "Academic Entrepreneurs or Entrepreneurial Academics? Research-Based Ventures and Public Support Mechanisms." *R&D Management* 33 (2): 107–115.

Min, Dahong. 1992. "The Epoch-Making Changes in China's Newspaper Industry Technology." *Journalism and Communication Research*, no. 3.

Nakamura, S. 1991. "GaN Growth Using GaN Buffer Layer." *Japanese Journal of Applied Physics* 30 (10A): L1705.

Nakamura, S., T. Mukai, M. Senoh, et al. 1992. "Thermal Annealing Effects on p-Type Mg-doped GaN Films." *Japanese Journal of Applied Physics* 31 (2B): L139.

Nakamura S, Mukai T, and Senoh M. 1994. "Candela-Class High-Brightness InGaN/AlGaN Double-Heterostructure Blue-Light-Emitting Diodes." *Applied Physics Letters* 64(13): 1687–1689.

Nakamura, S., M. Senoh, N. Iwasa, et al. 1995. "Superbright Green InGaN Single-Quantum-Well-Structure Light-Emitting Diodes." *Japanese Journal of Applied Physics* 34 (10B): L1332.

Nakamura, S., S. Pearton, and G. Fasol. 2000. *The Blue Laser Diode: The Complete Story*. Berlin: Springer Science & Business Media.

O'Shea, R., T. J. Allen, C. O'Gorman, et al. 2004. "Universities and Technology Transfer: A Review of Academic Entrepreneurship Literature." *Irish Journal of Management* 25 (2).

Shimomura, O., F. H. Johnson, and Y. Saiga. 1962. "Extraction, Purification and Properties of Aequorin, a Bioluminescent Protein from the Luminous Hydromedusan, Aequorea." *Journal of Cellular and Comparative Physiology* 59 (3): 223–239.

———. 1963. "Microdetermination of Calcium by Aequorin Luminescence." *Science* 140 (3573): 1339–1340.

Tsien, R. Y. 1998. "The Green Fluorescent Protein." *Annual Review of Biochemistry* 67 (1): 509–544.

Wang, Xuan. 1996. "From 'Beifangzheng' to the Industrialization of Scientific Research Results." *China Science and Technology Forum* (2): 15–17.

Way, J. C., and M. Chalfie. 1988. "Mec-3, a Homeobox-Containing Gene That Specifies Differentiation of the Touch Receptor Neurons in C. elegans." *Cell* 54 (1): 5–16.

Xu, Zhihong, Yu Xiangdong, and Wang Xinyu. 1996. "Technological Changes Caused by Computers in the Editing and Publishing Industry." *Journal of Editing* (4).

Yang, Ning. 1999. "A Model for the Combination of Industry, Academia, and Research—the Inspiration of the Road of Academician Wang Xuan." *Educational Development Research* (3).

Zhang, Qingzhi, Duan Yongqian, and Lei Jiaxiao. 2015. "A Study of Science-Based Innovation—an Example of Nobel Prize Scientific Achievements to Commercial Products." *Research in Science* 33 (12): 1770–1778.

Zhang, Qingzhi, Yang Yacheng, Zhao Tianyi, et al. 2019. "Scientist Engagement, Knowledge Transfer and Continuous Innovation in Science-Based Firms." *Science Research* (11).

Zheludev, N. 2007. "The Life and Times of the LED—a 100-Year History." *Nature Photonics* 1 (4): 189–192.

Zhou, Cheng. 2010. "How Can the 'Valley of Death' Be Crossed?—a Study of the Industrialization Process of Chinese Character Laser Typesetting System." *Nature Dialectics Letters* (2): 30–42.

CHAPTER 5

Science-Based Industrial Innovation: Science-Based Enterprises

5.1 Science-Based Enterprises

5.1.1 Crucial Role of Innovation in Science-Based Industries

Analyzing the business transformation cases of Nobel Prize achievements over the years reveals the emergence of "science-based enterprises," which are distinct from conventional businesses in the realm of science-based industries. These enterprises play an indispensable role in the commercial conversion of scientific discoveries.

From a management structure perspective, these enterprises leverage a blend of "star scientists and a professional management team" to possess dual capabilities: scientific-technological and commercial. This structure not only maintains a focus on scientific research but also facilitates the efficient utilization of various resources, enabling the rapid commercial transformation of scientific achievements.

Regarding capital sources, the initial funding for these enterprises typically comprises government grants, angel investments, and venture capital. As these enterprises progress beyond their inception phase, their development stage financing primarily stems from venture capital, public offerings, or business collaborations, which may include patent transfers or licensing fees.

The collaboration partners for these enterprises usually consist of PRIs and other businesses. Their partnerships with public scientific research institutions often involve joint scientific research projects, obtaining patent licenses, co-developing products, or transferring patent licenses.

The products developed by these enterprises fall into two categories: commercial products intended directly for consumers and business technologies that offer technology platforms to other institutions or businesses. This approach allows science-based enterprises to navigate and bridge the gap between scientific innovation and market needs effectively.

5.1.2 Science-Driven Enterprise Innovation

The enterprise-led innovation model, grounded in science, involves businesses conducting basic scientific research and undertaking a series of scientific, technological, and commercial efforts to transform scientific discoveries into marketable products. In this model, scientists are embedded within enterprises—meaning these award-winning scientists were initially corporate personnel, and the innovation originates within these enterprises rather than universities or PRIs. This encompasses enterprises that conduct independent basic scientific research to generate new scientific discoveries or collaborate with other businesses for the same purpose. Subsequent stages, including applied research, technology development, product development, and commercialization, are also executed within these enterprises.

Basic scientific research is a catalyst for innovation and enterprise growth. In the mid-to-late 20th century, the emergence of biopharmaceuticals, nanomaterials, new materials, and other fields led to the rise of a new type of entrepreneurial enterprise in the science-based sector, known as the "science-based entrepreneurial firm" (SBEF). According to Pisano (2006), these enterprises engage in basic scientific research with the aim of achieving financial returns. Colombo et al. (2010) describe SBEFs as businesses intending to commercialize scientific achievements from universities and other public research organizations. Karvonen et al. (2013) view such enterprises as derivatives of universities or research institutions, drawing their knowledge primarily from these academic or research sources.

The entrepreneurial teams of these enterprises are typically composed of scientists from universities or research institutions. Their knowledge foundation is rooted in evolving scientific disciplines, and their growth journey is fraught with unpredictable risks. Research indicates that these enterprises face three main challenges: scientific uncertainty, due to the uncodified nature of knowledge in science-based fields requiring extensive research with long, unpredictable outcomes; the need for knowledge integration across multiple disciplines; and the necessity for continuous learning to remain at the forefront of knowledge.

From a policy perspective, given the significant R&D investment, lengthy development cycles, and high risk associated with these enterprises, government support is crucial, especially in the early stages without tangible outcomes. However, some scholars argue against government subsidies, citing the high failure rate of such enterprises and suggesting that government support might reduce their competitiveness, lead to inefficient subsidies, and distort competition. Moreover, there's a concern that government subsidies could crowd out private investment.

At the enterprise level, the composition of the team within such enterprises is dynamic, with new members joining and some founding members departing over time. Initially, the core founding team might lack commercial operation experience, necessitating the establishment of a formal board of directors as the enterprise grows. Research by Colombo and Grilli (2005) indicates that entrepreneurs with prior start-up experience can significantly enhance the development of these enterprises. Audretsch and Lehmann (2004) found that venture capital positively impacts the growth of these businesses.

5.1.3 Review of Relevant Research

Scholars have conducted research on the transformation of university achievements and the growth of university-derived enterprises. Zhang et al. (2017) highlighted that transforming university achievements necessitates "secondary innovation," which stands as a critical challenge in China's current efforts to convert achievements. Yi et al. (2018) and Pang Wen explored the development of university-derived enterprises and the external environment they require. As conduits for the transformation of basic university achievements, science-based entrepreneurial enterprises are pivotal. However, the academic examination of SBEFs, especially detailed studies on their development and evolutionary processes at the micro level, remains insufficient. This research aims to address this gap by focusing on enterprises founded by Nobel Prize-winning scientists to commercialize their basic research findings.

It examines the development and evolution of SBEFs from various angles, including the management team, funding sources, enterprise collaboration, and product development, thereby enriching academic understanding and offering theoretical insights for universities and research institutions in establishing new ventures for technology transfer.

Universities' roles in "knowledge creation, talent cultivation, cultural dissemination, and social service" place them at the forefront of national competitiveness and social development. With unique advantages in original scientific research, universities have become strategic focal points for countries aiming to enhance their scientific and technological innovation capabilities. According to the Ministry of Science and Technology statistics as of 2016, Chinese universities have led over 80% of National NSFC fund projects and major national science and technology projects like the 973 and 863 projects. They have significantly contributed to addressing national economic development challenges, serving major strategic needs, accelerating scientific and technological innovation, fostering industry-academia-research collaboration, and securing a competitive edge in the global arena.

For a considerable period, universities' scientific and technological outputs have predominantly centered around basic research, culminating in publications, monographs, and laboratory prototypes. Bridging these achievements with industrial production has proven challenging, leading to a notably low rate of transformation for scientific and technological accomplishments. Less than 30% of university-generated innovations manage to secure transfer agreements. Of these transferred achievements, only about 30% generate economic benefits, with merely 10% achieving significant economic returns.

In recent years, universities and research institutions have been actively facilitating the commercialization of "SBI achievements" through patent licensing or the establishment of new ventures. SBI achievements are defined as scientific and technological breakthroughs rooted in fundamental science discoveries, capable of creating new technology platforms or developing novel product lines, thereby significantly advancing industry development. "Science-based enterprises" are businesses that transform scientific knowledge into foundational and application-specific technologies, further translating scientific discoveries and theoretical insights into commercial products.

Enterprises grounded in scientific discovery often exhibit business model evolutions distinct from traditional businesses. Typically initiated by universities or PRIs to marketize scientific findings from these entities, these enterprises are characterized as SBEFs. A theoretical framework has been developed to outline their growth, acknowledging their critical role in bridging laboratory knowledge and market transfer, potentially more impactful in technological and economic development than conventional high-tech firms.

SBEFs diverge from high-tech enterprises in their objectives of advancing science and generating wealth. They encounter unique external challenges, such as divergent market applications, a knowledge gap with end-users, and the need for complementary innovations. Internally, SBEFs face significant hurdles, including a lack of commercial expertise and the intensive use of scarce resources.

Typically, SBEFs' products or services represent the cutting-edge of knowledge, encompassing the refinement and advancement of scientific discoveries or innovations. Founders often import their prior experiences from scientific research and academic endeavors into these new ventures, adhering to specific institutional logics to foster and disseminate knowledge. This approach, however, tends to overlook market dynamics, leading to limited management and market adaptability.

The operation of SBEFs hinges on specific resources, fostering the accumulation and assimilation of knowledge across various domains such as science, technology, market, management, and organization. In many science-based fields like biotechnology, new materials, new energy, and nanotechnology, knowledge remains largely uncodified, necessitating prolonged basic research, extended timelines, high R&D costs, and yielding unpredictable outcomes. When research products transition from universities or research institutions to enterprises, the absorptive capacity of these enterprises becomes a significant barrier to technology transfer. Thus, SBEFs must possess robust knowledge integration capabilities. Research by Knockaert et al. (2011) established that higher scientist involvement correlates with quicker development of the first commercial product. Kotha and George (2010) further validated that the costs associated with scientists' technology transfer and direct product development participation significantly influence the commercialization outcomes. Rickne (2006) explored the creative and innovative capacities of SBEF employees within 73 life science industries, concluding that strategic adjustments could enhance these capabilities.

At a macro level, the intricate relationships affecting the inception, growth, and development of SBEFs, including interactions among educational institutions, enterprises, government bodies, and partners, are crucial.

Miozzo et al. (2016) differentiated SBEFs into "externally supported" versus "not externally supported," indicating that those with external backing (such as external investors, institutional support, policy assistance) tend to grow rapidly due to the high uncertainty surrounding the commercialization of their technological achievements, while those lacking such support struggle. Henrekson et al. (2001) highlighted the importance of fostering entrepreneurial environments conducive to start-up creation, comparing scenarios in the United States and Switzerland. Miozzo and colleagues advocated for sustaining and even strengthening ties between core scientists, laboratories, universities, and PRIs. Etzkowitz (2002) emphasized the need for institutional reform, funding and system adjustments, patenting of scientific knowledge, leveraging science-based industries for regional development, and sustaining innovation through the "science-based achievements" transformation model exemplified by MIT. Gambardella and Torrisi (2000) examined the synergy between the knowledge economy's value and SBEFs, proposing that both governments and entrepreneurs should focus on nurturing innovation networks.

The literature review reveals that international research on SBEFs primarily examines the outcomes of their evolution, exploring characteristics and focusing on growth and development post-commercialization, yet lacks a comprehensive theoretical model for their evolutionary process. Domestic research in this field is still in its initial stages.

5.2 Nobel Prize Case Analysis

5.2.1 Case Study and Data Sources

This chapter employs an inductive case study method, finding qualitative multi-case studies particularly effective for ongoing observation of samples over time. In our research, we delved into the founding and development strategies of each sample enterprise, scrutinizing changes within the management team, funding sources, and the progress of technology R&D. The primary focus is on analyzing the characteristics and growth of SBEFs and their pivotal role in SBI.

The selection of enterprises for this study includes those with involvement from Nobel Prize laureates in Physiology or Medicine, Chemistry, and Physics between 1990 and 2017, specifically established to commercialize Nobel Prize-winning achievements. This criterion was chosen because most Nobel Prize-winning contributions in these three natural sciences stem from basic scientific research. The enterprises aiming to commercialize these achievements are deeply intertwined with basic research, epitomizing the quintessential "SBEF." Additionally, Nobel Prize laureates and their achievements garner significant attention, and the enterprises they are involved in typically have abundant information available, facilitating data collection.

The case selection adhered to the following principles:

a. The enterprise originates from a university or research institution, with a Nobel Prize-winning scientist as one of the co-founders.
b. The enterprise's objective is to commercialize Nobel Prize scientific achievements, engaging in application research, development of these achievements, and dedication to their commercialization.
c. The enterprise has been established for a minimum of eight years, i.e., before 2010. Given the close ties to basic science and the extended, risky R&D cycles involved, enterprises with a longer history were chosen to explore their development and evolution. Based on these criteria, this study ultimately selected ten science-based start-ups as case studies, as detailed in Table 5-1. Information on the companies' progression from their inception to August 2018 was gathered.

Data sources included official websites, annual reports, press releases, media coverage, and other channels. Insights into the experiences of founders and managers were primarily obtained through Wikipedia, company websites, personal university web pages, LinkedIn, and the Crunchbase database. For key events and information requiring verification, emails were sent to relevant enterprise personnel for further confirmation.

Table 5-1 Science-based enterprises

Year	Award	Nobel Prize laureates involved in the foundation	Companies founded	Year of foundation	Purpose of foundation
2014	Physics	Shuji Nakamura	Soraa	2008	LED lighting
2009	Chemistry	Thomas A Steitz	Rib-X Pharmaceuticals	2000	New broad-spectrum antibiotics (clinical)
2008	Chemistry	Roger Y. Tsien	Avelas Biosciences	2009	Development of luminescent maps of cancerous tissues

Year	Award	Nobel Prize laureates involved in the foundation	Companies founded	Year of foundation	Purpose of foundation
2006	Chemistry	Roger Kornberg	Cocrystal Discovery	2008	Genetic interventions in clinical trials
2005	Chemistry	Robert Grubbs	Materia	1998	Development and production of catalysts
2000	Chemistry	Alan Heeger	Konarka	2001	Developing organic solar cells
2002	Biomedical	Robert Horvitz	Idun Pharmaceuticals	1993	Targeted drug development for cancer treatment
2000	Biomedical	Paul Greengard	Intra-Cellular Therapies	2002	Development of innovative small molecule drugs
1994	Biomedical	Alfred Gilman	Regeneron Pharmaceuticals	1988	Development of compounds for neurodegenerative diseases
1993	Biomedical	Phillip Sharp	Alnylam Pharmaceuticals	2002	Toward genetically defined target RNAi therapies

5.2.2 Case Results and Analysis

This chapter examines ten Science-Based Entrepreneurial Projects (SBEPs) founded by Nobel Prize laureates to commercialize their Nobel Prize-winning achievements, meticulously tracing the growth trajectories of these SBEPs. Among these, one has declared bankruptcy, two have been acquired, four have gone public, and three remain privately held. The subsequent sections delve into the analysis of SBEPs from four perspectives: the management team, sources of capital, enterprise collaboration, and product R&D.

1. Management Team

This study gathered information on the founding team members and their resumes for ten enterprises from corporate websites, university professors' home pages, LinkedIn, and Crunchbase databases,[1] as outlined in Table 5-2. The

1. Crunchbase is a database covering startup companies and investment institutions (https://www.crunchbase.com/).

founding teams of these ten enterprises comprise a total of 34 members, with team sizes ranging from a minimum of two to a maximum of seven members. Among these founders, 29 possess doctoral degrees, representing 85.29% of the total. Additionally, 23 are university professors, accounting for 67.65% of the total. Importantly, 13 individuals have prior business experience, including founding companies or holding senior management positions in other firms, making up 38.24% of the total. This indicates a high prevalence of academically distinguished scientists within these founding teams.

Table 5-2 Composition of the science-based enterprises' founding teams

Company	Number of founding team members	Hold a doctorate degree	College professor	Have business experience
Soraa	3	2	3	1
Rib-X Pharmaceuticals	5	5	4	1
Avelas Biosciences	2	1	1	1
Cocrystal Discovery	3	3	1	2
Materia	3	2	1	2
Konarka	2	1	1	1
Idun Pharmaceuticals	2	2	2	1
Intra-Cellular Therapies	3	3	1	1
Regeneron Pharmaceuticals	4	4	3	1
Alnylam Pharmaceuticals	7	6	6	2
Total	34	29	23	13

Source: The data was compiled from website data and LinkedIn data.

For instance, Rib-X Pharmaceutical Company, established in 2000 by Nobel Prize-winning scientist Professor Thomas Steitz of New York University, along with professors from UCSC and Yale University, concentrates on creating new broad-spectrum antibiotics to combat antibiotic-resistant infections. Another example is Soraa, founded in 2008 by Nobel Prize-winning scientist Shuji Nakamura, with semiconductor expert Professor Stephen and materials expert Professor Sipek from the University of California, Santa Barbara. Their focus is on the R&D of high-end LEDs.

Moreover, these enterprises often include business-savvy individuals among their founders. Avelas Biosciences, created in 2009 by Nobel laureate Roger Tsien and investor Kevin Kinsella, aims to develop fluorescent protein technology applications for cancer surgery and therapeutic interventions. Kevin Kinsella brings extensive investment experience as the founder of Avalon Venture Capital. Similarly, Sam Lee, co-founder of Cocrystal Discovery, has 17 years of experience in anti-infective drug development, having previously led a team at Icos specializing in this area. Phillip Sharp, co-founder of Alnylam Pharmaceuticals, is not only a Nobel laureate and MIT professor but has also founded companies such as Biogen and Magen Biosciences, demonstrating a blend of scientific excellence and entrepreneurial expertise within these teams.

As the enterprises evolve, changes within the management team exhibit two distinct trends. First, there is a continued effort to attract top-tier scientists as scientific advisors or board members, aiming to either maintain or amplify the enterprise's research capabilities. Second, there is a strategic recruitment of professionals with extensive management experience across various domains, including business development, product development, marketing, finance, and human resources.

For instance, Soraa's development journey, illustrated in Figure 5-1, exemplifies these trends. Founded in 2008 by Shuji Nakamura alongside Professors Steven P. DenBaars and James S. Speck, experts in semicon-

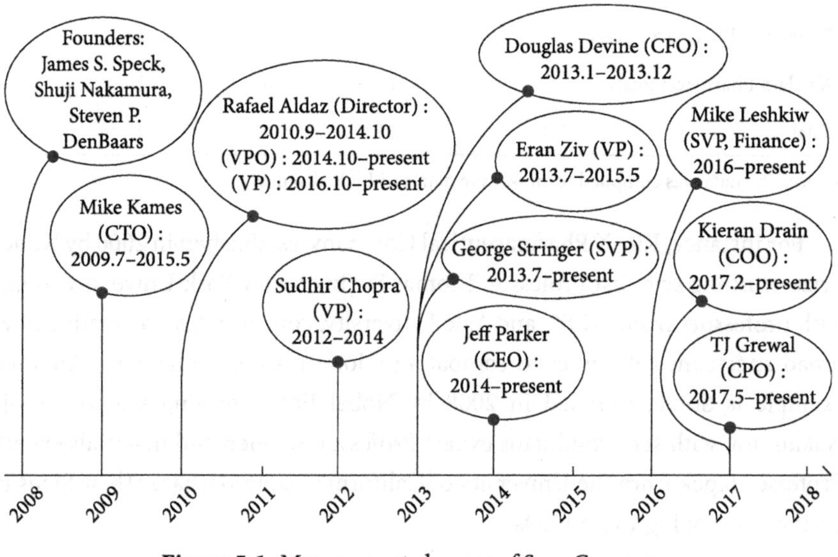

Figure 5-1 Management changes of Sora Company

ductors and materials from the University of California, Santa Barbara, Soraa quickly began to enhance its team. In 2009, Dr. Mike Krames joined as Chief Technology Officer. Prior to Soraa, Dr. Krames was the Executive Vice President at Philips Lighting's laboratory, overseeing product development and technology transfer, bringing a wealth of industry expertise to the role. In 2010, Dr. Rafael Aldaz was brought on board, initially as Development Director, before progressing to Vice President of Operations, and then Vice President of the Enterprise, focusing on LED product development. Dr. Aldaz, who earned a PhD in electrical engineering from Stanford University, previously managed equipment at Philips Lighting Company, spearheading the design and development of advanced high-power LED devices.

With ongoing growth, Jeff Parker was appointed CEO in 2014. Before his tenure at Soraa, Parker served as a senior manager at Rambus, primarily responsible for patent licensing of display technology and the production of LED lamps and lighting fixtures. He is also the founder and CEO of Global Lighting Technologies. Parker brings over 25 years of management experience in the LED, medical, and lighting industries to Soraa, holding more than a hundred patents related to lighting technology.

The management evolution of Regeneron, as depicted in Figure 5-2, illustrates a dynamic blend of scientific innovation and business acumen. Founded in 1989 by Alfred Gilman, a Nobel Prize-winning scientist in Physiology or Medicine, Regeneron initially focused on researching nerve factors and their regenerative potential. Early on, the company made a pivotal decision by recruiting Dr. George Yancopoulos, a renowned young molecular immunologist from Columbia University, as its chief scientist. Under Dr. Yancopoulos's leadership, Regeneron's molecular and cellular biologists achieved numerous significant discoveries and breakthroughs.

As Regeneron progressed, it consistently appointed vice presidents with strong scientific research backgrounds, each tasked with overseeing research in distinct company fields. This strategy underscored Regeneron's dedication to pioneering scientific inquiry.

Parallel to its scientific pursuits, Regeneron recognized the necessity of incorporating seasoned business professionals into its management team to ensure its growth and development. In 2002, Suzanne Blaug, bringing over 15 years of pharmaceutical industry experience, was named Vice President of Marketing and Sales. In 2009, Ned Braunstein, MD, joined Regeneron as Senior Vice President. Before joining Regeneron, Dr. Braunstein had spent 13 years

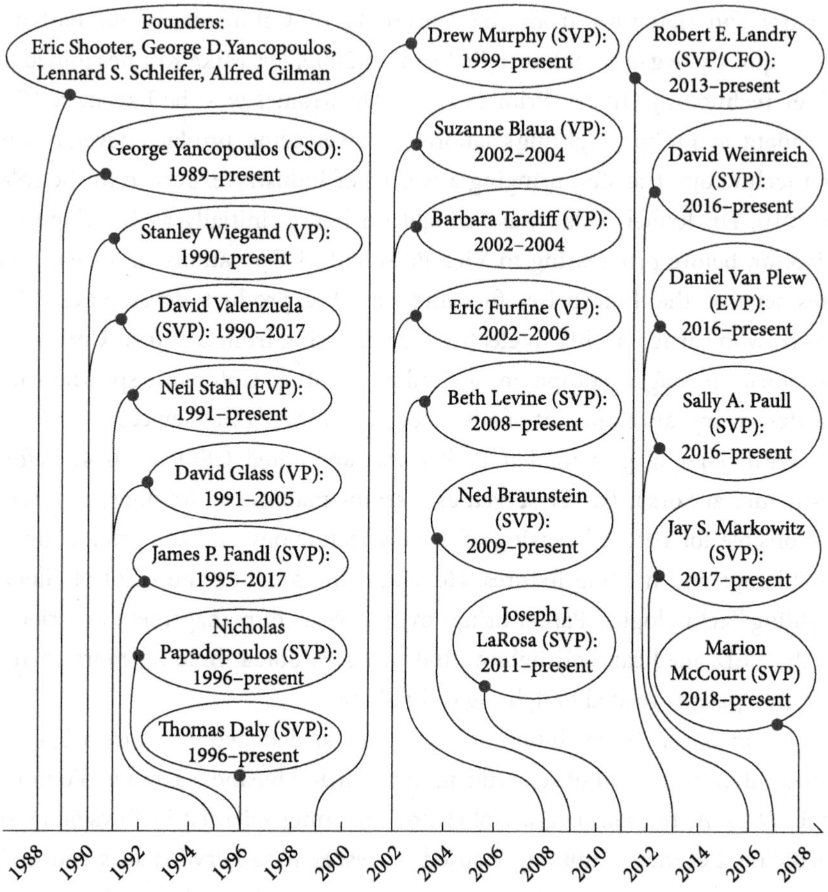

Figure 5-2 Management changes of Regeneron

at the Columbia University College of Physicians and Surgeons, followed by a 9-year tenure at Merck, accumulating extensive expertise in clinical research and technology management.

Regeneron's management team, deeply rooted in the scientific community, is characterized by a profound commitment to research over financial gain. The Vice President of Human Resources highlighted that the company's scientists prioritize research outcomes above financial reports, demonstrating a long-term dedication to scientific advancement rather than immediate financial returns.

The research reveals that a science-based management team exhibits two distinctive features. First, there is a high proportion of scientists within the team who play a pivotal role. The presence of doctoral degree holders in the management team is notably high. Some scientists juggle dual roles, serving as university or research institute professors while also participating in the establishment and management of companies. They are integral to the core management team. On the one hand, a management team comprised of scientists ensures that the enterprise remains at the cutting-edge of scientific research, keeping abreast of the latest scientific developments. On the other hand, it facilitates collaboration with top-tier scientific research institutions. In essence, a scientist-led management team positions SBEFs not just as consumers but as innovators of science. Second, there's an ongoing enhancement of the management team through the inclusion of business-experienced individuals. Beyond incorporating leading scientists, companies also onboard managers with backgrounds in venture capital, investment banking, finance, or product R&D, and even scientists with entrepreneurial experience. This diversified team composition effectively secures the enterprise's resource acquisition and operational management, alongside R&D endeavors. Thus, the SBEFs management team, characterized by a blend of "frontier scientists and business professionals," ensures efficient enterprise operation while maintaining a continuous focus on cutting-edge basic science research.

2. Funding Sources

This research identifies the funding sources for SBEFs through the Crunchbase database and the official databases of the Small Business Innovation Research (SBIR) and Small Business Technology Transfer (STTR) programs.[2] At the outset of their entrepreneurial journey, the primary funding sources were government grants and venture capital, with a few enterprises also securing funds through public offerings. In 1982, the United States enacted the SBIR Act, aimed specifically at funding new small enterprises by providing competitive R&D grants to encourage their participation in commercializing achievements from universities or PRIs. Additionally, the STTR program was established to foster collaboration between small businesses and academic or research institutions. A distinctive aspect of the STTR program is its requirement for small businesses to form formal research partnerships with research institutions, bridging the gap between basic scientific research and the commercialization of its outcomes.

2. SBIR and STTR are two government programs specifically designed to fund small businesses (https://www.sbir.gov/).

Except for Avelas Biosciences, Cocrystal Discovery, and Regeneron, the other seven enterprises discussed in this paper have benefited from SBIR or STTR funding, as detailed in Table 5-3. These seven enterprises have received a total of 37 grants amounting to $28.085 million. The US government's R&D support for these emerging small enterprises is sustained and recurring, with five enterprises receiving SBIR/STTR support more than once, including one enterprise that was supported up to ten times. For example, Soraa received SBIR/STTR funding for six consecutive years from 2009 to 2014 to develop a new generation of energy-saving LED lamps, while Avelas Biosciences was awarded nine grants over three years for technology R&D.

Table 5-3 Science-based enterprises obtaining SBIR/STTR funding

Company	Number of awards	Fee for access ($million)	Year
Soraa	10	1,012.5	2009–2014
Rib-X Pharmaceuticals	3	111.7	2003, 2005
Avelas Biosciences	0	0	—
Cocrystal Discovery	0	0	—
Materia	8	946.3	2006, 2009, 2011, 2012, 2014, 2015
Konarka	8	198	2002-2008
Idun Pharmaceuticals	1	10	1999
Intra-Cellular Therapies	6	470	2003, 2005, 2006, 2008, 2014, 2016
Regeneron Pharmaceuticals	0	0	—
Alnylam Pharmaceuticals	1	60	2006
Total	37	2,808.5	—

Source: The data was compiled from the SBIR/STTR official website database.

Additionally, other government entities like the National Institutes of Health (NIH) and the US Department of Energy provide substantial yearly funding to numerous enterprises. For instance, although Regeneron Pharmaceuticals did not receive SBIR/STTR funding, it was awarded R&D funding by the NIH for five consecutive years from 2006 to 2010, totaling nearly $25.32 million for basic research in new drug development. In 2013, Soraa received $7.95 million in R&D funding from the US Department of Energy, while Materia was awarded $3.8 million and $2 million in 2003 and 2014, respectively.

In conclusion, these nascent enterprises have received varying degrees of R&D support from government agencies at the initial stages of their development. Given the scientific uncertainty and significant R&D risks facing these start-ups, continuous government funding plays a crucial role in supporting early-stage research while mitigating the risk associated with private investment to some extent.

In addition to government support, early-stage funding for enterprises also comes from venture capital, as indicated in Table 5-4. Notably, five enterprises secured their initial investment from investment firms or angel investors in their founding year. For instance, Soraa received a $5 million venture capital investment from Khosla Ventures; Cocrystal Discovery garnered a $10 million angel investment from Phillip Frost; Konarka secured a seed round investment of $1 million from Zero Stage Company upon its establishment; Regeneron Pharmaceuticals was funded with a $1 million seed fund from investors; Alnylam Pharmaceuticals obtained $17 million in venture capital from Polaris Ventures. Additionally, within three years of their inception, another three enterprises received their first venture capital: Rib-X Pharmaceutical Co., Ltd. was awarded round A financing of $2.2 million; Avelas Biosciences received a round A financing of $7.7 million; and Alnylam Pharmaceuticals secured a seed round investment of $24.6 million in private equity. These venture investments were crucial in supporting the early establishment and growth of these enterprises.

It is noteworthy that at their inception, two enterprises sourced capital through public offerings. Regeneron Pharmaceuticals, founded in 1988, raised $99 million through an initial public offering in 1991, just three years post-establishment. Alnylam Pharmaceuticals, established in 2002, went public in 2004, raising $30 million to fund its early basic research. The ability of these two enterprises to successfully go public at such an early stage, capturing market attention, is attributed to their promising scientific prospects, experienced management teams, and strategic alliances.

Table 5-4 Science-based enterprises obtaining SBIR/STTR funding

Company	Year/$/investment source	Company	Year/$/source
Soraa	2008, 5 million, Khosla Ventures 2011, 88.6 million, Khosla Ventures 2013, 8 million, Trinity Capital Investment	Idun	2005, 298 million, acquired by Pfizer 2015, 2 million, venture financing 2015, 1.1 million, debt financing
Rib-X (now Melinta)	2002, 22 million, Warburg Pincus 2003, 63.5 million, Warburg Pincus 2006, 50 million, Warburg Pincus 2009, 25 million, Warburg Pincus 2011, 20 million, Warburg Pincus 2012, 70.5 million, Sanofi Aventis 2014, 70 million, Vatera Healthcare 2015, 97 million, Bond Finance & Venture Capital 2018, 123 million, equity deals	Konarka	2001, 1 million, seed round 2002, 11.2 million, Series B 2004, 18 million, Series C financing 2006, 20 million, Series D 2007, 45 million, 3i Group 2010, 43.8 million, Konica Minolta 2012, unknown, Chapter 11 filing
Avelas Biosciences	2012, 7.7 million, Avalon Ventures 2014, 14.2 million, Avalon Ventures 2016, 20 million, Pharmstandard	Intra- Cellular	2013, 15.3 million, debt financing 2013, 60 million, secondary market 2017, 15 million, equity fundraising
Cocrystal Discovery	2008, 10 million, angel investment 2009, 7.7 million, venture capital 2011, 7.5 million, Teva Pharmaceutical 2014, unknown, acquired by Biozone 2015, 20 million, Series C funding	Alnylam	2002, 17 million, Polaris Venture 2003, 24.6 million, private placement 2004, 30 million, public offering 2011, 10 million, Takeda Pharmaceuticals 2014, 70 million, equity financing
Materia	2014, 14.9 million, Venture Capital	Regeneron	1988, 1 million, angel investment 1991, 99 million, public offering 2016, 8.9 million, equity financing

Source: The data was compiled from the Crunchbase database.

In addition to government support, early-stage funding for enterprises also comes from venture capital, as indicated in Table 5-4. Notably, five enterprises secured their initial investment from investment firms or angel investors in their founding year. For instance, Soraa received a $5 million venture capital investment from Khosla Ventures; Cocrystal Discovery garnered a $10 million angel investment from Phillip Frost; Konarka secured a seed round investment of $1 million from Zero Stage Company upon its establishment; Regeneron Pharmaceuticals was funded with a $1 million seed fund from investors; Alnylam Pharmaceuticals obtained $17 million in venture capital from Polaris Ventures. Additionally, within three years of their inception, another three enterprises received their first venture capital: Rib-X Pharmaceutical Co., Ltd. was awarded round A financing of $2.2 million; Avelas Biosciences received a round A financing of $7.7 million; and Alnylam Pharmaceuticals secured a seed round investment of $24.6 million in private equity. These venture investments were crucial in supporting the early establishment and growth of these enterprises.

It is noteworthy that at their inception, two enterprises sourced capital through public offerings. Regeneron Pharmaceuticals, founded in 1988, raised $99 million through an initial public offering in 1991, just three years post-establishment. Alnylam Pharmaceuticals, established in 2002, went public in 2004, raising $30 million to fund its early basic research. The ability of these two enterprises to successfully go public at such an early stage, capturing market attention, is attributed to their promising scientific prospects, experienced management teams, and strategic alliances.

Due to the ongoing nature of R&D, enterprises entering their growth phase face increased financial demands and must secure continued funding. At this stage, funding sources typically expand to include venture capital, public offerings, business collaborations, and leveraging operational IP rights. For instance, Rib-X Pharmaceutical Company underwent nine rounds of financing, amassing $540 million for drug R&D; Alnylam Pharmaceuticals experienced five financing rounds, securing $780 million for foundational R&D. Among the ten enterprises analyzed, four successfully went public: Rib-X (listed in 2012), Intra-Cellular Therapies (listed in 2014), Regeneron (listed in 1991), and Alnylam (listed in 2004), thereby acquiring funds to sustain their R&D activities through public offerings. Additionally, some enterprises gained funding through business partnerships and the strategic use of IP rights.

For example, in 2011, Rib-X Pharmaceutical entered into a global research collaboration and licensing agreement with Sanofi to develop and commercialize new antibiotics. Under this agreement, Rib-X received an initial payment of $10 million from Sanofi for R&D, with future capital injections promised for reaching certain milestones. Similarly, in 2005, Alnylam licensed its patented technology to Novartis, receiving an upfront payment of $56.8 million. In 2007, Alnylam granted Roche Pharmaceuticals exclusive rights to its RNAi technology patent, securing an advance of $331 million in cash and a $42.5 million equity investment. Regeneron established a strategic partnership with Novartis in 2003, through which Novartis paid Regeneron $27 million and made a $48 million equity investment. That same year, Regeneron and Aventis entered a global partnership to co-develop and commercialize anti-vascular complex drugs, with Aventis paying Regeneron $125 million, including a $45 million investment in new common shares, an $80 million advance for R&D, and an additional $25 million for clinical research funding. Aventis also agreed to pay Regeneron $360 million for achieved milestones. Notably, despite receiving six rounds of financing in addition to government funding over ten years, Konarka filed for bankruptcy protection in June 2012 due to its inability to secure further funds.

In summary, the initial financing for SBEFs primarily originates from government grants and venture capital, with continuous government support for early-stage technology R&D. As enterprises grow, their financial needs escalate, necessitating further financing or public offerings to back basic R&D. Once enterprises achieve significant R&D milestones and possess independent patents or technologies, they can also access funding through business collaborations and the management of IP rights. This diversification of funding sources effectively underpins the substantial R&D expenditures of these enterprises.

3. Business Collaborations

The progress of SBEFs is inextricably linked to extensive collaboration. In reviewing the development trajectories of the enterprises featured in our case studies, their partnerships broadly fall into two categories: academic and business cooperation. Academic cooperation involves engaging in basic scientific research with universities, research institutes, and other PRIs, along with securing technology and patent licenses from these entities. Business cooperation encompasses patent licensing, product R&D, strategic alliances, and establishing business partnerships.

Most of the enterprises examined have engaged in both types of cooperation throughout their development. For instance, Materia Inc., as illustrated in Figure 5-3, secured patent licensing for olefin metathesis technology from the California Institute of Technology in 2001, followed by acquiring patent rights for complementary metathesis catalyst technology from Boston College in 2002. In 2007, Materia obtained a technology license for complementary metathesis catalyst technology from the University of New Orleans, enhancing its product R&D efforts. On the business cooperation front, Materia was granted patent rights for Grubbs catalyst technology from Cymetech in 2004, licensed its metathesis technology platform to Merck in 2006, and in 2008, partnered with Cargill to establish a biochemical enterprise specializing in the production of chemicals and chemical materials.

For another example, Rib-X Pharmaceutical Company, which was renamed Melinta Therapeutics (MT) in 2013, showcases its business collaboration as depicted in Figure 5-4. Its strategic business moves include acquiring the antibiotic Baxdela from Wakunaga Pharmaceutical Company in 2006, which facilitated key clinical trials on Lafarfloxacin. In 2009, MT collaborated with Ligand Company to acquire Captisol® Technology for the development of Rafafloxacin. By 2012, Lafafloxacin had received the FDA's priority review designation, leading to FDA approval for marketing in 2017. The partnership with Wakunaga Pharmaceutical Company significantly expedited the R&D process for new drugs. Furthermore, in 2017, MT acquired The Medicines Company for $270 million, gaining the sales rights in the United States for three drugs: VABOMERE™, Minocin IV®, and ORBACTIV®. This acquisition cemented MT's status as the world's premier pure-play antibiotic company. According to MT's CEO, this acquisition represented a pivotal milestone, merging two companies to harness renowned experts in antibiotic discovery, development, and commercialization. Moreover, this merger maximized synergies between the two entities, enhancing treatment options for patients.

In summary, science-based enterprises not only maintain their leading position in scientific innovation but also, through academic collaboration, they timely access the latest patents from basic scientific research. Their business collaborations significantly reduce R&D timelines, expedite product market entry, and strengthen the market presence of SBEFs.

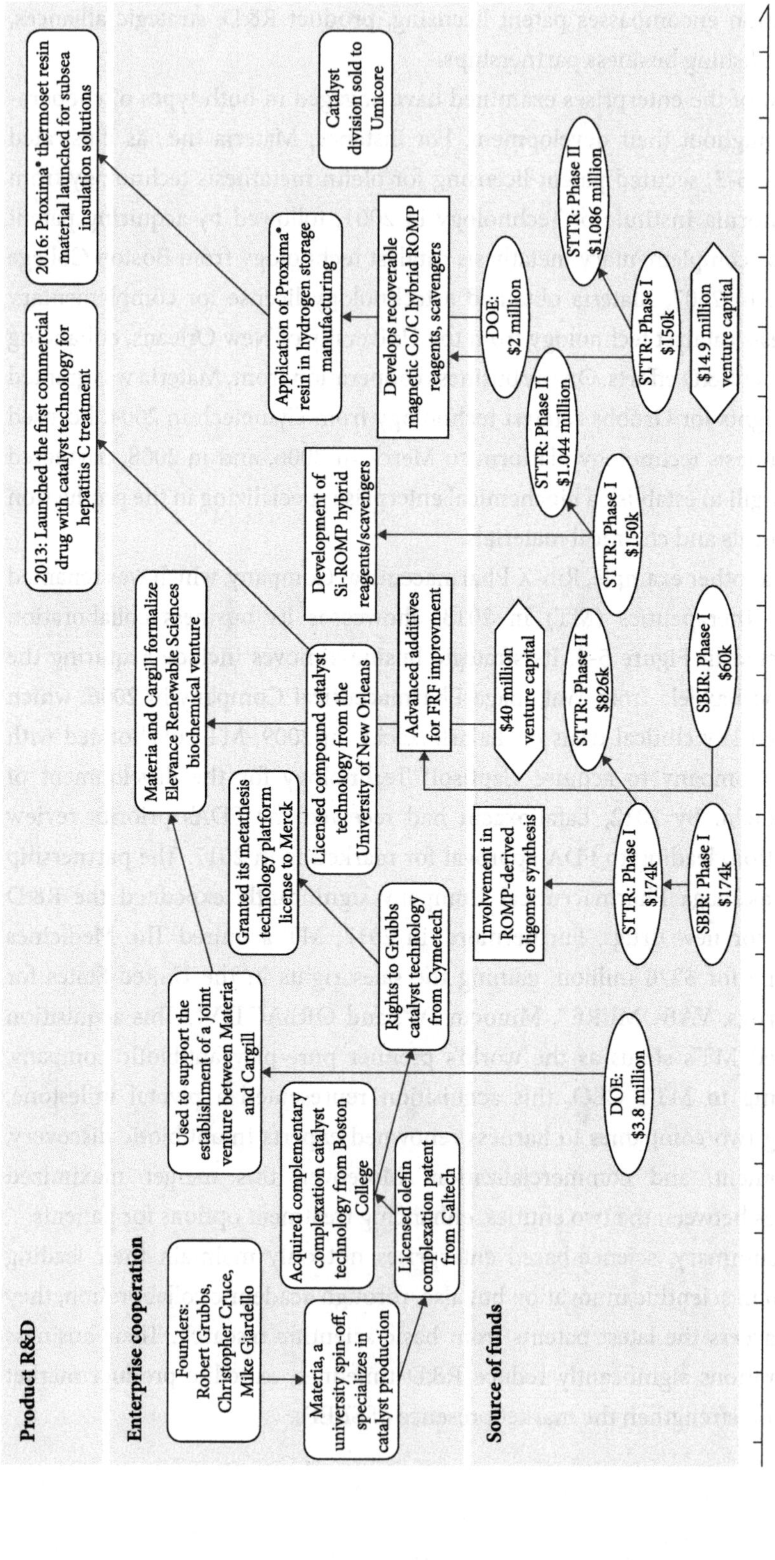

Figure 5-3 Development and evolution of Materia Company

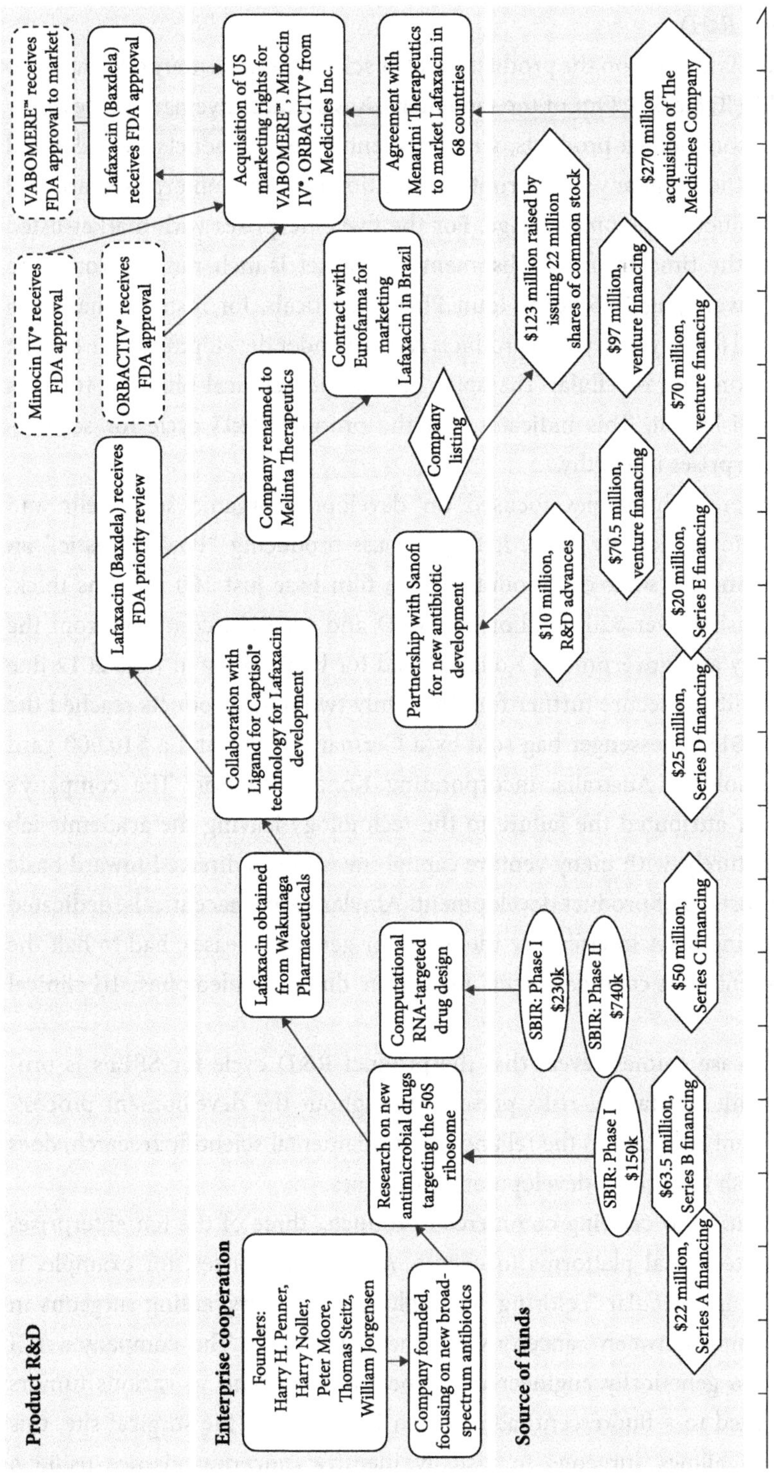

Figure 5-4 Development and evolution of Melita Therapeutics

4. Product R&D

This analysis focuses on the product R&D of science-based enterprises, as summarized in Table 5-5. Out of the ten enterprises studied, five have successfully launched commercial products, while one enterprise's products were delisted following the company's bankruptcy. Additionally, four enterprises are still in the product development stage. For the five enterprises with market-listed products, the time from establishment to market launch ranged from 5 to 20 years, averaging 14.6 years. Idun Pharmaceuticals, for instance, has been operational for 25 years, yet its products remain under development; the earliest product from Intra-Cellular Therapies has reached clinical phase 3, 16 years post-establishment. This indicates that the product R&D cycle for science-based enterprises is lengthy.

Konarka Technologies focused on developing organic solar cells and photovoltaic fabrics. By 2008, it began mass-producing "Power Plastic," an organic thin-film solar cell module with a film base just 100 microns thick. Despite raising over $200 million for R&D and securing contracts from the US military and government, Konarka filed for bankruptcy in June 2012 due to its inability to secure further funding. Only two of its products reached the market: a $180 messenger bag sold by a German retailer and a $10,000 yard umbrella sold in Australia, incorporating Konarka's fabric. The company's co-founder attributed the failure to the technology leaving the academic lab too prematurely, with many venture capital investments directed toward basic research instead of product development. Alnylam Pharmaceuticals, dedicated to developing RNA interference therapies for genetic diseases, had to halt the development of its candidate drug, Revusiran, due to a failed phase III clinical trial.

These case studies reveal that the product R&D cycle for SBEFs is protracted, with substantial risks present throughout the development process. This inherent risk, tied to the reliance on fundamental scientific research, does not diminish as product development progresses.

In addition to creating commercial products, three of the ten enterprises also offer technical platforms to clients. Avelas Biosciences, for example, is advancing a molecular "coloring" technology for tumors, aiding surgeons in distinguishing between cancerous and healthy tissues. The company's ACI AVB-620, a genetically engineered polypeptide, can bind to various tumors and is linked to a fluorescent label. When injected into the surgical site, this compound allows surgeons to visually identify cancerous tissues using a fluorescent imaging device, while healthy tissues remain unlit. This innovative technology is currently in phase 2 clinical trials, demonstrating the diverse applications and potential impacts of science-based enterprises on medical practice.

Table 5-5 Product R&D of SBEFs

Company	Year of foundation	First product availability	Commercial technology	Product description
Soraa	2008	2013	No	LED lighting mainly for commercial environments
Rib-X Pharmaceuticals	2000	2017	No	The company currently has four FDA-approved drugs
Avelas Biosciences	2009	No	Under development	Cancer illumination platform technology for fluorescence guided surgery
Cocrystal Discovery	2008	Clinical Phase 1	No	Discovery and development of new antiviral drugs
Materia	1998	2013	No	Development of new materials using catalytic technology
Konarka	2001	2008 (delisted)	No	R&D of solar cells, photovoltaic fabrics, etc.
Idun Pharmaceuticals	1993	Clinical Phase 2	No	Development of anti-apoptotic and anti-inflammatory drugs
Intra-Cellular Therapies	2002	Clinical Phase 3	No	For preclinical screening of candidate molecules
Regeneron Pharmaceuticals	1988	2008	No	Developing drugs and providing technology platforms for companies
Alnylam Pharmaceuticals	2002	2018	No	RNA-based drugs for rare diseases

Source: The data was compiled based on information gathered from corporate websites.

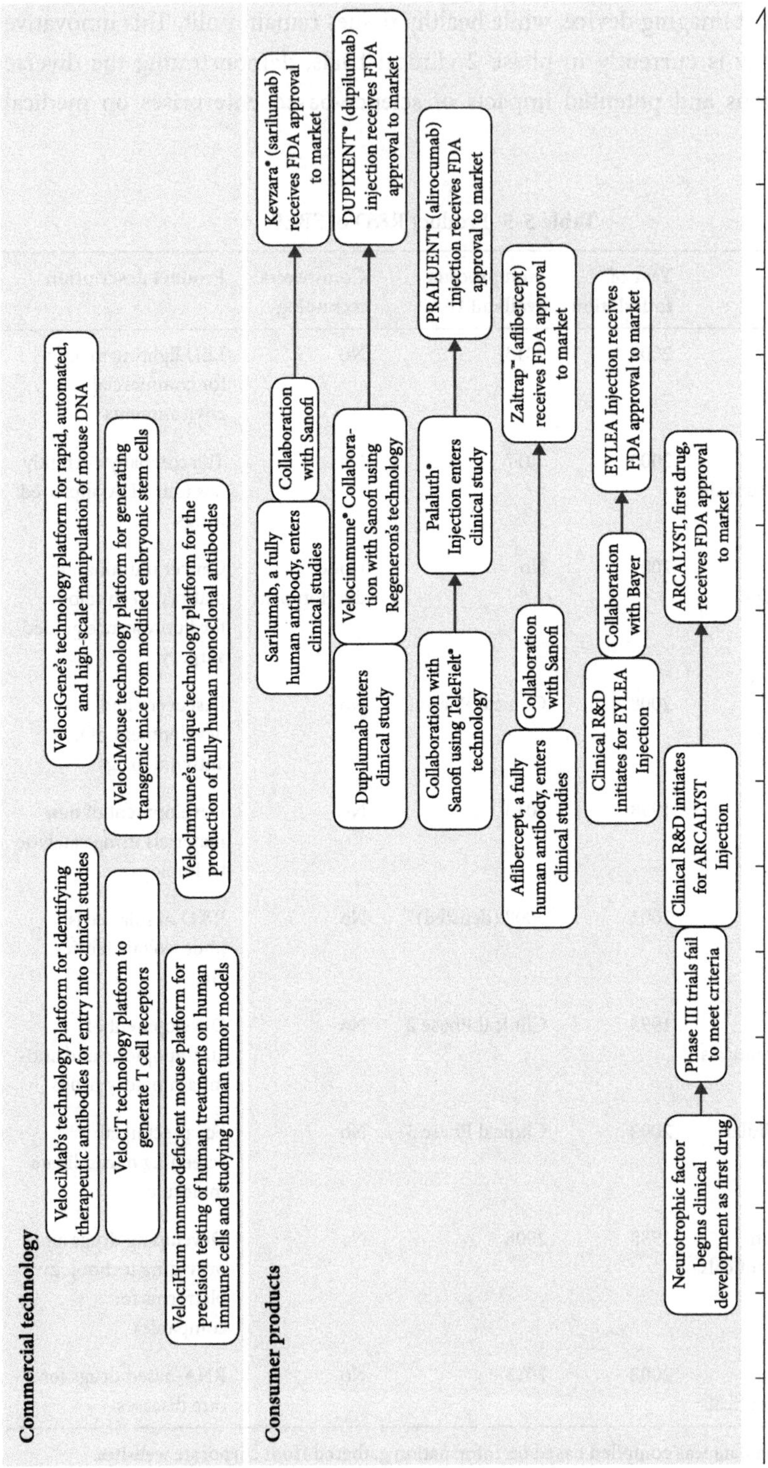

Figure 5-5 Product R&D of Regeneron

Regeneron (as shown in Figure 5-5), established in 1988, had six new drugs approved by the FDA by 2018. The company's inaugural drug, aimed at treating amyotrophic lateral sclerosis with fibro neurotrophin, entered the clinical R&D phase in 1992. ARCALYST® injection, discovered in 2000, entered the clinical stage and received FDA approval in 2008. The company's second product, developed in partnership with Bayer, was EYLEA®, intended for age-related macular degeneration treatment. This product commenced clinical trials in 2004, concluded phase III trials in 2010, and gained FDA approval in 2011. The subsequent four new drugs were developed in collaboration with Sanofi, including Zaltrap™ (aflibercept), which was FDA-approved in 2012; PRALUENT® (alirocumab) injection in 2015; and both DUPIXENT® (dupilumab) injection and Kevzara® (sarilumab) in 2017. Beyond these six self-developed drugs, Regeneron has also created six commercial technology platforms for basic research and drug development. For instance, VelocImmune® is a platform for producing human monoclonal antibodies, with the drug DUPIXENT® developed using this technology. In 2007, Regeneron licensed AstraZeneca to use the VelocImmune® platform for its drug R&D projects, requiring AstraZeneca to pay an annual platform usage fee of $20 million to Regeneron. Additional royalties are due upon the commercialization of antibodies developed with VelocImmune technology.

This analysis highlights that SBEFs face lengthy product development cycles and high risks inherent to their reliance on scientific research. Product R&D within these enterprises can be categorized into two types: commercial products directly used by consumers, such as specific pharmaceuticals, and commercial technologies that offer platform services to other businesses or research entities, such as the VelocImmune® for drug screening and molecular labeling, and other new drug screening platforms.

5.3 Insights from Chinese Case Studies

5.3.1 Evolution and Market Entry of Dawning Computers

On February 17, 2001, the Institute of Computing Technology of the CAS announced a significant accomplishment: the "Dawning 3000 Super Server," a major achievement of the National 863 Program and the CAS Knowledge Innovation Project, successfully reached the international advanced level of similar products at that time. This milestone signifies China's substantial progress in the research, development, and industrialization of independent high technology within the high-performance computing field (Li 2015).

1. Dawning Computer Development Trajectory

Rooted in the Institute of Computing Technology of the CAS, the Dawning series of computers have flourished under the auspices of the 863 Program. Since the "High-Performance Computer Research Center" was founded in 1990 and the development of the Dawning computer commenced, under the guidance of Academician Li Guojie, the Institute has successively unveiled the Dawning No. 1 multiprocessor, Dawning 1000 massively parallel computer, Dawning 1000A, Dawning 2000-I, Dawning 2000-II, and Dawning 3000 cluster architecture super servers.

Furthermore, with the backing of the "9th Five-Year Plan," the Institute of Computing Technology of the CAS, along with its spin-off company "Dawning Company," introduced the Dawning nIetmet server, a high-availability server, NT cluster system, and security server. The architecture of Dawning computers has evolved from symmetric multiprocessor to massively parallel processing and then to cluster architecture. Over more than a decade, the development and industrialization of the Dawning series of high-performance computers have yielded significant achievements, expanding from a single product line to three series—Wochao, Tianyan, and Tiankuo—comprising over 30 models and progressively capturing the market.

(1) Development of Dawning No. 1 parallel computer

The Dawning No. 1 parallel computer, developed successfully in 1993, stands as China's first fully symmetric multiprocessor. It pioneered the implementation of a multi-threading mechanism and fine-grain parallelism within the country. Remarkably, the development cycle of Dawning No. 1 was reduced from the previous five to six years to just one year, compared to the mainframes and supercomputers developed in China during the 1980s. This efficiency was achieved by adopting a strategic approach of focusing on specific tasks while adhering to international standards, significantly reducing the input of human resources and financial investment and resulting in a market-competitive product. Dawning No. 1 charted a new course for the development of high-performance computing in China, earning high praise from users and government agencies.

The development of the Dawning 1000 large-scale parallel machine, initiated in 1993, saw the Intelligent Machine Center lead the breakthrough in China's key technology of "resident routing." This breakthrough led to the successful development of a routing chip connecting a multitude of processors, paving a viable path for China to develop scalable large-scale parallel machines. Dawning 1000 became the first parallel computer in China to achieve an actual operational speed exceeding one billion floating-point operations per second (with a peak speed of 2.5 billion), significantly advancing the application of parallel computing within the country. In 1997, Dawning 1000 was honored with the first prize of the National Science and Technology Progress Award in China's information field, the only award of its kind that year.

(2) Expansion strategy post Dawning 1 and 1000 models

Following the successful development of Dawning 1000 in 1995, the researchers did not rest on their laurels but instead focused on the serialization, commercialization, and value-added upgrading of their existing achievements over the next two years. They expanded their product lineup based on Dawning No. 1 and Dawning 1000, launching more than ten types of multiprocessors tailored to different market demands and began to introduce smaller cluster systems. This move into commercialized high-end computers effectively opened up the market. Dawning Information Industry Co., Ltd., established with an IP investment of RMB 20 million from Dawning No. 1, has gradually emerged as the sole high-end server manufacturer and supplier in China capable of challenging and competing with large international companies.

(3) Evolution of Dawning cluster-structured super server

Since 1997, the development of cluster-structured super servers commenced. Launching the Dawning 2000-I at the end of 1995, followed by Dawning 2000-II at the start of 2000, and Dawning 3000 at the beginning of 2001, essentially introduced a new generation of products annually. The computational speed escalated from 20 billion to 110 billion and then to 400 billion floating-point operations per second, marking a four to five folds increase each year. Concurrently, the processor scale expanded from 34 (Dawning 2000-I) to 164 (Dawning 2000-II) and then to 250 (Dawning 3000). Both Dawning 2000-II and Dawning 3000 utilized multiprocessors as nodes.

The advancement and proliferation of the Dawning series of high-end computers have garnered accolades from both domestic users and international experts.

(4) Milestones with Dawning 3000

The Dawning 3000's computing speed not only achieved but exceeded the original goal of the 863 Plan by forty times, demonstrating its market value in information services, transaction processing, and scientific computing. The Dawning 3000, equipped with 16 processors, is capable of handling eight billion web page visits daily, matching the advanced international level of similar products at that time. Moreover, its cluster operating system and parallel programming environment for users have achieved global recognition.

Dawning 3000 has set several precedents. First, users financed the Dawning 3000 system in its early development phase to establish high-performance computing centers. Among these, the BGI utilizes it for gene sequencing and protein calculations. Second, even before the project's formal evaluation, many users expressed interest in purchasing the official Dawning 3000 series products. To meet user demand, a batch of Dawning 3000 series super server products, was produced successfully based on Dawning 3000 technology. Third, the computational capacity of Dawning 3000 surpassed the high-end computers restricted from export to China by an order of magnitude, breaking the technological embargo imposed by foreign countries.

Ji Fusheng, the former director of the Department of High Technology at the Ministry of Science and Technology, praised the Dawning computer, stating, "As a domestic brand, the Dawning computer has rewritten the rules of the game in China's high-performance computer market. In international bidding projects involving Dawning, all competing manufacturers felt the pressure from Dawning Company. The development of the Dawning computer has directly challenged the embargo containment strategy of the United States against China." In the 1998 evaluation report by the United States Government Accountability Office, the Dawning computer was recognized as a high-performance computer manufactured by China, leading to an adjustment in the US restrictions on computer exports to China to a level that coincided with that of the Dawning computer available in the market at that time.

(5) Timely capital market entry following product market success

Since its establishment in 1995, the Dawning Company's high-end computers have been upgraded in sync with major international firms. In the domestic market, Dawning's upgraded products have been launched earlier than those of foreign competitors, capturing a significant share of the super server market. In 2000, Dawning Company sold over 40 units of the Dawning 2000 super servers. Considering China imports more than 100 large-scale computers annually, the Dawning super server has claimed more than 20% of the market share in terms of sales volume.

In 2001, the Ministry of Finance of the People's Republic of China and the Securities Regulatory Commission approved Dawning Company's backdoor listing on the Hong Kong Main Board Market. Following its listing in Hong Kong, Dawning's net capital surged past $100 million. Over a decade later, leveraging its IP rights, Dawning Company has grown into an enterprise boasting net assets exceeding RMB 800 million, making steady strides in "developing high technology and achieving industrialization."

(6) Introduction of Dawning 4000A

In June 2004, "Dawning 4000A" achieved a "double leap" in both technology and application. With a computing speed of ten trillion operations per second, it became the most powerful supercomputer in China and entered the top ten supercomputers globally for the first time. The launch of "Dawning 4000A" positioned China as the third country, following the United States and Japan, to develop and apply the capability to produce computers with a computing speed of ten trillion operations per second.

The Dawning 4000A supercomputer marked significant advancements in numerous core technologies. Its motherboard and a vast array of system software were independently developed by the Institute of Computing Technology and Dawning Company. Additionally, the Dawning 4000A achieved the world's highest Linpack efficiency among supercomputers utilizing AMD chips. The in-house developed cluster system software suite includes a cluster management system, deployment system, work management system, parallel file system, monitoring system, parallel communication system, high-availability system, and load balancing system, among others. Dawning 4000A also featured various independently developed grid-enabling technologies, including rigid grid computing environment software and grid components developed by Baixing.

Table 5-6 Dawning computer series: Milestones in innovation and enterprise

Period	Product innovation	Enterprise development
1993	Aurora I launched in October	—
1995	Dawning 1000 MPP launched in May	—
1996	—	Aurora established, embarked on industrialization, achieved $20 million in sales
1998	Dawning 2000-I Super Server passed national appraisal in December	—
2000	Dawning 2000-I1 Super Server passed national appraisal in January; Dawning Scalable Parallel Computer System passed national appraisal in November	Achieved market operation and successful listing in Hong Kong, sales exceeded $100 million
2001	Dawning 3000 Super Server passed national appraisal in February	—
2002	Grid-Oriented Linux Super Server launched in September	—
2003	Dawning 4000L Super Server passed acceptance by the Academy of Sciences in March	Dawning's 1,000th supercomputer delivered, boosting domestic high-performance applications
2004	Dawning 4000A grid-oriented HPC passed national appraisal in June	Dawning 4000A Entered the world's top 10 supercomputers, marking China's entry into the top 10
2007	—	Dawning achieved nearly 30% growth for the third consecutive year
2008	Dawning 5000 developed in August, China became the second country to develop a petaflop supercomputer	Dawning 5000A ranked among the world's top 10 supercomputers
2009	—	Dawning achieved first place in China's HPC TOP100 with a 27% market share
2011	—	Dawning topped China's HPC TOP 100 for three consecutive years
2012	—	Dawning maintained high growth and topped China's HPC TOP 100 for four consecutive years
2014	—	Dawning listed on the Shanghai Stock Exchange

In terms of volume, power consumption, usage efficiency, and cost, Dawning 4000A surpassed high-performance computers produced in the United States and Japan. It set multiple global records and applied for 38 patents, including 31 for inventions. As one of the world's top ten supercomputers and a major node of China's State Grid, Dawning 4000A has successfully executed over thirty applications across various fields such as weather forecasting, petroleum seismic data processing, nuclear energy development and utilization, computational fluid dynamics, gene and protein analysis, and material science. This demonstrates its robust capabilities in scientific computing, transaction processing, and information services.

2. Strategic Decisions in Dawning's Growth and Market Introduction

(1) First major decision: Shift from intelligent to parallel processing

In March 1990, leveraging the expertise of the Institute of Computing Technology of the CAS, the High-Performance Computer Research Center, also known as the "Intelligent Center," was established. It was tasked specifically with the development of Dawning high-performance computers. Li Guojie served as the director of the "Intelligent Center" and was the project leader for Dawning No. 1 (Li 2016; Fu 2009).

The decision to develop the Dawning Machine involved choosing between pursuing an intelligent machine or a parallel machine, a choice that would dictate the future direction of high-performance computing. Traditionally, both domestic and international mainframes predominantly relied on integrated circuits for designing operational controller motherboards. Japan's development of fifth-generation intelligent computers also followed this technical path. However, despite the promising application prospects and alignment with international industrial standards, the early development of parallel computers was fraught with great uncertainty. Consequently, the initial aim within the 863 Plan's computer domain was focused on intelligent machines.

Before the development of the Dawning No. 1 parallel machine, a thorough evaluation was conducted by experts including Li Guojie, Ji Fusheng, and Wang Cheng. Li Guojie's expertise lies in intelligent machines, efficient search algorithms, VLSI processor arrays, among other areas. Nevertheless, upon closer examination of the domestic and international trends in computer development, the experts recognized several critical insights. First, the computer industry had established a series of international standards, making the future of "intelligent computers" that diverge from these standards and mainstream computer technology less promising. Second, compared to traditional minicomputers (VAX) and mainframes (IBM mainframe), multiprocessor servers offered distinct cost-effectiveness advantages. Third, the pivotal technology for multiprocessors was software, a field where Chinese expertise could shine, facilitating the transition of technical challenges. Possessing multiprocessor technology would simplify the creation of a product series. Fourth, parallel computer technology was still immature internationally, providing China with an opportunity to catch up.

With the backing of the expert group, the "Intelligent Center" opted to forgo the development of intelligent machines in favor of focusing on general-purpose machines enhanced with intelligent applications. The research direction was set on high-performance computers utilizing parallel processing technology, with "shared memory multiprocessors" identified as the target product.

During its design phase, Dawning No. 1 embraced a clear concept: to be a marketable product rather than merely a scientific research outcome. By adopting a technical route aligned with international standards, the investment in human resources and funding was significantly reduced, and the R&D timeline was considerably shortened. Academician Song Jian, then director of the National Science and Technology Commission, explicitly directed that Dawning 1000 be utilized to establish several high-performance computing centers nationwide.

(2) Second major decision: Transition from supercomputer to super server

After the successful development of the Dawning 1000, a pivotal decision on the future technical direction was required: whether to continue developing "supercomputers" or pivot to "super servers." Supercomputers, primarily utilized for scientific and engineering computations, focus on maximizing computing speed and are highly regarded within the academic community. Super servers, on the other hand, represent a broader category of high-end computers capable of handling scientific and engineering computing, transaction processing, and network services simultaneously, catering to computing-intensive, data-intensive, and communication-intensive applications, respectively. The distinction between the two lies not only in their "applications" but also in their underlying "technologies."

To expedite the commercialization of the research achievements, the Institute of Computing Technology of the CAS founded "Dawning Information Industry Co., Ltd." (hereafter referred to as "Dawning Company") in 1995. The Intelligence Center of the Institute has worked closely with Dawning Company, taking charge of the development of "Dawning series computers."

Upon the completion of the Dawning 1000 "massively parallel machine," 90% of the world's top 500 high-performance computers were categorized as vector machines and massively parallel machines, with cluster systems holding a minor market share. However, the evolution of high-performance computing was already trending toward networking, mainstream architecture, openness, standardization, and diversified applications, with networked applications emerging as a key developmental direction. The Client/Server model was also evolving into its second generation, namely, server aggregation mode. Given these application prospects, super servers were seen as the way forward. Hence, guided by computer standardization and Moore's Law, the Intelligence Center made a bold technological pivot: instead of striving to match the world's top performance in single metrics like computing speed, the focus shifted toward developing super servers with a cluster structure and advancing cluster technology, particularly cluster operating systems, which had yet to become standardized industrially.

Following Dawning 1000, Dawning 2000 was successfully developed, validating the soundness of this strategic decision. By the end of 1999, super servers comprised over 300 of the world's 500 fastest computers. Currently, more than 90% of high-end computers globally are deployed for information services and data processing, with less than 10% dedicated to scientific computing. The success of this second technology choice underscores that the foundation of successful innovation lies in aligning development goals with real needs and technological trends.

Subsequent technology decisions for the Dawning Machine "comprehensively considered factors of technological development, product application, and industrialization," marking a historic contribution to the Dawning Machine's industrial development.

(3) Third major decision: Focused specialization

While Dawning No. 1 and Dawning 1000 marked significant technological achievements, their applications fell short of expectations, primarily due to operating system limitations. The Dawning 1000, having modified the source code of the AT&T UNIX operating system it acquired, successfully developed SNIX, which complied with POSIX industrial standards. However, this alteration in the operating system rendered application software object codes, purchased by users from abroad, incompatible with Dawning machines, thus restricting their broader application.

To enhance the applicability of Dawning machines, Academician Li Guojie resolved to ensure that thousands of commercialized application object codes could operate on Dawning machines without altering the UNIX operating system (IBM AIX operating system) on the nodes. Instead, the strategy was to develop cluster operating systems, which had yet to establish an industrial standard, atop the node operating system. This approach aimed to manage the system, resources, jobs, and files of hundreds of processors within the entire cluster.

The success of both Dawning 2000 and Dawning 3000 validated the soundness of this technical direction. This shift marked the beginning of the transformation in R&D of the Dawning series high-performance computers from a "big and comprehensive, small and comprehensive" approach to a more focused strategy of "doing certain things while refraining from doing others." This shift also represented a significant innovation for Dawning 2000 and Dawning 3000.

(4) Fourth major decision: From general-purpose to niche-targeted

After the launch of Dawning 3000, cluster systems emerged as the mainstream in the high-performance computing market. However, as high-performance computing evolved, the technical barrier for general-purpose clusters lowered, and the unique features of high-end machines prevented rapid updates by users. This necessitated market segmentation based on user needs.

Addressing the bottleneck of traditional general cluster systems became a significant technical challenge for Dawning Company and the Intelligent Center. They faced a decision to transition from supercomputers to super servers and from "general-purpose" super servers to "specialized" products. To broaden the application of Dawning machines, Dawning's R&D objectives shifted from creating a "universal" super server to developing specialized servers tailored for industrial applications.

In the development of the Dawning 4000A, Dawning Company and the Intelligent Center devised several grid components, making the Dawning

4000A a truly grid-oriented server. Starting in 2002, Dawning initiated a "downsizing plan" for super servers, marking the transition from "universal" to "specialized" servers. In 2003, Dawning Company explicitly outlined its high-performance computing development strategy as "integrated computing and specialized applications." Subsequently, the Dawning 4000A and 5000A secured the 10th position in the global top 500 supercomputers list in June 2004 and November 2008, respectively.

3. Impact of Commercialization

(1) Development of the Dawning computer industry

Over the years, with the continuous development of the Dawning series computers, the Dawning computer industry has gradually taken shape. Beginning with Dawning No. 1 and Dawning 1000, and following the establishment of Dawning Company in 1995, Dawning has risen to become one of the top three server brands in China by 2002. Dawning high-performance computers have secured the leading position in domestic high-performance computer market share for 13 consecutive years. The Dawning computer has outperformed imported products in the high-performance cluster field, capturing over 70% of the domestic high-performance computers market and more than 70% of the market share in oil exploration.[3]

(2) Contributions to domestic high-performance computing

Dawning high-performance computer technology has not only provided the company with core technology, but it has also been disseminated to industry key players like Lenovo. The transfer of server storage testing technology to Lenovo has significantly enhanced the quality of Lenovo's servers. Moreover, the joint laboratory established by the Institute of Computing Technology and Chaohua Technology, a listed company, ensures the latter's transition from traditional industry sectors to the information service industry. The information security technology developed for the Dawning Security Server has been invested in Beijing Jingtai Network Technology Co., Ltd., in the form of IP rights. Dawning

3. Li Jun, "The Industrialization of Dawning High-Performance Computers," *Science and Technology Herald* 34, no. 14 (2016); Success story: "The Development Path of 'China Speed'—the Past and Present of Dawning High-Performance Computers," *Computer and Network*, no. 13 (2008).

computer technologies have even made their mark overseas, notably altering the dynamics of China's restrictions by developed countries in this sector.

(3) Enhancing national defense and economic security

Dawning high-performance computers have been integrally linked with national strategic needs, finding extensive applications across various scientific research and production sectors, thereby bolstering China's national defense security and economic development. The Dawning 4000 series supercomputers played a crucial role in computing the entire trajectory of the manned spacecraft, from launch to recovery. They were instrumental in target orbit calculations, space debris orbit determination, spacecraft orbit control, launch meteorological climate monitoring, and spacecraft launch window analysis.

In the biomedical research arena, Dawning high-performance servers are employed in gene computing and sequencing as well as drug molecular design, achieving significant accomplishments in gene computing, sequencing, and pharmaceutical research. Furthermore, Dawning high-performance computers have been successfully utilized in ship design, regional aircraft design, automotive collision simulations, metal catalysis, drug molecules, geological structure and seismic performance analysis, nuclear energy development, electromagnetic radiation, computational fluid dynamics, materials science, and more.

4. Dawning Computers' Scientific Leadership: Li Guojie

In the R&D, as well as the industrialization of Dawning computers, the contributions of Li Guojie have been pivotal. He spearheaded the Dawning Team, significantly accelerating China's efforts to catch up with advanced technology.[4]

(1) Lifelong dedication to computer science

Li Guojie enrolled in the Department of Physics at Peking University in 1962. In 1960s, he worked at the Hunan Shaoyang Wireless Power Plant (now Shaoyang Computer Factory), contributing to the development of desktop computers and focusing on hardware development. After the release of the "733 desktop computer" by the Shaoyang Wireless Power Plant, the Ministry of Electronic

4. Li Jun, "Industrialization of Dawning High-Performance Computers," *Science and Technology Herald* 34, no. 14 (2016); Fu Xianghe, "The Innovation History and Inspiration of Dawning High-Performance Computers," *Engineering Research—Engineering in Interdisciplinary Perspective* 1, no. 3 (September 2009): 282–291.

Industry took significant interest in the project. Subsequently, Li Guojie also engaged in the development of the "154 computer" and "140 computer" for the Ministry of Electronic Industry, marking the beginning of his lifelong commitment to computing.

In 1978, Li Guojie was admitted to the Graduate School of the University of Science and Technology of China, where he studied under Professor Xia Peisu, a pioneer in the computer industry. In 1981, he went on to pursue a doctoral degree at Purdue University in the United States, under the mentorship of Professor Hua Yunsheng, a leading authority in the computer industry. During his doctoral research, Li Guojie made remarkable contributions in three areas: parallel computer systems, efficient search methods, and VLSI array processing. He published numerous papers in prestigious international academic journals and presented at significant international conferences.

(2) Aligning research direction with national needs

In 1985, Li Guojie earned his doctorate from Purdue University and subsequently conducted postdoctoral research on computer architecture at the CSL Laboratory of the University of Illinois. Returning to China with his family in 1987, he became the inaugural director of the National Intelligent Computer Research Center in 1990. Confronted with the challenges in China's computer sector at that time, Li Guojie was acutely aware of the daunting task ahead and resolved that "China must catch up." To inspire his team, he displayed a motivational banner in the Research Center's lobby stating, "How many fights can one have in life," and initiated intensive, dedicated research efforts.

In May 1993, the Dawning No. 1 was unveiled, boasting a computing speed of 640 million operations per second, matching the world's advanced level. Early in 1994, the Dawning No. 1 underwent an extraordinary "trial" in Changsha. When the van carrying the computer overturned, Dawning No. 1 continued to "operate normally and was safe," creating a buzz in Changsha.

The Dawning 1000 and Dawning 2000 were introduced in 1995 and 1998, respectively, followed by the Dawning 3000 supercomputer, a tribute to the new century, reaching a computing speed of 400 billion operations per second, the highest in China at that time. The gap between the Dawning 3000 supercomputer and the latest international supercomputers had significantly narrowed. Upon reviewing the Dawning machines, the esteemed scientist Wang Daheng remarked emotionally, "The Dawning high-performance computer is as significant as two bombs and one satellite."

Under Li Guojie's leadership, the Institute of Computing Technology continued to achieve new heights. In June 2004, the Dawning 4000A was launched, operating at a speed of 11.2 trillion operations per second, making it the most powerful supercomputer in China and placing it among the top ten in the global top 500 computers list.

(3) Bridging scientific research, development, and marketing

Li Guojie contends that the development of computers transcends mere academic pursuit and accolade collection. It primarily serves to fulfill the demands of both the country and the market. When he assumed the role of director at the Research Center in March 1990, China had a mere 757 computers, each with a computing capability of just ten million operations per second from the 1980s, yet there was no market for these computers. The high-performance computer market in China, beyond workstations, was nearly entirely dominated by foreign manufacturers.

Consequently, upon taking office, Li Guojie resolved to concentrate on crafting intelligent computers that could either match or surpass Western advancements. At that time, the prevailing belief among foreign companies was that "no one in China has the capability to develop supercomputers." As such, these companies prioritized launching their higher-performance computers in American and European markets, leaving a gap in the Chinese market for supercomputer research.

Li Guojie turned to the domestic market to overcome these challenges. The Dawning No. 1, introduced in May 1993, performed five times better than similar products previously imported and operated at a speed of 640 million operations per second, yet its cost and size were only a fifth of those counterparts. It quickly gained favor from users, including the software base at Wuhan University. The emergence of Dawning No. 1 also served as a wake-up call to foreign supercomputer manufacturers that they could no longer monopolize China's supercomputer market and had to compete at "relatively fair prices."

Always with an eye on the market, Li Guojie saw the Dawning 2000, with its 110 billion operations per second capability, swiftly enter and win bids for domestic supercomputer projects, including the "BGI Gene Research Center," where it became the primary computer for China's undertaking of 1% of the human gene sequencing tasks.

The introduction of Dawning 4000A soon captured market attention, with Shanghai users promptly expressing their intent to purchase. Three months later, the Dawning 4000A was delivered to Shanghai by six trucks for installation and testing. The test party installed nearly thirty types of large-scale commercial and scientific computing software, with none of the over 500 CPU motherboards needing replacement. At the Shanghai installation signing ceremony, Li Guojie proudly stated, "The significance of Dawning 4000A is not only that we have developed a supercomputer capable of more than ten trillion operations, but also that it satisfies the needs of Chinese users represented by Shanghai for ten trillion operations computers. It stands as one of the world's least demanding computers in terms of room requirements and best performance." Since then, Dawning 4000A has successively offered powerful computing services to domestic sectors including meteorology, shipping, aircraft, automobile, construction, steel, petroleum, and more.

5. *Summary and Insights*

The journey of catching up and innovating with Dawning computers has been both challenging and remarkable, warranting attention to the following aspects:

a. Ambition and confidence. From the inception of the Intelligent Center, the Dawning Team, under Li Guojie's leadership, has always harbored the ambition and confidence to excel, embedding this ethos into the rigorous and winding path of R&D and industrialization efforts.
b. Strategic directional choices. The success of the Dawning computers has hinged on making correct decisions regarding scientific research directions and commercial market niches. Throughout its development and commercialization, four pivotal decisions were made: transitioning "from intelligent machines to parallel machines," shifting "from supercomputers to super servers," evolving "from a broad and comprehensive approach to a focused and specialized strategy," and moving "from general to specific" applications. These strategic adjustments have ensured that Dawning computers not only align with international trends but also meet market demands.
c. Steady and incremental progress. The development and commercialization of Dawning computers began with the Dawning No. 1 parallel computer, subsequently expanding its range based on Dawning No. 1 and Dawning 1000, leading to the development of Dawning cluster structure super servers.

This progression from Dawning 3000, which set multiple precedents, to the emergence of Dawning 4000A, illustrates a methodical and innovative path of continuous improvement.

d. Leadership in science. The pivotal figure behind Dawning computers is Dr. Li Guojie, a dedicated computer science enthusiast who has always believed that "the country's needs direct scientists' efforts." Committed to leading the team from research and computer development to marketization, he has fostered the growth of the Dawning computer industry, advanced the domestic high-performance computer sector, and significantly contributed to enhancing China's national defense security and economic development through his expansive vision and collective team effort.

5.3.2 Zhongwang Boyun's Brake Material Industrialization

In the mid-1980s, the United States, Britain, and France had developed and monopolized the production and preparation technology for carbon / carbon composite materials, essential for aircraft brake pairs. Over the years, China imported a significant number of aircraft, relying on imports for the carbon / carbon composites and brake devices, which are consumable equipment, costing a substantial amount of foreign exchange annually.

In 2003, a research team led by Huang Boyun from Central South University successfully completed the test flight of a domestically produced carbon / carbon brake pair for a large passenger aircraft. This breakthrough involved a theoretical discovery of the microscopic mechanism of atmosphere atom accumulation and friction film formation in the CVI microregion. It marked the first use of all carbon fiber preforms both domestically and internationally, moving away from the foreign approach of using pre-oxidized wire preforms. The team pioneered the reverse directional flow radial thermal gradient CVI pyrolysis carbon deposition technology, representing an integrated innovation. To date, this effort has resulted in 11 national invention patents, with nine already authorized. Additionally, 30 sets of key process equipment across 6 categories, all holding independent IP rights, have been developed (Yang 2012).

This unique technical pathway not only led to the production of a new generation of aviation brake pairs but also resulted in performance metrics surpassing those of international counterparts: service intensity increased by 30%, wear resistance improved by 20%, service life extended by 9%, price reduced by 21%, production efficiency doubled, and high-energy braking performance exceeded by 25% (liu 2012).

Currently, this technology supports an industrial production line capable of producing 10,000 carbon / carbon brake pads annually, generating an output value of RMB 200 million. This achievement has yielded substantial social and economic benefits, breached the foreign high-tech blockade, and secured the localization of carbon / carbon brake materials for hundreds of imported large trunk aircraft in China, bolstering national aviation strategic security, especially in defense.

1. Carbon / Carbon Aviation Brake Material Industrialization Journey

(1) Technology inception

International aviation brake pads come in two varieties: metal disks and carbon disks. The carbon disk, known as "black gold," is lightweight, performs well, boasts high-temperature resistance, and has a long service life. Weight significantly impacts aircraft performance, necessitating efforts to reduce even a single gram. Carbon disks weigh merely a quarter of their metal counterparts. However, China has historically depended on imports for these components, which are not only costly but also subject to restrictions.

Carbon / carbon aviation brake material is a sophisticated composite material reinforced with carbon fiber and embedded in a carbon matrix. Carbon fiber acts much like the steel reinforcement in concrete, while carbon atoms resemble the cement and sand. Carbon fibers are about one-tenth the thickness of human hair, with carbon atoms being invisible and intangible. This composite material leverages carbon fiber's reinforcement capabilities and carbon's matrix properties to create a substance with low specific gravity, low density, and excellent performance. The preparation process for this material is complex, requiring the orderly arrangement of countless carbon atoms among carbon fibers, with controllable arrangement structures and processes.

By the late 1960s, various countries began developing carbon / carbon composites for aircraft brakes. By the mid-1980s, the technology in the United States, Britain, and France had matured, and these materials had been in production for over two decades.

Although China initiated research in the late 1970s, it had yet to achieve significant technological breakthroughs. The technology and production of carbon / carbon composites were monopolized by companies in a few countries, with the knowledge being closely guarded. About 50% of China's large civil aviation and military aircraft utilize carbon / carbon composite aviation brake pairs. Specifically, large civil aviation aircraft alone require the replacement of 10,000 units annually, all relying on imports. This not only drives up costs, with an annual foreign exchange expenditure of nearly $50 million, but also subjects the country to restrictions, jeopardizing aviation strategic safety.

In pursuit of breaking the international technical blockade and catching up with or surpassing the global pace of research in high-performance carbon / carbon aviation brake materials, the research group at Central South University, focusing on "preparation technology of high-performance carbon / carbon aviation brake materials," embarked on basic research in 1986.

(2) Lab-scale research

At the time, the prevailing manufacturing technologies globally utilized uniform temperature furnaces. Faced with the choice between uniform temperature furnaces and gradient furnaces, the decision was clear: uniform temperature furnaces were simpler and technologically mature, whereas gradient furnaces presented significant risks. After thorough comparisons, Huang Boyun concluded that as scientists and technologists, there was a duty to innovate for the nation's strength. He stated, "I realized that other countries' technologies were not the most advanced. If we were to merely follow them, we would never surpass them. We must dare to innovate and take risks, even at the risk of failure."

However, the process of developing carbon / carbon brake materials was not a simple act of repetition or imitation but a new venture and creation, significantly more challenging than the preparation of metal materials. Attempts to send team members abroad for study were made. During one of Huang Boyun's visits to a renowned foreign company, he was told, "I'm sorry, you cannot visit our production workshop. Our technology is twenty years ahead of yours," implying an insurmountable technological gap. Upon purchasing a sample for study, the team discovered it was a defective product, fueling their determination. Huang Boyun declared, "With the foreign technology blockade, we cannot depend on others. We must innovate independently. We should not only develop such products themselves but also aim to surpass the existing technology!"

Scientific endeavor requires not just bravery but substantial expertise. The research group, comprised of experts in powder metallurgy materials, had ample experience in preparing metal-based brake disks. However, powder metallurgy focuses on metal materials, while carbon / carbon composites are inorganic non-metallic materials, representing divergent research paths within materials science. To build a solid research foundation, they began exploring the distinct principles and properties of powder metallurgy and carbon / carbon materials.

Research group members Huang Boyun, Xiong Xiang, Huang Qizhong, Zou Zhiqiang, Yi Maozhong, Zhang Hongbo, Jiang Jianchun, and others diligently acquired comprehensive knowledge on carbon / carbon composites through extensive reading and rigorous study, culminating in significant research outcomes:

a. Rapid CVI technology for carbon / carbon composites. The team discovered the corresponding relationship between CVI parameters, intermediate products, and pyrolytic carbon, unveiling the pyrolytic deposition mechanism for both small and macromolecular products. They identified how carbon source concentration affects the content of intermediate products under H2 and N2 carrier gases, resolving the bottleneck in efficiently preparing carbon / carbon composites and enhancing the CVI densification rate by 30%. These advancements were applied to the CVI densification of carbon / carbon composite engine components.
b. Ablation resistance technology of carbon / carbon composites. The distribution and formation mechanism of residual stress in (Zr, Ti) C matrix modified carbon / carbon composites were elucidated, alongside proposing a thermal stress damage mechanism. The team developed methods for preparing ZrB2 SiC ceramic layers using SPS and RSI, creating coating / matrix modified gradient structure components. This innovation addressed the high-temperature oxidation and ablation challenges in carbon / carbon composites, with applications in space engine nozzles and C/C gas rudders.
c. Low-cost preparation technology of carbon / carbon composites. In-depth studies on carbon fiber preforms, chemical vapor deposition, and high-temperature heat treatment processes led to the proposal of a multi-column chemical vapor deposition furnace method. This breakthrough in rapid chemical deposition addressed low-cost manufacturing challenges, significantly enhancing thermal field materials technology. These achievements have been utilized in new energy sectors.
d. Carbon/ceramic friction material technology. The group invented technologies for increasing friction and reducing wear, including a low-cost method for preparing C/C-SiC friction materials through "warm

compaction in situ reaction," a non-immersion directional silicon infiltration technique, and a "carbon ceramic metal dual" friction pair technology. These innovations extended the service life of friction pairs to over four times that of powder metallurgy brake pads and marked the first successful application of such friction pairs in high-speed, heavy-load, and complex environment brake systems. The application scope of carbon/ ceramic friction materials has been significantly broadened.

In 1996, under Huang Boyun's leadership, the research group completed the basic laboratory research on the "preparation technology of high-performance carbon / carbon aviation brake materials" after extensive experimentation, mastering the fundamental preparation methods. In 1997, their findings passed the evaluation and moved to industrial testing. By 1998, they progressed to the industrial experimentation phase.

(3) Industrial trials

In 1998, the project transitioned to industrial experimentation as a national key initiative, backed by an investment of RMB 150 million from the former State Planning Commission. The transition from laboratory research to industrial testing, scaling from small to large samples, was not a straightforward technology transfer. Parameters varied significantly, leading to numerous experimental failures, re-analyses, and retries before success was achieved.

Early in 1998, the research team designed a small set of equipment they believed could produce high-performance carbon / carbon aviation brake materials. However, the experimental results yielded incomprehensible carbon clusters, far from meeting practical application standards. Yet another experiment ended in failure ...

Faced with repeated setbacks, the team looked to Academician Huang Boyun, questioning whether success was attainable following this path. Huang Boyun understood that conquering this project meant achieving a major breakthrough through the integration of numerous technological inventions. He was prepared for the monumental challenges ahead, resolving to proceed despite the obstacles.

To expedite progress on the "preparation technology of carbon / carbon aviation brake materials," Huang Boyun, as the project's lead, organized over sixty engineering and technical personnel from disciplines such as materials science, chemistry, metallurgy, machinery, electronics, and aviation. The project was divided into six subtopics, including manufacturing methods, key process equipment, oxidation coating technology, material structure and properties, performance testing techniques, and airworthiness standards, tackled concurrently.

By 1999, the sub-research groups had achieved new breakthroughs, including the invention of the differential thermal vapor phase precipitation furnace, which sped up carbon atom deposition. In August, the first batch of samples was released. However, the path to innovation was fraught with challenges. In September 2000, after extensive testing, the strength performance of the samples was found to be significantly inferior to similar products, a significant setback that, instead of discouraging the team, spurred them to intensify their efforts.

Their unwavering sense of responsibility fueled relentless work, culminating in a major breakthrough in 2002. They discovered the friction film formation mechanism under micro atmosphere control and braking, pioneered directional flow thermal gradient carbon atom deposition technology, and established a novel technical route distinct from foreign methodologies, with key technologies reaching international leadership levels.

Additionally, the team developed laboratory material performance testing and evaluation methods, established China's first ground test device for carbon / carbon brake materials, and formulated the country's inaugural airworthiness standard.

(4) Industrialization

To rapidly convert scientific achievements into cutting-edge productivity, Central South University established an industrial demonstration production line capable of producing 10,000 carbon / carbon brake pads annually. On January 20, 2003, the domestically developed carbon brake pair for the B757-200 aircraft underwent a successful flight test at Haikou Meilan Airport. A subsequent reinstallation and test flight on September 20, 2003, also proved successful. The successful landing of the B757-200 at the airport was a moment of triumph for the "preparation technology of high-performance carbon / carbon aviation brake materials" research team, marking the culmination of two decades of effort. On December 27, 2003, Central South University received the Civil Aviation Administration of China's first approval for manufacturing carbon / carbon brake pairs for large aircraft and the aerospace product process approval, leading to widespread adoption of their products in aviation.

In July 2001, Hunan Boyun New Materials Co., Ltd. was founded with a registered capital of RMB 36 million. In May 2006, the company increased the registered capital to RMB 58 million and giving employees a 14.56% share of the company.

The construction of Hunan Boyun New Materials Co., Ltd.'s entrepreneurship base began on January 15, 2004, with an investment of RMB 150 million. Once operational, it was projected to generate an annual output value of RMB 200 million, establishing a significant production base for high-performance carbon / carbon aviation brake materials.

Boyun New Materials and Changsha Xinhang, instrumental in transforming new material achievements, partnered with Honeywell Group, a leading aerospace product supplier, to secure the wheel and brake system project for the C919, leading to the establishment of Honeywell Boyun Aviation Systems (Hunan) Co., Ltd. in 2012. This collaboration marked a significant milestone for domestic production in the C919 large aircraft project.

The partnership aimed to leverage the historic opportunity presented by the large aircraft project to enhance technological and manufacturing capabilities. Despite the daunting scale of the joint venture, Huang Boyun's persistence saw the negotiation through to success.

The development of carbon / carbon composites has evolved, with production time reduced from nearly half a year to two months, alongside efforts to improve performance and extend service life. Significant progress has been made, including reducing the cost of civil carbon / carbon materials by over 50%.

Boyun Company's technological innovation system is shown in Figure 5-6.

2. Industrialization Catalysts

(1) National research funding support

Upon his return from abroad in 1988, Huang Boyun was awarded a research start-up fund of RMB 300,000. Since 1997, Huang Boyun and his innovation team have embarked on approximately 150 scientific research projects. This influx of research funding in the initial stages provided crucial support, encouraging and enabling Huang Boyun and his team to complete the fundamental laboratory research on the "preparation technology of high-performance carbon / carbon aviation brake materials" and to master the essential preparation techniques.

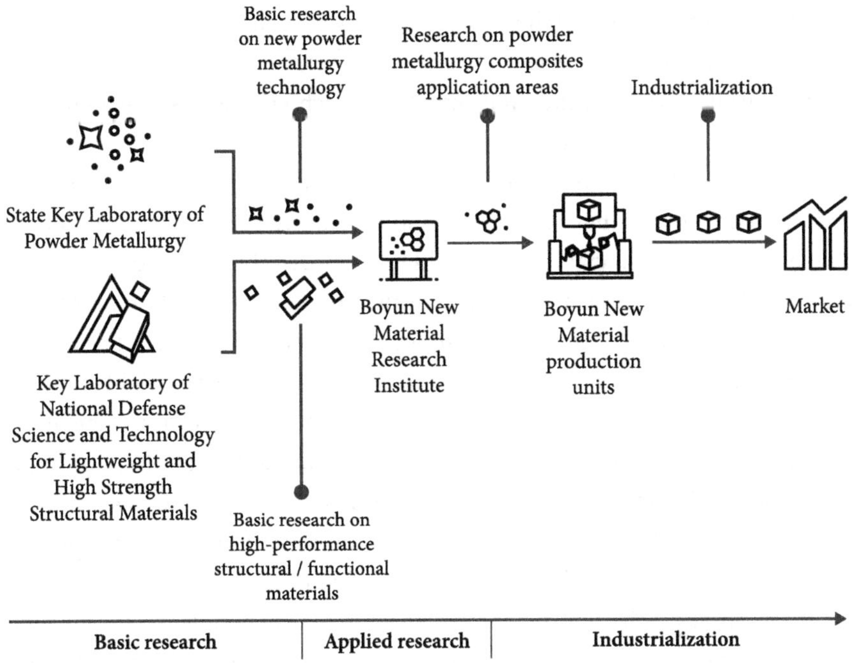

Figure 5-6 Technology innovation system of Boyun Company

By 1996, the research group led by Huang Boyun had finished the basic laboratory research on the "preparation technology of high-performance carbon / carbon aviation brake materials" after conducting numerous experiments and had acquired the fundamental preparation methods. Following a successful appraisal of their results in 1997, the team applied for industrial trials. In 1998, their project was designated as a national key project by the former State Planning Commission, receiving the investment and commencing industrial experimentation. It was acknowledged as a high-tech demonstration project, marking a significant milestone in the journey toward technological innovation and industrial application.

(2) University incentives for tech transfer

In March 2000, Central South University enacted the Implementation Measures for the Implementation of the National Policy of Valuing High-Tech Achievements as Shares to boost the innovative drive of scientists and engineers, ensure prompt conversion of research findings into productive forces, and minimize the squandering of scientific achievements. The essence of the Measures was encapsulated in the "two 70%s" policy: 70% of the equity was to be allocated to researchers directly involved in the creation of intangible assets when such assets were contributed as capital; and when the surplus from scientific research funds was invested in tech enterprises, research team members would retain 70% of the equity.

The "two 70%s" policy had an undeniable motivational impact on researchers. It meant that academics, who previously spent years in scholarly pursuit with little financial reward, could be rewarded through entrepreneurial ventures. This policy effectively liberated the potential of scientific personnel. Over the following five years, Central South University garnered 25 national science and technology awards. Notably, in 2005, it clinched eight national science and technology awards for achievements including the first prize in the national technological invention award for "preparation technology of high-performance carbon / carbon aviation brake materials." This success instilled a deep understanding within the university community of the "three biggest losses": the squandering of human resources due to a lack of enthusiasm and creativity among scientific personnel; the loss of intangible assets through ineffective transformation of scientific and technological achievements; and the tangible asset loss from underutilized scientific research and experimental equipment.

Furthermore, initiatives like the "preparation technology of high-performance carbon / carbon aviation brake materials" gained momentum for further industrialization and institutional innovation. Supported by the Powder Metallurgy Engineering Research Center of Central South University, in collaboration with China Northwest Aviation Supplies I.&E. Corp, Hunan Hi-tech Venture Capital Co., Ltd., Shenzhen Shengcheng Investment Development Co., Ltd., and Huang Boyun as co-founders, Hunan Boyun New Materials Co., Ltd. was established in July 2001. The company was initially capitalized with shares in the powder metallurgy institute valued at RMB 36 million. Through subsequent capital increases and share expansions, the registered capital grew to RMB 80 million.

(3) Cross-disciplinary synergy

Enterprises are typically at the forefront of technological innovation, yet the overall capacity for such innovation within Chinese enterprises remains limited. Their intrinsic innovation awareness and risk tolerance significantly lag behind the seasoned multinational corporations from developed nations, leading to a stark mismatch in their ability and preparedness for international competition. Engaging universities in industry-academic alliances emerges as an effective strategy to foster intrinsic innovation and boost enterprises' innovative capabilities.

Leveraging the existing National Key Laboratory of Powder Metallurgy, National Powder Metallurgy Engineering Research Center, and National Powder Metallurgy Product Testing Center, Central South University rapidly established an innovation platform focused on "high-performance carbon / carbon aviation brake material preparation technology." This initiative quickly attracted over sixty top-level experts across six disciplines, including materials science, chemistry, metallurgy, mechanical engineering, electronics, and aviation, creating a cohesive and resilient scientific team.

The university's unique advantage lies in its capacity to orchestrate intrinsic innovation through the integration of multiple disciplines. Mobilizing multi-disciplinary intrinsic innovation stands as a strategic approach to addressing significant technological challenges within national economic development.

(4) Local government policy backing

In an effort to facilitate the project's achievement transformation, the local government, Changsha City secured acres of land at the Lugu Industrial Base within the Changsha High-Tech Zone and allocated finance in support. Led by Huang Boyun, Hunan Boyun New Materials Co., Ltd., was in the process of setting up an industrial base in Changsha.

Deeply moved by the city's support and conducive entrepreneurial environment, Academician Huang Boyun and his team decided to invest RMB 150 million. They constructed 30,000 square meters of new facilities at the "Lugu Industrial Base," establishing a large-scale production capacity. Annually, the plant is capable of producing 10,000 sets of carbon / carbon composite aircraft brake pairs, rocket nozzle materials, combustion chamber materials, and a variety of other products. With the first phase of the project operational in the first half of the next year, annual sales revenue is projected to exceed RMB 1 billion.

3. Role and Structure of the Scientific Team

(1) Team dynamics

This "task force," comprised of over sixty engineering and technical personnel from six disciplines at Central South University, including materials, chemistry, metallurgy, machinery, electronics, and aviation, is spearheaded by Academician Huang Boyun. The core team, with an average age of 45, possesses top-tier research capabilities in material science but also a deep commitment to serving their country.

The leader of this formidable group is Professor Huang Boyun, a member of the Chinese Academy of Engineering and President of Central South University. Xiong Xiang, the "deputy commander" and a doctoral tutor, led numerous national and provincial scientific research projects. The team also includes key members such as Yi Maozhong, Huang Qizhong, Jiang Jianchun, Zhang Hongbo, and Zou Zhiqiang, among others.

(2) Key scientist profiles

Back in China in 1988, Huang Boyun led projects like the "High-Performance Powder Metallurgy Aircraft Brake Materials," achieving results that not only matched but exceeded foreign standards, positioning them at the forefront of global technology. He then turned his attention to the pioneering research field of carbon / carbon aviation brake pads, a project many deemed too challenging. However, Huang was driven by national need, asserting, "Researchers should not only undertake minor tasks. We must be prepared to take on significant challenges that meet the country's needs."

Carbon / carbon aviation brake material, comprising carbon fibers (akin to steel bars in reinforced concrete) and a carbon matrix (similar to cement and sand), represents a sophisticated composite material. The process of arranging hundreds of millions of carbon atoms among carbon fibers to create lightweight, low-density, high-performance materials is incredibly complex.

Embarking on industrial experiments in 1998, the team faced a lengthy and arduous process, periodically checking the furnace for key metrics like weight and density, only to be met with incomprehensible results like charcoal balls—another setback. In 2000, a high-stakes inertial platform test ended in failure, causing Huang Boyun great distress. Yet, he rallied his team with a powerful message of perseverance and commitment to the project, emphasizing the value of their collective effort and the inevitability of setbacks in scientific research. He declared his unwavering dedication to the project, stating he would have no regrets, even if it meant sacrificing his life for the cause.

During his most challenging periods, Huang Boyun resorted to sleeping pills for rest. If one pill didn't suffice, he would take two. He believed that failure was merely a phase in the process of undertaking tasks. "When we undertake tasks, we must have the courage to scale high mountains and construct bridges across rivers. We will always come up with more good ideas than obstacles. Don't easily give up," Huang Boyun maintained. To achieve greatness, he argued, one must endure hardships and exhibit perseverance.

Huang Boyun was adamant about the practical application of research. "What's the point of conducting scientific research? Why push for scientific and technological progress? To me, it's about utilizing the results. Outcomes that cannot be applied are not successful outcomes," he stated, emphasizing that research without practical application is futile.

As a proponent of pragmatism, Huang Boyun also implemented significant changes at Central South University. Despite facing resistance, he introduced the "two 70% incentive policies," fostering the growth of several high-potential disciplinary companies and creating the nationally recognized "Central South University Model."

Huang Boyun, who places his career above life itself, is selfless and industrious. He values his time greatly, dedicating nearly all his energy to his work. Whether it's a holiday or the middle of the night, he is always ready to work tirelessly with his colleagues to see tasks to their successful completion. Despite his numerous responsibilities as an academician, university president, and board chairman, Huang Boyun is known for his fast-paced lifestyle. His secretary once remarked on the difficulty of keeping pace with him on walks. Huang is known to work more than 12 hours a day, rarely taking breaks. Over the 18 years since his return to China, he has spent nearly every Spring Festival working intensely.

In 2000, shortly after undergoing surgery for small intestinal tumors, Huang rushed back to the laboratory without proper rest. During an experiment, he experienced severe abdominal pain and bleeding but chose to return to the lab after minimal treatment. His unwavering dedication was driven by a sense of urgency to advance research on carbon / carbon composites and stay ahead of international competition.

In 2004, Huang and his team traveled to Beijing for a project defense, a culmination of months of preparation. Despite a delayed flight home, they worked tirelessly, reflecting Huang's relentless work ethic. Now in his seventies, Huang does not indulge in leisure activities like smoking, drinking, or playing poker. Instead, he finds joy in contemplation and problem-solving, likening the intellectual challenge to treasure hunting. "The more challenging the problem, the more exhilarating the process. There's a sweetness in the struggle, awaiting discovery at the end," Huang shared, encapsulating his philosophy toward work and innovation.

4. Strategy for High-Performance Material Industrialization

This project has independently invented, designed, and manufactured thirty sets of key process equipment across six categories. The mechanical and braking properties of the products exceed those of similar international products and have been successfully applied to the brake pairs of aircraft. It is the first to receive the Civil Aviation Administration of China's approval as a manufacturer of large aircraft carbon brake pairs. An industrial production line with an annual output of 10,000 carbon / carbon brake pads and an output value of RMB 200 million has been established. Additionally, brake pairs for a series of aircraft, including A320, Y8W, JH7, and Tu204, have been developed.

The innovation platform for "high-performance carbon / carbon aviation brake material preparation technology" includes a vast array of self-developed equipment with endogenous innovation IP rights, some imported equipment, and numerous new plants, totaling nearly RMB 250 million in fixed assets.

The completion of this innovation platform has led to several major scientific and technological achievements:

a. A series of technical prototypes for high-performance carbon / carbon aviation braking materials have been developed, supporting the advancement of braking technologies for China's large civil aircraft and thousands of military aircraft.
b. A prototype of ablation-resistant and thermal protective carbon / carbon materials has been established, paving the way for the development of China's advanced propulsion systems for high-performance rockets, strategic and tactical missiles, and supersonic aircraft.
c. Prototypes of heat conduction and insulation, thermal structure, corrosion-resistant, and high-performance carbon / carbon materials have been created, offering material-technical support for the national large-scale manufacturing industry, chemical industry, and major national projects.

As of 2009, the company emerged as China's largest manufacturer of similar products. The company's civil aircraft brake pairs, which qualify for production on over 67% of domestic aircraft, including about 85% of powder metallurgy brake pairs and 52% of carbon / carbon composite aircraft brake pairs, are progressively replacing imported products and being exported to former Soviet Union countries.

5. Innovation Ecosystem at Central South University

(1) Equity incentive frameworks

As early as 2000, Central South University was at the forefront in China, bravely pioneering equity incentives. It issued the Implementation Measures for the Implementation of the National Policy of Valuing High-Tech Achievements as Shares, which clearly stipulated that when scientific and technological personnel establish enterprises, their technological intangible assets can be evaluated and converted into shares, with 70% of the total value of these shares awarded to the holders of the technology. Additionally, when surplus funds from horizontal scientific research projects are invested in technology companies, research group members are entitled to hold 70% of the investment amount. The adoption of equity incentives has significantly boosted the enthusiasm of professors and researchers for innovation and entrepreneurship, leading to the establishment of a large number of discipline-based companies.

(2) Entrepreneurial management enhancements

Central South University adopts a hands-off management approach, refraining from meddling in the internal affairs of enterprises while simultaneously providing exemplary entrepreneurial services. Its primary aim is to serve society and advance academic disciplines. In essence, the university does not act as the corporate headquarters, nor does it depend on discipline-specific companies for its survival. Although numerous discipline-based enterprises have emerged, the university has not reaped significant financial rewards. However, the university perceives its true gains in the enhancement of academic disciplines and improvements in talent cultivation. The prestige and impact Central South University has achieved nationally are considered invaluable benefits beyond monetary measurement. Additionally, the university's evaluation and management system for teaching and research is notably adaptable. Professors are allowed to hold part-time positions in companies, and as long as they fulfill their academic and research obligations, they are compensated by both the university and the company. This relaxed and flexible management policy has proven to be a significant driving force behind the growth of discipline-based companies.

(3) Talent development strategies

Central South University emphasizes a practical learning approach where students step out of the classroom for hands-on training in industrial, academic, and research settings. The university holds the view that traditional classroom instruction is merely one aspect of education, not its entirety. According to reports, over 70% of students' thesis topics are derived from real-world scientific research and production experiences, leading to the development of graduates with stronger innovative and entrepreneurial skills. This educational method has proven successful and serves as a model worthy of emulation. Data reveals that among the more than 1,800 companies listed on China's Shanghai and Shenzhen stock exchanges, nearly seventy are led by Central South University alumni. This figure includes chairs and presidents but does not account for other executive roles. The alumni network spans more than thirty heads of state-owned enterprises and over thirty private entrepreneurs who have founded and taken their companies public. Notable examples include Wang Chuanfu of BYD, Liang Wengen of Sany Group, and Zhong Faping of Liyuan New Materials.

(4) Industry-academia collaboration innovations

Numerous disciplinary companies have flourished with the nurturing and support of scientific and technological advancements, sparking private investment and fueling economic growth. These companies not only serve as practical platforms for research and education, offering internships and experimental opportunities but also ensure research aligns more closely with societal needs and education meets the demands of the workforce. Furthermore, the growth of these companies contributes to the development of academic disciplines through financial support, creating a beneficial cycle of industry, education, and research collaboration.

On October 8, 2006, Central South University passed a resolution allowing Xiong Xiang and eight other colleagues to take unpaid leave, meaning they would not hold any positions at the university while working full-time at the company and its subsidiaries. Despite their new roles, their personnel and organizational affiliations with Central South University would be maintained. These nine individuals, including Xiong Xiang, entered into open-ended contracts with the company.

The organizational structure of the company is detailed in Figure 5-7.

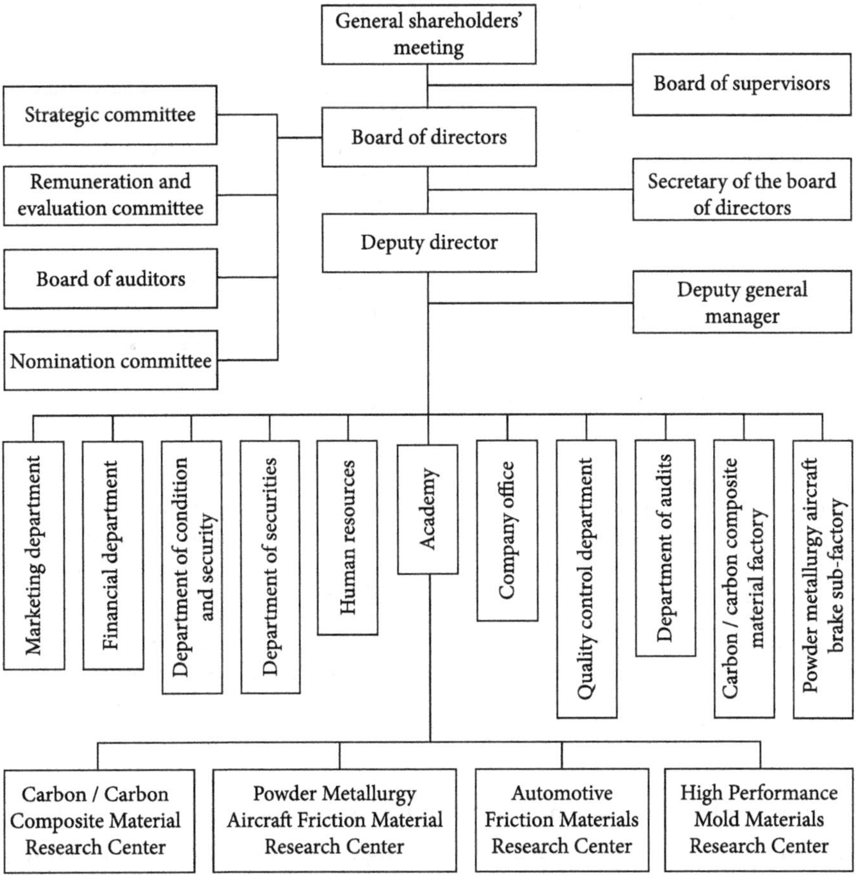

Figure 5-7 Organization of the company

5.4 Commercialization Evolution Model

SBEFs significantly contribute to transforming basic scientific research achievements into commercial successes. This chapter examines the development and evolutionary traits of these enterprises during the innovation process from four perspectives: the management team of SBEFs, sources of capital, enterprise collaboration, and product development, as outlined in Table 5-7.

Table 5-7 Development and evolution characteristics of SBEFs

Variable	Characteristics	The analysis of characteristics
Management team	Large proportion of scientists in key roles; recruiting experienced business people to join	Keeps companies at the forefront of research and facilitates cooperation with research organizations; effectively safeguard enterprise resource acquisition and operation management
Source of funds	Initial stage: Government funding, venture capital; developing stage: Venture capital, public offerings, business partnerships, operating IP, etc.	Continuous government funding supports early-stage R&D and reduces the risk of private investment; diversified sources of funding effectively support the company's huge R&D expenditures
Enterprise cooperation	Academic cooperation with universities and research institutions; business cooperation with related enterprises	Keeping the company at the forefront of science and obtaining the latest patents in a timely manner; shorten R&D cycle, accelerate product launch, and consolidate market position
Product R&D	Long cycle time and high risk; business products and business technologies	Dependence on basic scientific research determines; provide products for customers and a technology platform for companies

The analysis of the management teams of SBEFs reveals that these enterprises possess dual capabilities through a combination of "pioneering scientists and business professionals." This arrangement not only places the enterprise at the cutting-edge of scientific research and facilitates collaboration with research institutions but also effectively secures the enterprise's resource acquisition and operational management. Regarding capital sources, initial entrepreneurial funding primarily consists of government public funds and venture capital, with a few enterprises also securing funds through public offerings. Continuous government support bolsters early R&D efforts while mitigating the risk to private investment. Beyond the entrepreneurial phase, enterprises' development-stage capital sources expand to include venture capital, public offerings, business collaboration, and the operationalization of IP rights. These diversified funding streams significantly underpin the substantial R&D expenses of the enterprise. Enterprise cooperation is bifurcated into academic and commercial collaborations. Academic partnerships enable enterprises to remain at the forefront of scientific advancement and secure the latest patents; commercial collaborations considerably shorten the product

R&D cycle, hasten market entry, and bolster market positioning. SBEFs are characterized by lengthy product R&D cycles and substantial risks, stemming from their reliance on foundational scientific research. These enterprises typically develop not only consumer-directed commercial products but also commercial technologies that offer technical platform services to research institutions or other enterprises.

This case analyses outline the evolutionary process of SBEFs, described in broad strokes as follows:

a. Scientists, driven by market applicability and a commitment to societal benefit from scientific achievements, assemble teams to transition laboratory breakthroughs to practical applications, initiating SBI efforts.
b. Initial support from national and university science and technology funds nurtures innovative achievement prototypes. Concurrently, system designs align scientists' innovative outcomes with commercialization prospects, fostering confidence in the commercial viability of scientific advancements. This, along with the initial step, catalyzes the formation of SBEFs.
c. Scientists spearhead the engineering or industrial validation of innovative prototypes, confronting technical challenges through intensified innovation activities and ensuring ongoing technological leadership through prescient innovation planning. National industrial policies facilitate market entry for enterprises' inaugural products, addressing SBEFs' financial needs during the engineering phase.
d. As SBEFs engage the market, extensive innovation activities revolve around market demands, diversifying product lines to accommodate customer preferences. This phase demands additional R&D personnel and foundational research to navigate future market shifts. The inherent connectivity between scientific teams or academic institutions and SBEFs enables lasting partnerships with universities or research institutes, ensuring enduring innovation capabilities.
e. Post-initial commercialization, SBEFs enter a phase of sustainable enterprise development, necessitating risk management strategies to safeguard against potential pitfalls in ongoing innovation endeavors, including industry, market, technical, and organizational risks.

This book categorizes the growth of science-based enterprises into four stages, as illustrated in Figure 5-8.

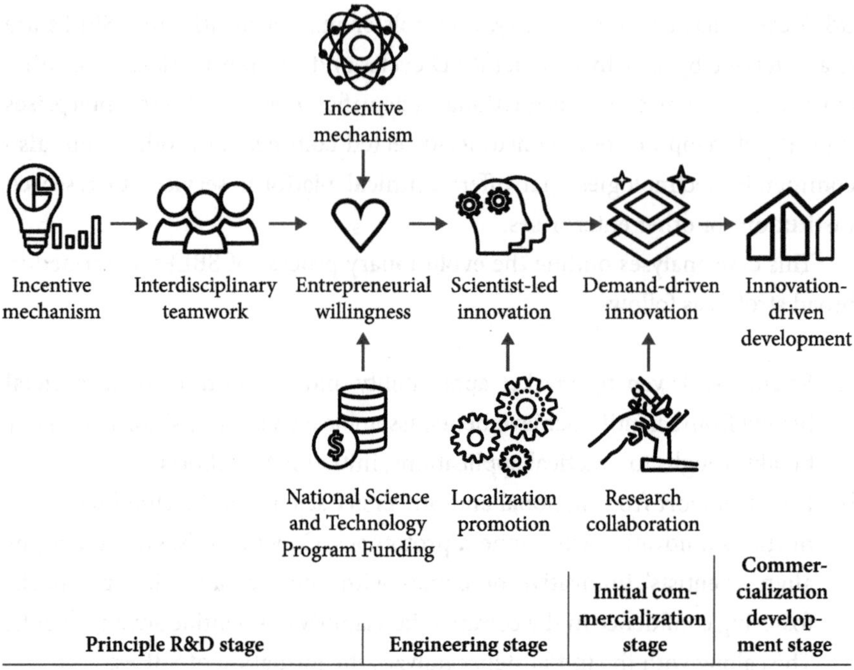

Figure 5-8 Evolution model of science-based enterprises

5.4.1 Initial Prototyping Phase

Marketing awareness is a crucial component of successfully turning scientific and technological breakthroughs into industrial successes. If scientists solely focus on publishing their findings in academic journals or securing personal patents without a keen eye for practical application, their drive to industrialize their discoveries may wane. Market awareness equips scientists with the foresight to assess the potential application value of their lab results. This vision can steer their research direction and fuel their dedication and perseverance.

Cross-disciplinary teamwork is vital for the industrialization of scientific and technological achievements. It necessitates the collaboration of experts from various fields, the creation of teams that span different professions and departments, the influential presence of team leaders, and shared values among team members. Such a foundation enables the team to confront challenges fearlessly, swiftly achieve its objectives, and enhance the pace and quality of industrialization efforts.

Entrepreneurial intention is influenced not just by scientists' innate personal traits but also by their awareness of the market and their capability to form entrepreneurial teams. These elements are pivotal in motivating scientists to take the helm in operating SBEFs.

National scientific research funding plays a significant role in the early stages of R&D, facilitating the rapid generation of innovative outcomes. Moreover, through the establishment of specific scientific and technological projects, the state can effectively direct scientists toward developing discoveries that hold strategic importance for the nation's economic progress.

5.4.2 *Engineering and Refinement Phase*

Scientist-led initiatives are pivotal at the inception of the innovation model, where the groundwork of innovative scientists' basic research lies. As the journey toward industrialization unfolds, continually refining the technological path is imperative. Without the scientists' leadership in steering technical innovation during the engineering phase, propelling the industrialization of scientific and technological advancements becomes daunting.

The incentive mechanism plays a critical role in the operational dynamics of a company. To unleash the team's maximum potential, it's essential to motivate and empower them through a robust corporate governance structure. This entails clearly delineating the distribution of rights and responsibilities among the scientists' teams across the shareholders' meeting, the board of directors, and the management, alongside crafting corresponding incentive mechanisms.

Promoting localization offers a strategic lever to boost the growth of SBEFs during the engineering phase. This can be achieved through various approaches, such as allocating funds to engineering projects, encouraging market acquisition of the first product via localization policies, and aiding enterprises in setting industry standards. Notably, facilitating market entry for domestic technology and products through localization policies presents a significant opportunity to level the playing field with international competitors. This not only secures a timeframe for domestic technologies to potentially overtake their foreign counterparts but also significantly contributes to the competitive positioning of domestic innovations globally.

5.4.3 *Early Commercialization Efforts*

Demand drives innovation. Once the initial products of SBEFs reach the market, they encounter a spectrum of diverse market demands. Only those innovative products that align with customer needs can achieve sustained acceptance in the market. Building on their inaugural offerings, SBEFs engage in relentless innovation to expand their product line or enhance the technical performance of their initial products, ensuring they remain competitive in the market.

Scientific research collaboration is crucial for the market competitiveness of SBEFs, which hinges on their innovative technologies and products. This necessitates ongoing fundamental research. By forging long-term partnerships between academia and industry, SBEFs can funnel investments into R&D projects within universities and research institutes, bolstering the foundations of basic research. This symbiotic relationship ensures a steady pipeline of innovation, reinforcing the competitive edge of SBEFs in the market.

5.4.4 Advanced Commercialization Development

Innovation propels development forward. As a company begins to flourish, a team of scientists must not only possess the capability for technological innovation but also develop a knack for managerial innovation. These two skills complement and strengthen each other. Managerial abilities are essential across all facets of technological innovation, encompassing technology and product strategy, supply chain management, marketing, organization, and more.

To construct a model for the evolution of science-based enterprises, it's crucial to incorporate ten fundamental components: market awareness, collaboration across disciplines, a drive for entrepreneurship, a robust incentive framework, support from national science and technology programs, leadership by scientists in innovation, encouragement of local production, innovation spurred by demand, development driven by innovation, and partnerships in scientific research.

References

Audretsch, D. B., and E. E. Lehmann. 2004. "Financing High-Tech Growth: The Role of Banks and Venture Capitalists." *Schmalenbach Business Review* 56 (4): 340–357.

Colombo, M. G., and L. Grilli. 2005. "Founders' Human Capital and the Growth of New Technology-Based Firms: A Competence-Based View." *Research Policy* 34 (6): 795–816.

Colombo, M. G., D. D'Adda, and E. Piva. 2010. "The Contribution of University Research to the Growth of Academic Start-Ups: An Empirical Analysis." *The Journal of Technology Transfer* 35 (1): 113–140.

Etzkowitz, H. 2002. *MIT and the Rise of Entrepreneurial Science*. Routledge.

Gambardella, A., and S. Torrisi. 2000. "The Economic Value of Knowledge and Inter-Firm Technological Linkages: An Investigation of Science-Based Firms." *Dynamo TSER Project* (contract no. SOE1-CT97-1078).

Henrekson, M., and N. Rosenberg. 2001. "Designing Efficient Institutions for Science-Based Entrepreneurship: Lesson from the US and Sweden." *The Journal of Technology Transfer* 26 (3): 207–231.

Knockaert, M., D. Ucbasaran, M. Wright, et al. 2011. "The Relationship between Knowledge Transfer, Top Management Team Composition, and Performance: The Case of Science-Based Entrepreneurial Firms." *Entrepreneurship Theory and Practice* 35 (4): 777–803.

Karvonen, M., and T. Kässi. 2013. "Patent Citations as a Tool for Analysing the Early Stages of Convergence." *Technological Forecasting and Social Change* 80 (6): 1094–1107.

Kotha, R., and G. George. 2010. "Academic Entrepreneurs: The Role of Star Scientists in Commercialization of Radical Science."

Miozzo, M., and L. DiVito. 2016. "Growing Fast or Slow?: Understanding the Variety of Paths and the Speed of Early Growth of Entrepreneurial Science-Based Firms." *Research Policy* 45 (5): 964–986.

Pisano, G. 2006. "Profiting from Innovation and the Intellectual Property Revolution." *Research Policy* 35 (8): 1122–1130.

Rickne, A. 2006. "Connectivity and Performance of Science-Based Firms." *Small Business Economics* 26 (4): 393–407.

Fu, Xianghe. 2009. "The Innovation History and Inspiration of Dawning High-Performance Computer." *Engineering Research—Engineering in Interdisciplinary Perspective* 1 (3): 282–291.

Li, Jun. 2015. "Supercomputing, High-Performance Computer, Supercomputing Industry." *Proceedings of the Chinese Academy of Sciences* 30 (1).

———. 2016. "Industrialization of Dawning High-Performance Computer." *Science and Technology Herald* (14): 29–32.

Liu, Weiyuan. 2012. "Boyun New Material: Large Aircraft Project Takes Substantial Steps." *China Metal Bulletin* (47): 36–36.

Yang, Chengxiao. 2012. "BoYun New Material: Composite Material Watch Brake Pad Strikes." *China Metal Bulletin* (30): 34–35.

Yi, Chaohui, and Guan Lin. 2018. "Scholars' Entrepreneurial Roles, Entrepreneurial Orientation and Entrepreneurial Performance of University-Derived Enterprises." *Scientific Research Management* 39 (11): 166–176.

Zhang, Hu, Yang Liu, and He Wei. 2017. "The Current Situation and the Crux of the Transformation of Scientific and Technological Achievements in Universities." *Research Management* (S1): 687–690.

CHAPTER 6

Science-Based Industrial Innovation: Industry-University-Research Cooperation

In SBI, the collaboration between industry, universities, and research institutes plays a pivotal role. In the journey toward industrialization, enterprises can engage in two primary ways. First, by participating in or funding the basic research at public institutions during the stage of scientific discovery, obtaining patent licenses, conducting application R&D, and creating marketable products. Notable examples include the "synthetic ammonia industry," honored with the Nobel Prize in Chemistry in 1931, and the "discovery and application of streptomycin," recognized with the Nobel Prize in Physiology or Medicine in 1952. Second, after universities or PRIs generate research outcomes with strong applicability, including patentable inventions or laboratory outputs ready for direct application and commercialization, enterprises can get involved in the subsequent application-oriented research and market product development by acquiring patents for further R&D or by collaborating with universities and public entities for continued R&D. Emblematic instances include the application of the phase contrast microscope, awarded the Nobel Prize in Physics in 1953, the ECG measuring device recognized in the Nobel Prize in Physiology or

Medicine in 1924, and the discovery and application of the GMR effect, which won the Nobel Prize in Physics in 2007.

6.1 Enterprise Participation in Early Scientific Research

6.1.1 Synthetic Ammonia: From Research to Industrial Production

The journey to the industrial production of synthetic ammonia is a prime example of innovation rooted in the nascent stages of scientific development. It benefited from the continuous R&D investments and contributions of three Nobel Prize laureates in Chemistry between 1909 and 1931, showcasing various forms of collaboration between enterprises and research institutions (scientists) at each stage. In the early 1900s, Professor Ostwald, awarded the Nobel Prize in 1909, after years of researching catalysts, believed he had successfully synthesized ammonia and sought follow-up research funding from the German company Badische Anilin- & Sodafabrik (later renamed BASF). His request was declined due to the inability to verify the success of his experiments. Nevertheless, Ostwald's theoretical contributions on catalysts laid the groundwork for their industrial application. This episode illustrates that enterprises prioritize application value over theoretical value, with the assessment of application potential not influenced by the theoretical depth.

Subsequently, in 1904, chemist Haber, who would go on to win the Nobel Prize in 1918, successfully produced ammonia at low concentrations, attracting support from two Viennese entrepreneurs. However, by July 1905, due to slower than anticipated experimental progress and the inability to demonstrate economic value, the financial backing was withdrawn, leaving Haber in a predicament. Persisting based on the theoretical potential of his experiments, Haber achieved a breakthrough in 1907, marking a significant step toward the laboratory production of synthetic ammonia. In 1908, the Baden Aniline and Soda Factory stepped in to provide financial and technical support, acquiring all subsequent patents through a reservation fee and awarding Haber a stake. This early model of collaboration with research institutions (scientists) shows that enterprises mitigate risks by setting expected outcomes and choosing the optimal time to engage. The specific commercial process is illustrated in Figure 6-1.

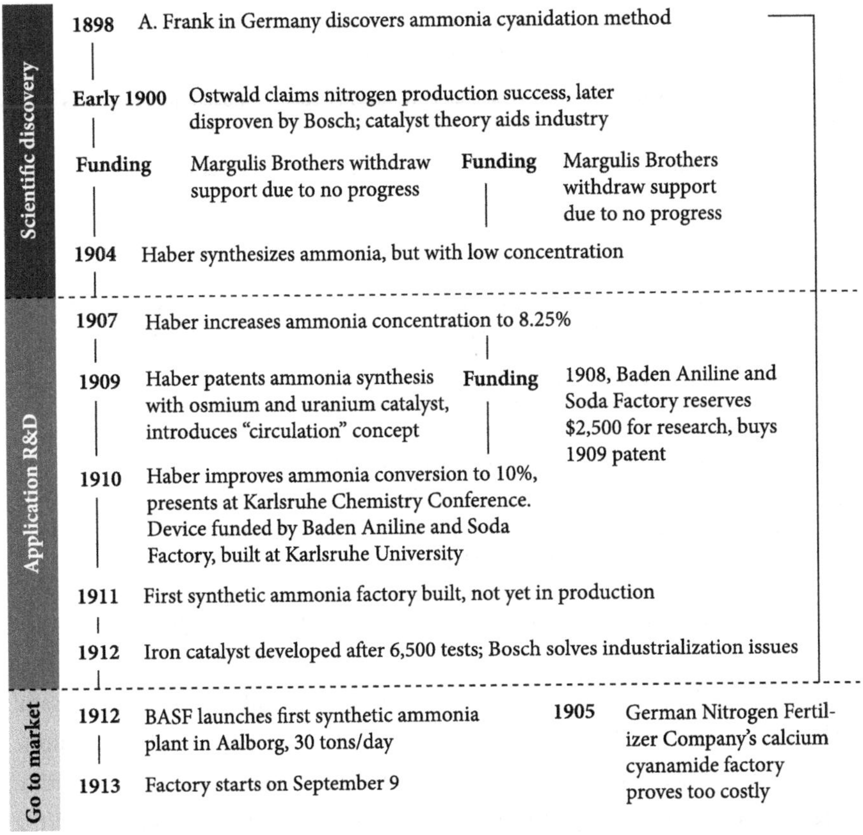

Figure 6-1 Commercialization process of synthetic ammonia

6.1.2 *Streptomycin: Pathway from Development to Industrial Scale Production*

After penicillin revolutionized the treatment of many bacterial infections, the search intensified for a powerful antibacterial drug to combat tuberculosis, one of the deadliest infectious diseases known as the "white death" before the 1940s. This quest culminated in the discovery of streptomycin by soil microbiologist Selman Waksman, marking the beginning of a new era in the fight against tuberculosis.

In 1932, Waksman began researching anti-tuberculosis drugs under the sponsorship of the American Anti-tuberculosis Association. Recognizing the potential, pharmaceutical giant Merck started funding the research in 1939 and secured all patents for streptomycin through an agreement. Waksman isolated

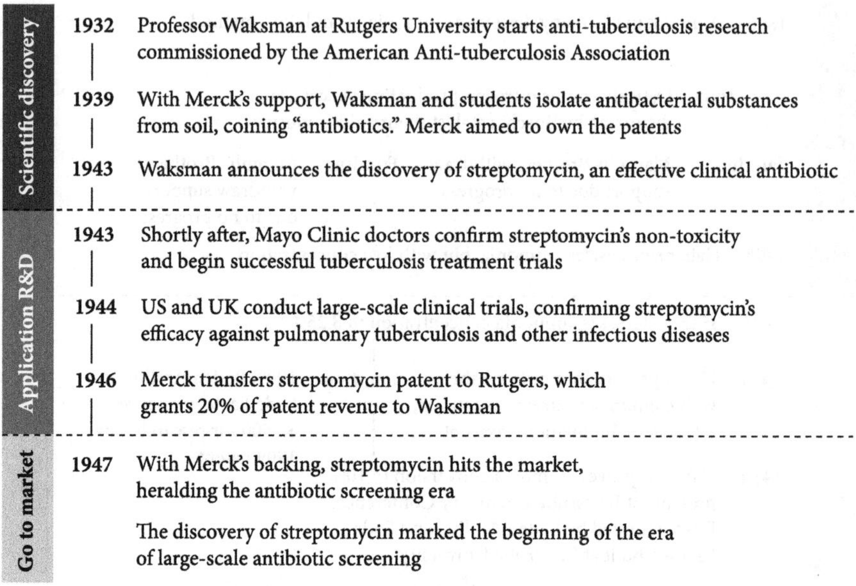
Scientific discovery
1932 Professor Waksman at Rutgers University starts anti-tuberculosis research commissioned by the American Anti-tuberculosis Association
1939 With Merck's support, Waksman and students isolate antibacterial substances from soil, coining "antibiotics." Merck aimed to own the patents
1943 Waksman announces the discovery of streptomycin, an effective clinical antibiotic
Application R&D
1943 Shortly after, Mayo Clinic doctors confirm streptomycin's non-toxicity and begin successful tuberculosis treatment trials
1944 US and UK conduct large-scale clinical trials, confirming streptomycin's efficacy against pulmonary tuberculosis and other infectious diseases
1946 Merck transfers streptomycin patent to Rutgers, which grants 20% of patent revenue to Waksman
Go to market
1947 With Merck's backing, streptomycin hits the market, heralding the antibiotic screening era
The discovery of streptomycin marked the beginning of the era of large-scale antibiotic screening

Figure 6-2 Commercialization process of streptomycin

an actinomycete producing streptomycin in 1943, and by 1944, successful large-scale clinical trials were underway. By 1946, concerned that Merck alone couldn't meet the production demands and to foster market competition to reduce streptomycin's price, Waksman negotiated the cancellation of the 1939 agreement. Merck agreed to transfer the streptomycin patent to Rutgers University in 1946, retaining only the production rights. Rutgers then allocated 20% of the patent income to Waksman.

With Merck's backing, eight pharmaceutical companies joined the production efforts by the late 1940s, significantly accelerating streptomycin's journey from discovery to market, ensuring wide-scale production and distribution. The specific commercial process is detailed in Figure 6-2.

6.2 Enterprise Participation in Application Stage R&D

6.2.1 Phase Contrast Microscope: Journey from Development to Commercialization

In 1953, Frits Zernike, a physicist from the University of Groningen in the Netherlands, was awarded the Nobel Prize in Physics for inventing the phase contrast method and, notably, the phase contrast microscope. This innovation is particularly adept at observing highly transparent objects such as biological specimens, oil films, and phase gratings, which typically alter only the phase, not the amplitude, of light waves passing through them. Since human eyes and energy detectors can only discern intensity differences, not phase changes, traditional microscopes struggled with these subjects.

Zernike's journey began in 1930 with his discovery of the wave phase difference interference phenomenon. By 1932, he was pioneering the prototype of a phase contrast microscope and applied for a patent in Germany. Despite initial skepticism and rejection from peers and potential industrial supporters like Zeiss in Jena, Germany, Zernike's persistence paid off. By 1941, Zeiss had produced phase contrast objective lenses and accessories, followed by further advancements, including the achromatic phase village microscope objective lens developed in collaboration with Brink in 1944, and H. Heine's annular lighting device for the condenser in 1951.

The global adoption and production of phase contrast microscopes followed, with companies such as Zeiss Winkel, American Optical Company, and Cooke, Troughton & Sims contributing to its widespread use. Today, phase contrast microscopes are invaluable tools in biology and medicine, enabling detailed studies in bacteriology, pathology, and mineral crystal micromorphology.

6.2.2 ECG Measuring Device: Path from Innovation to Market Entry

In 1924, the Nobel Prize in Physiology or Medicine was awarded to Willem Einthoven (1860–1927), a Dutch physiologist, for his discovery of the electrocardiogram's mechanism and his invention of the earliest ECG and measuring device. The problem of cardiac action currents has always been a subject of research among medical scientists. The first electrical signal map recording a heartbeat was created in 1872, and by 1887, the first ECG capable of displaying potential changes was developed. However, due to the complex calculations and lengthy debugging time required, this method could not display heart rate changes in real-time, limiting its clinical value to merely indicating the presence of a problem.

In 1891, Einthoven began his research into the electrocardiography of heartbeats. He first designed a simple correction method in 1894, obtaining an actual human ECG. By 1903, he had successfully replaced the capillary electrometer with a string galvanometer, marking the first instrument capable of directly reflecting the potential changes in mental processes. This innovation led Einthoven to become the first person to produce an electrocardiogram with practical application value (Einthoven 1903).

The string galvanometer Einthoven manufactured in 1901 was more of an improved experimental instrument in the field of pure physics rather than a practical product. After its creation, it was utilized to explore the practical feasibility of documenting the current effects in organisms, such as the heart, representing one of his significant contributions. Due to its enormous size, this early galvanometer had to be located in a laboratory a mile away from the Leiden University Affiliated Hospital. To capture the physiological currents of patients in the hospital, Einthoven had to use signal wires to connect the patients to the instrument.

In 1903, Einthoven began collaborating with German Edelman and Sans Instruments to produce the string galvanometer he invented. However, the German partners soon terminated the contract and chose to work with another designer. At this juncture, partnering with the Cambridge Scientific Instrument Company marked a significant turning point. Einthoven's research on the relationship between the string galvanometer and cardiac currents continued to progress. In 1906, he explored the impact of string quality and tension on the current curve. Between 1908 and 1909, he successfully detected retinal and vagal currents, while Dudel from the Cambridge Scientific Instruments in England aided in translating his theories into practice. Efforts were made to minimize the size of the equipment, while simultaneously enhancing the sensitivity of the galvanometer. The involvement of commercial entities significantly accelerated the R&D of electrocardiographs. These collaborations not only provided funding for R&D but also offered the necessary manpower and intellectual support for the practical application of theories. In 1911, the world's first practical electrocardiograph was officially launched on the market by the company (Barold 2003; Moukabary 2007; Cajavilca 2008).

Before Einthoven, early electrocardiographs lacked real practical value. He was the first to create an instrument theoretically capable of clinical application. However, the instrument he developed was only theoretically suitable for clinical use, and the ECG still faced issues, such as its large size. The engagement with Cambridge Scientific Instruments greatly sped up the research and application of the ECG, facilitating the product's quick market entry and industrialization.

6.2.3 The GMR Effect and Its Commercial Applications

The magnetoresistive effect refers to the phenomenon where the resistance of certain metals or semiconductors changes with variations in the external magnetic field. This effect was discovered by British physicist William Thomson in 1857. However, the research on the magnetoresistive effect did not see significant breakthroughs for over a century until the advent of another technology—MBE.[1] Between 1968 and 1973, Bell Laboratories[2] and IBM[3] developed a new semiconductor manufacturing technology, which involved attaching molecular (atomic) beams generated in a high vacuum onto a crystal plate to produce a nano-scale film through MBE. Since 1974, with the continuous advancements in industrial technology, MBE technology has been capable of producing a variety of fine semiconductor single-crystal films, single-crystal metal films, and insulating films. Around 1980, MBE technology moved from the experimental research phase into production and application, enabling the study of nanomaterials. It was such films that Fert and Grunberg were investigating when they layered magnetic and non-magnetic materials with nanometer thickness into multilayer films to study their magnetic distribution.

At the time, Alain Friederich, a former student of Fert, was conducting research on MBE at Thomson CSF. In 1985, they met at a conference in San Diego. Through discussions, they decided to collaborate on exploring the magnetic effects of multilayers. Consequently, experts from Thomson CSF and Fert's students formed a research group. In their experiments, they used a structure composed of strongly magnetic layers and less magnetic layers, discovering that the thickness of the spacer between the strongly magnetic layers was a crucial factor in determining the GMR. One day, after creating numerous iron and chromium multilayer plates and testing their magnetoresistance individually,

---

1. MBE (molecular beam epitaxy) is a technology that crystallizes atoms and molecules in the same direction on a metal crystal plate in a high vacuum. This technology was jointly developed by Bell Laboratories and IBM Laboratories in the 1960s and was widely used in semiconductor manufacturing.
2. In 1968, in order to make ultra-thin planar structures and multilayer stacked structural films with precisely controlled depth direction doping elements, Bell Laboratories of the United States first proposed MBE technology and developed a piece of equipment for manufacturing MBE.
3. IBM was funded by the Army Research Office of the United States, proposed the concept of "superlattice," and developed its own MBE equipment from scratch.

they observed that the magnetoresistance increased as the chromium layer became thinner. When the chromium layer's thickness reached 0.9 nm, the magnetoresistance soared to 80%. Fert's team had witnessed the emergence of a new discovery, which they named GMR. Meanwhile, Phil's research team experimented with sixty multilayer films. Simultaneously, Grunberg, on the other side of the world, was conducting similar research. They too achieved the same results using iron-chromium-iron triple-layer films (Baibich et al. 1988; Binasch et al. 1989).

Since the discovery of the GMR effect, the physical properties and GMR of multilayers have become a focal point of research. The GMR effect has given rise to a new discipline and technical field—spintronics. Grunberg's team quickly recognized the significance of the GMR effect. At that time, leading companies in the computer industry were developing read head technology for hard disks using the magnetoresistive effect. They found that GMR technology offered superior characteristics, prompting Grunberg to wisely patent the hard disk technology based on GMR. This decision proved to be astute, as many large companies recognized the potential value of this technology, resulting in Forschungszentrum Juelich earning tens of millions of euros in patent licensing fees.

Among many companies, IBM has played a significant role in advancing the application of GMR in industry. Following the discovery of the GMR effect, Stuart Parkin, a researcher at IBM, took a keen interest in GMR. He aimed to replicate Fert's experiment but lacked access to the costly MBE equipment needed to manufacture multilayer metal films. Seeking an affordable and straightforward method to create multilayer films, Parkin turned to the sputter-deposition technique. This method involves using high-energy ions to dislodge atoms from a solid surface, which then form a thin film. It is extensively used in the production of thin film semiconductor materials (integrated circuits), glass, optical fiber, and other products. Although sputter-deposition does not achieve the same precision as MBE equipment in fabricating multilayer films, it is an economical and accessible means of obtaining multilayer films. This enabled Parkin to investigate the GMR effect across various materials.

As GMR is a relatively new field, numerous challenges remain, such as its application in data reading. Traditional hard disk head reading employs the anisotropic magnetoresistance principle, where the resistance decreases when the magnetic field direction is orthogonal to the current direction and increases when parallel. This property allows the read head's storage capacity to quadruple compared to the previous induction coil head, enabling smaller hard disks. However, as hard disks shrink, the magnetic areas representing binary 0 and 1 also decrease, weakening each bit's magnetic field and complicating data reading. The more information stored on the disk, the greater the sensitivity required by the reading technology. The high sensitivity of the GMR effect is crucial for read heads, as it can detect weaker magnetic field changes, significantly enhancing memory capacity. Parkin's research team conducted extensive experiments, testing up to 30,000 combinations of elements and layers to identify the optimal material combination and structure for hard disk reading, known as a spin valve[4] (Dieny et al. 1991). The introduction of the spin valve structure rapidly made the application of GMR a reality. In 1997, just nine years after the discovery of GMR, IBM launched the highly sensitive data reading head "spin valve" to the market. This breakthrough revolutionized data reading technology transformed the magnetic data storage landscape, and dramatically increased storage capacity, making it the most practical GMR structure. IBM licensed this technology to Western Digital, NEC, Honeywell, and other companies, enabling them to produce data reading heads for IBM computers. Currently, this type of magnetic head dominates the magnetic recording head market with a 95% share, generating a quarterly revenue of $1 billion (Day 2007). The commercialization process is detailed in Figure 6-3.

6.3 Analyzing and Learning from Industry-University-Research Collaboration Models

The innovation model of industry-university-research collaboration in SBI can be categorized into two models of participation, depending on the stage of enterprise involvement. The first model involves participating in or funding basic research at public institutions during the scientific discovery phase, securing licenses for patents, conducting applied R&D, and developing marketable products. The second model activates after scientific research findings become more defined, with corresponding patent outputs or laboratory results ready for direct application and transformation. In this scenario, enterprises engage in the subsequent application-oriented research

4. IBM applied for a patent for this technology in 1991, and it was approved in 1992. The patent number is 5,159,513.

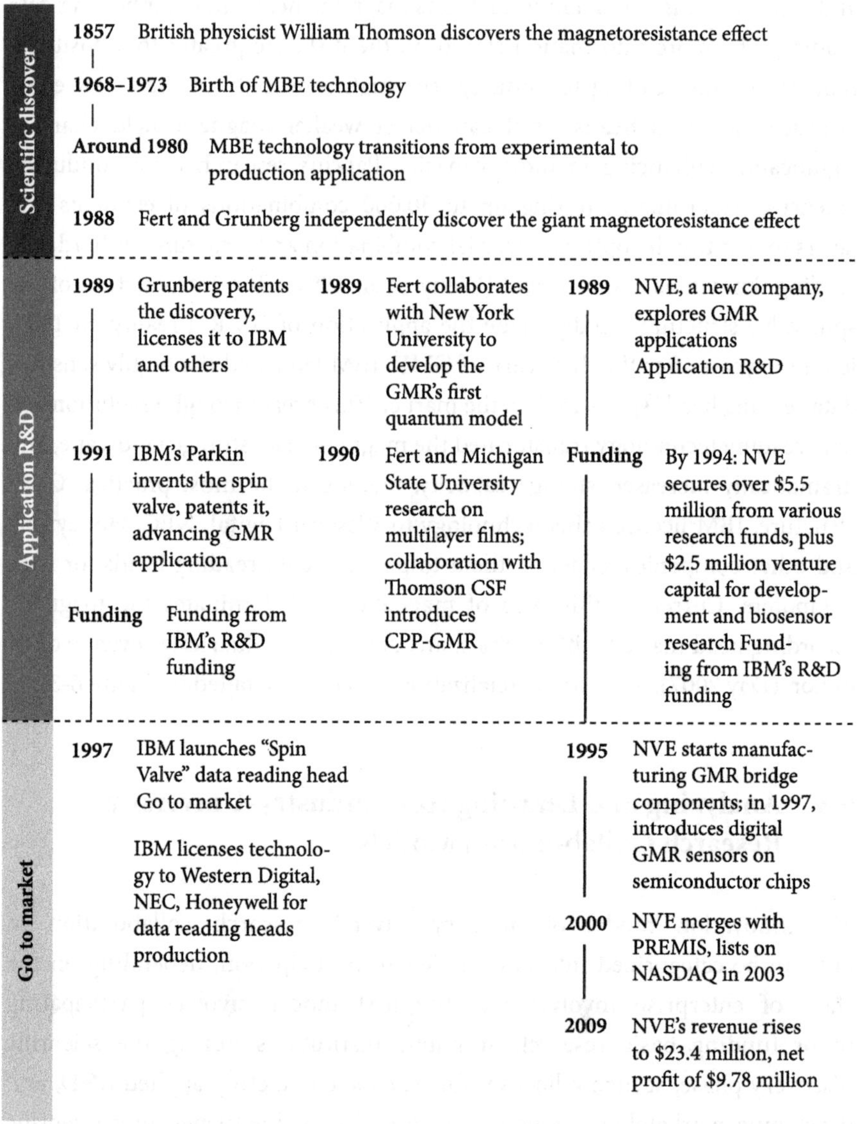
Scientific discover
1857 British physicist William Thomson discovers the magnetoresistance effect
1968–1973 Birth of MBE technology
Around 1980 MBE technology transitions from experimental to production application
1988 Fert and Grunberg independently discover the giant magnetoresistance effect
Application R&D
1989 Grunberg patents the discovery, licenses it to IBM and others
1991 IBM's Parkin invents the spin valve, patents it, advancing GMR application
Funding Funding from IBM's R&D funding
1989 Fert collaborates with New York University to develop the GMR's first quantum model
1990 Fert and Michigan State University research on multilayer films; collaboration with Thomson CSF introduces CPP-GMR
1989 NVE, a new company, explores GMR applications Application R&D
Funding By 1994: NVE secures over $5.5 million from various research funds, plus $2.5 million venture capital for development and biosensor research Funding from IBM's R&D funding
Go to market
1997 IBM launches "Spin Valve" data reading head Go to market
IBM licenses technology to Western Digital, NEC, Honeywell for data reading heads production
1995 NVE starts manufacturing GMR bridge components; in 1997, introduces digital GMR sensors on semiconductor chips
2000 NVE merges with PREMIS, lists on NASDAQ in 2003
2009 NVE's revenue rises to $23.4 million, net profit of $9.78 million

Figure 6-3 Commercialization process of 2007 Nobel Prize in Physics—GMR effect

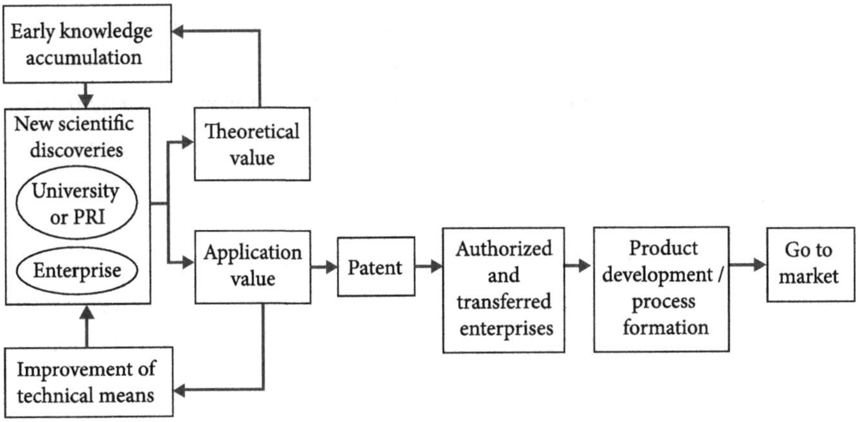

Figure 6-4 Innovation mode of industry-university-research cooperation

and product development process, either by obtaining patent licenses for further R&D or by partnering with universities and public institutions for continued R&D. The innovation model is depicted in Figure 6-4, while Table 6-1 compares the two participation models.

Table 6-1 Comparison of industry-university-research cooperation modes

	Enterprise participation in early scientific research	**Enterprise participation in application stage of R&D**
R&D characteristics	Universities and PRIs lead in basic scientific research with some enterprise involvement	Basic scientific research primarily conducted by universities and PRIs
Source of funds	R&D funding primarily sourced from business operations	R&D funding predominantly from public funds
Intellectual property	Joint ownership between universities or research institutions and enterprises	Enterprises collaborate with universities or PRIs post-basic research breakthrough to secure patent licenses or transfers, focusing on "application research and development"

In the early scientific research model, where enterprises participate, basic research is primarily conducted by universities and PRIs, with enterprises and universities collaboratively engaging in basic research to a certain extent. R&D funding is predominantly provided by the enterprises. After achieving a breakthrough, IP rights are jointly held by universities or research institutions and the enterprises. The enterprise then leads the subsequent application R&D, bringing the results to market. In the model where enterprises participate in R&D during the application stage, basic research is conducted by universities and PRI, with R&D funding largely sourced from public funds. Following a basic research breakthrough, the enterprise collaborates with universities or PRI to acquire patent licenses or transfers, dedicating efforts to "application R&D" to market the results. In both models, enterprises work closely with universities or research institutions to achieve the commercialization of outcomes.

References

Baibich, M. N. 1988. "Giant Magnetoresistance of (001) Fe/(001) Cr Magnetic Superlattices." *Physical Review Letters* 61 (21): 2472.

Barold, S. S. 2003. "Willem Einthoven and the Birth of Clinical Electrocardiography a Hundred Years Ago." *Cardiac Electrophysiology Review* 7 (1): 99–104.

Binasch, G. 1989. "Enhanced Magnetoresistance in Layered Magnetic Structures with Antiferromagnetic Interlayer Exchange." *Physical Review* B 39 (7): 4828.

Cajavilca, C. 2008. "Willem Einthoven: The Development of the Human Electrocardiogram." *Resuscitation* 76 (3): 325–328.

Dieny, B. 1991. "Giant Magnetoresistive in Soft Ferromagnetic Multilayers." *Physical Review* B 43 (1): 1297.

Einthoven, W. 1903. "The String Galvanometer and the Human Electrocardiogram." *Proceedings of the KNAW* 6: 107–115.

Haber, F. 1913. "The Production of Synthetic Ammonia." *Industrial & Engineering Chemistry* 5 (4): 328–331.

Kingston, W. 2004. "Streptomycin, Schatz v. Waksman, and the Balance of Credit for Discovery." *Journal of the History of Medicine and Allied Sciences* 59 (3): 441–462.

Moukabary, T. 2007. "Willem Einthoven (1860–1927): Father of Electrocardiography." *Cardiology Journal* 14 (3): 316–317.

Perley, G. A. 1920. "The Commercial Oxidation of Ammonia." *Industrial & Engineering Chemistry* 12 (1): 5–16.

Perman, E. P. 1905. "The Decomposition of Ammonia by Heat." *Proceedings of the Royal Society of London* 74 (497): 110–117.

Wainwright, M. 1991. "Streptomycin: Discovery and Resultant Controversy." *History and Philosophy of the Life Sciences*: 97–124.

Yoshioka, A. 2002. "Streptomycin in Postwar Britain: A Cultural History of a Miracle Drug." In *Biographies of Remedies*, 203–227. Leiden: Brill Rodopi.
Zernike, F. 1942. "Phase Contrast, a New Method for the Microscopic Observation of Transparent Objects Part II." *Physica* 9 (10): 974–986.
Zernike, F. 1955. "How I Discovered Phase Contrast." *Science* 121 (3141): 345–349.

CHAPTER 7

Science-Based Industrial Innovation: China's Path

7.1 Science-Based Industries in Strategic Emerging Industries

7.1.1 Catalog of Strategic Emerging Industries in the Science Sector

The term "science-based industries" within China's strategic emerging industries can be succinctly referred to as "science-based strategic emerging industries." Based on the Guiding Catalogue of Key Products and Services of Strategic Emerging Industries issued by the National Development and Reform Commission, China's critical strategic emerging industries are segmented into seven categories, encompassing 171 products and services. We have identified above that "science-based industries" among these seven strategic emerging industries in China by calculating the ISCI for related industries, revealing that "science-based strategic emerging industries" are listed in Table 7-1.

Table 7-1 Science-based industries in China's strategic emerging industries

Primary industry	Secondary industry	Tertiary industry
New generation information technology industry	1.1 Next generation Information network industry	1.1.1 Network equipment; 1.1.2 Information terminal equipment
	1.3 Electronic core industry	1.3.1 Integrated circuits; 1.3.2 New display devices; 1.3.3 New components; 1.3.4 High-end energy storage; 1.3.5 Key electronic materials; 1.3.6 Electronic specialized equipment and instruments
	1.4 Network information security products and services	1.4.1 Network and information security hardware
	1.5 AI	1.5.3 Intelligent robots and related hardware
High end equipment manufacturing industry	2.1 Intelligent manufacturing equipment industry	2.1.3 Industrial robots and workstations; 2.1.4 Intelligent processing equipment
	2.2 The aviation industry	2.2.3 Aviation equipment and systems; 2.2.4 Aviation materials
New materials industry	3.1 New functional material industry	3.1.6 High-quality new organic active materials; 3.1.7 New membrane materials; 3.1.9 Eco-environmental materials; 3.1.10 High-quality synthetic rubber; 3.1.11 High-performance sealing materials; 3.1.12 New catalytic materials and auxiliaries; 3.1.13 New chemical fibers and functional prevention materials
	3.2 Advanced structural materials Industry	3.2.4 Engineering plastics and synthetic resins
	3.3 High-performance composite material industry	3.3.1 High-performance fibers and composites; 3.3.2 Metal matrix composites and ceramic matrix compliant materials
Bio-industry	4.1 Biomedical industry	4.1.1 New vaccines; 4.1.2 Biotechnology drugs; 4.1.3 Chemical drugs and API manufacturing; 4.1.4 Modern traditional Chinese medicines and ethnic pharmaceuticals; 4.1.5 Biomedical key equipment and raw materials and accessories
	4.2 Biomedical engineering industry	4.2.4 Implant intervention biomedical materials
	4.3 Bio-agriculture industry	4.3.1 Bio-breeding; 4.3.2 Bio-pesticides; 4.3.3 Bio-fertilizers; 4.3.4 Bio-feeds; 4.3.5 Bio-veterinary medicines, veterinary bioproducts, and vaccines: 4.3.6 Bio-foods
	4.4 Biomanufacturing industry	4.4.1 Bio-based materials; 4.4.2 Bio-chemicals: 4.4.3 Special fermentation products and bioprocess equipment; 4.4.4 Marine bioactive substances and biological products
Instruction	New energy automobile industry, new energy industry, energy conservation and environmental protection industry "no science-based industry"	

7.1.2 Overview and Elucidation

From the discussion above, we can summarize the following points.

First, among the seven strategic emerging industries (referred to as "primary industries" in Table 7-1) that China plans to prioritize, four industries (the new generation information technology industry, high-end equipment manufacturing industry, new materials industry, and biotechnology industry) are identified as containing "science-based industries." The remaining three industries (new energy vehicle industry, new energy industry, energy conservation, and environmental protection industry) do not primarily include "science-based industries."

Second, the seven strategic emerging industries that China intends to focus on are further divided into forty industries (referred to as "secondary industries" in Table 7-1), covering 171 product and service categories (referred to as "tertiary industries" in Table 7-1). Of these, 13 industries qualify as "science-based industries." A more detailed analysis reveals that, within the 171 product and service categories, there are forty that are considered "science-based products and services."

Third, some of the tertiary industries exhibit characteristics of both science-based industry and technology-based industries. However, since the focus of this book is on "science-based industries," industries that embody attributes of both types are not included in this analysis.

7.2 Huawei's Innovation and Evolution as a Model for China's Science-Based Industries

7.2.1 Background on Huawei

1. Business Orientation

Founded in 1987, Huawei Technologies Co., Ltd. (hereafter "Huawei") is a high-tech enterprise owned by its employees and stands as a leading global provider of information and communications technology solutions. The company primarily focuses on the R&D, production, and sales of communication network technologies and products. Huawei specializes in delivering network solutions for telecom operators across various sectors such as optical networks, fixed networks, mobile networks, and value-added services.

Huawei's product and solution portfolio encompasses mobile communication (including LTE/HSPA/WCDMA/EDGE/GPRS/GSM, CDMA2000 1xEV-DO/CDMA 2000 1X, TD-SCDMA, and WiMAX technologies), core networks (featuring IMS, Mobile Softswitch, and NGN), networking equipment (such as FTTx, xDSL, optical networks, routers, and LAN switches), and telecommunication value-added services (including IN, mobile data service, and BOSS) as well as terminals (UMTS/CDMA).

2. Corporate Development

Huawei was registered in Shenzhen with an initial capital of RMB 20,000 in 1988. After years of innovation and development, Huawei's sales revenue surged to RMB 185.176 billion in 2010, marking a 24.2% increase year over year. Huawei's products and solutions now serve over 140 countries, including 45 of the world's top 50 telecom operators, and reach one-third of the global population. It has become the world's second-largest provider of integrated communication equipment, ranking 351st among the world's top 500 companies. Additionally, Huawei is recognized as the 18th most innovative company in the world. Through its journey, Huawei has evolved into a global enterprise with significant competitive strength.

7.2.2 Main Facts of Huawei's Innovation/Catching-Up

1. Initial Phase as an Agent

At its inception in 1988, Huawei started as a sales agent for a company producing PBX systems. Over more than two years of agency work, Huawei developed its marketing network and team, gained a deep understanding of the domestic communication industry and market, and became well-acquainted with the market and products. Building on this foundation, a renowned international telecom equipment manufacturer, proposed a joint venture with Huawei to develop router products. However, Huawei was stipulated to produce low-end routers and forsake the manufacture of high-end routers, essentially aiming to make Huawei their OEM base in China. This condition motivated Huawei to start developing its own products and establish its own brand (Wu and Zhao 2007; Burgelman 2021).

2. Transition to Independent R&D

In 1990, Huawei began independently developing PBX technology tailored for hotels and small businesses, launching the PBX BH03. By 1991, Huawei had introduced the 512-port PBX HJD48 and the vertical-horizontal office system JK1000. Early in 1993, Huawei unveiled the C&C08, a large switching system indicating Huawei's own technological development and initial R&D capabilities. The C&C08 system featured unique technology by employing optical fiber as the switch's connection material for the first time, addressing specific needs for lightning protection, power efficiency, and remote modules. In contrast, many foreign switches at the time relied on cable connections, which required high maintenance expertise and were costly to install in areas with sparse user distribution, making them unsuitable for remote markets. Huawei's C&C08, with its optical fiber connections, was ideally suited for distant locations and met the requirements of China's extensive rural areas. At a time when large foreign switches were cable-connected, Huawei's devices used optical fiber—a medium that was particularly well-suited for rural markets, thereby distinguishing Huawei's products in the Chinese market.

3. Patent Acquisition and Collaborative Innovation

Before 1995, Huawei primarily focused its market efforts on rural areas. After 1995, Huawei expanded into the international market, undertaking several strategic actions.

First, Huawei sought to bridge the technology gap by acquiring patents. To gain entry into the international market, it secured international market access for its products by purchasing necessary core technologies and paying for patent licenses, thus maintaining competitiveness. Huawei dedicates over 10% of its annual sales revenue to R&D expenses. This investment not only enhances the functionality and features of the acquired patented technologies but also advances technology in engineering design and implementation.

Second, Huawei fostered its innovation capabilities through collaborative innovation. On one side, Huawei partners with colleges and universities, allocating special funds annually to establish long-term R&D collaborations. This approach leverages its information platforms and channels to stay abreast of the latest electronic information technologies and industry trends, both domestically and internationally. On the other side, Huawei has formed strategic alliances with large international companies possessing strong technical capabilities to jointly pursue innovative projects and foster the transformation and development of the industrial value chain. Notable partnerships include joint laboratories with world-class enterprises like Motorola, Intel, AGERE, ALTERA, SUN, Microsoft, NEC, and collaborations such as YuMeng Communication Technology Company with Panasonic and NEC, H3C Technologies Company with 3COM, and a 3G development laboratory.

Third, Huawei has established a customer demand-oriented innovation process. Focused on the field of communication equipment, Huawei aims to meet any customer need. The company operates under the belief that products that can be manufactured and sold in advance reflect the real needs of customers. Adopting an "advanced quantity" mindset, Huawei develops, produces, and sells products based on an understanding of customers' potential needs, whether it involves core technology or product design.

4. Shift to Endogenous Innovation and Global Recognition

Building on a foundation of introduction, improvement, and adoption, Huawei embarked on endogenous innovation. In 2003, it launched the world's first complete set of 3G R4 commercial products, achieved the world's first commercial network with R4 architecture in the United Arab Emirates, and completed the world's first interworking of R4 equipment from different manufacturers. It also made the world's largest mobile soft switch tandem network commercially available on the B plane of China Mobile's first-level long-distance tandem network, reaching a peak IP bearer network resource occupancy rate of 40%.

In 2004, Huawei began supplying 3G data communication cards, which it had successfully developed, to operators in Hong Kong (China) and Europe in batches, becoming one of only two manufacturers worldwide to do so. In 2005, at the 3GSM World Conference in Cannes, France, it unveiled an innovative UMTS distributed base station solution that supports rapid networking. By 2006, Huawei's H3C had expanded the deep expansion of IP network construction from layers 1–3 to layers 4–7, committing to the transformation from a network equipment supplier to a full-service solution provider.

In 2007, Huawei's Qualcomm test terminal based on MSM6280 successfully completed a video phone call and HSDPA 3.6 Mbps high-speed download test on a UMTS900 network in Europe and completed the IOT test of the UMTS900 terminal and system in Shanghai. In 2008, *Business Week* rated Huawei as one of the world's top ten most influential companies. For the first time, it deployed UMTS/HSPA networks on a large scale in North America to build a next-generation wireless network for Telus and Bell, Canadian operators. In 2009, Huawei led the industry by releasing end-to-end 100 GB solutions from routers to transmission systems, successfully delivered the world's first LTE/EPC commercial network, and led globally in the number of LTE commercial contracts. Its wireless access market share climbed to the second highest in the world.

By 2010, Huawei had deployed over 80 SingleRAN commercial networks globally, with 28 already having commercially released or soon to release LTE/EPC services. This progression signifies Huawei's evolution from a private enterprise focused on agency business to a large technological multinational company with robust innovation capabilities (Low 2007; Zhang 2009; Zhu 2008; Luo 2011).

5. Emphasis on Management Innovation alongside Technical Progress

Since its inception, Huawei has emphasized the importance of institutional innovation, organizational innovation, and innovation in management practices. As a result, after eight years of operation, Huawei drafted and adopted the Basic Law of Huawei in 1995. This significant step transitioned its internal management from being person-centered to being governed by an "internal legal system" for the enterprise, thus establishing a solid institutional foundation for its consistent growth (Wu 2009).

In 1997, two years after establishing its Basic Law, Huawei began to systematically engage international consulting firms. With the assistance of global management expertise, Huawei developed an IT-based management system aligned with international standards. This system emphasized key business processes such as market management, Integrated Product Development, Integrated Supply Chain, and Customer Relationship Management as its backbone, supported by financial, human resources, and other reform initiatives. These efforts led to comprehensive changes in the company's business processes, the adoption of industry best practices, and the construction of an IT infrastructure to support these operations. Financial management initiated the IFS project to bolster operational capabilities, particularly in supply chain management, where the "ISC" reform was implemented to enhance procurement performance management and the TQRDCE supplier certification process, drawing on industry best practices.

After more than five years of enhancements and changes, including the implementation of the "customer demand-driven development process and ISC process," Huawei's differentiated competitive advantage has become increasingly prominent, further strengthening its core competitiveness.

7.2.3 Stages and Paths of Huawei's Innovation/Catching-up

The aforementioned details of Huawei's innovation journey highlight that its innovation and catch-up process has distinct phases and unique path characteristics. These have enhanced its innovation capabilities and enabled it to achieve leapfrog advancements.

1. Stages of Huawei's Innovation/Catching-Up

Huawei's journey began with acting as an agent and producing products to supply China's rural market. As it expanded into international markets, the company purchased foreign patents and engaged in innovation through international collaborations. By 2003, Huawei had begun to pursue comprehensive endogenous innovation. This progression illustrates that Huawei's technological innovation can be broadly categorized into three phases: "introduction and imitation innovation, cooperative R&D, and endogenous innovation."

(1) The first stage: Imitation innovation

Initially, Huawei's innovation strategy was primarily based on imitation, such as manufacturing low-end routers for rural areas. Subsequently, it replicated and produced low-end enterprise switches. In 1990, Huawei introduced the Yangchun model, targeting small, mid-tier, and budget hotels. In 1991, it launched the 512-port PBX HJD48 and the multi-functional office device JK1000. Early in 1993, Huawei unveiled the C&C08, a system with a capacity of 2,000 units.

To bring these products to market, Huawei utilized common mature technologies in the industry and licensed technologies from multinational corporations. At the same time, it needed to develop some technologies that would distinguish its own products. Throughout this process of "imitation and follow-up," Huawei naturally accumulated R&D experience, as well as production and manufacturing technology capabilities.

(2) The second stage: Cooperative innovation

An incident in 2003 marked a pivotal moment for Huawei, propelling it into a phase of cooperative innovation. That year, Huawei found itself embroiled in an IP dispute with Cisco. Although the dispute ultimately concluded with a settlement, the experience profoundly influenced Huawei, leading the company to completely abandon the "imitation and follow-up" method of innovation. Instead, Huawei began to seek collaboration with international counterparts for innovation. This shift ushered Huawei into the "cooperative innovation stage," during which it formed strategic alliances with large international companies boasting significant technical expertise. Huawei's approach to innovation became "anchored in an international perspective, leveraging global resources and standards."

(3) The third stage: Endogenous innovation

Collaboration and innovation with leading international companies quickly elevated Huawei's R&D capabilities to a new level. The R&D process has become increasingly aligned with international standards, becoming more systematic, coordinated, and efficient. With the ability and opportunity to compete with top international companies, Huawei began to pursue endogenous innovation.

At this stage, Huawei aimed to become an "innovation leader" within the telecommunications equipment industry. As part of this effort, it consistently invested more than 10% of its annual sales revenue into R&D. In 2013 alone, Huawei's R&D investment surpassed $5 billion, representing 12.8% of its sales revenue. By the end of 2013, Huawei had approximately 150,000 employees globally, with 45% engaged in R&D activities. Up to that point, it had applied for 44,168 Chinese patents and 18,791 patents in other countries, including 7,848 in the United States, 5,944 in Europe, and 4,555 under the international PCT system, with 36,511 patents granted. Huawei has led China in the number of invention patent filings for seven consecutive years, and its number of patent applications and grants in Europe and the United States has consistently ranked in the top twenty and fifty, respectively (as shown in Table 7-2).

Table 7-2 Number of PCT patents submitted by Huawei (pcs.)

Year	Quantities	Global ranking	Year	Quantities	Global ranking
2007	1,365	4th	2008	1,737	1st
2009	1,847	2nd	2010	1,528	4th
2011	1,831	3rd	2012	1,801	4th
2013	2,094	3rd	—	—	—

2. Strategies for Huawei's Innovation Progress

(1) R&D strategy: From technology-driven to market-driven

Huawei's R&D strategy has evolved from being purely "technology-driven" to a blend of "technology + market-driven." A pivotal moment was its failure to win the Unicom CDMA project bid in 2002, which highlighted the flaw of overlooking market preferences in R&D efforts. To prevent R&D personnel from focusing solely on new and advanced technologies without market sensitivity, Huawei mandated an annual transfer of 5% of its R&D staff to market roles, and vice versa. This approach ensures the development of world-class, marketable technologies while fostering a culture of "engineering businessmen" over mere scientists. Huawei's leadership maintains that technology only holds value when it generates profit, emphasizing market adaptation over technology-led R&D, prudent innovation over blind creativity, and a market strategy that encompasses both rural outreach and international expansion.

(2) R&D direction: From local market focus to capturing the international market

In the global arena, control over core technologies equates to mastering strategic market competition highlands. Thus, Huawei emphasizes "market-driven innovation and R&D-driven market" strategies. Initially focusing on establishing research institutes within China, Huawei's growing international competitiveness prompted the expansion of R&D facilities abroad, including in Silicon Valley, Dallas, Sweden, India, Russia, and more. Recognizing the importance of localized products and technologies for securing customer loyalty in host countries, Huawei adopted a strategy of "localization of R&D in the host country," leading to a global but locally sensitive R&D approach.

Despite initial low recognition among customers in developed nations, unfamiliar with Huawei as opposed to giants like Nokia, Ericsson, Siemens,

GE, and others, strategic alliances with these international firms have raised awareness of Huawei's brand. Through equity participation and leveraging well-known brands and channels, Huawei has expanded its global presence based on its products and technologies.

(3) R&D path: From following to leading development

In its early years, Huawei's R&D focused on following industry peers and learning from their mature technologies. However, as Huawei closed the technological gap with international counterparts and began competing directly with multinational corporations, the strategy of merely following others became unsustainable for maintaining competitiveness. This realization propelled Huawei toward a path of "leading R&D."

Determined to break the monopoly held by European and American companies in high-value communication equipment, Huawei aimed for a high starting point to match the pace of multinational corporations, focusing on high-end, cutting-edge, and marketable industry products. With sustained, intensive R&D investment and technology accumulation, Huawei has emerged as a world leader in various fields such as ultra-long distance DWDM, MSTP, NGN, and many more. It has not only reached the forefront in technologies like intelligent optical network ASON, switches, and 3G terminals but has also progressed from participating to dominating the formulation of international standards.

3. Huawei's Global Expansion Aligned with Innovation

Huawei's innovation and catch-up journey, along with its process of internationalization, is marked by distinct stages and a clear path of gradual advancement.

(1) First stage (1996–2000): Early international explorations

After eight years of domestic success, Huawei set its sights on the international arena in 1996, starting with developing countries before aiming for a broader global market. Achieving success in some Asian and African countries, Huawei planned its entry into the "marginal markets" of European and American (developed) countries, marking its first significant step into Russia in 1998. Securing the initial contract of $380,000 in this "marginal market" took nearly three years of diligent effort.

(2) Second stage (2001–2004): Growth in international presence

By the third year of its venture into Russia's marginal market, Huawei secured a GSM equipment supply contract worth tens of millions of dollars with the Russian National Telecommunications Department in 2001. Its commendable technology and services led to sales exceeding $300 million in the CIS countries by 2003, making Huawei a top telecom equipment supplier in the region. The company established R&D centers globally to cater to more country-specific products and services, including in Bangalore, India (1999), Stockholm, Sweden (2000), and the United States (2001). Huawei also made strides in Southeast Asian markets, as well as regional markets in the Middle East and Africa, actively collaborating with operators in these developing regions.

(3) Third stage (2005–2009): Penetration into European markets

Huawei successfully entered markets in Eastern and Southern Europe, gradually making its way into the high-end markets of Western Europe and North America. It established its European center in Paris, France. On November 21, 2005, Huawei signed a global procurement framework agreement with Vodafone, the world's largest mobile communication operator, marking its entry into the "high-end supplier club" of global communication equipment, alongside Ericsson, Nokia, Siemens, and Lucent.

(4) Fourth stage (2009–present): Deepening and broadening global market engagement

Despite the global financial crisis starting in 2008, which led to a downturn in the international telecommunications manufacturing industry, Huawei achieved an annual sales figure of $30 billion, becoming the world's second-largest mobile equipment manufacturer by 2011. Focusing on terminals, enterprise business, and telecommunications management services, Huawei aimed to transcend its "telecommunications equipment manufacturer" image. It has continued to innovate based on customer needs and engage in "open cooperation" with business partners to build "end-to-end solutions" across telecommunications networks, enterprise networks, consumer segments, and cloud computing. Committed to providing competitive ICT solutions and services for telecom operators, enterprises, and consumers, Huawei strives to enhance customer experiences and create maximum value for its clients.

4. Huawei's Environmental Strategy Supporting Innovation

As Huawei embarked on innovation, development, and international market expansion, European countries were championing the "green economy." Specifically, the signing of the Global Climate Change Convention necessitated that the production and usage of products adhere to the principles of being "green, low-carbon, and emitting minimal emissions." In response, Huawei has endeavored to enhance its innovation capabilities and align with international trends through a "green life cycle R&D system design," providing a "self-guarantee" for its innovation, development, and internationalization efforts.

Huawei introduced a strategy encompassing "green pipeline, green operation, green partner, and green world." It has woven the concept of green ICT into the life cycle of all its products, continuously boosting product efficiency, and constructing green communication networks.

(1) Raw material acquisition

Huawei aims to minimize raw material use, favor renewable resources, and employ biological materials wherever feasible. It exercises strict control over harmful materials and pursues minimalistic design. All new Huawei products undergo green product certification before production to enhance their environmental performance. This initiative seeks to diminish resource consumption, elevate energy efficiency, cut production and operation costs, and lessen the environmental impact throughout the product's life cycle.

(2) Production and transportation

To reduce energy and resource consumption, Huawei employs "manufacturability design, transportability design, green packaging design, and lightweight design." It continuously innovates in product energy efficiency, explores new energy sources, and develops energy-saving products and solutions to help customers cut energy use and carbon emissions. Huawei has implemented a green packaging strategy, dubbed 6R1D, focusing on Right packaging design, Reduction, Returnability, Reuse, Recycling, Recovery, and Degradation, alongside green logistics practices.

(3) Utilization and installation

Emphasizing energy and resource efficiency, Huawei has innovated in durability, refined energy-saving designs, efficient cooling, power supply, and new energy use. It has optimized global network layouts and transportation routes, improved supply modes and logistics schemes, thereby reducing logistics costs, greenhouse gas emissions, and environmental impact.

(4) Waste management

Committed to energy reuse and recycling, Huawei focuses on technologies that facilitate easy disassembly and ensure the quality of reused components. Packaging materials are printed with environmentally friendly soy ink, which is safe, renewable, free of VOCs, and resistant to friction and heat, contributing to human health and equipment maintenance. This approach also simplifies the recycling of packaging materials.

(5) Internal management

Huawei has transformed its internal structure from being divided by equipment, terminals, and software services into a "full-featured service enterprise" catering to operators, enterprises, and consumers. This shift has enabled Huawei to catch up with and surpass international leaders in internal management.

7.2.4 Key Drivers of Huawei's Innovative Growth

In Huawei's journey of innovation and catch-up, several key factors have played pivotal roles.

1. The Innovation Spirit of Entrepreneurship

The innovative spirit of entrepreneurs is crucial for businesses to surpass their limits and sustain endogenous innovation. Huawei's ability to innovate and catch up effectively is largely attributed to the entrepreneurial team led by Ren Zhengfei, which forms the enterprise's soul. An early testament to this spirit was Huawei's decision to borrow money at high-interest rates for R&D, making a bold move to develop switches despite facing numerous failures and a loss of RMB 60 million. Huawei's persistence in investing resources led to the successful development of its first switch.

2. Talent Valuation as an Innovation Cornerstone

Huawei has established an effective incentive mechanism and a culture of innovation. The launch of Huawei University in 2005 and the establishment of 29 training centers worldwide underscore its commitment to building a learning organization and promoting employee localization. Huawei's comprehensive human resource management system covers business rules, work environment, employee training, career development, and communication between leaders and employees, ensuring high professional ethics and standards. The company regularly evaluates the work environment and employs external authorities for inspections, guaranteeing a positive workplace. Career development at Huawei offers dual promotion paths, allowing management-capable employees to become managers and technically skilled employees to become experts. Compensation is competitive and regularly adjusted based on performance and market research. Effective recruitment and utilization strategies have significantly contributed to staff growth.

3. Essential Role of Core Technologies and Intellectual Property

Huawei annually invests over 10% of its sales revenue in R&D, with around 10,000 professionals contributing to these efforts. This commitment has led to a wealth of core technologies under independent IP rights. Huawei's patent application rate, especially for invention patents, is exceptionally high, with a significant number of patents granted both domestically and internationally. As of December 31, 2010, Huawei had filed for tens of thousands of patents worldwide and actively participated in 123 industry standard organizations, contributing over 23,000 proposals. Huawei's involvement in shaping industry standards and its substantial contribution to LTE/EPC proposals highlight its R&D prowess and the strategic value of holding independent IP rights. This foundation has been instrumental in securing and enhancing Huawei's international brand and market position.

7.3 Strategic Approach to Technology Catch-Up and Intrinsic Innovation in Science-Based Industries

7.3.1 Integration of Technology Catch-Up and Intrinsic Innovation

At the strategic management level, it's essential to view technology catch-up and endogenous innovation as a cohesive whole.

First, technology catch-up serves as the foundation for "high-level endogenous innovation." For laggards aiming to achieve "high-level endogenous innovation" and hoping that their innovative outcomes will establish a competitive edge among peers, it's crucial to first develop their inherent innovation capabilities through "technology catch-up."

Second, "low-level endogenous innovation" typically represents a phase of technology accumulation and catch-up. When laggards are unable to directly acquire technology from leaders to enhance their innovation capacity, they must engage in "low-level endogenous innovation activities." This involves independent research and commercial development to create products for the "low-level market," while gradually building their own "technology accumulation." Once this "technology accumulation" reaches a certain "threshold," it may enable laggards to "catch up with the leaders."

Third, the relationship between technology catch-up and endogenous innovation is reciprocal, making it challenging to distinctly separate the two. In terms of development, technology catch-up underpins and facilitates high-level endogenous innovation, which, in turn, propels the former. At the activity level, distinguishing between technology catch-up and endogenous innovation is not straightforward.

Therefore, considering technology catch-up and endogenous innovation as a "unity" is beneficial for strategically addressing the positioning, mode, path, market selection, and other aspects of technology catch-up and endogenous innovation.

7.3.2 Defining the Roles of Technology Catch-Up and Intrinsic Innovation

Based on the analysis, the strategic positioning for science-based technology catch-up in strategic emerging industries should be as follows.

First, the essence of technology catch-up is "to catch up with and surpass their technological innovation capabilities," with the core being "to catch up with and surpass their capacity to acquire new scientific knowledge." The goal extends beyond merely reaching parity at a technical level. Achieving technological innovation capabilities that match or exceed those of leading countries, combined with an effective catch-up and innovation model, path, mechanism design, and implementation efforts, is essential for "synchronizing with or even surpassing" the innovation achievements of leading nations.

Second, the process outcome of technology catch-up should be seen as the "coordinated advancement of both hard and soft capabilities." Here, "catching up in hard capabilities" refers to "narrowing the technological gap." It ensures that in the same scientific and technological field, achieving at least the same level as the leaders or even surpassing them. "Catching up in soft capabilities" implies that within science-based industries, "mechanism construction" also catches up with or surpasses the efficiency of the leaders' mechanisms in terms of scientific progress, technological breakthroughs, and endogenous innovation.

Third, a significant milestone in technology catch-up is "the considerable improvement in the quantity and quality of independent IP." Given the current lag behind leading nations in "science-based strategic emerging industries" due to scientific development and technological upgrading, as well as the constraints of the "IP lock" and the "technology paradigm" and "development path" of similar industries, technology catch-up must aim for the milestone of "significantly enhancing the quantity and quality of independent IP rights to break through the IP lock of leading countries."

The strategic positioning of endogenous innovation in science-based strategic emerging industries should include the following perspectives.

First, intensifying investment in fundamental scientific research is crucial to support domestic original new knowledge for the endogenous innovation of science-based strategic emerging industries. Innovation grounded in science relies on the advancements of basic scientific research, necessitating significant investment in this area. The technological gap between China and leading countries in many "science-based strategic emerging industries" fields partly results from these countries' early investment in basic scientific research and subsequent applied scientific research. To catch up, China must bolster its basic scientific research investment, serving both as a catch-up effort and a proactive strategy for future endogenous innovation.

Second, it's essential to fully leverage the new achievements in international basic science. In today's knowledge economy, monitoring global basic scientific progress and utilizing existing human knowledge for the endogenous innovation of China's "science-based strategic emerging industries" are critical. This approach requires universities, non-profit scientific and technological information institutions, and industries to focus on collecting and researching basic science information. Notably, initiatives like "patent early warning research" and "discipline development research based on big data technology" are steps toward making informed use of international basic science advancements.

Third, addressing the major needs of the national economy should be a priority for endogenous innovation. The development of China's science-based strategic emerging industries faces challenges, including significant technology gaps. Given the historical underinvestment in basic research and the long cycle of exploration in basic research, focusing on industries with a solid scientific, technical, and market foundation, especially those with significant national needs, is advised. Prioritizing "endogenous innovation" in industries crucial to national interests is expected to not only meet these major needs but also stimulate the accelerated development of science-based strategic emerging industries.

7.3.3 Modelling Technology Catch-Up and Intrinsic Innovation

When considering the technology catch-up mode for "science-based strategic emerging industries" to catch up and surpass international leaders, it's essential to understand the following aspects.

First, the essence of the technology catch-up mode lies in "the logical approach and method for technology catch-up." This method should encompass several critical aspects: a. the approach and method for technology catch-up across different stages of innovation capability development, b. strategies for technology catch-up under varying levels of basic scientific support, and c. the organizational structures necessary for the effective implementation of these strategies. Overall, the technology catch-up mode that China could employ for its "science-based strategic emerging industries" is outlined in principle in Figure 7-1.

Second, the technology catch-up in "science-based strategic emerging industries" primarily involves "catching up with scientific discovery and its commercial transformation capability." While the essence of technology catch-up encompasses surpassing technological innovation capabilities, within the realm

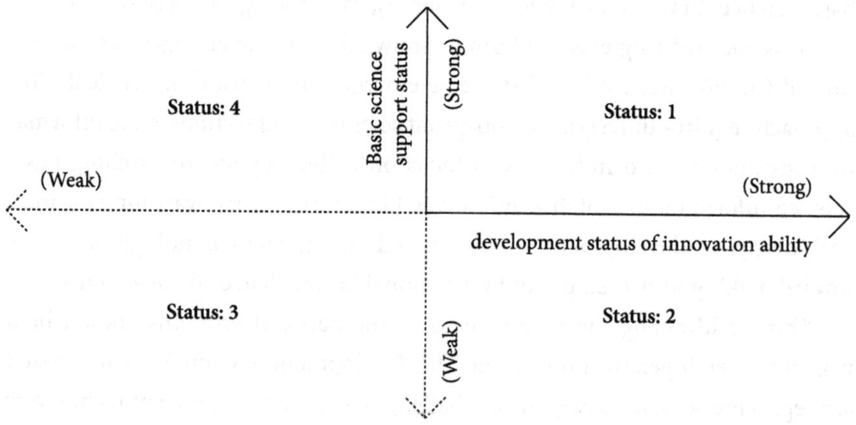

Figure 7-1 Schematic diagram of technological catching-up mode for science-based strategic emerging industries

of "science-based strategic emerging industries," such innovation capabilities are integrally linked to "scientific discovery capabilities, application research capabilities, technology development capabilities, and business transformation capabilities." Consequently, technology catch-up in these industries initially focuses on "the catch-up of scientific discovery and its commercial transformation capacity." Given that China's "science-based strategic emerging industries" are generally in a "dual weakness state" at this stage (as depicted in Figure 7-1), the fundamental catch-up mode must leverage advancements in basic science, both domestically and internationally, to "compensate for the domestic shortfall in scientific discovery ability." Simultaneously, utilizing the existing domestic foundation, through imitation and innovation, it's imperative to enhance "application research capability, technology development capability, and commercial transformation capability."

Third, establishing "science-based enterprises" is recognized as an effective means for implementing technology catch-up in "science-based strategic emerging industries" and may even serve as a mechanism for "leapfrogging or rapid catch-up." As noted, a science-based enterprise is formed by scientists and professional management teams aiming to commercialize scientific achievements swiftly while continuing scientific research. Regardless of whether domestic basic scientific research supports the industry's technology catch-up, forming a "science-based enterprise" to specialize in the commercial transformation of domestic and foreign basic scientific achievements can enhance the technological innovation capability of the respective industry. In scenarios where there's an international "technology paradigm" shift in an industry, business, or product and service category, such enterprises can quickly undertake application research of relevant scientific findings and subsequent technology development and commercialization. This approach, thanks to their nimble understanding and precise grasp of the latest basic science developments, enables rapid establishment of technological innovation capabilities that are on par with international counterparts.

In light of the feasible "technology catch-up mode" for China's "science-based strategic emerging industries," considering the dynamic interplay (akin to a "double helix") between "endogenous innovation" and "technology catch-up," there are three prevalent modes of endogenous innovation within this sector in China at the current stage.

First, there's the enterprise-led innovation model grounded in science. In this model, scientists within enterprises undertake basic scientific research to generate new scientific discoveries. Alternatively, enterprises might collaborate with each other to engage in basic scientific research, leading to new scientific findings. Following these discoveries, the processes of application research, technology development, product development, and commercialization are also carried out within these enterprises.

Second, the scientific innovation model involves enterprise-university-research cooperation. Here, leveraging the scientific achievements of university or PRI scientists, enterprises collaborate with universities or PRIs in application R&D. This collaboration might also extend to obtaining patent licenses and transfers for commercial product development and market introduction. Enterprises can engage in this process in two ways: by participating in or funding basic research at universities or public institutions during the discovery phase to gain preferential access to patent licenses for further R&D and commercial product development, or by stepping in after universities or PRIs have developed scientifically robust achievements with applicable patents or lab prototype products, to then take on or be authorized for further technology development and commercial product development through to market launch.

Third, the innovation model based on scientists establishing enterprises is characterized by scientists from universities or PRIs initiating "science-based enterprises" after achieving scientific breakthroughs, to then navigate the commercial development of these scientific achievements until product market entry. In this scenario, scientists take the lead in the R&D and operational aspects of the enterprise.

7.3.4 Market Strategies for Technology Catch-Up and Intrinsic Innovation

In the realm of "science-based strategic emerging industries," the choice of market for technology catch-up and endogenous innovation primarily concerns the selection of products for endogenous innovation and the identification of the initial customer base for most enterprises.

First, product market selection should adhere to market principles. The advancement of "science-based strategic emerging industries" in China is undeniably a national strategic imperative aimed at securing an international competitive advantage. Nonetheless, success ultimately hinges on customer acceptance of the innovators' products or services, enabling the transformation of these products into marketable goods and realizing their value. This necessitates innovators to initially tailor their products and services to meet market demands, especially latent demands. Given that the product market in science-based industries is largely untapped, innovators must endeavor to identify, develop, create, and steer the market. Therefore, product innovators in China's "science-based strategic emerging industries" must operate in accordance with market principles.

Second, when selecting the initial customer base, innovators should prioritize markets with public demand. Historical observations from the early phases of developing "science-based strategic emerging industries" in China reveal that the first group of customers essentially comprises a "public demand user market." For instance, the military was among the first clients for artemisinin-based drugs, while airports, ports, and customs were initial buyers of Nuctech's security screening equipment. Similarly, Dawning Computers' debut customers included national high-performance computing centers, as well as numerous universities and research institutions. Huawei's initial clientele for its communication equipment were small hotels and guesthouses operated by rural grassroots organizations and urban governments, and BGI's early customers encompassed international organizations and scientific research institutions. Moving forward, innovators within "science-based strategic emerging industries" should continue to target public demand users as their primary clientele. However, it's important to acknowledge that the "continuous demand cycle" from such customers is likely to be brief.

References

Burgelman, R. A. 2021. "Xiaobo Wu, Johann Peter Murmann, Can Huang, and Bin Guo: The Management Transformation of Huawei: From Humble Beginnings to Global Leadership." *Administrative Science Quarterly*: 000183922110043.

Low, B. 2007. "Huawei Technologies Corporation: From Local Dominance to Global Challenge?" *Journal of Business & Industrial Marketing.*

Luo, Y., M. Cacchione, M. Junkunc, et al. 2011. "Entrepreneurial Pioneer of International Venturing: The Case of Huawei." *Organizational Dynamics* 40 (1): 67–74.

Wu, D., and F. Zhao. 2007. "Entry Modes for International Markets: Case Study of Huawei, a Chinese Technology Enterprise." *International Review of Business Research Papers* 3 (1): 183–196.

Zhang, Y. 2009. "Alliance-Based Network View on Chinese Firms' Catching-Up: Case Study of Huawei Technologies Co. Ltd."

Zhu, B. 2008. "Internationalization of Chinese MNEs and Dunning's Eclectic (OLI) Paradigm: A Case Study of Huawei Technologies Corporation's Internationalization Strategy."

Mao, Wuxing, Chen Jin, and Wang Yi. 2006. "A Study on the Evolution of Core Technology Capabilities in a Dynamic Environment: An Example of the Evolution of Technological Capabilities of Lucent Technologies and Huawei Technologies." *Journal of Management Engineering* 20 (1): 124–129.

Wu, Yajun. 2009. "Strategic Duality in Chinese Local Emerging Firms: A Theoretical Exploration Based on the Practices of Huawei, Lenovo and Haier." *Management World*, no. 12: 120–121.

Index

M

N

O

P

Q

R

S

T

ABOUT THE AUTHORS

Dr. Wang Ling is a professor and doctoral supervisor specializing in Innovation Economics and Management at the China University of Political Science and Law (CUPL). She is also the director of the Center for Enterprise Patent Strategy at CUPL. She brings a unique perspective to her field with a remarkable academic journey that spans the fields of patent system economics, enterprise patent strategy, innovation management, and industrial economics. Before joining CUPL in 2006, she conducted postdoctoral research at Tsinghua University. She worked as a visiting scholar at Stanford University (2009–2010) and the University of Surrey (2022–2023). She has authored or coauthored more than fifty articles in academic journals, including *Technovation, IBM Journal of Research and Development,* and *Expert System with Application*. She has received numerous awards, including the Excellent Teaching Achievement Award of CUPL and the Beijing Teaching Achievement Award.

Dr. Zhang Qingzhi is an associate professor and master's supervisor at the School of Public Policy and Management, University of Chinese Academy of Sciences. With a PhD in Management and a postdoctoral research background at Tsinghua University, she specializes in innovation management, science and technology policy, IP management, and industrial economics. She worked as a visiting scholar at Boston University (2010–2011) and Nottingham University (2020–2022). Zhang has actively contributed to various national research projects and has published extensively in renowned domestic and international journals. Her remarkable achievements include receiving prestigious awards such as the Beijing Social Science Award and the China Soft Science Award, recognizing her significant contributions to her field.

Dr. Lei Jiasu is a professor and doctoral supervisor at Tsinghua University's School of Economics and Management. He is also the director of the Center for Chinese Enterprise Growth and Economic Security at Tsinghua University. He is renowned for his innovation, entrepreneurship, enterprise growth expertise, and dedication to national economic security. Dr. Lei has an impressive publication record, comprising over two hundred academic papers and thirty monographs and textbooks. Primary funding agencies have supported his research and have earned him recognition, including first prizes in Science and Technology Progress and the National Excellent Achievement Award of Universities. He is highly regarded for his exceptional teaching achievements. He has received numerous awards, including the Excellent Teaching Achievement Award of Tsinghua University and the National Education Reform and Innovation Teacher Excellence Award.